Born in Chatham, Kent, **Henry Stedman** has been writing guidebooks for over fifteen years now and is the author or co-author of half a dozen titles, including Trailblazer's *Dolomites Trekking*, *Coast to Coast Path* and *Hadrian's Wall Path*, as well as *The Bradt Guide to Palestine* and the *Rough Guides* to *Indonesia* and *Southeast Asia*. Travel remains his abiding love, a passion surpassed only by his obsession with Kilimanjaro – an obsession that has seen him climb all the routes, collect books, maps and other paraphernalia about it, and even set up the leading website dedicated to climbing it (see p15). He now also leads groups up the mountain.

When not travelling, Henry lives in Hastings in England, editing other people's guidebooks, writing travel brochures and books, arranging climbs for clients and putting on weight. Friends describe him as living proof that almost anyone can climb Kilimanjaro.

Kilimanjaro – The trekking guide to Africa's highest mountain
First edition 2003; second edition 2006; this third edition 2010

Publisher
Trailblazer Publications
The Old Manse, Tower Rd, Hindhead, Surrey, GU26 6SU, UK
Fax (+44) 01428-607571, info@trailblazer-guides.com
www.trailblazer-guides.com

British Library Cataloguing in Publication Data
A catalogue record for this book is available from the British Library

ISBN 978-1-905864-24-9

Editor: Nicky Slade
Series editor: Patricia Major
Typesetting and layout: Henry Stedman
Proof-reading: Jane Thomas
Cartography: Nick Hill
Index: Jane Thomas

Warning: mountain walking can be dangerous
Please read the notes on when to go (p20) and on mountain safety (p217).
Every effort has been made by the author and publisher to ensure that the information
contained herein is as accurate and up to date as possible. However, they are unable
to accept responsibility for any inconvenience, loss or injury sustained by anyone as a
result of the advice and information given in this guide.

Printed on chlorine-free paper by
D2Print (☎ +65-6295 5598), Singapore

Kilimanjaro

The trekking guide to
Africa's highest mountain

HENRY STEDMAN

TRAILBLAZER PUBLICATIONS

A request

The author and publisher have tried to ensure that this guide is as accurate and up to date as possible. However, things change quickly in this part of the world. Agencies come and go, trails are re-routed, prices rise and ... well, rise some more, governments are toppled and glaciers shrink. If you notice any changes or corrections for the next edition of this guide, please email Henry Stedman at 🖳 henry@climbmountkilimanjaro.com. You can also contact us via the Trailblazer website at 🖳 www.trailblazer-guides.com. Those persons making a significant contribution will be rewarded with a free copy of the next edition, an acknowledgement in the front of that edition, and my undying gratitude.

CLIMBING TACKLE
(FROM *ACROSS EAST AFRICAN
GLACIERS – AN ACCOUNT OF THE
FIRST ASCENT OF KILIMANJARO*
HANS MEYER, 1891)

Updated information will shortly be available on:
🖳 **www.climbmountkilimanjaro.com**

CONTENTS

ACKNOWLEDGEMENTS

For this third edition I would like to thank those trekkers, locals and expats who kindly offered advice and suggestions. These are the people who did the hard work, allowing me to sit back and collect both the glory and the royalties – so the least I can do is thank them. Thus, in no particular order (and Tanzanian unless otherwise stated), thanks are due to: Karen Valenti (US) at KPAP, as ever, for all her information and company; Eric Knox (US) of Indiana State University for his help in identifying the various groundsel species; Lazarus Mirisho Mafie and all at Shidolya for their help in organizing my Mount Meru trip, and Haleluja and Godbless for getting me to the top – with names like that, how was I ever going to fail?; Velly and Teddy, the receptionists at the Buffalo Hotel, for always making me feel so welcome; Joseph, the gentleman of Moshi; Cuthbert Swai, Methley and Timba at Ahsante for their help and expertise; Janet Bonnema (US) for her lesson on air pressure and burning damp toilet roll(!); Martin Fehr (Den); Jack Hollinghurst (UK); Sharon Edwards (UK); Martin Pennington (UK); Hannah Cunningham and Nicola Woods (UK); Andreas Kallkvist, Torbjorn Wilund and Niklas Johansson (Swe); Kristian De la Riva (UK); Dr Gurudas Harshe (India); Michael Bolton (UK via Ethiopia); brother and sister Frank Wildermann and Leigh Wynn (US); Linsley Green (UK); Richard Oliver (UK); Laura van der Ploeg-Vermerris and Wietze van der Ploeg (Ned); Peter Stansfield (Aus via Saudi Arabia); Weilun Lin, Scott Cassano and Matthew Ratcliffe (US); Chris Baker, Ben Seelaus and Michael Carvin (US); Michael Hayden (Aus); Jane Andrews, Preet and Sandeep Grewal (Aus); Bjorn Havemann (SA); Muriel Niffle and Orjan Anderberg (Bel); Ann Fisher and Michael Spilsbury (UK via Kenya); Jonathan Boxall (Aus); Christian and Matthew Brash (UK); Stephen Donaldson, Sue Bloomfield, Bill Flynn, Alexandra Gosden and Frank Richards (Aus); Michael Annand, Ray Beattie, JR Cruickshank, Ian Young, Gregor Thomson, Graeme Morrison, Gordon Duncan, Stephen Reid, Colin Morrison and Colin Brown (all from Scotland); Rob and Gareth Blakesley (UK); Mark, Shona, Caitlin and Patrick Synnott (UK), Nigel, Kim and William Binks (UK), Kim and Charlie McGuire (US); Tom Stoa (US); Jenny Bennett (US); Jorge Campos-Vallejo and Carlos Martin Ruiz De Gordejuela (Spain via Belgium and Greece); Arielle Goodley; John Rees-Evans of Team Kilimanjaro; guides Freddie Achedo, Deodatus Na'alli, James Matu, John Naiman, Joshua Ruhimbi, Deo Shayo, Simon Kahya, Patric Moshi, Felix Akas, Saumu Burhani Myusa, and Alex Minja; thanks to Frank Mtei for his help with the Chagga guide and Amina Malya and Vincent Munuo for checking; and Shafi Msiru and all the crew at TK; Joe Ventura and Valerie Todd at Amani; and Dr Doug Hardy for his help with the climate section of the book. I hope you all find that, thanks largely to your input, this third edition is even better than the previous two.

At Trailblazer I would like to thank Nick Hill for transforming my childlike scribbles into maps of beauty; Patricia Major for turning my incoherent ramblings into something approaching English in the first edition, Jim Manthorpe for performing similar miracles in the second, and Nicky Slade for this edition; Jane Thomas for proof-reading and for the index; and Bryn, as ever, for making the whole thing possible.

INTRODUCTION

Kilimanjaro is a snow covered mountain 19,710 feet high, and is said to be the highest mountain in Africa. Its western summit is called the Masai 'Ngà'je Ngài', the House of God. Close to the western summit there is the dried and frozen carcass of a leopard. No one has explained what the leopard was seeking at that altitude.

Ernest Hemingway in the preamble to *The Snows of Kilimanjaro*

On the 26 October 2007 Gérard Bavato of France stood at the Marangu gates on the south-eastern slopes of Africa's greatest mountain, Kilimanjaro. We can imagine the scene that day, for it's one that's repeated there every day of the year. There would be the noisy, excitable hubbub as porters, guides and rangers packed, weighed, re-packed and re-weighed all the equipment; the quiet murmur of anticipation from Gérard's fellow trekkers as they stood on the threshold of the greatest walk of their lives; maybe there was even a troop of blue monkeys crashing through the canopy, or the scarlet flash of a turaco's underwing as it glided from tree to tree, surveying the commotion below.

Monsieur Bavato's main goal that day was no different from the ambitions of his fellow trekkers: he wanted to reach the summit. Unlike them, however, Gérard planned to forego many of the features that make a walk up Kili so special. Not for him the joys of strolling lazily through the mountain's four main ecozones, pausing occasionally to admire the views or examine the unique mountain flora. Nor did Gérard want to experience the blissful evenings spent scoffing popcorn, sharing stories and gazing at the stars with his fellow trekkers. Nor, for that matter, was M Bavato looking forward to savouring the wonderful *esprit de corps* that builds between a trekker and his or her crew as they progress, day by day, up the mountain slopes; a sense of camaraderie that grows with every step until, exhausted, they stand together at the highest point in Africa.

It is these experiences that make climbing Kilimanjaro so unique and so special. Yet Gérard had chosen to eschew all of them because, for reasons best known to himself, he had decided to *run* up the mountain. Which is exactly what he did, completing the 36.5km from base to summit in an incredible 5 hours, 26 minutes and 40 seconds – on a trail that takes the average trekker anywhere from five to six days to complete!

A mountain for eccentrics

Barking mad though Gérard may be, in his defence it must be said that he isn't exactly alone in taking an unorthodox approach to tackling Kilimanjaro. Take the Crane cousins from England, for example, who cycled up to the summit, surviving on *Mars* bars that they'd strapped to their handlebars. Or the anonymous Spaniard who, in the 1970s, drove up to the summit by motorbike. Or what about Douglas Adams, author of the *Hitchhikers' Guide to the Galaxy*, who in 1994 reached the summit for charity while wearing an eight-foot rubber rhinoceros costume. Then there's the (possibly apocryphal) story of the man who walked *backwards* the entire way in order to get into the *Guinness Book of Records* – only to find out, on his return to the bottom, that he had been beaten by somebody who had done exactly the same thing just a few days previously.

And that's just the ascent; for coming back down again the mountain has witnessed skiing, a method first practised by Walter Furtwangler way back in 1912; snowboarding, an activity pioneered on Kili by Stephen Koch in 1997; and even hang-gliding, for which there was something of a fad a few years ago.

Don't be fooled

Cyclists to skiers, heroes to half-wits, bikers to boarders to backward walkers: it's no wonder, given the sheer number of people who have climbed Kili over the past century, and the ways in which they've done so, that so many people believe that climbing Kili is a doddle. And you'd be forgiven for thinking the same.

You'd be forgiven – but you'd also be wrong. Whilst these stories of successful expeditions tend to receive a lot of coverage, they also serve to obscure the tales of suffering and tragedy that often go with them. To give you just one example: for all the coverage of the Millennium celebrations, when over 7000 people stood on the slopes of Kilimanjaro during New Year's week – with 1000 on New Year's Eve alone – little mention was made of the fact that well over a third of all the people who took part in those festivities failed to reach the summit, or indeed get anywhere near it. Or that another 33 had to be rescued. Or that, in the space of those seven days, three people died.

The reason why most of these attempts were unsuccessful is altitude sickness, brought about by a trekker climbing too fast and not allowing his or her body time to acclimatize to the rarified air. Because Gérard Bavato didn't just set a record by climbing Kilimanjaro in under six hours; he also, unwittingly, set a bad example. For once, statistics give a reasonably accurate impression of just how difficult climbing Kili can be. According to the park authorities, almost one in four people who climb up Kilimanjaro fail to reach even the crater. They also admit to there being a couple of deaths per annum on Kilimanjaro; though independent observers put that figure nearer ten.

There's no doubt the joys of climbing Kili are manifold; unfortunately, so are the ways in which it can destroy you. Because the simple truth is that Kilimanjaro is a very big mountain and, like all big mountains, it's very adept at killing off the unprepared, the unwary or just the plain unlucky. The fact that the Masai call the mountain the 'House of God' seems entirely appropriate, given the number of people who meet their Maker every year on Kili's slopes.

At one stage we were taking a minute to complete thirty-five small paces. Altitude sickness had already hit the boys and two were weeping, pleading to pack up. All the instructors with the exception of Lubego and myself were in a bad way. They were becoming violently ill. It was becoming touch and go. The descent at one stage was like a battlefield. Men, including the porters, lying prone or bent up in agony. Tom and Swato though very ill themselves rallied the troops and helped manhandle the three unconscious boys to a lower altitude.
From the logbook of **Geoffrey Salisbury**, who led a group of blind African climbers up Kilimanjaro, as recorded in *The Road to Kilimanjaro* (1997).

The high failure and mortality rates speak for themselves: despite appearances to the contrary, climbing Kilimanjaro is no simple matter.

'Mountain of greatness'

But whilst it isn't easy, it *is* achievable. After all, no technical skill is required to reach the summit of Africa's highest mountain beyond the ability to put one foot in front of the other; because, unless you go out of your way to find a particularly awkward route, there is no actual *climbing* involved at all – just lots and lots of walking. Thus, anyone above the age of 10 (the minimum legal age for climbing Kilimanjaro) *can*, with the right attitude, a sensible approach to acclimatization, a half-decent pair of calf muscles and lots of warm clothing, make it to the top. Even vertigo sufferers are not excluded, there being only one or two vertical drops on any of the regular trekking routes that will have you scrabbling in your rucksacks for the Imodium.

Simply put, Kilimanjaro is for everyone. Again, statistics can back this up: with the youngest successful summiteer aged just seven and the oldest, the venerable Frenchman Valtée Daniel, aged 87, it's clear that Kili conquerors come in all shapes and sizes. Amongst their number there are a few who have managed to overcome enormous personal disabilities on their way to the summit. Virtually every year there is at least one group of blind trekkers who, incredibly, make it to the top by using the senses of touch and hearing alone. And in January 2004 four climbers who had been disabled on previous expeditions on other mountains all managed to make it to the summit. The party consisted of Australian Peter Steane, who has permanent nerve damage and walks and climbs with the help of two leg braces; his compatriot Paul Pritchard, who has limited control over his right side; Singaporean David Lim, partially disabled in his right leg and left hand after contracting the rare nerve disorder Guillain-Barre Syndrome; and Scotland's Jamie Andrew, an amazing man who had to have his hands and feet amputated after suffering severe frostbite during a climbing expedition near Chamonix, France, in January 1999, and yet who made it to the top of Kilimanjaro with artificial limbs and prosthetic arms.

It is this 'inclusivity' that undoubtedly goes some way to explaining Kilimanjaro's popularity, a popularity that saw 40,701 trekkers visit in the 2006-7 season, thereby confirming Kili's status as the most popular of the so-called 'Big Seven', the highest peaks on each of the seven continents.

The sheer size of it must be another factor behind its appeal. This is the Roof of Africa, a massive massif 60km long by 80km wide with an altitude that reaches to a fraction under 6km above sea level. Writing in 1924, the renowned anthropologist Charles Dundas claimed that he once saw Kilimanjaro from a point over 120 miles away. This enormous monolith is big enough to have its own weather systems (note the plural) and, furthermore, to influence the climates of the countries that surround it.

The aspect presented by this prodigious mountain is one of unparalleled grandeur, sublimity, majesty, and glory. It is doubtful if there be another such sight in this wide world.
Charles New, the first European to reach the snow-line on Kilimanjaro, from his book *Life, Wanderings, and Labours in Eastern Africa* (1873).

See pp349-51 for more sights
and sounds of Kili

But size, as they say, isn't everything, and by themselves these bald figures fail to fully explain the allure of Kilimanjaro. So instead we must look to attributes that cannot be measured by theodolites or yardsticks if we are to understand the appeal of Kilimanjaro.

In particular, there's its beauty. When viewed from the plains of Tanzania, Kilimanjaro conforms to our childhood notions of what a mountain should look like: high, wide and handsome, a vast triangle rising out of the flat earth, its sides sloping exponentially upwards to the satisfyingly symmetrical summit of Kibo; a summit that rises imperiously above a thick beard of clouds and is adorned with a glistening bonnet of snow. Kilimanjaro is not located in the crumpled mountain terrain of the Himalayas or the Andes. Where the mightiest mountain of them all, Everest, just edges above its neighbours – and looks less impressive because of it – Kilimanjaro stands proudly alone on the plains of Africa. The only thing in the neighbourhood that can even come close to looking it in the eye is Mount Meru, over 60km away to the south-west and a good 1420m smaller too. The fact that Kilimanjaro is located smack bang in the heart of the sweltering East African plains, just a few degrees (330km) south of the equator, with lions, giraffes, and all the other celebrities of the safari world running around its base, only adds to its charisma.

Then there's the scenery on the mountain itself. So massive is Kilimanjaro that to climb it is to pass through four seasons in four days, from the sultry rainforests of the lower reaches through to the windswept heather and moorland of the upper slopes, the alpine desert of the Saddle and Shira Plateau and on to the arctic wastes of the summit. There may be 15 higher mountains on the globe but there can't be many that are more beautiful, or more tantalizing.

In sitting down to recount my experiences with the conquest of the "Ethiopian Mount Olympus" still fresh in my memory, I feel how inadequate are my powers of description to do justice to the grand and imposing aspects of Nature with which I shall have to deal. **Hans Meyer**, the first man to climb Kilimanjaro, in his book *Across East African Glaciers – an Account of the First Ascent of Kilimanjaro* (1891)

Nor is it just tourists that are entranced by Kilimanjaro; the mountain looms large in the Tanzanian psyche too. Just look at their supermarket shelves. The nation's second favourite lager is called Kilimanjaro. There's Kilimanjaro coffee (grown on the mountain's fertile southern slopes), Kilimanjaro tea (ditto), Kilimanjaro mineral water (bottled on its western side) and Kilimanjaro honey (again, sourced from the mountain). While on billboards lining the country's highways, Tanzanian models smoke their cigarettes in its shadow and cheerful roly-poly housewives compare the whiteness of their laundry with the mountain's glistening snows. And to pay for all of these things you may use Tanzanian Ts500 or Ts2000 notes – both of which just happen to have, on the back of them, a member of Tanzania's vaunted animal kingdom (namely a buffalo and a lion respectively) posing in front of the distinctive silhouette of Africa's highest mountain.

It was perhaps no surprise, therefore, that when Tanganyikans won their independence from Britain in 1961, one of the first things they did was plant a torch on its summit; a torch that the first president, Julius Nyerere, declared

would '...shine beyond our borders, giving hope where there was despair, love where there was hate, and dignity where before there was only humiliation.'

To the Tanzanians, Kilimanjaro is clearly much more than just a very large mountain separating them from their neighbour Kenya. It's a symbol of their freedom and a potent emblem of their country. And given the tribulations and hardships willingly suffered by thousands of trekkers on Kili each year – not to mention the money they spend for the privilege of doing so – the mountain obviously arouses some pretty strong emotions in non-Tanzanians as well.

Whatever the emotions provoked in you by this wonderful mountain, and however you plan to climb it, we wish you well. Because even if you choose to walk rather than run, leave the bicycle at home and forego the pleasures of wearing a latex rhino outfit, climbing up Kilimanjaro will still be one of the hardest things you ever do.

But it will also, without a doubt, be one of the most rewarding.

We were in an amiable frame of mind ourselves and, notwithstanding all the toil and trouble my self-appointed task had cost me, I don't think I would that night have changed places with anybody in the world.
Hans Meyer on the evening after reaching the summit, as recorded in
Across East African Glaciers (1891)

IN THIS EDITION

The main change we have made for this third edition is the addition of **GPS waymarks** for each of the routes up Kilimanjaro. Though these aren't essential for your trek – the chances of you getting lost on the mountain are minimal given that you will be accompanied the whole way by a licensed guide – from the emails we receive I know that many people like to use their GPS receiver when trekking, and many would like to preprogram their machine with waymarks so they can plot their route. We have printed the waymarks at the back of this book (p352) and also published them on the website, from where you can download them (for free).

Other than the addition of waymarks, we have kept the book pretty much the same as the last edition in terms of style and structure. We have of course given everything a thorough update, including our guides to the cities and towns. We have also walked the routes again, both on Kilimanjaro and Meru, to satisfy ourselves that our descriptions of them are still accurate. And as with the last edition, we have once again called upon the services of Karen Valenti at KPAP (see pp46-49) to help us tackle the problem of porter mistreatment. We do, of course, also welcome updates from readers on *any* aspect of the book.

🖳 www.climbmountkilimanjaro.com – the website!

The website that was set up a couple of years ago to accompany this book is still going strong. Originally designed to keep our readers informed of the latest news and developments on the mountain, it now also hosts details of the **climbs that we organize on Kilimanjaro**.

So what exactly can you find on the site? Well, pay a visit to the site and you will see:

● **Updates on the book** From new restaurants in Moshi to route changes on Machame, if we discover something new or altered since the publication of the book, this is where you can find out all about it.

● **Links to weblogs** Compiling a weblog for your Kili climb? Then why not link it to our site so others can follow your progress?

● **Charity climbs** If you're involved in a charity climb or trying to organize one, you'll find space on the website for you to tell the world about your climb.

● **Links to Kili-based websites** Links to sites that we think are worth a look.

● **Kili news** Route alterations, park-fee increases and the tragedies and triumphs that occur on the mountain – we have the latest news.

● **The Kilimanjaro Hall of Fame** Celebrate your achievements with the world by posting your photos of yourself and your friends on the summit!

With a group or on your own?

INDEPENDENT TREKKING NOT AN OPTION

In 1991, the park authorities made it compulsory for all trekkers to arrange their walk through a licensed agency. Furthermore, they insist that all trekkers must be accompanied throughout their walk by a guide supplied by the agency. Even after these laws were introduced, for a while it was still feasible to sneak in without paying, and many were the stories of trekkers who managed to climb Kilimanjaro independently, tales that were often embellished with episodes of encounters with wild animals and even wilder park rangers.

Fortunately, the authorities have tightened up security and clamped down on non-payees, so these tedious tales are now few in number. Don't try to climb Kilimanjaro without a guide or without paying the proper fees. It's very unlikely you'll succeed and all you're doing is freeloading – indeed, stealing isn't too strong a word – from one of the poorest countries in the world. Yes, climbing Kilimanjaro is expensive. But the costs of maintaining a mountain that big are high. Besides, whatever price you pay, trust us, it's worth it.

WITH FRIENDS . . .

It's Kili time! Time to kick back, relax and take it easy with your friends.
Printed on the labels of Kilimanjaro Beer

So you have decided to climb Kilimanjaro, and have thus taken the first step on the path that leads from the comfort and safety of your favourite armchair to the untamed glory of the Roof of Africa. The second step on this path is to consider with whom you wish to go.

This may not be as straightforward as it sounds, because Kilimanjaro breaks friendships as easily as it breaks records. The tribulations suffered by those who dare to pit themselves against the mountain wear down the most even of temperaments, and relationships are often the first to suffer. Idiosyncrasies in your friend's behaviour that you previously thought endearing now simply become irritating, while the most trivial of differences between you and your chum could lead to the termination of a friendship that, before you'd both ventured onto its slopes, you thought was as steadfast and enduring as the mountain itself. Different levels of stamina, different levels of desire to reach the top, different attitudes towards the porters and guides, even differences in your musical tastes or the colour of your socks: on Kilimanjaro these things, for some reason, suddenly matter.

PLANNING YOUR TRIP

Then there's the farting. It is a well-known fact that the regular breaking of wind is a sure sign that you are acclimatizing satisfactorily (for more about acclimatization, see pp217-225); while the onset of a crushing headache, combined with a loss of sleep and a consequent loss of humour, are all classic symptoms suffered by those struggling to adapt to the rarified atmosphere. Problems occur, of course, when two friends acclimatize at different rates: ie, the vociferous and joyful flatulence of Friend A is simply not appreciated by Friend B, who has a bad headache, insomnia and ill-temper. Put the two parties together in a remote, confined space, such as that provided by a two-man tent on the slopes of a cold and lonely mountain, and you have an explosive cocktail that can blow apart even the strongest of friendships.

It rained terrible all night, and we put most of the Wachaga porters in our tent. It was rather distressing to the olfactory nerves ... At 4am a leopard visited us but did not fancy our scent.
Peter MacQueen, *In Wildest Africa* (an account of an expedition of 1907, published in 1910)

Of course, the above is just one possible scenario. It may be that both of you adapt equally well/badly to the new conditions and can draw pleasure/comfort from each other accordingly. People from Northern Europe seem particularly good at making the best of the windy conditions: while researching the first edition of this book we encountered a party of four Germans holding a farting competition, and one particularly talented Dutch pair who even managed a quick game of Name that Tune. (It probably won't surprise you to know that all but one of the participants in these events was male.)

And there are plenty of advantages in going with a friend too. There's the companionship for a start. It's also cheaper, because you'll probably be sharing rooms, which always cuts the cost, and if you are planning on booking your climb through an agency in Tanzania your bargaining position is so much stronger if there are two of you. Having a companion also cuts the workload, enabling, for example, one to run off and find a room while the other looks after the luggage. It also saves your being paired with someone you don't know when you book with an agency; someone who may snore or blow off more violently than your friend ever would. And, finally, if you *do* both make it to the top, it's good to know that there will be somebody to testify to your achievements upon your return.

Climbing Kili with a companion has its problems, but there's no doubting the extra pleasure that can be gained as well. As the graffiti on the walls of the Kibo Huts tells us: '*What does not break us makes us stronger*'. If you are planning on travelling with a friend this, perhaps, should be your motto for the trek.

. . .OR ON YOUR OWN?

Those without friends, or at least without friends willing to climb a mountain with them, should not worry. For one thing, you'll never truly be on your own, simply because the park authorities forbid you from climbing without a guide (see previous page) and you'll need at least one other crew member to act as porter. Furthermore, planning to go on your own means you can arrange **the trek that you want**; you choose the trail to follow, the time to go and for how long; the pace of the walk, the number of rest-stops, when to go to bed – these are all your decisions, and yours alone. You are the boss; you have nobody else's feelings to consider but your own.

If you want to join up with others, for companionship or simply to make the trek a little cheaper, that's not a problem: you can book your trek in your home country with a tour operator (they nearly always insist on a minimum number of participants before the trek goes ahead); or you can book in Tanzania and ask to be put with other trekkers (which will often happen anyway, unless you specifically say otherwise). And even if you are walking alone, you can always meet other trekkers at the campsite in the evening if you so desire.

Trekking by yourself is fun, and not the lonely experience many imagine; unless, of course, you enjoy the bliss of solitude and *want* to be alone. That's the beauty of walking solo: everything is up to you.

Budgeting

The most significant cost of your holiday, unless you opt for a few days at one of Tanzania's top-of-the-range lodges (US$2400 per night is the highest – and most ridiculous – rate I've heard for a night's accommodation, though there may be other even higher ones), is the walk itself. Set aside US$1000-plus for a budget trek, more if you plan on ascending by the Lemosho/Shira or Rongai routes or insist on walking without other trekkers. Once on the mountain, however, you won't need to pay for anything else throughout the trek, except for the occasional chocolate bar or beer which you can buy at the ranger's huts on the way.

Away from the mountain and the other national parks, by far the most expensive place in Tanzania is Zanzibar. Elsewhere, you'll find transport, food and accommodation, the big three day-to-day expenses of the traveller's life, are pretty cheap in Tanzania and particularly in Moshi and Arusha – it's just unfortunate that Zanzibar and the national parks are pretty much all most visitors want to see of the country!

The Tanzanian shilling (Ts) is the national currency. For exchange rates and more on money see p83.

ACCOMMODATION

Basic tourist accommodation starts at around £5/US$7.50. You can get cheaper, non-tourist accommodation, though this is often both sleazy and unhygienic and should be considered only as a last resort. We have not reviewed these cheap hotels individually in the book.

At the other end of the spectrum, there are hotel rooms and luxury safari camps going for anything up to US$2000 or more per night in the high season.

FOOD

Food can be dirt cheap if you stick to the street sellers who ply their wares at all hours of the day – though dirt is often what you get on the food itself too, with hygiene standards not always of the highest. Still, even in a clean and decent budget restaurant the bill should still be only £2.50-3.50/US$4-5.50.

TRANSPORT

Public transport is cheap in Tanzania, though it could be said you get what you pay for: dilapidated buses, potholed roads, inadequate seating and narcoleptic drivers do not a pleasant journey make, but this is the reality of public transport, Tanzanian-style. Then again, at around £1/US$1.50 per hour for local buses and Coasters (the local minibuses that ply the route between Arusha and Moshi; see p189), it seems churlish to complain. That said, given the appalling number of accidents on Tanzanian roads (they say that after malaria and AIDS, road accidents are the biggest killer in the country), if your budget can stretch to it do consider spending it on transport: extra safety and comfort are available on the luxury buses, and at only a slightly higher price.

When to go

The two main trekking seasons for Kilimanjaro correspond with the mountain's two dry seasons (an imprecise term, the weather being occasionally inclement during these periods too) namely January to mid-March and June to October. Of course you can walk in the rainy season but not only is there a much higher chance of walking in the rain, your views of Kibo and Mawenzi are likely to be obscured by thick cloud and you may be trudging through thigh-high snow to the summit. Indeed, several agencies even suspend their operations in April and May, deciding that any trek is foolhardy at this time and the rewards for the trekkers considerably less. Curiously, however, Christmas and New Year, when the weather is far from perfect, are actually amongst the most popular times to go. (You can read peoples' experiences of climbing during the low season on p22.)

As to the relative merits of the two trekking seasons, the differences are small though significant. The **January to March** season tends to be colder and

DAR ES SALAAM

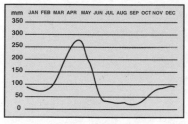

Average rainfall (mm)

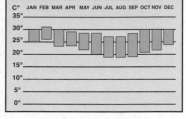

Average max/min temp (°C)

ARUSHA

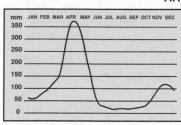

Average rainfall (mm)

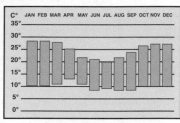

Average max/min temp (°C)

For statistics and graphs on the weather on Kilimanjaro, please see pp98-101.

there is a much greater chance of snow on the path at this time. The days, however, are often clearer, with only the occasional brief shower. It is usually an exceptionally beautiful time to climb and is often a little quieter than the other peak season of **June to October**, which coincides with the main academic holidays in Europe and the West. In this latter season the clouds tend to hang around the tree-line following the heavy rains of March to May. Once above this

---

❏ Star gazing

Having decided in which period you wish to travel, you may wish to refine your dates still further by timing your walk so that on the final push to the summit, which is usually conducted at night, you will be walking under the brightness of a **full moon**. The weather is said to be more stable at this time, too – though, of course, the night sky is less spectacular when it's a full moon as fewer stars are visible to the naked eye.

On that subject, stargazers may wish to try to coincide their trip with a major astronomical happening; the views of the night sky from Kili are, after all, quite exceptional. It's good to know that it isn't just the costs of climbing Kilimanjaro that are astronomical; the rewards can be too.

❏ Trekking in the rainy season

For those who absolutely have no choice but to walk during the rainy season, don't get too downhearted. We have had letters from several readers who positively recommend the experience. Take, for example, trekker Jack Hollinghurst, from the UK, who wrote the following way back in 2006:

'...*I do think that you don't give enough encouragement to walking in the rainy season. I was forced to walk at this time by holiday dates and thought it excellent. Due to the hugely reduced numbers of trekkers on the mountain me and my friend were given our own room at all of the huts (including Kibo, where it is about 12 beds to a room) and* [your] *advice about having dinner early at Horombo is irrelevant as there were about five other groups there at the most.*

'...*the walking is* [also] *much more enjoyable when you have some peace and quiet...Maybe you should advise walkers to wear waterproof trousers at this time of year (although I didn't take any and was fine) but otherwise I wouldn't walk at any other time of year.*'

His sentiments were endorsed by Martin Fehr from Denmark, who wrote to me early in 2009:

'*Don't be afraid to recommend climbing the mountain* [at the end of] *April. Our porters were so happy to have work in low season, we didn't get a lot of rain, and there were absolutely no climbers on the mountain besides us, which made our climb exceptionally great! Plus the top of the mountain was all covered in snow – a challenge, but soooo beautiful (and it was great to be able to "sleigh" down the mountain as well).*

However, Martin does go on to warn '*Of course, by climbing the mountain during the low season you are very much at the mercy of the elements – and conditions can be quite extreme at this time.*'

Martin's experience – and his opinion of walking in the low season – seems similar to that of Tom Stoa, another reader and Kili conqueror who sticks up for the rainy season:

'*I went in April, 2008, despite the recommendations of you and everyone else to avoid April due to weather, simply because that is when I could go. No regrets. I chose the Marangu route, 6 days, because of the huts – I figured that despite the rain, we would be warm, dry and comfortable in the huts at least. And that was correct (and we were lucky, it mostly just rained at night). Being the off season, my son and I had a hut to ourselves each night, and the big dining hut was also nearly empty.*

'*We made the summit just fine. My only regret was not having crampons for the big icy snowfield between Hans Meyer Cave and before Gillman's Point. We were gingerly kicking steps in the snow, or trying to step in the steps of others. Having some alpine climbing experience, I know that a slip would have resulted in a nasty, long slide with a crash onto the rocks below. I know that crampons are not customary on Kili, but for that route, on that day, they would have made all the difference between a very sketchy and slow slog, versus an "easy" and safe walk up.*'

So there you have it. It would seem that if you have an adventurous spirit, take the Marangu Route (the only route on the mountain where you sleep in huts rather than under canvas), consider taking crampons and/or ice axes, can put up with some pretty extreme conditions and are prepared for some possibly treacherous walking – then the low season is a fine time to climb!

altitude, however, the skies are blue and brilliant and the chance of precipitation minimal (though still present).

Although the June to October season tends to be busier, this is not necessarily a disadvantage. For example, if you are travelling independently to Tanzania but wish, for the sake of companionship or simply to cut down on costs, to join up with other travellers for the trek, then the high visitor numbers in the June to October peak season will give you the best chance of doing this. And even if you do crave solitude when you walk, it can still be found on the mountain during this peak season. The trails are long, so you can always find vast gaps between trekkers to allow you to walk in peace; some of the routes – Umbwe, for example, or the two trails across the Shira Plateau – almost never have more than one or two trekking groups on them at any one time and are sometimes completely deserted. And besides, Kilimanjaro is just so huge that its presence will dwarf your fellow trekkers to the point where they become, if you wish them to be, quite unnoticeable.

Booking your trek

With the decision over whether or not to climb independently taken out of your hands, and once you've chosen who is going to join you on this trip of a lifetime, the next thing to decide is which agency is going to get your business.

The next few pages deal with exactly this matter. This may seem like overkill but booking with the right agency is perhaps **the single most important factor in determining the success or otherwise of your trek**: they are the ones who arrange everything, supply the equipment, and designate somebody to be your guide. So take your time choosing one. Because unless you are a guide, porter, guidebook writer or just plain daft, climbing Kili will be a once-in-a-lifetime experience – and an expensive one too – so make sure that you get it right.

BOOKING WITH AN AGENCY AT HOME

The overwhelming majority of trekkers book their Kilimanjaro climb before they arrive in Tanzania, either through an agency in their home country or, usually via the internet, with an agency in Tanzania or abroad. This is only sensible – you will have enough on your plate once you get to Tanzania just trying to get to the top of Africa's highest mountain without having to sort out the whole trek beforehand as well. (That said, there is a fair case to be made for waiting until you arrive in the country before booking, particularly if you are on a tight budget; see p37.)

Booking your trek with an agency in your home country gets rid of the hassle of arranging everything when you arrive. It depends what kind of package you have booked, of course, but few tour companies will sell you a climb up Kilimanjaro and nothing more. Nearly all will include in their Kili package such things as airport pick-up, accommodation, sightseeing trips, transport to and from the mountain, and maybe even the odd safari or Zanzibar excursion. Pay them some more and they'll throw in the flights and insurance and sort out your visas too. With no need to arrange these things yourself, booking from home will save you a considerable amount of time. It also ensures that you know exactly when you'll be walking, rather than having to hang around for a few days as you may have to if you wait until you've arrived in Tanzania before booking.

Booking with an agency in your country also means you can plan your trek more precisely months in advance, and ask your agent any questions you may have well before you even arrive in Tanzania. Your agency at home will also either have their own guide to lead you up the mountain or, more probably, will be acting on behalf of one of the larger and better trekking operators in Moshi or Arusha, providing you with peace of mind. And if the trek still turns out to be a disaster, then the big advantage of booking from home is that you have a lot more comeback and thus more chance of receiving some sort of compensation.

A run-down of the larger tour operators who arrange treks up Kilimanjaro follows. Before booking with anybody, have a look at *Booking with an agency in Tanzania* on p37, and in particular the advice given in the sections headed *Choosing an agency in Tanzania* (p37) and *Signing the contract* (p39). Both contain useful hints that could also be relevant when dealing with agents and operators in your own country.

The agencies

All prices quoted in the following list include park fees unless stated otherwise but exclude flights – again, unless stated. For details of the various routes up Kilimanjaro that are mentioned here, please see p55. You'll see a wide range of prices listed below; remember to ask each agency exactly what is included. Most companies will provide airport transfers and a night or two in a hotel but do make sure this is the case. Some prices also include return flights from your home country – we have tried to highlight where this is the case in the reviews below. Some companies specialize in certain routes only; others offer all official routes and, in some cases, have devised (or, rather, the agency they use in Africa has devised), their own route up the mountain.

You should also check each supplier's ethical credentials. A disappointing number of foreign agencies make bold claims about how well they treat their porters, because this is what their Tanzania operator has told them they do. Unfortunately, the foreign agency rarely verifies these claims – so you will have to. If you can find out the name of the African supplier they use, read our opinion of them in the reviews on p182, p205 and p215 and check on the porters' charity KPAP's (see pp46-49) website too (🖥 www.kiliporters.org) to get their opinion. On the subject of the treatment of porters, in the following reviews you'll find that we have noted where the company is a KPAP partner; this means, in essence, that they have received the seal of approval from KPAP for the way their porters are treated. You may also wish to dismiss the agencies' claims for certain routes – eg that the Marangu Route is easy or Machame is quiet; at the risk of sounding arrogant, trust our descriptions of the trails rather than theirs.

If it transpires that two companies use the same African supplier, but charge different amounts for the same trek, don't necessarily opt for the cheaper agency. The companies may offer different services – more nights in a hotel, for example, or free one-day tours before or after the trek.

Finally, if you are planning on a safari after your trek, take this into account when choosing which agency to book with: often booking a safari and Kilimanjaro trek with the same company will work out cheaper than booking each leg with a separate company.

Trekking agencies in the UK

● **Aardvark safaris** (☎ 01980-849160; 🖳 www.aardvarksafaris.com), RBL House, Ordnance Road, Tidworth, Hants SP9 7QD. With a name that guarantees that it will always be at the top of any list of companies, this agency offers tailor-made trips to Africa and are the agents for KPAP partner Summits Africa. As such, they specialize in Machame and Lemosho Route ascents – because that is what Summits Africa do – and have three standards of trek: lightweight, luxury and VIP (the latter including proper beds, wash tents and also includes tips for the crew, which saves you the trouble of having to sort them out yourself); see the Summits Africa review, p188, for more details. Prices: for the Machame Route, their prices were: 'Lightweight' scheduled trip £1637 per person; 'Luxury' scheduled/private trip, £2390/£2665 per person.

● **Abercrombie & Kent** (☎ 0845-618 2200; 🖳 www.abercrombiekent.co.uk). Upmarket holiday company which will send you big, glossy brochures at the click of a mouse (sadly, with very little information inside, though the photos are nice). You'll have more joy phoning them and the staff do seem pretty knowledgeable, especially so when you consider how many other types of holiday they sell. Unfortunately, they do still perpetuate the myth that the Machame Route is a less busy route and they also claim that they have their own operation in Arusha and don't delegate out to a third party – which must come as something of a surprise to Summits Africa who operate their treks. Still, at least their choice of Summits Africa is a good one! Prices are around £2800, though as every trek is private and tailor-made, that's a ballpark figure only. KPAP partner.

● **Acacia Africa** (☎ 020-7706 4700; 🖳 www.acacia-africa.com), Lower Ground Floor, 23A Craven Terrace, London W2 3QH. Africa specialist using Springlands as a base (so it looks like Moshi's Zara Tours, see p210, are the local trekking agency here). Prices start at £530 (or £715 including Nairobi transfers) for the basic 5-day Marangu trek plus a further US$540 local payment which is collected at the start of the trip. As with most UK travel agents, Acacia offer you the chance to combine your trek with a Zanzibar trip or safari.

● **Action Challenge** (☎ 020-7354 1465; 🖳 www.actionchallenge.com) AH 216, 22 Highbury Grove, London, N5 2EA. 'A specialist organizer of challenge events across the globe', Action Challenge's main business is helping with the organization of various charity treks and adventures. Currently they organize a trek a month on the Machame Route. As is often the case with these sorts of charitable expeditions, it can be a terrifically cheap way to climb if you can raise a minimum amount of sponsorship. With Action Challenge, they ask for a deposit (£299) to book your place, but then an extra £3400 is required in sponsorship before they allow you on the mountain; alternatively, you can forget trying to raise the sponsorship money and just pay for your trek yourself (another £1696 in addition to the deposit). KPAP partner using Duma Explorer (see p186).

● **The Adventure Company** (☎ 0845-609 11137; 🖳 www.adventurecompany. co.uk) 15 Turk Street, Alton, Hampshire GU34 1AG. Offers Machame Route trips for £1379-1629, Marangu route packages starting from £1329 and Rongai Route trips from £1369, each package lasting around ten days of which six are actually spent on the mountain, the prices including flights but *excluding* park fees (estimated by them to be £430; see p41 for our calculations).

● **Africa Travel Resource** (☎ 01306-880770; 🖳 www.africatravelresource.com) Milton Heath House, Westcott Road, Dorking, Surrey RH34 3NB. Often recommended, very reliable and extremely knowledgeable outfit that uses African Walking Company (see p184) for their climbs. ATR's website is a no-nonsense place stuffed with information, for as well as promoting their own climbs they also have general stuff on booking a trek with other companies and a review of some of the local hotels. Offering only the Rongai and Shira/Lemosho routes (because, in their opinion, the Machame Route is overcrowded, as is the Marangu) as well as AWC's own 'North Route', their very helpful telephone staff quoted us ballpark figures only (as each climb is a little different in what it incorporates), namely US$2300 per person for seven days on the Lemosho Route, or US$2000 for six days on Rongai. For the North Route, which is eight days, they charge around US$3000-3500, though they accept private bookings only on this route (ie you can't join a scheduled climb on this route). KPAP partner and recommended by us too.

● **Audley Travel** (☎ 01993-838000, 🖳 www.audleytravel.com) New Mill, New Mill Lane, Witney, Oxfordshire, OX29 9SX. Tailor-made travel agents with multiple awards to their name and a KPAP partner to boot, thanks to their use of Nature Discovery as their ground operator. Offer eight days on Lemosho and seven days on Machame, though other routes can be arranged too. With no pretensions to being cheap, they use the lovely Onsea House as the base for their clients and charge £3560 each for a private Machame trek for two, or £4582 each for eight days on Lemosho, each including two nights at Onsea. Whack on another £300 each to the latter climb for a climb via the Western Breach. Not cheap – though if you've got the money you could do a lot worse.

● **Charity Challenge** (☎ 020-8557 0000; 🖳 www.charitychallenge.co.uk) 7th Floor, Northway House, 1379 High Road, London N20 9LP. This company arranges expeditions to various places in order to raise money for charity and helped in the organization of 2009's Comic Relief trek. Seeming to concentrate on the Lemosho and Rongai routes only, in order to participate you need to raise a substantial amount of sponsorship – in Kili's case, over £4000. Fail, and you could be kicked off the trip! Aside from all the fundraising, the cost for climbing Kili is £2554 for Lemosho, £2338 for Rongai – not cheap, though flights are included and you are paying for their expertise. KPAP partner, uses AWC (see p184).

● **Classic Journeys** (☎ 01773-873497; 💻 www.classicjourneys.co.uk) 33 High St, Tibshelf, Alfreton, Derbyshire DE55 5NX. Recommended by one reader for their efficient service and reputation for ethical tourism (a reputation that is well-founded, apparently, for they use KPAP partner Tanzanian Journeys (see p210) for their climbs). Classic Journeys uses the seven-day Rongai Route with Mawenzi Tarn diversion (including a rest day there) for their climbs, charging around £1445 for the latter, excluding flights but including three nights in Moshi. Also offers the Shira Route including a diversion to Moir Huts for £1655 including two nights' accommodation in Moshi.

● **Climb Mount Kilimanjaro** (💻 www.climbmountkilimanjaro.com) Fourth floor, 38 Eversfield Place, St-Leonards-on-Sea, East Sussex TN37 6DB. Company established by the author of this book with the aim of providing high-quality treks for clients at a reasonable price, using the knowledge gained over the past ten years of researching and writing this book; for more details on our service and the treks we offer, please visit our website.

● **Discover Adventure** (☎ 01722-718444 💻 www.discoveradventure.co.uk) Throope Down House, Blandford Road, Coombe Bassett, Salisbury, SP5 4LN. Organization specializing in expeditions to various far-flung parts of the world, where you participate on behalf of the charity of your choice. Recommended by one reader, as with many of these charity companies if you manage to raise a certain amount of sponsorship they'll pay for your climb. Climbs start at about £1749 if funding it yourself, or you must raise over £3500 to get a freebie.

● **Exodus Travels** (☎ 0845-863 9619; 💻 www.exodustravels.co.uk) Grange Mills, Weir Rd, London SW12 ONE. Long-standing British company that offers a number of different trips including a new North Circuit trek (so it's no surprise to find that African Walking Company are the African operator here; see p184). Also offer plenty of Kili-plus combinations (eg a 17-day Kilimanjaro, Serengeti and Zanzibar trip for £2799). Regarding their treks, they offer Rongai (6 days from £1399 including flights, although there is a land-only version for £999) or Shira/ Lemosho (8 days, £1549 including flights) and the new Northern Circuit route (9 days, £1629 including flights). All prices include return flights from the UK. Laudably, they also run the Porter Education Project to teach English to the porters during the low season of April-June, and have established three schools in the local area to facilitate this. KPAP partner.

● **Explore Worldwide** (☎ 0845-013 1539; 💻 www.explore.co.uk) Nelson House, 55 Victoria Road, Farnborough, Hants GU14 7PA. Long-established company offering treks on, rather unusually, the old Shira Route (£1419 land only), though they do divert to Moir Hut and the Lent Group. They also operate an interesting 'Tanzanian Volcano' trip taking in a safari in Ngorongoro, a four-day Meru climb and a seven-day Kili trek on the Rongai Route (from £2595). Prices exclude flights though these can be booked too. A *mzungu* (ie Western) guide accompanies every trek. For Kili they use Ahsante of Moshi (see p205). KPAP partner.

● **Footprint Adventures** (☎ 01522-804929; 💻 www.footventure.co.uk) 5 Malham Drive, Lincoln LN6 0XD. Offers guided treks on Kilimanjaro beginning at

£760 for a five-day yomp up the Marangu Route, though all other routes are £935. As they say that these prices include all park fees, this seems to us to be particularly low – ask carefully what's included before booking. Uses Zara Tours (p210) as their local trekking agent and thus accommodation away from the mountain is at the Springlands (see p199).

● **Gane & Marshall** (☎ 01822-600600; 🖳 www.ganeandmarshall.co.uk), Aldenham, 2 Deer Park Lane, Tavistock, Devon, PL19 9HD. Company whose co-founder, Richard Gane, was one of the organizers behind 2009's successful Comic Relief celebrity climb. Prices start from around US$1870 for seven days on Rongai, while eight days on Shira (that's the old Shira Route via the Morum Barrier) costs US$2100 per person – it's an unusual take on the route in that on day three they divert off to Moir Huts and spend some time studying the Northern Icefields and the Lent Group, which is a pleasing change from the standard walk. They also do a six-day, US$1650 Rongai climb that departs most Sundays during high season and also offer a Meru climb followed by a six-day trek up Kili on the Rongai Route (US$2535). They can also book flights. KPAP partner, using African Walking Company (see p184).

● **Imaginative Traveller** (☎ 0845-077 8802; 🖳 www.imaginative-traveller. com) 1 Betts Avenue, Martlesham Heath, Suffolk IP5 3RH. Runs small-group tours including six-day treks on the Rongai (£899) and Marangu (£699) trails, both with a local payment of US$685.

● **IntoAfrica Eco Travels Tanzania** (☎ 0114-255 5610; 🖳 www.intoafrica. co.uk) 40 Huntingdon Crescent, Sheffield, S11 8AX. Partner of Maasai Wanderings; see p187. KPAP partner. Costs, as usual, depend on how many people are booking but for solo travellers they start at US$1995 if joining a scheduled seven-day Machame trek, rising to US$3385 if undertaking a private expedition and climbing by yourself.

● **Intrepid Travel** (☎ 0203-147 7777; 🖳 www.intrepidtravel.com), Wessex House, 40 Station Road, Westbury, Wiltshire BA13 3JN. Now that they've taken over Guerba Expeditions, Intrepid are one of the bigger operators on Kilimanjaro with offices worldwide. Offers the Rongai (£1070 plus US$650), Machame (£1070 plus US$650) and five days on Marangu (£700 plus US$550) routes. Nothing unusual there, but what *is* out of the ordinary is the ethical nature of their company. Not only do they issue each client with guidelines regarding responsible travel – and themselves use the Marangu Hotel (p215) to ensure their porters are fairly treated – but they also organize treks for Amani Children's Home in Moshi that are free for those who can raise £2400 in sponsorship. Well worth checking out. KPAP partner.

● **Jagged Globe** (☎ 0845-345 8848; 🖳 www.jagged-globe.co.uk) The Foundry Studios, 45 Mowbray Street, Sheffield S3 8EN. Serious mountaineering company that leads 14-person trips up 'trekkable' Kili per year on the Lemosho Route (£2475-2785). Prior to all their expeditions and treks they host a pre-trip weekend in North Wales for their clients for instruction and to meet their fellow trekkers. Uses the Key's Hotel (see p207).

• **KE Adventure Travel** (☎ 01768-773966; 🖥 www.keadventure.com) 32 Lake Rd, Keswick, Cumbria CA12 5DQ. Worldwide trekking specialists running a seven-day Rongai Route trek (including a rest day at Mawenzi Tarn Hut) for £895 as well as a 13-day combination Mount Meru and Kilimanjaro holiday, climbing the latter via the Lemosho trail (though they, like many others, misleadingly call it the Shira trail). Prices for the Kilimanjaro/Meru climb start at £1295 plus US$960 park fees.

• **Kumuka** (☎ 0800-092 9595, 020-7937 8855; 🖥 www.kumuka.com) 40 Earls Court Rd, London, W8 6EJ. Offers a lightning seven-day trip starting and finishing in Nairobi and including a five-day trek up Kili on the Marangu Route for £480 plus local payment US$700. Experienced and reliable but with only a short Marangu climb available, seems Kilimanjaro is not too important to them.

• **The Mountain Company** (☎ 020-749 80953; 🖥 www.themountaincompany.co.uk) Flat 3, 190 Cedars Rd, Clapham, London SW4 0PP. Small company running four expeditions on the Machame Route every year, using Marangu Hotel as their local partner. Price: US$2340 for six days on Machame with two nights' accommodation at the Marangu Hotel included. KPAP partner by virtue of using the Marangu Hotel.

• **Outlook Expeditions** (☎ 01286-871888; 🖥 www.outlookexpeditions.com) The Outlook Development Centre, Deiniolen, Llanberis, Gwynedd, LL55 3NF. Company specializing in organizing expeditions for schools to various parts of the world. For Kilimanjaro they offer a Machame trek preceded by an acclimatization walk around the Ngorongoro Highlands, with the chance to take part in some charitable project afterwards, whether it be teaching English or helping children with special needs. KPAP partner using Duma Explorer (see p186) of Arusha.

• **Sherpa Expeditions** (☎ 020-8577 2717; 🖥 www.sherpaexpeditions.com) 131a Heston Rd, Hounslow, Middlesex TW5 0RF. Longstanding walking company offering a ten-day package including a six-day Machame trek for a very reasonable £1049 *including* park fees, or a 13-day Mount Meru-Machame combination for £1342.

• **Team Kilimanjaro** (☎ 020-7193 5895 – note the clever number, with the last four digits being the height in metres of Kili; 🖥 www.teamkilimanjaro.com) 5 Church Walk, Bideford, Devon EX39 2BP. Coming at Kilimanjaro from a whole different angle, this company offers treks on all the routes (although Marangu only reluctantly) including their own takes on Rongai and Lemosho. Sample prices: from US$1809-2611 for seven days on their Rongai Route, US$1713-2356 for seven on Machame, the exact price depending on the number of people in your group. We liked them in the last edition and we still like them now: a well organized and efficient company and worth checking out.

• **Terra Firma** (☎ 01691-870321; 🖥 www.terrafirmatravel.com) 'eunant', Lake Vyrnwy, Wales, SY10 0NF. Runs four seven-day Rongai treks per year for £845 (land only) plus US$740 local payment per person. Uses Zara Tours (see p210) so accommodation is at Moshi's Springlands Hotel (p199).

• **Tribes Travel** (☎ 01728-685971; 🖥 www.tribes.co.uk) 12 The Business Centre, Earl Soham, Woodbridge, Suffolk IP13 7SA. Award-winning, eco-friendly, fair-trade company offering all the routes including the Western Breach – although they sensibly recommend that you don't take this option. Prices start from £1395 for six days on Machame, £1140 for five days on Marangu, both excluding flights but including two nights at Key's Hotel (whom they use as their trek supplier). KPAP partner.

● **Ultimate Travel Company** (☎ 020-7386 4646; 🖳 www.theultimatetravel company.co.uk), 25-27 Vanston Place, London SW6 1AZ. KPAP partner and luxury tour operator with Marangu Hotel as their local supplier. Offer plenty of trips in Africa, including climbs on the Machame route which you can combine with a Mount Kenya climb (£2955 per person based on two sharing). Also offers a tailor-made mountain-bike tour around Kilimanjaro for £1875 including flights, while for Machame they charge £1780 for seven days. KPAP partner, using Marangu Hotel (see p215) for their climbs.

● **World Expeditions** (☎ 020-8545 9030; 🖳 www.worldexpeditions.co.uk), 81 Craven Gardens, Wimbledon, SW19 8LU. KPAP partner. See p36, *Trekking Agencies in Australia* for more details.

Trekking agencies in Continental Europe

● **Austria** **Clearskies Expeditionen und Trekking** (☎ 0512 28 45 61, 🖳 www. clearskies.at), Planötzenhofstraße 25/1, 6020 Innsbruck; **Hauser Exkursionen** (☎ 1-50 50 34 6; 🖳 www.hauser-exkursionen.de), Favoritenstraße 70, A-1040 Wien – branch of German agency, see p32; **Supertramp** (☎ 01-533 51 37;

It's not just about the climbing – other things to do on Kili
There are plenty of other things you can do with Kilimanjaro apart from climbing it. How about entering the **Kilimanjaro Marathon**, for example, which usually takes place in late February or early March (🖳 www.kili manjaromarathon.com)? The race is run over the standard 26 miles/42.2km and starts by heading out along the road to Dar before returning to Moshi via a climb to Mweka. As such, it doesn't actually enter into the national park at all – though given the levels of exhaustion suffered by your average marathon participant, it's probably just as well that they don't have to climb a mountain too. Disabled races and a half-marathon are also held at the same time and with prizes of Ts2,500,000 each to the winners of the men's and women's race this is turning into one of the biggest events in the social calendar in Northern Tanzania.

For those for whom a marathon is not testing enough, there is always the **Kiliman Challenge** (🖳 www.kilimanjaroman.com). This particular brand of torture begins with a seven-day saunter up the Machame Route to Uhuru Peak, followed by a two-day circumnavigation by mountain bike around the base of the mountain, before rounding it all off with participation in the marathon described above. The organizers are at pains to point out that only the last two events are races; with the climb, of course, it's too dangerous to race up. If it all sounds too much, you can opt to take part in just one or two of the activities.

For details of how to participate in either the marathon or the Kiliman challenge, contact the South African operator Wild Frontiers (see p36) who organize the latter event and are the official tour agency for the marathon.

🖳 www.supertramp.co.at), Helferstorferstraße 4, A-1010 Wien; Islaverde Reisen eU (☎ 1-660 55 52 775; 🖳 www.islaverde.at), Andreas Misar, A-1170 Wien, Schumanngasse 67.

● **Belgium** Africa Tours (☎ 051-708 171; 🖳 www.africatours.be/) Sint Jansstraat 78, 8840 Staden; **Joker Tourisme** (☎ 02-502 19 37; 🖳 www.joker.be) Handelskaai 27, Brussels, and ten offices throughout the country.

● **Denmark** Inter-Travel (☎ 33-15 00 77; 🖳 www.intertravel.dk), Frederiksholms Kanal 2, 1220 Kobenhavn K; **Marco Polo Tours** (☎ 70-12 03 03; 🖳 www.marcopolo.dk), Borgergade 16, 1300 Kobenhavn K; **Topas** (☎ 86-89 36 22; 🖳 www.topas.dk), Bakkelyvej 2, 8680 Ry.

● **France** Allibert (☎ 08-25 090 190; 🖳 www.allibert-trekking.com) Route de Grenoble, 38530, Chapareillan, and three other offices around the country; **Club Aventure** (☎ 08-26 88 20 80; 🖳 www.clubaventure.fr), 13 rue Séguier, 75006 Paris; **Terres d'Aventure** (☎ 08-25 700 825; 🖳 www.terdav.com) 30 rue Saint Augustin, 75002 Paris and 13 other offices around the country – KPAP partner, using Corto of Arusha (see p185).

● **Germany** Chui Tours (☎ 0611-18249-13; 🖳 www.chui-tours.de), Biebricher Allee 58, 65187 Wiesbaden – KPAP partner using both Tanzania Journeys (see p210) and Summit Expeditions and Nomadic Experience (see p209);

While all of these events will doubtless test your stamina and teach you much about yourself, if you'd rather learn more about the country instead then may we recommend that you try a **bike tour around Kilimanjaro**. Chagga Tours (see p206) of Moshi currently organize a nine-day, 176-mile circuit of the mountain for €990-1250 (depending on the number of participants), including an escort vehicle for your luggage and a security guide who accompanies you. Considering the tour takes you through the remote north-west side of the mountain, sandwiched between Kili and Kenya's Amboseli National Park, we think this is a great trip. Accommodation is either at guesthouses or camping and the tour encompasses Lake Chala, Kilimanjaro's only crater lake, as well as isolated Maasai and Chagga villages.

Another option is **horseriding**. Makoa Farm near Machame Gate organizes horseback safaris in the West Kilimanjaro Wildlife Management Area, where you stay in permanent luxury camps and mobile camps, farmhouse accommodation next to Kilimanjaro Forest Reserve, comfortable cottages or at the guesthouse on Makoa Farm. Some experience is necessary to make the most of these rides but an alternative tour can be drawn up for those for whom this is their first time in the saddle. Costs are €1800 for four days on the Kilimanjaro Wilderness Trail (an itinerary where you don't move camp), €990 for the tour that's suitable for those with no riding experience; while for the 8-day West Kilimanjaro Big Game Trail (where you do move camp every night), prices rise to €2800. It's certainly a unique experience and being on horseback allows you to go where four-wheel drives and mountain bikes never could.

Hauser Exkursionen (☎ 089-2 35 00 60; 🖳 www.hauser-exkursionen.de/main.asp), Spiegelstraße 9, D-81241 München – also has offices in Berlin, Frankfurt and Hamburg; **DAV Summit Club** (☎ 089-64 240-0; 🖳 www.dav-summit-club.de), Am Perlacher Forst 186, 81545 München; **Olifants Tours and Safaris** (☎ 04293-78 98 89; 🖳 www.olifants.de) Wilhelmshauser Straße 3, D-28870 Fischerhude; **Skantur** (☎ 047-61 21 53 55; 🖳 www.skantur.de), Skandinavisches Reisezentrum DA, Ulvoldsveien, N-2670 Otta.

● **Luxembourg** Bel Africa (☎ 26 30 59 03; 🖳 www.belafrica.fr) KPAP partner using Maasai Wanderings (see p187) for their climbs.

● **Netherlands** 7 Summits (🖳 http://7summits.com/). Company run by one-man band Harry Kilkstra that specializes in climbs up each of the continents' highest peaks, with a website that has a good FAQ section about Kilimanjaro; uses Zara Tours. Land-only prices start at US$1475 for seven days on Machame, US$1250 for six days on Marangu. **Explore Tanzania** (☎ 055-53 32 550; 🖳 www.exploretanzania.nl), Koppellaan 11, 7314 BP Apeldoorn – KPAP partner using African Walking Company (see p184); **Flach Travel Company** (☎ 0343-59 26 59; 🖳 www.flachtravel.nl), Volderstraat 27, 3961BA Wijk bij Duurstede; **Himalaya Trekking** (☎ 052-22 41 146; 🖳 www.htwandelreizen. nl), Noordeinde 4A, 7941 AT Meppel; **Nederlandse Klim en Bergsport Vereniging** (☎ 0348-40 95 21; 🖳 www.nkbv.nl), Houttuinlaan 16A, 3447 GM Woerden; **Snow Leopard Adventure Reizen** (☎ 070-38 82 867; 🖳 www.snowleopard.nl), The Globe, Outdoor & Travel Center, Waldorpstraat 15M; **SNP Reiswinkel** (☎ 024-32 77 000; 🖳 www.snp.nl), Bijleveldsingel 26, Nijmegen; **Tanzaniaonline** (☎ 071-51 62 035, 🖳 www.keniaonline.nl), Pompoenweg 9, 2321 DK Leiden – KPAP partner, using Tanzania Journeys (see p210).

● **Norway** EcoExpeditions (☎ 47-90 04 13 30; 🖳 www.ecoexpeditions.no/), PO Box 2028 Hillevåg, 4095 Stavanger; **Explore Travel** (☎ 47-69 36 18 50; 🖳 www.exploretravel.no/), PO Box 458, N-1601 Fredrikstad – KPAP partner using Marangu Hotel (see p215); **Hvitserk** (☎ 23 21 30 70; 🖳 www.hvitserk. no), Prof Dahlsgt 3, 0355 Oslo; **Kilroy Travels** (☎ 026 33; 🖳 www.kilroytravels.no), Nedre Slottsgate 23, 0157 Oslo; **Skandinavisches Reisezentrum DA** (☎ 61-23 03 23, 🖳 www.myafrica.no), Terje Ulvolden, Ulvoldsveien 1, N-2670 Otta; **Worldwide Adventures** (☎ 22-40 48 90; 🖳 www.worldwide.no), AS Nedre Slottsgate 12, Oslo 0157.

● **Spain** Giroguies (☎ 972-30 38 86; 🖳 www.giroguies.com), c/Ample, 126 baixos, 17200, Palafrugell, Girona.

● **Sweden** Aventyrsresor (☎ 08-55 60 69 00; 🖳 www.aventyrsresor.se) Box 19573, Tulegatan 39, 104 32, Stockholm; **Kilroy Travels** (☎ 0771-545769; 🖳 www.kilroytravels.se), Kungsgatan 4, S-103 87 Stockholm.

● **Switzerland** Acapa Tours (☎ 056-443 32 21; 🖳 www.acapa.ch) Underdorfnstrasse 35, CH5107, Schinznach Dorf; **Aktivferien AG** (☎ 052-335 13 10; 🖳 www.aktivferien.com) Weidstrasse 6, Postfach 27, CH-8472 Seuzach; **b&b**

travel (☎ 01-380 4343; 🖳 www.bandbtravel.ch) Seefeldstrasse 210, 8008 Zürich; **Hanspeter Kaufmann** (☎ 041-822 00 55, 🖳 www.kaufmanntrekking.ch/), Wylen 1, 6440 Brunnen/Schweiz; KPAP partner using Marangu Hotel (see p215).

Trekking agencies in the USA

North American trekking agencies tend to quote land cost only.

● **Aardvark Safaris** (☎ Toll free from USA 1-888-776-0888; Outside USA: 1-858-794-1480; 🖳 www.aardvarksafaris.com), 12707 High Bluff Drive, Suite 200, San Diego, California CA 92130. Agent for Summits Africa (see p188).

● **Adventure Center** (☎ 510-654 1879, 800-228 8747; 🖳 www.adventurecenter.com) 1311 63rd St, Suite 200, Emeryville, CA 94608. Agents for Intrepid (see p28) amongst others, offering Marangu, Machame, Shira and Rongai routes, with prices starting from around US$1055 plus a local payment of US$685.

● **Adventures within Reach** (☎ 877-232 5836; 🖳 www.adventureswithinreach.com) Boulder, Colorado. Award-winning 'adventure company', now working with Moshi's Eco Tours. Supports the Tunahaki Centre for Street Children in Moshi. Offers all routes, the itinerary of their treks being fairly standard and their prices reasonable: US$1365 for six days on Marangu; US$1640 for seven days on Machame. Add another US$50 for the Western Breach Route.

● **Alpine Ascents International** (☎ 206-378 1927; 🖳 www.alpineascents.com) 121 Mercer St, Seattle, WA 98109. Highly regarded, very professional and efficient agency that, a little surprisingly, uses Big Expeditions of Arusha. All of their climbs are accompanied by one of their own mountain guides and they do have a very good success rate. Price: US$5700 with flights from the US for seven days on the Machame Route, US$4800 land only. KPAP partner.

● **Deeper Africa** (☎ 888-658 7102; 🖳 www.deeperafrica.com) 4450 Arapahoe Avenue, Suite 100, Boulder, Colorado 80303. Small company specializing in East Africa and winners of National Geographic's Best Safari Outfitters for 2009. Offer an eleven-day trip including a seven-day Machame Route trek for US$4999 excluding international flights, with a trip to Arusha National Park thrown in too. Not cheap, though their concern for the welfare of porters shines through on their website and, thanks to their use of African Environments as the local supplier, they are a KPAP partner.

● **F&S Kiliwarrior** (☎ 0703-3493215; 🖳 www.go-kili.com). US contact of Arusha-based company; (see p186).

● **Geographic Expeditions** (☎ 415-922 0448, 800-777 8183; 🖳 www.geoex.com), 1008 General Kennedy Ave, San Francisco, CA 94129-0902. Offer an 18-day 'Real Kilimanjaro' trek up the Lemosho/Western Breach Route with trips to Ngorongoro Crater and Serengeti afterwards as a reward for your exertions. Prices start at a jaw-dropping US$7400 plus US$1565 park fees, with internal airfares a further US$850.

● **Global Adrenaline** (☎ 866-884-5622; 🖳 www.globaladrenaline.com) 25 East Washington Street, Suite 1458, Chicago, Illinois 60602. KPAP partner offering a nine-day trip including a seven-day Machame trek, using African Environments as their local supplier.

- **Global Alliance for Africa** (☎ 312-382-0607 ⌨ www.globalallianceafrica. org) 703 West Monroe Street, Chicago IL, 60661. Organization that teams up with local African NGOs to help orphans and children affected by HIV/AIDS. Organizes occasional treks up Kili to boost fundraising and is a partner of KPAP.
- **Good Earth** (☎ 888-776-7173; ⌨ www.goodearthtours.com), 1936 Bruce B Down Blvd, Suite # 334, Wesley Chapel, Florida 33543. American office of Arusha-based company (see p187).
- **International Mountain Guides** (☎ 360-569-2609, ⌨ www.mountain guides.com) PO Box 246, Ashford, WA 98304. Long-established company that's conducted over 150 climbs on Kilimanjaro, each accompanied by one of IMG's American guides (with the Key's Hotel as the local supplier). The climb only – seven days on Machame – is US$4025; for roughly double that you can join one of their unique 'Mount Kilimanjaro Photoworkshop' climbs in the company of professional snapper Adam Angel, with every climber accompanied by his or her own porter who carries the photographic equipment; a safari is also included. The cost for all this opulence is US$8450, land only. KPAP partner.
- **Journeys International** (☎ 734-665 4407, 800-255 8735; ⌨ www.journeys. travel/) 107 Aprill Drive, Suite 3, Ann Arbor, MI 48103-1903. Does Rongai and Shira routes (from US$3675-3895/US$3795 respectively).
- **Journey to Africa** (☎ 877-558 6288; ⌨ www.journeytoafrica.com) 1302 Waugh Drive 504, Houston, TX 77019. Currently organizes 16-day trips including a Machame, Shira (check whether they actually mean Lemosho) or Rongai Route trek for US$6680/US$7380 per person for 4/2 people respectively, with a safari trip to Tarangire, Ngorongoro and Serengeti national parks included.
- **Mountain Madness** (☎ 206-937 8389, 800-328-5925; ⌨ www.mountainma dness.com) 3018 SW Charlestown Street, Seattle, WA 98126. Founded by the late Scott Fischer, after whom Kili's (now disused) Fischer Campsite is named, the highly regarded Mountain Madness and their sister company African Environments (see p183) have a long association with the mountain, pioneering Kili's Lemosho Route across the Shira Plateau and boasting a success rate in reaching the top of greater than 90%. These days in addition to Lemosho they also offer the Umbwe Route, combining the trip with an optional jaunt to the Serengeti. Climb-only prices are US$5300/US$5100/US$4875 for parties of 4-5/6-9/10-14 respectively on the 8-day Lemosho Route. One of the best. KPAP partner.
- **Mountain Travel & Sobek Expeditions** (☎ 510-594 6000, ☎ 888-831 7526; ⌨ www.mtsobek.com) 1266 66th Street, Emeryville, CA 94608. Upmarket trekking company offering ten-day hikes on the Machame/Western Breach trail (with eight days actually on the mountain), including a night at Crater Camp, for US$5095/US$4595/US$4295 per person for 4-6/7-11/12–14 members. Rongai climbs are also available. NBC's Ann Curry climbed with them in November 2008. KPAP partner, using African Enviroments (see p183) as their local supplier.
- **Peak Planet** (⌨ www.peakplanet.com) 2415 E Camelback Rd #700, Phoenix, AZ 85016. Exclusive US agent for African Walking Company (p184).

Prices start from US$1999 for the Rongai Route with Mawenzi Tarn diversion, rising to US$3199 for AWC's new Northern Circuit Route. KPAP partner.

● **Thomson Safaris** (☎ 617-923 0426, toll free 800-235 0289; ☐ www.thomsontreks.com) 14 Mount Auburn Street, Watertown, MA 02472. The first US tour company in Tanzania and one recommended by David Breasher, the director of the IMAX film *Kilimanjaro: To the Roof of Africa*. They are also a KPAP partner (see pp46-49) with their local operator, Nature Discovery, boasting a good reputation for looking after their porters. They offer just the 9-day Lemosho Route with a night in Crater Camp from US$5390, and 6 days on Umbwe from US$3630.

● **Tusker Trail** (☎ toll free 800-231-1919; ☐ http://tusker.com) 924 Incline Way, Suite H, Incline Village NV 89451-9423. Highly recommended, highly regarded and very experienced company that's been operating for over 30 years, now using their own company, Tembo Trails, as their supplier. Cited by Kilimanjaro Porters Assistance Project for their exemplary treatment of porters (see pp46-49), Tusker claim to have the highest guide-to-climber ratio and a success rate that hovers around the 97% mark; their guides also receive the best medical training on the mountain. The two routes they offer are the Machame and Lemosho routes. Their guides, weirdly, often sing for their clients, sometimes virtually all the way to the summit! Trips start at US$3890 for the Machame (seven days), or US$4790 for Lemosho. KPAP partner.

● **Wilderness Travel** (☎ 510-558 2488, toll free 800-368 2794; ☐ www.wildernesstravel.com) 1102 9th St, Berkeley, CA 94710. Offers an 18-day trek on an unusual version of the 'Shira Plateau' (Lemosho) and Western Breach Route combined with a Serengeti safari add-on. Prices US$7495/US$7295/$6995 for 7-8/9-11/12-14 members). KPAP partner, using African Enviroments (see p183) as their local supplier.

Trekking agencies in Canada

● **Canadian Himalayan Expeditions** (☎ 416-360 4300, toll free 1-800-563 8735; ☐ www.himalayanexpeditions.com) 2 Toronto St, Suite 302, Toronto, Ontario M5C 2B6. Focuses on private treks, running a couple of standard treks on the Marangu and Machame routes. Land costs are around US$1695 (CA$1745) and US$1895 (CA$1950) respectively.

● **GAP Adventures** (☎ 1-800 708 7761; ☐ www.gapadventures.com) 19 Charlotte Street, Toronto, Ontario, M5V 2H5. Run treks on all routes. Prices start at US$729 for five days on the Marangu Route, using Zara as the local agency.

● **Intrepid Travel** (☎ 1-866-360 1151; ☐ www.intrepidtravel.com). KPAP partner. See p28 for more details.

● **Trek Escapes** (☎ 1-866 338 TREK; ☐ www.trekescapes.com). Agent for companies such as Exodus, Gecko's, Imaginative Traveller (see *Trekking Agencies in the UK*, p28) and Australia's Peregrine Adventures (see p36).

● **World Expeditions** (☎ 613-241 2700; ☐ www.worldexpeditions.ca) 78 George Street, Ottawa (ON) K1N 5W1; also **Montreal** 1705 St-Denis Street, Montreal (QC) H2X 3K4. KPAP partner, using African Walking Company (see p184) as their local supplier.

Trekking agencies in Australia

● **Intrepid Travel** (☎ 1300 360 887; 🖳 www.intrepidtravel.com) 11 Spring Street, Fitzroy, Victoria. See p28. KPAP partner.

● **Peregrine Adventures** (☎ 03-8601 4444; 🖳 www.peregrineadventures.com) Level 4, 380 Lonsdale St, Melbourne, Vic 3000. One of Australia's larger agencies. Offers Rongai and Machame routes with optional Zanzibar/safari add-ons.

● **World Expeditions** (☎ 1300-720-000; 🖳 www.worldexpeditions.com/au) Level 5, 71 York St, **Sydney** NSW 2000. Also in **Melbourne** (☎ 03-8631 3300) 1st Floor, 393 Little Bourke St; **Perth** (☎ 08-9486 9899), Level 4, Gledden Building, Corner Hay & William St; and **Brisbane** (☎ 07-3216 0823). This KPAP partner (see pp46-49) offers a challenging 16-day Twin Peaks trekking trip encompassing both Mount Kenya and Kilimanjaro (Rongai Route; from A$5790 for both treks), or simple Rongai/Shira treks (A$2790/3450). They also organize a 17-day 'Tanzania on Foot' (A$5790) tour, a combination of safari and trekking including climbs of Lemagrut, Meru and Kili. Uses African Walking Company (see p184) for their treks.

Trekking agencies in New Zealand

● **Adventure Consultants** (☎ 03-443 8711, 🖳 www.adventureconsultants. com) PO Box 739, 58 McDougall St, Lake Wanaka, 9343. KPAP partner, using Nature Discovery (see p187) for their climbs.

● **Adventure World** (☎ 0800 238 368, 09-524 5118; 🖳 www.adventure world.co.nz) 101 Great South Rd, Remuera, PO Box 74008, Auckland. Offers six-day treks on the Marangu Route for NZ$1671.

● **Aspiring Guides** (☎ 03-443 9422; 🖳 www.aspiringguides.com) 99 Ardmore Street, PO Box 345, Lake Wanaka 9192. Partners of Jagged Globe (see p28).

● **Intrepid Travel** (☎ 0800 450 883; 🖳 www.intrepidtravel.com); see p28. KPAP partner.

● **World Expeditions** (☎ 09-368 4161, toll free 0800 350 354, 🖳 www.world expeditions.com/nz/) Level 2, 35 High Street, Auckland CBD. Branch of World Expeditions of Australia (see above).

Trekking agencies in South Africa

● **Acacia Africa** (☎ 21-556 1157, 🖳 www.acacia-africa.com) Unit 4, 23A Kilarney Avenue, Kilarney Gardens, Cape Town 8051. See *Trekking agencies in the UK*, p25.

● **Destination Africa Tours** (☎ 12-333 7110; 🖳 www.climbingkilimanjaro. co.za) 671 31st Avenue, Villeria, Pretoria 0186. Agency covering all routes that *claims* to have a 96% success rate for getting trekkers to Uhuru. Their website includes full-moon dates, Swahili terms, a fitness programme and a menu.

● **Wild Frontiers** (☎ 11-702 2035; 🖳 www.wildfrontiers.com). Organizes regular trips up Kili and are involved in the annual Kilimarathon. Uses Key's as their local supplier. KPAP partner.

For a review of **trekking agencies in Tanzania and Kenya**, see p145 (Dar es Salaam), p154 (Nairobi), p182 (Arusha), p205 (Moshi) and p215 (Marangu); and read the following section.

BOOKING WITH AN AGENCY IN TANZANIA

The main advantage of booking in Tanzania is one of economy: simply put, you're cutting out the middleman. Many foreign tour operators don't actually use their own staff to organize and lead the treks but use the services of a Tanzanian tour operator. By booking in Tanzania, therefore, you are dealing directly with the people who are going to take you up the mountain and not the Western agent.

So it can be a bit cheaper waiting until after you've arrived in Tanzania before booking your trek, particularly if you are willing to shop around and especially if you are willing to bargain. There are other advantages too. If you ask, there should be no reason why you cannot meet the guides and porters before you agree to sign up – and even your fellow trekkers, all of whom have a huge role to play in making your trek an enjoyable one. You can also personally check the tents and camping equipment before booking. Furthermore, the fact that you can book a trek up to 24 hours beforehand (though see the note on p242) gives you greater flexibility, allowing you to alter your plans so that you can pick a day that suits you – whereas when booking with an agency at home you often have to book months in advance, the tour is usually organized to a pretty tight schedule and altering this schedule at a later date is often impossible. Another point: while the money you spend on a trek may not be going to the most destitute and deserving of Tanzania's population, at least you know that *all* of it is going to Tanzanians, with none going into the pockets of a Western company. And finally, thanks to the internet you don't even need to wait until you arrive in Tanzania before booking: most agencies in Arusha and Moshi (see p182 and p205) now have internet booking services and, while it may seem a little scary sending a four-figure sum to people in East Africa whom you've never met, the bigger companies at least are used to receiving bookings this way and are trustworthy. What's more, if you go with an agency that's been recommended in this book or by friends, then there's no reason why it should be any more risky than if you were booking at home; indeed, there's a slim chance that you might even end up joining a group who *did* book their tour abroad and paid more as a consequence.

Choosing an agency in Tanzania

The best place to look for an agency is either **Arusha** (see p182), which has the greatest number of tour and trekking operators, or **Moshi** (see p205). A third option, **Marangu**, is smaller and has fewer agencies (see p215). Agencies in Dar es Salaam and other Tanzanian towns are usually nothing more than middlemen for the operators in Moshi, Arusha or Marangu: book a tour with an agency in Dar, for example, and the chances are you'll still end up on a trek organized by an agency in Moshi or Arusha, only you would have paid more for it. Furthermore, if you book outside of Arusha or Moshi, you have less chance of inspecting the equipment or testing your guide before you set off.

Regarding the difference between Arusha and Moshi: in general the former is the home of the more established and larger safari companies/trekking agencies. However, perhaps due to its location, the Arusha-based companies tend to concentrate just as much on safaris in the Serengeti, Ngorongoro and Arusha

National Park (including climbs up Meru) as they do on treks up Kilimanjaro. Indeed, some just act as middlemen for one of the agencies in Moshi, and don't actually arrange Kili treks themselves. Moshi, on the other hand, is a smaller place and one where the agencies tend to focus more on climbing Kilimanjaro than on safaris. It would also be fair to say that the Moshi-based companies tend to be a little cheaper than those in Arusha, and most budget operators have their offices in Moshi.

Reading the above, therefore, it would seem that you should base yourself in Moshi rather than Arusha if you are in the market for a budget trek. But it's not that simple. In particular, if you are thinking of taking a safari before or after your Kili climb, the Arusha-based companies may be able to offer you a better package for both than those in Moshi. Furthermore, it is an unfortunate truth that of those that KPAP (the Kilimanjaro Porters Assistance Program) recommend for treating their porters well, only six are based in Moshi.

Our advice, therefore, is as follows. If you want a budget trek, the operators in Moshi tend to be cheaper. But before booking with any of them, do check out KPAP's website, download their questionnaire, and use this to grill any agency about their treatment of porters (many of them are cheaper because they pay porters poorly); and if you're unsatisfied with any of the answers given by an agency, let your conscience be your guide and go somewhere else. And don't dismiss the Arusha companies, particularly if a safari also features in your plans.

Wherever you decide to shop for your trek, check out our reviews of the agencies on p182 (Arusha) and p205 (Moshi), which should help in your quest. The golden rule when shopping around in either town is: **stick to those agencies that have a licence** and check that licence thoroughly to ensure it covers trekking. If they don't have a licence, or the one that they show you looks a bit suspect, is out of date, or looks fake, take your business elsewhere.

Other advice includes:
● Decide what sort of trek you want, what route you wish to take, how long you wish to go for, and with how many people.
● Ask other travellers for their recommendations of a good agency.
● Shop around. Don't sign up with the first agent you talk to but consult other agencies first to compare.
● Read the section on p39 on signing contracts and learn it off by heart (or take this book with you!), so you know what to ask the agency.
● Ask about the number of other people on your trek and the number of porters you'll be taking.
● Ask if you can see their **'comments book'**. This is a book where previous clients have written their thoughts on the agency. Nearly every agency will have one and if they are any good they will show it to you with little or no prompting. Indeed, if they don't have one, or are reluctant to show you, be suspicious.
● If you have any dietary requirements or other special needs, ask them if these will be a problem, if it will cost any more, and how exactly they propose to comply with your requirements. For example, if you are a vegetarian, ask the agent what kind of meals you can expect to receive on the trek.

● Ask to see a print-out of the day-to-day itinerary (though some, admittedly, will not have this, all agencies should be able to describe the trekking routes and their itineraries without any problem); if you're negotiating with an agency at the upper end of the market, you may even be able to get a preview of the daily menus.

● If you think you've found a good company, ask to see the equipment you will be using and make sure the tent is complete, untorn and that all the zips work.

● Check the sleeping arrangements, particularly if you're not trekking with friends but have joined a group: are you going to have a tent to yourself, or are you going to be sharing with somebody you've never met before?

● If you are alone and on a budget, ask if it is possible to be put with a group, which should make things cheaper. (This is normally done automatically anyway; indeed, if you are travelling alone and were quoted a very low price, you can expect to be put with another group.)

Following on from the last point, many of the operators at the budget end often band together to lump all their customers into one large trekking group, thereby making it cheaper for them as certain fixed costs can be shared. So don't be surprised if, having signed up with one company, you end up being joined by trekkers who booked with another company. Once again, make sure you know in advance about any arrangements like this *before* you sign anything or hand over any money. And if you want to be on your own, tell them.

The sleeping arrangements are just one of the potential hazards of booking with a budget company. Or rather, it's one of the advantages of paying a bit more and going with a company that won't spring any nasty surprises on you. Sign up with a more expensive company and you should find that they have better safety procedures and emergency equipment and more knowledgeable guides. So unless money is really tight don't look for the cheapest company but the *best value* one; and hopefully our reviews will help you to decide which agencies offer the best deals.

For a list of trekking agencies in Tanzania, see the relevant sections in the Arusha, Moshi and Marangu chapters on p182, p205 and p215 respectively.

SIGNING THE CONTRACT

This section is mainly for those who are in Tanzania and dealing with agencies face to face, though much of it is relevant to those booking with an agency in their own country – or with a company online – too.

So, you've found a suitable agency offering the trek you want for the required duration at an acceptable price. Before you sign on the dotted line, however, there are a number of questions to be asked, matters to consider and points to discuss with the agency. (And if there is no dotted line to sign on – ie no contract – then don't even think about handing over any money or going with them.) What is vitally important is that you **sort out *exactly* what is and isn't included in the price of the trek**. Don't just ask what is included in the price: ask what *isn't* included – ie what you yourself will need to pay for as this will give you an idea of exactly how much extra you need to pay in addition to the basic cost of the trek.

The following is a brief checklist of **items that should be included**:

● All park fees, rescue fees, hut/camping fees for both yourself and the porters and guides.

● Hire of porters, assistant guides and guides, their wages and food.

● Food and water for the entire trek. Get a breakdown of exactly how many meals per day you will be getting: normally trekkers are served three main meals per day plus a snack – typically a hot drink with popcorn and biscuits – upon arrival at camp at the end of the day; see p245 for more details on food on the trek.

● Transport to and from the park at the beginning and end of the trek.

● Hire of camping and cooking gear. If you have brought your own gear, you might be able to persuade the agency to reduce the cost of your trek, though it will be only by a small amount.

● Hire of any equipment – torches, ski poles, spare water-bottles etc – that you have forgotten to bring with you. There will probably be a small surcharge for these – just make sure that whatever you agree is included in the contract.

● Any special dietary requirements or other needs, all of which should be stipulated in the contract.

● Any free night's accommodation at the beginning or end of your trek that the trekking company has agreed to pay for.

In addition to the above, clients who are booking from abroad and have agreed that transfers from and to Kilimanjaro Airport are included should again make sure that it's stipulated in the contract.

Please note that items that are rarely, if ever, included in the package include cigarettes, soft drinks and the tips you dish out to your crew at the end.

Having sorted that out, you then need to make sure that *everything* that the agency has said they will provide, including everything listed above, is **specified in the contract**. This is important because, as you probably already know, a verbal contract is simply not worth the paper it isn't written on. The trekking companies all have standard contracts already drawn up which should include most of the above but will not include specific things such as the hire of any equipment that you need or any free nights' accommodation that you have managed to negotiate into the package. However, these will need to be written in as well.

THE COST: WHY IS IT ALL SO EXPENSIVE?

With little change from US$1200 for even the rock-bottom cheapest trek, it cannot be denied that climbing Kili is a relatively expensive walk, particularly when compared to other famous treks (the Annapurna Circuit in Nepal, for example, has a 'conservation fee' of Rs2000 – less than US$30 – while the Inca Trail has an entrance fee of around US$80, and it's US$450 for an all-inclusive tour); with no refund available to those who fail either, even if you are forced to give up after only a few minutes on the mountain, at first sight this trek can seem very bad value too – though to those who successfully reach the summit, of course, the sense of achievement and the enjoyment of the trek makes any amount seem worth it.

Since January 2006 and the doubling of the park entry fees, the cost of the trek has become even more extortionate. To give you some idea of where your US$1000-plus is going, the following is a breakdown of fees, wages and other costs incurred on the trek, while the box on p42 is an example of the breakdown of costs for an average trek. Don't forget that, in addition to the official costs outlined below, there is also the matter of **tips**: see p43 for further details.

Park fees

Rescue fee	US$20 per trip
Park entry fee	US$60 per day (US$10 for U16s)
Hut fee (Marangu Route only)	US$50 per night
Porter/guide entrance fees	US$1 per person per trip
Camping fee	US$50 per night (US$10 for under 16s)

(Note: residents of Tanzania pay Ts20,000 in park fees per trip)

Take a quick look at these figures and already you can see just why the cost of climbing Kilimanjaro is so high. Even if you took the quickest (and thus not recommended) five-day yomp up the Marangu Route, your fees alone still come to $520 plus porter/guide entrance fees. See p42 for how much a typical trek could cost.

Other costs

The following are the other major expenses involved in an expedition up Kilimanjaro. Note that, unlike park fees, with all of the following the more people in your group, the lower the per-person charge.

Wages (per trip) Wages vary from company to company, of course. Currently KINAPA, with assistance from KPAP (the Kilimanjaro Porters

---

Extending your time on the mountain

Although it's never made clear, it is possible to extend your permit while you're on the mountain. So, for example, if you are booked on a six-day trek, you can actually extend it to seven days or more. All you have to do is pay for the extra day(s) spent in the national park when you leave, either at Mweka or Marangu Gate. This means, of course, that should you fail to reach the summit, you can wait a day and try again. (The exception to this rule is those people on the Marangu Route who have to book their hut spaces in advance. As such, they have to specify the number of days they will be on the mountain before they start their trek and stick to it.)

At least, that's the theory. In practice, of course, it's not that easy. For a start, you have to make sure you have enough food for everyone to cover the extra time spent on the mountain. Secondly, you have to get permission from everybody else on your trek, including the guides, porters, the trekking company and, of course, other trekkers, that it's OK to delay your return back to civilization – and work out who's going to pay for the extra fees involved. This shouldn't be too difficult if you're the only trekker in the group, or the other trekkers you're with failed to reach the summit too and want another try at it. But both of these situations are unlikely – and it's perhaps unsurprising that we've never yet met anyone who has actually extended their time on the mountain. Still, it's worth knowing that the option exists.

Assistance Project), are trying to set a minimum wage on the mountain. The ambitious figures they have come up with are as follows:

Porters:	US$10 per day
Assistant guides (and presumably cooks):	US$15 per day
Guides:	US$20 per day

However, many in the industry consider these wages to be simply too generous and the figures have been widely criticized by many trekking agencies as simply unsustainable. Perhaps the success of this policy should be measured by the number of agencies who have actually tried to adopt this pay structure – namely two out of the 125 or so companies who operate on the mountain. So, instead, KINAPA have been forced to take a step backwards for the moment, and are instead concentrating on trying to ensure that companies at least meet the *old* wage levels, which were agreed between TATO (Tanzanian Association of Tour Operators) and KINAPA in March 2006 as follows:

Porters:	Ts6000 (Marangu Route) to Ts8000 (other routes) per day
Assistant guides:	Ts8000 (Marangu) to Ts10,000 (other routes) per day
Guide:	Ts10,000 (Marangu) to Ts12,000 (other routes) per day

❏ AN EXAMPLE: THE MACHAME TREK

A seven-day Machame trek, taking one guide, one assistant guide/cook and two porters, would cost as follows:

Park fees

Rescue fee	US$20
Park entry fee (US$60 x 7 days)	US$420
Camping fee (US$50 x 6 nights)	US$300
Porter/guide entrance fees	US$4

Wages

Two porters (assuming they're paid a wage of Ts8000 per day)	Ts112,000
Assistant guide/cook (assuming Ts10,000 per day)	Ts70,000
Guide (assuming Ts12,000 per day)	Ts84,000

Food

One person plus crew	Ts179,000

Transport

Estimate per person	Ts150,000

TOTAL US$744 + Ts595,000 = US$744 + US$458 = **US$1202**

Obviously if there are more of you then some costs, such as the food, wages and the transport costs, can be divided between the group, thus making it cheaper. Nevertheless, the above example gives you an idea of just how quickly the costs add up. Any excess over these costs goes straight to the agency but they have significant costs of their own, including an annual licence fee of US$2000, not to mention tax that amounts to nearly 30%. Remember, too, when working out your budget, to add on **tips** for your crew; see p43 for details.

The trouble is that these amounts have never been enshrined in law, and there is little anybody can do if an agency wants to pay less than these minimum wages (the lowest wage we have heard about, incidentally, is Ts20,000 for seven days.) It should be noted, too, that whilst KINAPA have for the moment relented from trying to enforce their higher wages, they prefer to see it as a temporary postponement only and are hoping to reintroduce the new pay scale in 2010. If they are successful, expect the cost of a trek to rise significantly from the figures given in this book.

Transport A gallon of premium petrol at the time of writing is Ts1700 per litre (about US$1.30), with diesel a little more. According to one company's price schedule, the cost of transport from Arusha to Machame is Ts150,000 (around US$110), while for Marangu it's Ts170,000 (US$130), Lemosho Ts240,000 (US$185) and Rongai Ts400,000 (US$310) – which is why the latter two routes are usually the most expensive to climb. Of course, the per-person charge may change dramatically if you need to hire a second vehicle for your crew.

Food Your total bill has to cover not only *your* food but the food of the porters and guides too. One agency boss told me that a rough estimate for a seven-day climb of the cost of food if there are more than three people in a group can be gleaned by using the following magnificent formula:

Ts291,000 + [Ts50,000 x (number of trekkers - 2)] = total cost of food in Tanzanian shillings.

He goes on to say that for a single person on the same seven-day Machame Route the cost is around Ts179,000, for two it's about Ts146,000 per person.

TIPPING

Like a herd of elephants on the African plains, the subject of tipping is a bit of a grey area. What is certain is that, in addition to the cost of booking your trek, you will also need to shell out tips to your crew at the end of it all. The gratuity system on Kilimanjaro follows the American style: that is to say, a tip is not so much a bonus to reward particularly attentive service or honest toil as a mandatory payment to subsidize the poor wages the porter and guides receive. In other words, **tipping is obligatory**.

To anybody born outside the Americas this compulsory payment of gratuities seems to go against the very spirit of tipping. Nevertheless, it is very hard to begrudge the guides and porters a decent return for their labours – and depriving your entourage of their much-needed gratuities is not the way to voice your protest against this system.

As to the **size of the remuneration**, there are no set figures or formulas, though we do urge you to let your conscience instruct you on this matter as much as your wallet. The best advice I have found is on the KPAP website (💻 www.kiliporters.org), which I have reproduced here. They suggest that guides should receive $10 per day, assistant guides $8 per day, cooks $7 per day and porters $5 per day.

They give a few examples of how this might work in practice. The following is for a six-day trek (you may want to quibble over their estimates for the number of porters per trekker but it gives you an idea at least).

No of trekkers	Guide	Assistant Guide	Cook	Porter	Total	Total per trekker
1	60	-	42	30 x 2	US$162	US$162
2	60	48	42	30 x 3	US$240	US$120
3	60	48	42	30 x 6	US$330	US$110
4	60	48	42	30 x 8	US$390	US$97.50

These are mere guidelines, and you may wish to alter them if you feel, for example, a certain porter is deserving of more than his normal share, or if your trek was particularly difficult.

Having collected all the money, the usual form is to hand out the individual shares to each porter and guide in turn. **Do not hand all your tips to the guide** unless you are happy that the distribution of the tips will be fair and honest; sadly, no matter how much respect and affection you have towards your guide, often he'll end up trousering most of it. A survey by KPAP found that while porters received an average of Ts27,969 in tips when the tourists gave it to them individually, that figure dropped to Ts20,270 if the guide distributed them instead.

For more details on this, see the KPAP box on pp46-49.

The crew

PORTERS

My guide was as polite as Lord Chesterfield and kindly as the finest gentleman of the world could be. So I owe much to the bare-footed natives of this country, who patiently for eight cents a day bear the white man's burden. **Peter MacQueen** *In Wildest Africa* (1910)

The wages may have gone up – a porter today earning KPAP's proposed new minimum will be on US$60 for a six-day trip (though do see the box on pp46-49 for details of just how low it can be) – and all now have footwear of some description, but the opinion expressed way back at the beginning of the twentieth century by the intrepid MacQueen is much the same as that voiced by thousands of trekkers at the beginning of the twenty-first.

These men (and the ones hired by trekkers are nearly always male, though female porters are becoming increasingly common on the mountain) never fail to draw both gratitude and, with the amount they carry and the minimum of fuss they make it about it, admiration from the trekkers who hire them. Ranging in age from about 18 (the minimum legal age, though some look a good deal younger) to 50 (and occasionally beyond this), porters are amongst the hardest workers on Kilimanjaro. To see them traipsing up the mountain, water in one hand, cooker in another, rucksack on the back and picnic table on the head, is staggering to behold. And though they are supposed to carry no more than 20kg (plus 5kg of their own luggage), many, desperate for work in what is an over-supplied market, manage to bypass KINAPA's own weight checks at the gates to carry much more.

And if that isn't enough, while at the end of the day the average trekker spends his or her time at camp moaning about the hardships they are suffering – in between cramming down mouthfuls of popcorn while clasping a steaming hot cup of tea – these hardy individuals are putting up the tents, helping with the preparation of the food, fetching more water and generally making sure every trekker's whim is, within reason, catered for.

Yet in spite of appearances, porters are not indestructible. Though they rarely climb to the summit themselves, a few still die each year on the slopes of Kilimanjaro. The most common cause of death, perhaps unsurprisingly given the ragged clothes many wear, is exposure. For this reason, if you see a porter dozing by the wayside and it's getting a bit late, put aside your concerns about depriving him of some much needed shut-eye and wake him up: many are the tales of porters who have perished on Kilimanjaro because they took forty winks and then couldn't find their way back to camp in the dark. It's this kind of horror story that has caused so much concern over recent years and led to the formation of organizations such as the Kilimanjaro Porters Assistance Project (see pp46-49).

How many . . .

As a general rule, the larger the number of trekkers, the fewer porters per person required and, if you take the Marangu Route (where no tent is needed), you can probably get away with two per trekker, and maybe even fewer. *(Cont'd on p48)*

A PORTER'S LOT IS NOT A HAPPY ONE

Nobody should underestimate the achievement of reaching the summit of Kilimanjaro. For five days or so you've dragged yourself up 4500m-plus of vertical height, through four different seasons, on terrain that may be as alien to you as the moon. Imagine then, trying to do the same trek while eating only one square meal a day, with nothing but a pair of secondhand plimsolls on your feet and tatty cast-offs for clothes; that your days on the mountain are spent carrying up to 30kg on your back or head, while your nights are spent sharing a draughty four-man tent with up to nine other people, often with no ground mats and inadequate sleeping bags. And that, should anything go wrong – which, given the conditions you're expected to work in, they very well might – there'll be no insurance to cover you.

Imagine, furthermore, climbing not out of desire to be on Africa's highest mountain, but out of necessity, for if you don't submit yourself to these deprivations then you won't be able to fund yourself through college (which costs about US$300 per year) or feed your children. Imagine, too, that your reward for putting up with such conditions is somewhere around Ts4500 per day (the average in 2008 for those companies that aren't KPAP partners); and that, out of this, you have to pay for your transport to and from the mountain (Ts5000 each way from Arusha to Marangu Gate), your food whilst on the mountain (which is why you eat only once a day) and even have to bribe the guide (at least Ts5000) in order to be allowed on the mountain in the first place. No wonder you often end up relying on tips from tourists in order to take home any money from your labours. Tips that, if you're unlucky, may end up in the pocket of that same guide you bribed in order to get a job in the first place.

Such is the lot of the porters on Kilimanjaro: a precarious existence that, at best, involves hardship and indignity, and at worst can lead to death, as happens every year on the mountain. It is these kinds of conditions that various organizations are now trying to improve. Foremost amongst these, without a doubt, is KPAP.

The Kilimanjaro Porters Assistance Project (KPAP)
🖳 *www.kiliporters.org*

Registered at the beginning of 2003, KPAP is an initiative of the American-based International Mountain Explorers Connection (🖳 www.mountainexplorers.org), which fights for porters' rights worldwide including those working in other tourist hotspots such as Nepal's Annapurna Sanctuary. With offices (open roughly Mon-Sat 8am-1pm, though occasionally later) on the ground floor of the Kilimanjaro Backpackers in Moshi, KPAP has been run for the past few years with both skill and bravery by American Karen Valenti.

According to their manifesto, the organization's focus is on improving the working conditions of the porters on Kilimanjaro. They do this in three main ways:

● Lending trekking equipment and clothing at no charge. KPAP have a couple of wardrobes full of good quality trekking gear, much of it donated by American skiing companies and couriered over by American trekkers. For a returnable deposit (which can be anything from a school certificate to a mobile-phone charger) the porter can borrow items of clothing such as fleeces, boots etc.

● Providing classes on English, first-aid, HIV awareness and money management for the benefit of porters.

● Educating the climbers and general public on proper porter treatment.

In addition, we think it's fair to say that they are also trying to educate the trekking agencies and, hopefully, with a mixture of pressure and incentives, encourage them to treat their porters better – and pay them better too.

Among those incentives, KPAP run an '**African Partnership for Responsible Travel**' scheme. In order to join the scheme, companies have to conform to certain guidelines issued by KPAP. They include directives on porters' wages, the amount the porters are required to carry, the food and water they receive on the mountain, what the sleeping conditions are like and how they are treated in the event of an accident or sickness. In order to be considered as a partner, the trekking agency must not only adhere to these guidelines but must allow KPAP to monitor them, too, to make sure they continue to stick to them.

Manage to fulfil all these criteria and the benefits, in terms of increased marketing opportunities and the extra demand that comes from being known as a Partner for Responsible Travel, are considerable. Yet so many companies fail to meet the criteria, which may explain why there are a couple of unfair rumours that often circulate about KPAP's Partners scheme. One is that they push foreign companies ahead of local ones (a rumour that presumably started after it was noticed that their list of partner companies is largely made up of companies with foreign owners); and that it costs money to be a partner (it doesn't – though donations are, of course, always welcome!). Instead, we think that KPAP are actually the only organization that, thanks to their work on the ground, properly monitors what is happening on the mountain, and as such their opinions should be relied upon even more than more established campaign groups such as Tourism Concern.

In addition to the partnership scheme, KPAP also promotes the rights of porters in other ways. For one thing, at the end of your trek you may well bump into a KPAP staff member at Marangu or Mweka gates conducting a survey. If you should see one, do go out of your way to help them by filling in one of their questionnaires (if you haven't already picked one up from their website or office). It is these questionnaires that help KPAP to maintain a comprehensive and accurate picture of exactly which companies treat their porters well...and which don't. KPAP also sell maps and T-shirts from their office, the proceeds of which go towards their campaign.

So how can you help?

There are many things trekkers can do to help the campaign. Signing up for a trek with one of the companies recommended by KPAP is one obvious way, of course. The following Tanzanian-based companies have joined KPAP's African partners scheme. All but three are owned by foreigners, perhaps reflecting the fact that the fight to end the mistreatment of porters has a higher profile abroad than it does in Tanzania. The companies are: **African Environments** and **Africa Walking Company** from Arusha, Moshi's **Ahsante** (the one company, according to KPAP, which has really improved since the last edition), **Big Expeditions**, French-established **Corto Safaris**, **Duma Explorer**, **F&S Kiliwarrior** (another company with a large American input), **Keys Hotel**, **Kibo Slopes** (whose parent company is in Nairobi), **Maasai Wanderings**, **Marangu Hotel** in Marangu Village, **Real Life Adventure**, **Rift Cross Expeditions**, **Summits Africa**, **Summit Expeditions and Nomadic Experience**, **Tanzanian Journeys**, **Thomson Safaris** (who are actually American-based, though they use Arusha's **Nature Discovery** for their treks) and the American **Tusker Trail** (who use their own local company **Tembo Trails** for their own climbs). You can read reviews of each of these companies in their relevant sections in this book; while to find out the latest situation and see if any other companies have become partners, access the 'Partner' section on the KPAP website.

(*Continued on p48*)

❏ A PORTER'S LOT IS NOT A HAPPY ONE *(Continued from p47)*

Other ways to help

Another way to help is to donate your camping equipment and clothing at the end of your trek to KPAP. You can also give it directly to a porter on your trek, though note this should not be seen as a substitute for a tip but a supplement to it, no matter how good the equipment/clothing you're donating. Furthermore, you have to accept that the porter will probably sell those clothes when money is tight.

In addition, KPAP recommend the following on their website:

● 1 **Make sure your porters are outfitted with appropriate clothing** Porters need adequate footwear, socks, waterproof jackets and pants, gloves, hats, sunglasses, etc. Clothing can be borrowed at the KPAP office in Moshi – make sure they know this.

● 2 **Fair wages should be paid to the porters** The Kilimanjaro National Park recommends a minimum Ts6000 day on the Marangu Route and Ts8000 per day on all of the other routes (where you camp, so equipment is heavier and there's more work to do). Unfortunately, they don't enforce this very well. Ask your porters how much they are paid and if it includes food. Showing that you care about such things will encourage all operators and guides to treat their porters fairly.

● 3 **Make sure porters have proper food and water** If they are required to purchase their own food, wages should be increased accordingly.

● 4 **Check the weights of porters' loads** The Kilimanjaro National Park has a maximum carrying weight per porter of 25kg, which includes the porter's personal gear which is assumed to be 5kg. Thus the load they carry for the company should not exceed 20kg. If you can, be there at the weighing of the luggage at the start of the trek to make sure no funny business is going on. If additional porters need to be hired, do make sure that the tour company is paying each porter their full wage when you return.

● 5 **Count the number of porters every day** Know the number of people in your crew. After all, you are paying for them. If there are any missing, ask where they are. If they've been sent down the mountain, ask why, and whether they will still receive both a fair wage and their share of the tips.

● 6 **Make sure your porters are provided with proper shelter** Where no shelter is available (ie on all routes other than Marangu), porters need proper accommodation: that means their own tents and sleeping bags.

(Continued from p45) On other routes, where tents are necessary, around three porters or more per person is the norm. (Just for the record, and just in case taking porters up a mountain makes you feel a little less virile, you may like to know that the great Count Teleki – see p116 – took no less than 65 porters up the mountain with him!)

Those looking to save every last shilling often ask the agency to cut down on the number of porters. But this is neither easy nor – given that the cost of a porter's wages is a relatively minor part of the overall cost – a particularly brilliant idea. Remember that even if you do carry your own rucksack, there is still

● **7 Ensure that your porters are given the tips you intend for them** Give your tips to the guide and you run the risk that they won't pass on the full amount to your crew. Tipping directly to each individual crew member ensures they receive their fair share. Alternatively, see that your tour company has a transparent method of distributing tips.

● **8 Take care of any sick or injured porters** Porters deserve the same standard of treatment and care as their clients. Sick or injured porters need to be sent back with someone who speaks their language and understands the problem.

● **9 Get to know your porters and thank them** Some porters speak English and will appreciate your making an effort to speak with them. The Swahili word *pole* (pronounced 'polay') – which translates loosely as 'I'm sorry for you' – shows respect for porters after a hard day of carrying your bags. *Ahsante* ('asantay') means 'Thank you'.

● **10 Report any instances of abuse or neglect** To both the trekking agency concerned and, more importantly, to KPAP on 🖳 info@kiliporters.org.

● **11 Complete the post-climb survey** This is perhaps the most important and easiest thing you can do. Before heading off up the mountain, pick up a questionnaire from the KPAP office or the website 🖳 www.kiliporters.org, as this will remind you of what to look out for on the mountain. By providing KPAP with your feedback regarding the tour company's treatment of its staff, they will be able to share with the company any problem areas that need to be corrected.

In addition to the above, you can also help KPAP directly by shopping for T-shirts, maps etc in their office in Moshi and donating your climbing gear to KPAP. Their publicity department would also welcome photos of porters etc wearing KPAP clothing. What's more, if you're travelling from America and have some spare luggage allowance, you may wish to contact IMEC to see if you can help courier some of their donated clothing to Moshi; please email jack@mountainexplorers.org about this.

Further details
Kilimanjaro Porters Assistance Project (KPAP) 🖳 www.kiliporters.org
International Mountain Explorers Connection 🖳 www.mountainexplorers.org
IMEC is the umbrella organization of which KPAP is a part.
International Porter Protection Group (IPPG) 🖳 www.ippg.net

all the food, cooking equipment, camping gear and so forth to lug up the mountainside. What's more, you're also tempting the agency to overload each porter in order to reduce their total number – leading to the kind of illegal practices described in the box on pp46-49. So, in general, accept the agency's recommendations as to the number of porters on your expedition and make sure that they're not overloaded.

. . . and how much?

The porters' wages are paid by the agency you sign up with. All you need to worry about is how much to give them as a **tip** at the end of the trek. Given the privations they suffer over the course of an average trek and their often desultory wages, their efforts to extract as much money as possible from the over-privileged *mzungu* (Swahili for 'white person') are entirely forgivable. One elaborate yet surprisingly common method is for the porters to pretend that there are more of them than there actually are; which, given the vast numbers of porters running around each campsite and the fact you don't actually walk with them on the trail, is a lot easier to achieve than you may think. It's a technique hinted at by John Reader in his excellent 1982 book *Kilimanjaro*:

I hired four porters for part of my excursion on Kilimanjaro. The fourth man's name was Stephen, or so the other three told me. I never met Stephen himself. Our gear seemed to arrive at each campsite without his assistance and I am not aware that he ever spent a night with us. I was assured that he was engaged elsewhere on tasks essential to the success of my journey, but I occasionally wondered whether Stephen actually existed. I was particularly aggrieved when he failed to collect his pay in person at the end of the trip. The other guides collected it for him. They also collected his tip.

This sort of thing shouldn't happen if you're with a reputable company but it's a good idea anyway to **make sure you meet your team at the start of the trail before you set off**. This will help to prevent this sort of scam and it's good manners too. While at the end, to ensure each porter gets his fair share, dish the tips out yourself – *do not* give them to your guide to hand them out on your behalf; see the box on pp46-49 for why this is so.

Please note that however much money and equipment you lavish on them at the end, the porters' reaction will usually be the same. Simply put, porters are not above play-acting, in the same way that the sea is not above the clouds.

Breaking camp in the early morning at a chilly Karanga Camp with Kibo overseeing all the activity.

On being given their gratuity some porters will grimace, sigh, tut, shake their head, roll their eyes in disgust and stare at the money in their hand with all the enthusiasm and gratitude of one who has just been handed a warm jar of the contents of the Barranco Camp toilets. Several of the more talented ones may even manage a few tears. Nevertheless, providing you have paid a reasonable tip (and for guidance over what is the correct amount, see pp43-44), don't fall for the melodramatics but simply thank them warmly for all their endeavours over the course of the trek. Once they realize your conscience remains unpricked it will all be handshakes and smiles and, having pocketed the money, they'll soon trot off happily enough.

GUIDES

Mzee Yohana Lauwo, the porter guide who accompanied the first Europeans up the Kilimanjaro Mountain a century ago, was the centre of attention in a commemorative ceremony in Moshi on Friday.

Mzee Lauwo, now over 118 years, was presented with a prize in cash. The Deputy Minister for Lands, Natural Resources and Tourism, Ndugu Chabanga Hassan Dyamwalle, suggested that Mzee Lauwo also be given a house to be built in his own village.

The ambassador to the Federal Republic of Germany (FRG) to Tanzania, Christel Steffler, presented Mzee Lauwo with a letter which expressed gratitude for his service in cementing German-Tanzanian relations. She said it was high time porters and guides were given the recognition they deserved for their work.

Press cutting from the *In Brief* section of a local newspaper, found stuck on the wall of the *Kibo Hotel*, Marangu.

If portering is the first step on the career ladder of Kilimanjaro, then it is the guides who stand proudly on the top rung. Ornithologist, zoologist, botanist, geologist, tracker, astronomer, butler, manager, doctor, linguist and teacher, a good guide will be all of these professions rolled into one. With luck, over the course of the trek they'll also become your friend.

The metamorphosis from porter to guide is a lengthy one. Having served one's apprenticeship by lugging luggage as a porter, a few talented and ambitious ones are eventually promoted to the position of **summit porter**. In addition to carrying their fair share of equipment, they are also expected to perform many of the duties of a fully fledged guide – including, most painfully of all, the escorting of trekkers on that final, excruciating push to the summit.

From there the next logical step is to become a fully fledged guide – though standing between them and a licence is a period of intensive training conducted by the park authorities. This mainly involves a two- to three-week tour of the mountain, during which time they are supposed to cover every designated route up and down Kilimanjaro. On this course they are also taught the essentials of being a guide, including a bit about the fauna and flora of Kili, how to take care of the mountain environment, how to spot the symptoms of altitude sickness in trekkers and, just as importantly, what to do about it.

Training complete, they receive their licences and are free to tout themselves around the agencies looking for work. While a few of the better guides

Interview with a female guide

Though I have heard of three female guides working on Kilimanjaro, Saumu Burhani Myusa, aged 27, is the first I've come across during my time on the mountain. Originating from the Pare region, on the way to Tanga to the east of Moshi, she's been working on the mountain for over two years. This interview was conducted in August 2008, when I had the privilege of leading a trek with Saumu on the Machame Route.

How did you start off being a guide? I started off as a porter, a job I did for about 6 months. I was then an assistant guide for just 2 months before I was lucky enough to lead my first trek.

How did people react when you told them you wanted to be a guide? My mum and dad were very scared; they thought I would die up there! They're OK now, as they see that I come down safely. As for my son, Nicos, he knows I go on the mountain but is too young to understand that it may be a little bit dangerous. [Nicos is aged five and lives with his gran in Arusha while Saumu is on the mountain.]

What made you want to be a guide? I love it! The money's OK, of course, but I really love meeting people – that's the main reason. I also love the mountain. The top, in particular, with all the snow and glaciers, is just beautiful.

Do you not mind sharing your life with 30 male porters for a whole week? I don't mind – even if there are even 60 of them! They know I am the guide so they listen to what I say if I tell them to do something as they all know me by now and respect me. Indeed, maybe they respect me more because I don't fight with them.

Do you think they're frightened of you? Yeah!

What is the best bit about your job? To see my clients happy.

And the worst? When somebody gets sick and cannot try for the top.

What's your favourite route? Machame. It's got some lovely views of Meru and it's a challenge.

And your favourite part of the mountain? It would have to be the top – it's so beautiful. I also love being there with the clients – to see them so happy, having made it after all that effort.

And your favourite nationality? British. [I made her say this.]

are snapped up by the top agencies and work exclusively for them, the majority are freelance and have to actively seek work in what is already an over-supplied market. This helps to explain why a newly qualified guide will probably have to settle for being an **assistant guide** in order to secure work, for which they'll receive a higher wage than a porter and a commensurately greater proportion of the tips – though not as much as they would receive if leading the climb themselves.

Getting to Kilimanjaro

One of the gladdest moments in life, methinks is the departure upon a distant journey into unknown lands. Shaking off with one mighty effort the fetters of habit, the leaden weight of routine, the cloak of many cares and the slavery of home, man feels once more happy... The blood flows with the fast circulation of childhood ... afresh dawns the morn of life.
Diary entry of **Richard Burton** (the explorer, not the actor), 2 December 1856

BY AIR

Tanzania has three major international airports: Dar es Salaam, Zanzibar and Kilimanjaro. The latter, as you may expect, is the most convenient for Kilimanjaro, standing only 42km away from the mountain town of Moshi and 50km from Arusha. An approximate timetable of international flights to and from KIA (the acronym for Kilimanjaro International Airport, though the three-letter international airport code is JRO) can be found in *Appendix B*, p340. Unfortunately, the lack of airlines flying into Kilimanjaro – with Air Tanzania's operations suspended, KLM, Ethiopian Airlines and Kenyan Airways are the only major ones – means that airfares from Europe and elsewhere are rather inflated due to lack of competition; this, combined with the fact that many trekkers will want a few days on a beach at the start or end of their holiday, means that many visitors to Tanzania fly to one of the other two airports. Of the two, Zanzibar is often, surprisingly, the cheaper destination. It is, however, rather inconveniently located for Kilimanjaro, being around 40km off the Tanzanian coast, and as such those flying out for the specific purpose of climbing the mountain should really discard this option: Dar es Salaam, too, is a day's bus journey from Moshi or Arusha and thus not ideal.

In addition to the Tanzanian destinations, you may also wish to consider Nairobi in Kenya, which is fairly conveniently situated for Kilimanjaro and to which it is usually a little cheaper to fly. This also gives you the chance of taking in one of Kenya's world-renowned game reserves (which have lower park fees than their Tanzanian counterparts). Note, however, that by choosing this option you may need a multiple-entry visa for Kenya (if you are also flying back home from Kenya, for example, and spend longer than a fortnight in Tanzania), which for Brits and others can be as much as £70/US$119 – thereby reducing or eliminating any saving you may have made in airfares. (For details of whether you will require a multiple-entry visa for Kenya, or can get away with a single-entry one for Kenya, see p83.) Furthermore, there is all the extra travelling to and from Kilimanjaro to consider: Arusha is a six- (minimum) to eight-hour (usual) shuttle bus journey from Nairobi. (Incidentally, Kenya's second airport, Mombasa, is less convenient, the journey to Kilimanjaro from Mombasa currently entailing a drive to Nairobi; though with the highway between Marangu and Kenya via the border at Tarakea improving quickly, in future this may be a good option. Our website, ⌨ www.climbmountkilimanjaro.com, will have the latest details on the progress of this route.)

You will find brief guides in this book to Dar es Salaam (p142) as well as Nairobi (p151) and Kilimanjaro International Airport (p161).

From the UK

A cheap flight to Kilimanjaro from London with KLM via Amsterdam will set you back a minimum of £550, or £800 in the July-August high season, while for Dar the determined may be able to find one for around £450 (but don't forget to factor in the cost of getting to the Kilimanjaro region from there).

In addition to the travel agencies listed below, net-heads may also like to check out ⌨ www.cheapflights.co.uk, which gives a summary of the flight offers to your destination from a number of different agents. A couple of other online agencies to recommend are Airline Network (⌨ www.airline-network.co.uk) and Expedia (⌨ www.expedia.co.uk), while Last Minute (⌨ www.lastminute. com) is useful in that it provides a table which shows the price of flights using various different arrival and departure dates (so if you're flexible as to when you want to fly to and from Tanzania, you could save yourself a couple of hundred pounds by flying on dates when the price is lower). Larger high-street travel agents include STA Travel (☎ 0871 230 0040; ⌨ www.statravel.co.uk), Flight Centre (☎ 0870 499 0040; ⌨ www.flightcentre.co.uk) and Trailfinders (☎ 0845 058 5858; ⌨ www.trailfinders.com), all with branches countrywide.

From North America

Try Air Brokers International of San Francisco (⌨ www.airbrokers.com; ☎ 1-800-883-3273), Travel Cuts (⌨ www.travelcuts.com; ☎ 1-800-592-2887, Canada ☎ 1-866-246-9762) and STA Travel (⌨ www.statravel.com; ☎ 1-800 781 4040).

From Australia and New Zealand

Try Flight Centre (⌨ www.flightcentre.com; Australia ☎ 133 133, New Zealand ☎ 0800 2435 44), Trailfinders (⌨ www.trailfinders.com.au; ☎ 1300 780 212) and STA Travel (⌨ www.statravel.com.au; ☎ 134 782).

OVERLAND

A big country lying at the heart of East Africa, Tanzania has borders with many countries including Burundi, Kenya, Malawi, Mozambique, Rwanda, Uganda and Zambia. Now reopened, the border between Tanzania and Burundi is most easily crossed on the venerable old *MV Liemba* that sails to Kigoma, cutting across the northern corner of Lake Tanganyika from Bujumbura.

The borders with **Rwanda**, **Uganda** (most commonly crossed at Mutukula, north-west of Bukoba), **Zambia** (main crossing Tunduma), **Mozambique** (Kilambo), **Malawi** (Songwe River Bridge) and **Kenya** (see the Nairobi chapter for details) are all relatively straightforward and served by public buses. Tanzania and Zambia are also linked by express train, running twice weekly between Dar es Salaam and Mbeya.

The routes up Kilimanjaro

GETTING TO THE MOUNTAIN

This book aims to take you from your armchair to the summit of Africa's highest mountain. If you have booked a package from home, of course, your transport to and from the mountain will already have been sorted out and you needn't worry. If you haven't then this book will tell you about the city you are flying to and the towns of Arusha, Moshi and Marangu that lie nearest to the mountain. It also goes into some detail about which trekking company to book with and where you can find them; and having booked your trek with a company in Tanzania, you will invariably find that it includes transport to and from the Kilimanjaro National Park gates. From there, it's all about the walking...

GETTING UP THE MOUNTAIN   [See colour map inside back cover]

Kilimanjaro has two main summits. The higher one is Kibo, the glacier-clad circular summit that stars on all the pictures of Kilimanjaro. While spiky Mawenzi, to its east, is impossible to conquer without knowledge of advanced climbing techniques and no small amount of courage, it is possible to *walk* up to the top of Kibo at a height of 5895m above sea level.

Look down at Kilimanjaro from above and you should be able to count seven paths trailing like ribbons up the sides of the mountain. Five of these are ascent-only paths (ie you can only walk *up* the mountain on them and you are not allowed to come down on these trails); one, Mweka, is a descent-only path, and one, the Marangu Route, is both an ascent and descent trail. At around 4000m these trails

PLANNING YOUR TRIP

meet up with a path that loops right around the Kibo summit. This path is known as the Kibo Circuit, though it's often divided into two halves known as the Northern and Southern circuits. By the time you reach the foot of Kibo, only three paths lead up the slopes to the summit itself. For a *brief* description of the trails and a look at their relative merits, read on; for a map, see inside back cover, while for further details check out the **full trail descriptions**, beginning on p241. Note that some trekking agencies vary the routes slightly, particularly on the Shira Plateau, but any agency worth its salt will provide you with a detailed itinerary so you can check exactly which path you'll be taking each day.

The topography of Kilimanjaro

And surely never monarch wore his royal robes more royally than this monarch of African mountains, Kilimanjaro. His foot rests on a carpet of velvety turf, and through the dark green forest the steps of his throne reach downward to the earth, where man stands awestruck before the glory of his majesty. Art may have colours rich enough to fix one moment of this dazzling splendour, but neither brush nor pen can portray the unceasing play of colour – the wondrous purples of the summit deepening as in the Alpine afterglow; the dull greens of the forest and the sepia shadows in the ravines and hollows, growing ever darker as evening steals on apace; and last, the gradual fading away of all, as the sun sets, and over everything spreads the grey cloud-curtain of the night. It is not a picture but a pageant – a king goes to his rest.

Hans Meyer *Across East African Glaciers* (1891)

Kilimanjaro is not only the highest mountain in Africa, it's also one of the biggest volcanoes on the entire planet, covering an area of approximately 388,500 hectares. In this area are three main peaks that betray its origins as the offspring of three huge volcanic eruptions.

The oldest and lowest peak is known as **Shira**, and lies on the western edge of the massif. This is the least impressive of the three summits, being nothing more than a heavily eroded ridge, 3962m tall at its highest point, **Johnsell Point**. This ridge is, in fact, merely the south-western rim of the original Shira crater, the northern and eastern sides being covered by later material from Kibo (see below).

The Shira Ridge separates the western slopes from the **Shira Plateau**. This large, rocky plateau, 6200ha in size, is one of Kilimanjaro's most intriguing features. It is believed to be the caldera of the first volcano (a caldera is a collapsed crater) that has been filled in by lava from later eruptions which then solidified and turned to rock. The plateau rises gently from west to east until it reaches the youngest and main summit on Kilimanjaro, **Kibo**. This is the best preserved crater on Kilimanjaro; its southern lip is slightly higher than the rest of the rim, and the highest point on this southern lip is **Uhuru Peak** – at 5895m the highest point in Africa and the goal of just about every Kilimanjaro trekker.

Kibo is also the only one of the three summits which is permanently covered in snow, thanks to the large **glaciers** that cover much of its surface. Kibo is also the one peak that really does look like a volcanic crater; indeed, there are not one but three concentric craters on Kibo. Within the inner **Reusch Crater** (1.3km in diameter) you can still see signs of volcanic activity, including fumaroles, the smell of sulphur and a third crater, the **Ash Pit**, 130m deep by 140m wide.

Ascending Kilimanjaro: the options

There are six ascent trails leading up to the foot of Kibo peak. These are (running anti-clockwise, beginning with the westernmost trails): the little-used Shira Plateau Route, Lemosho Route, Machame Route, Umbwe Route, Marangu Route and, running from the north-eastern side, the Rongai (Loitokitok) Route. Each of these six routes eventually meet with a path circling the Kibo cone, a path known as either the **Northern Circuit** or the **Southern Circuit** depending on which side of the mountain you are. (It is possible and very worthwhile to walk right around Kibo on this path, though this needs to be arranged beforehand with your agency,

---

The outer **Kibo Crater** (1.9 by 2.7km) is not a perfect, unbroken circle. There are gaps in the circumference where the walls have been breached by lava flows; the most dramatic of these is the **Western Breach**, through which some climbers gain access to the summit each year. The crater has also subsided a little over time, leading to a landslide 100,000 years ago that created the **Barranco** on Kibo's southern side. On the whole, though, Kibo's slopes are gentle, allowing trekkers as well as mountaineers to reach the summit (for details on the Kibo summit, see p334).

Separating Kibo from Kilimanjaro's second peak, Mawenzi, is the **Saddle**, at 3600ha the largest area of high-altitude tundra in tropical Africa. This really is a beautiful, eerie place — a dusty desert almost 5000m above sea level, featureless except for the occasional parasitic cone dotted here and there, including the **Triplets**, **Middle Red** and **West Lava Hill**, all running south-east from the south-eastern side of Kibo. (A parasitic cone is a mini cone on the side of a volcano caused by a later, minor eruption; amazingly, there are said to be some 250 parasitic cones on Kilimanjaro!)

Nothing could be more marked than the contrast between the external appearance of these two volcanoes – Kibo, with the unbroken, gradual slopes of the typical volcanic cone – Mawenzi with its bewildering display of many-coloured lavas and its fantastically carved outlines, the result of long ages of exposure, combined with the tendency of its component rocks to split vertically rather than horizontally. The hand of time has left its impress upon Kibo too, but the havoc it has wrought is not to be detected at a distance. **Hans Meyer** *Across East African Glaciers* (1891)

Seen from Kibo, **Mawenzi**, the second summit, looks less like a crater than a single lump of jagged, craggy rock emerging from the Saddle. This is merely because its western side also happens to be its highest, and hides everything behind it. Walk around Mawenzi, however, and you'll realize that this peak is actually a horseshoe shape, with only the northern side of the crater having been eroded away. Its sides too steep to hold glaciers, there is no *permanent* snow on Mawenzi, and the gradients are enough to dissuade all but the bravest and most technically accomplished climbers. Mawenzi's highest point is Hans Meyer Peak at 5149m but so shattered is this summit, and so riven with gullies and fractures, that there are a number of other distinctive peaks including Purtscheller Peak (5120m) and South Peak (4958m). There are also two deep gorges, the Great Barranco and the Lesser Barranco, scarring its north-eastern face.

Few people know this but Kilimanjaro does actually have a crater lake. **Lake Chala** (aka Jala) lies some 30km to the south-east, and is said to be up to 2.5 miles deep.

For details on how exactly Kilimanjaro came to be this shape, see the geology section on p93.

takes a long time, and permission from KINAPA may need to be sought before embarking on such an expedition.) The trails mix and merge at this point, so that by the time you reach Kibo just three trails lead up to the crater rim: the **Western Breach Route** (aka the **Arrow Glacier Route**), **Barafu Route** and the nameless third path which runs up from Kibo Huts to Gillman's Point, and which we shall call the **Kibo Huts Route**. Which of these you will take to the summit depends upon which of the six paths you took to get this far: the Shira, Lemosho, Machame and Umbwe routes can use either the difficult Arrow Glacier Route or the easier (but longer) Barafu Route, while the Marangu and Rongai trails use the Kibo Huts Route. You can deviate from this rule and design your own combination of trails to take you to the summit and back but it will require special permission from KINAPA and the agencies charge a lot more to organize such a trek.

A brief description of each of the six main trails follows:

The Marangu Route (5-6 days) is the oldest and has traditionally always been seen as the most popular trail on the mountain (though see the statistics opposite for the current story). It is also the one that comes closest (though not very) to the trail Hans Meyer took in making the first successful assault on the summit. Plus it is the only ascent trail where camping is not necessary, indeed not allowed, with trekkers sleeping in dormitory huts along the way. From the Kibo Huts, trekkers climb up to the summit via Gillman's Point. The trail should take a minimum of five days and four nights to complete, though an extra night is usually taken after the second day to allow trekkers more time to acclimatize.

The Machame Route (6-7 days) now vies with Marangu as the most popular trail on the mountain. It's certainly the one the majority of guides consider the most enjoyable. Though widely regarded as more difficult than the Marangu Route, the success rate on this trail is higher, possibly because it is a day longer at six days and five nights (assuming you take the Barafu Route to the summit) which gives trekkers more time to acclimatize; most trekkers also take an extra acclimatization day in the Karanga Valley. You can also take the more difficult Western Breach Route though this shortens the trek by a day or two so it would be wise to build in acclimatization days if taking this option.

The Shira Plateau and Lemosho routes (6-8 days each) Both of these routes run from west to east across the centre of the Shira Plateau. The **Shira Plateau Route** is the original plateau trail though it is seldom used these days, for much of it is now a 4WD track and walkers embarking on this trail often begin their trek above the forest in the moorland zone. After traversing the plateau the trekker has a choice of climbing Kibo via the Western Breach/Arrow Glacier Route or the longer and easier Barafu Route. If opting for the former, expect the trek to last a total of six days and five nights. By the latter trail the walk should last eight days if extra overnight stops on the plateau and in the Karanga Valley are taken – if not, seven days is more likely.

The **Lemosho Route** (aka the **Lemosho Glades Route**) improves on the Shira Plateau Route by starting below the Shira Ridge, thus providing trekkers with a walk in the forest at the trek's start, giving them more time to acclimatize.

So who climbs the most – and on what route?

After about eight years of pleading and digging, I have finally – finally! – managed to extract figures from KINAPA on which nationalities climb the most, and on what route. I'm not sure how reliable they are, but they are the best we can get; plus, to be fair, they do seem to conform to my own experience of which nationalities climb the most.

	2003/4	2004/5	2005/6	2006/7
Tanzanians	1745	1819	1561	1772
Kenyans and Ugandans	110	228	305	481
Other Africans	1006	1053	1552	1836
Americans/Canadians	5073	7645	9176	9961
Other Americans				174
British	4965	5458	7155	5427
Germans	2859	1750	3536	4217
Italians	636	644	611	570
Scandinavians	1522	3126	2789	2947
French	2050	2779	2744	1832
Other Europeans	6636	7942	8352	6705
Japanese	596	1701	1610	1004
Other Asians/Oceanians	1219	2884	2265	3775
Total	**28,417**	**37,029**	**41,656**	**40,701**

It would have been nice to have seen the split between the Americans and Canadians (who do send great numbers to Kilimanjaro every year) but it does appear that, even without the Canadians, the Americans are probably the nationality that climbs Kilimanjaro the most, which is surprising to those who know them as people who rarely travel beyond the borders of their own country. But for some reason the Americans love Kilimanjaro, a passion that I can only ascribe, maybe, to the 'Hemingway effect', his books doing much to publicize the mountain in his home country.

So which routes do all these climbers use? Once again, after much investigation I have managed to unearth the following: It's for 2007 only, but I think it applies fairly accurately to today too:

Marangu 15,334	**Shira/Lemosho** 3970
Machame 15,879	**Umbwe** 156
Rongai 5073	

The thing that leaps out at you about these figures is that Machame is now officially the most popular route, knocking Marangu into second place. This won't surprise anybody who's trekked on this trail for the past few years – but will surprise many of the foreign agents who still try to hype the 'Whiskey Route' as a wild and untrammelled path. Remember, too, that while the Marangu Route gets trekkers all year round, because people sleep in dormitories rather than under canvas, during the rainy season the Machame Route is very quiet; which means, of course, that during the rest of the year they must get many, many more people than the Marangu Route.

Other points to note? Well, it's interesting how much the Rongai Route has grown in popularity to become the third busiest route; if there is one thing that has changed since 2007, I would guess that Rongai has become even more popular.

Finally, I never realized just how unpopular the Umbwe Route was. It's a beautiful route and, being close to Marangu, a convenient one for the agencies to use. But its reputation as the 'hardest' route seems enough to deter most people from taking it.

Day trips

If for some reason you cannot climb all the way to the top but neverthe-less wish to experience the pleasure of walking on Africa's most beauti-ful mountain, it is possible to enter the Kilimanjaro National Park for one day only. There are some advantages in doing this. It's safer for one thing, for few will get beyond 3000m at most in one day so altitude sickness shouldn't be an issue. With no camping or rescue fees, porters' wages or food to pay, it will work out much cheaper too: just US$60 per day entry fee plus a wage for the compulsory guide. And as well as being wonderfully pleasant, if you're fit and start out early enough there's no reason why you can't climb above the treeline to the heathland, thereby covering two vegetation zones and giving yourself a good chance of a reasonably close-up view of Kibo and Mawenzi. There are even designated picnic spots on the way.

Marangu Gate has a **three-hour nature loop** through the cloud forest which is love-ly and from which you can descend either via the trekkers' trail or the less scenic but faster porters' route. There are also a number of seldom-visited waterfalls in the area. The ambitious can attempt to reach the Mandara Huts (p250) and descend again in one day. Furthermore, just 15 minutes beyond the Mandara Huts through a small patch of forest alive with monkeys is the Maundi Crater (p250), with excellent views of Kibo and Mawenzi to the north-west and the flat African plains stretching away to the east.

The other place where day trips are allowed is on the Shira Plateau, where your chances of spotting big game are much greater (though still very, very small). However, the time taken in entering the park from the west deters most day-trippers.

As with the Shira Plateau Route, you can ascend Kibo either by the Western Breach or by the Barafu Route; allow five nights for the former (though this is too fast for such a long trail) or a recommended seven nights for the latter.

It's common for trekking agencies to refer to the Lemosho Route as the Shira Route, which is of course confusing. If you have already booked your 'Shira' trek and want to know what route it is that you will actually be taking, one way to check is to see where your first night's campsite will be; if it's the Big Tree Campsite – or Mti Mkubwa in the local language – then it's actually the Lemosho Route that you'll be using.

The Rongai Route (5-6 days) is the only trail to approach Kibo from the north. Indeed, the original trail began right against the Kenyan border, though recently the trail shifted eastwards and now starts at the Tanzanian town of Loitokitok after which the new trail has been named (though everybody still refers to it as the Rongai Route; it is also sometimes called the Nalemuru Route, after the nearby river). For the final push to the summit, trekkers on this trail take the Kibo Huts Route, joining it either at the huts themselves or just below Hans Meyer Cave. Again the trek can be completed in five days and four nights though most trekkers take a detour to camp beneath Mawenzi peak, adding an extra day.

The Umbwe Route (5-6 days) is the hardest and least popular trail, a tough vertical slog through the jungle, in places using the tree roots as makeshift rungs on a ladder. Having reached the Southern Circuit, trekkers then traditionally continue north-west to tackle Kibo from the west and the more difficult Arrow

Glacier/Western Breach Route, though you can also head east round to Barafu and approach the summit from there. The entire walk up and down takes a minimum of five days if going via the Barafu Campsite (though this is entirely too rapid; take six minimum, with a day at Karanga Valley); or four/five minimum (again, this is way too short; six is better) if going via the Western Breach, with additional days if sleeping in the crater.

Descending Kilimanjaro: the designated descents

In an attempt to control the number of people walking on each trail, and thus limit the amount of soil erosion on some of the more popular routes, KINAPA introduced regulations regarding the descent routes and which ones you are allowed to take. In general, the main rule is as follows: those ascending Kilimanjaro from the west, south-west or south (ie by taking the Machame, Umbwe, Lemosho or Shira routes) must take as their descent route the **Mweka** trail; whereas if you have climbed the mountain from the south-east or north (ie on the Marangu or Rongai/Loitokitok trails) you must descend by the **Marangu Route**. See p324 for descriptions of these trails.

Those trekkers who wish to **deviate from these rules** should first seek permission from KINAPA.

What to take

CLOTHES

The best head-gear for all weathers is an English sun-helmet, such as are supplied by Messrs. Silver & Co., London; while a soft fez or smoking cap should be kept for wearing in the shade – one with flaps for drawing down over the ears on a cold night to be preferred.
Hans Meyer *Across East African Glaciers (1891)*

According to his book *Life, Wanderings, and Labours in Eastern Africa*, when Charles New attempted to climb Kili in 1861 he took with him a party of thirteen porters, all of whom were completely naked. New and his crew became the first to reach the mountain's snow-line, which is a rather creditable effort considering their lack of suitable apparel. Assuming your goal is to reach more than just snow, however, you will need to make sure you (and indeed your porters) are appropriately attired for the extreme conditions.

The fact that you will be paying porters to carry your rucksack does, to some degree, make packing simpler – allowing you to concentrate on warmth rather than weight. However, packing for warmth does not mean packing lots of big jumpers. The secret to staying warm is to **wear lots of layers**. Not only does this actually make you warmer than if you just had one single, thick layer – the air trapped between the layers heats up and acts as insulation – but it also means you can peel off the layers one by one when you get too warm, and put them on again one by one when the temperatures drop.

A suitable mountain wardrobe would include:

● **Walking boots** Mountaineering boots (ie ones with stiff soles that take a crampon) are unnecessary unless you're taking an unusual route that demands them. If you're not, a decent pair of trekking boots will be fine. The important thing about boots is comfort, with enough toe room, remembering that on the ascent up Kibo you might be wearing an extra pair or two of socks, and that on the descent the toes will be shoved into the front of the boots with every step. Remember these points when trying on trekking boots in the shop. Make sure they are also sturdy, waterproof, durable and high enough to provide support for your ankles. Finally, ensure you break them in *before* you come to Tanzania, so that if they do give you blisters, you can recover before you set foot on the mountain.

● **Socks** Ahhh, the joy of socks ... a couple of thick thermal pairs and some regular ones should be fine; you may stink but you'll be comfortable too, which is far more important. Some people walk in one thick and one thin pair of socks, changing the thin pair regularly, rinsing them out in the evening and tying them to their pack to dry during the day.

● **Down jacket** Not necessary if you have enough fleeces, but nevertheless wonderfully warm, light, compact – and expensive. Make sure it is large enough to go over all your clothes.

● **Fleece** Fleeces are light, pack down small, dry quickly and can be very, very warm. Take at least two: one thick 'polar' one and one of medium thickness and warmth. Make sure that you can wear the thinner one over all of the T-shirts and shirts you'll be taking, and that you can wear your thick one over all of these – you'll need to on the night-walk up Kibo.

● **Thermals** The value of thermal underwear lies in the way it draws moisture (ie sweat) away from your body. A thermal vest and long-johns are sufficient.

● **Trousers** Don't take jeans, which are heavy and difficult to dry. Instead, take a couple of pairs of trekking trousers, such as those made by Rohan, preferably one light and one heavy.

● **Sunhat** One reader wrote in to say that, because he wears glasses, a baseball cap or similar was much more useful than a regular sunhat as it kept the rain off his spectacles. This is a good idea but do make sure that you have something to cover the back of your neck too. Whatever you choose, headgear is essential as it can be hot and dazzling on the mountain ...

● **Woolly/fleecy hat** ... but it can also be very cold. Brightly coloured bobble hats can be bought very cheaply in Moshi; or, better still, invest in one of those knitted **balaclavas** which you can usually find on sale in Moshi, which look a bit like a pizza oven but which will protect your face from the biting summit wind.

● **Gloves** Preferably fleecy; many people wear a thin thermal under-glove too.

● **Rainwear** While you are more likely to be rained on during the walk in the forest, where it should still be warm, once you've got your clothes wet there will be little opportunity to dry them on the trek – and you will not want to attempt to climb freezing Kibo in wet clothes. A **waterproof jacket** – preferably made from Gore-tex or a similar breathable material, hopefully with a warm or fleecy lining too, and big enough to go over all your clothes so you can wear it for the night-walk on Kibo – is ideal; **waterproof trousers** are a necessity too. Alternatively, one reader suggests a cheap waterproof **poncho** 'from a dollar store', preferably one that goes over the backpack as well as yourself.

● **Summer clothes** T-shirts and shorts are the most comfortable things to wear under the humid forest canopy. You are strongly recommended to take a shirt with a collar too, to stop the sun from burning the back of your neck.

OTHER EQUIPMENT

Any trekking agency worth its licence will provide a **tent**, as well as **cooking equipment**, **cutlery** and **crockery**. You will still need to pack a few other items, however, if you don't want to return from your trek as a sunburnt, snow-blinded, dehydrated wretch with hepatitis and hypothermia. Some of these items can be bought or rented in Moshi or Arusha. Your agency can arrange equipment rental, which is the most convenient way, though you may well find it cheaper to avoid going through them as they will, of course, take their cut. Note that the following lists concern the trek only. It does not include items necessary for other activities you may have planned on your holiday, such as binoculars for your safari or a bucket and spade for Zanzibar.

Before buying or renting all of the following, check to see what your agency will supply as part of their trekking package. Many will provide mattresses and water purifiers, for example, which will save you a little.

Essentials

● **Sleeping bag** The warmest you've got. A three-season bag (up to -10°C) is probably the most practical, offering a compromise between warmth and cost. A two-season plus **thermal fleecy liner**, the latter available in camping shops back at home for about £20-30/US$30-45, is another solution.

● **Sleeping mat** Essential in camping but unnecessary if you're following the standard Marangu Route, when you'll be sleeping in huts. Trekking agencies sometimes supply these.

● **Water bottles/Platypus Hoser/Camelbak system** You'll need to carry two litres of water up Kibo *at the very least*. Indeed, many people take enough bottles to carry four litres, with one reader saying it's essential for summit day. It's certainly good to take a lot of water, though do remember that you've got to carry it with you and four litres is a lot of water to carry; we recommend three litres.

Make sure your bottles are thermally protected or they will freeze on the summit. Regular army-style water bottles are fine, though these days many trekkers prefer the new **Platypus Hoser-style systems**, or **CamelBaks**, a kind of soft, plastic bladder with a long tube from which you can drink as you walk along. They have a number of advantages over regular bottles in that they save you fiddling about with bottle tops and you can keep your hands in your pockets while you drink – great on the freezing night-time walk to the summit. But while they encourage you to drink regularly, which is good for dealing with the altitude, they also discourage you from taking a break, which is bad. What's more, these systems usually freeze up on the way to the summit, especially the hose and mouthpiece. One way to avoid this – or at least delay it – is to **blow back into the tube** after you have taken a drink to prevent water from collecting in the tube and freezing. (One reader suggested adding Dioralyte which also helps to delay freezing.) So if you are going to bring one of these with you, make sure it's fully insulated – and don't forget to take frequent breaks!

● **Water purifiers/filter** Also essential, unless you intend to hire an extra porter or two to transport your drinking water up from the start, or if your agency has stated that they will purify your water for you. While you can get your cooking crew to boil you some water at the end of every mealtime, you'll still find purifiers and/or a filter essential if you're going to drink the recommended three to four litres every day, for which you may have to collect water from the mountain streams. Of the two, purifying tablets such as iodine are more effective as they kill everything in the water, though they taste awful. A cordial will help to mask this taste; you can buy packets of powdered flavouring in the local supermarkets. Filters are less effective and more expensive, though the water they produce tastes much better.

There's now a third option, the **Steripen** (🖳 www.steripen.com/), which kills waterborne microbes by using ultraviolet light. The pen is simple to use. Simply hold the pen in a litre of water for 30 seconds and... that's it. I've seen one of these in action on the mountain and I have to say I found it a very impressive bit of kit. My only quibble was that you can use it on only one litre of water at a time, so it can be awkward if you have, for example, a three-litre bottle.

● **Torch** A head-torch, if you have one and don't find it uncomfortable, is far more practical than a hand-held one, allowing you to keep both hands free; on the last night this advantage is pretty much essential, enabling you to keep your hands in your pockets for warmth.

● **Sunscreen** High factor (35-40) essential.

● **Ice axe** Only really useful now if you are taking a highly unusual route on the mountain (ie none of the official ones) where you have to cross glaciers, or, possibly, if you're travelling out of season when snow can be heavy. **Crampons**, too, would be useful on these occasions, though ask your trekking agency first if they will be necessary before bringing them. Otherwise leave them, your snow boots, rope, karabiners and all that other mountaineering gear at home.

● **Glasses/contact lenses** For those who need them, of course. Contact lenses are fine but super-expensive ones should be avoided on the final assault to the summit as there's a risk that when the strong cold wind blows across the saddle on assault night the lenses can dry and go brittle very quickly and fall out of the eye. I suggest affordable disposable lenses be worn but that spare glasses be carried, especially during the assault on the summit. Obviously you'll need to be extra careful to keep your hands super clean and dry when putting them in.

Cameras and camera equipment

It's important to prepare properly when it comes to taking a camera on Kilimanjaro. After all, it's likely that your camera will not have spent seven days in constant use before and almost certainly not in the dusty and/or humid conditions one finds on Kili, with its extremes of temperature and weather.

The first thing to do is to make sure you have enough **memory cards**; I take an average of 400-600 shots each time I spend a week on Kilimanjaro and while that's probably a bit extreme, if you like taking photographs you could well match or even surpass these figures. Indeed it may feel like you've spent the entire trip with your camera attached to your face, such is the frequency with which you find something worth photographing on the mountain. Bring a **spare battery** or two, too, and make sure all batteries are fully charged before you set off on the mountain. More and more photographic equipment is becoming available for sale in Arusha and, to a lesser extent, Moshi, but I certainly wouldn't rely on them having the battery you require for your camera. And for goodness sake don't forget to bring the **charger**, so you can charge your batteries the night before you head off onto the mountain.

Regarding **lenses**, I always take a couple of zooms: a wide-angle (around 18mm-135mm) and a telephoto. This latter is far less useful on Kilimanjaro, of course, as panoramic shots of the mountain and stunning wide-angle views are the order of the day, but occasionally it's nice to zoom in on a bird of prey, or a particular part of the mountain. A telephoto zoom also comes into its own if you're going on safari after your trek (I suggest a 300m minimum for this).

Other useful equipment includes: a **polarizing filter** to bring out the rich colours of the sky, rocks and glaciers. A **tripod** is useful for those serious about their photography, in order to keep the camera steady and allow for maximum depth of field – though remember, you're the one who's going to have to carry it if you want to use it during the day (though you could ask your agency to provide a porter for this task); a **bean-bag** is a more portable alternative. One other essential investment is a **camera-cleaning kit**. Your camera goes through a lot of hardship on Kili, not least because of the different vegetation zones you pass through, from the humidity of the forest to the dusty desert of the Saddle. Either buy a ready-made kit from a camera shop or make one yourself by investing in a soft cloth, cotton buds, a blow brush and tweezers.

Many people with expensive SLR cameras also bring a cheap point-and-shoot **compact**; this is not a bad idea, as it doubles your chances of getting some photographic record of your journey. As an alternative, why not invest in a disposable panoramic camera – you can pick them up for about a tenner in the UK – which both acts as a back-up to your main camera *and* offers an alternative perspective of the mountain.

Finally for those people still using **regular film**, there is plenty of light on Kilimanjaro, so 100 or 200ASA film should be fine, or even slower if you are going to bring a tripod/bean bag. Film is available in the larger towns of Tanzania though the choice is limited and the films are sometimes either past their sell-by date or have been stored in the baking hot sun and have perished. Therefore, you are strongly advised to **bring all your film from home**.

A Kilimanjaro washbag
Hygiene is very, very important on Kilimanjaro. The last thing you want to get is a stomach bug on the mountain due to the poor hygiene regime of one of your fellow trekkers – or, indeed, yourself. The trouble is, of course, that opportunities to wash are minimal on the mountain and water is limited the further up Kilimanjaro you go. Put the following in your washbag, however, and you should be able to maintain some sort of standards on the mountain.

● **Soap** Though you won't get through much of it on the mountain and your trekking agency should provide some for you.
● **Bacterial handwash** This stuff is very effective and though you won't find it on most kit lists, I think it's essential.
● **Moist toilet tissues (Wet-wipes)** For mopping brows, mainly; use several at the end of the day and it's the closest thing to a shower on the mountain.
● **Toothbrush and toothpaste** Ensure your dental checks are up-to-date; if there is one thing more painful than climbing to the summit of Kili, it's climbing to the summit of Kili with toothache.
● **Toilet paper**
● **Tampons/sanitary towels**
● **Contraceptives** For those with too much energy. But gentlemen be warned: if she says she has a headache on the mountain, the chances are she *really does have* a headache.

In addition to the above, you should also carry a **towel** of course. The controversy here is over which sort of towel to bring. Many just bring one enormous beach towel because they plan to visit Zanzibar after the trek and don't see the point of packing two towels.

At the other extreme there are the tiny so-called 'travel towels', a sort of chamois-cloth affair sold in camping shops and airport lounges the world over. Some people swear by these things but others usually end up swearing at them, finding that they have all the absorbency of your average block of volcanic stone. Nevertheless, we grudgingly admit that they do have their uses on Kilimanjaro, where opportunities to wash anything other than face and hands are minimal. You can dry your towel by attaching it to the outside of your rucksack during the day (see p68).

● **Sunglasses** Necessary for the morning on the summit when the early morning light on Kibo can be really painful and damaging; could also be essential for preventing snow-blindness.
● **Money for tipping** For a rough guide as to how much you should take, see p43 – then add a few dollars, just in case.

Highly desirables
● **Plastic bags** Useful for segregating your wet clothes from the rest of your kit in your rucksack and for collecting rubbish to take off the mountain.
● **Trekking poles** If you've done some trekking before you'll know if you need trekking poles or not; if you haven't, assume you will. While people often use them the whole way, poles really come into their own on the descent, to minimize the strain on your knees as you trudge downhill. Telescopic poles can be

A Kilimanjaro medical kit

According to Meyer, the Chagga treated their cuts and scars with the liberal application of cow dung. We advise, however, that you don't. Instead, if you're going on a cheap trek, take a medical kit with you as few of the budget agencies will have one. (And even if you're going with a more luxurious operator, check to see what they pack in the way of medication, bandages etc.)

A medical kit should include the following:

● **Antiseptic cream and plasters** For small cuts and grazes.
● **Bandages** Useful for twists and sprains as well as for larger flesh wounds.
● **Compeed** For blisters.
● **Elastic joint supports** For steeper gradients if you have knee/ankle problems.
● **Ice packs** One of my clients brought 'Ice Paks', which turned icy cold when 'snapped' and provided great relief for painful joints. Can be bought online and are very reasonable; ideal if you know that your knees or ankles will play up on the mountain.
● **Anti-malarials** You won't catch malaria on the mountain but if you're on a course of anti-malarials you should continue taking them.
● **Ibuprofen/Aspirin/Paracetamol** Or other painkillers, though do read the discussion on AMS (p217) and the medical indications in the packet before scoffing these.
● **Imodium** Stops you going when you don't want to go, which could come in handy.
● **Rehydrating powders** Such as Dioralyte. Usually prescribed to people suffering from diarrhoea but useful after a hot day's trekking as well.
● **Lip salve or chapstick/vaseline** See under *Highly desirables*, below.
● **Throat pastilles** Useful, as the dry, dusty air causes many a sore throat.
● **Any current medication you are on** Bring with you all your needles, pills, lotions, potions and pungent unguents.
● **Diamox** Diamox is the brand name for Acetazolamide, the drug that fights AMS and which many people use prophylactically on Kilimanjaro. See the box on p223 to help you decide whether you want to bring a course of these with you.
● **Sterile needles** If you are having an injection in Tanzania, insist that the doctor uses your new needles.

Carry everything in a **waterproof bag or case** and keep at least the emergency stuff in your daypack – where hopefully it will lie undisturbed for the trek's duration.

bought from trekking/camping outfitters in the West, or you can invest in a more local version – a Maasai 'walking stick' from souvenir shops in Moshi or Arusha.
● **Boiled sweets/chocolate** For winning friends and influencing people. Good for energy levels too. And morale.
● **Bandanna (aka 'buff')** For keeping the dust out of your face when walking on the Saddle, to use as an ear-warmer on the final night, and to mop the sweat from your brow on those exhausting uphill climbs. Also useful for blocking out the odours when using the public toilets at the campsites.
● **Chapstick/ lip salve or vaseline** The wind on the summit will rip your sunburnt lips to shreds. Save yourself the agony by investing in a chapstick, available in strawberry and mint flavours from pharmacists in Moshi and Arusha.
● **Money** For sundry items on sale at huts en route.
● **Camera and equipment** See box on p65.

PLANNING YOUR TRIP

Usefuls

● **Earplugs** Some porters have stereos and mobile phones and they love advertising this fact by playing the former and speaking into the latter extremely loudly at campsites. A set of earplugs will reduce this disturbance.

● **Gaiters** Useful on the dusty Saddle. Indeed, more than one trekker has written in to say that gaiters are essential. However, we've also met more than one trekker who can't see the point of them. It's a matter of preference, really.

● **Aluminium sheet blanket** Provides extra comfort if your sleeping bag isn't as warm as you thought, though they do cause condensation overnight that can leave your sleeping bag wet.

● **Sandals/flip-flops** Useful in the evenings at camp, but make sure they are big enough to fit round a pair of thick socks.

● **Candles** But don't use them in the tent and keep them away from everybody else's tent too. Usually supplied by the trekking company for use in the mess tent.

● **Bootlaces/string**

● **Clothes pegs** Useful for attaching wet clothes to the back of rucksacks to allow them to dry in the sun while you walk; a reader wrote in to recommend **binder clips** (also known as bulldog or office clips) as a smaller, stronger alternative.

● **Penknife** Always useful, if only for opening beer bottles at the post-trek party.

● **Matches** As with the penknife, always useful, as any Boy Scout will tell you.

GPS waypoints

If you have a handheld GPS receiver you will be able to take advantage of the waypoints marked on the maps and listed in the appendix on p352 of this book. Essentially a GPS calculates your position on the Earth using a number of satellites and the results should be accurate to a few metres. It is, of course, not essential that you use a GPS; your chances of getting lost on the mountain are very slim, given that you will be accompanied at every step by a guide who may have climbed on your route a hundred times or more.

If you do decide to use a GPS unit in conjunction with this book don't feel that you need to be ticking off every waypoint as you reach it; you'll soon get bored with that method. But if you look it occasionally – when you stop for lunch, for example – it will give you an idea both of where you are on the trail, and also how far you have to go.

You have two ways of inputting the waypoints into your receiver. You can either manually key the nearest presumed waypoint from the list in this book on p352 as and when the need arises. Or, much less laboriously, and with less margin for keystroke error, download the complete list (but not the descriptions) for free from our website at ⌨ www.climbmountkilimanjaro.com.

● **Sewing kit** For repairs on the trail.
● **Insulating tape** Also for repairs – of shoes, rucksacks, tents etc, and as a last resort for mending holes in clothes if you have forgotten your sewing kit or are incapable of using it.
● **Watch** Preferably cheap and luminous for night-time walking.
● **Compass** Not essential, but useful when combined with ...
● **Map** See p345 for a list of our preferred maps; again not essential but will, in combination with a compass, help you to determine where you are on the mountain, and where you're going.
● **GPS receiver** See box p68.
● **Trowel** If you envisage needing to defecate along the trail at places other than the designated toilet huts, this will help to bury the evidence and keep the mountain looking pristine; see p227.
● **Whistle** It's difficult to get lost on Kilimanjaro but if you're taking an unusual route – on the northern side of the mountain, for example, or around Mawenzi – a whistle may be useful to help people locate which ravine you've fallen into.
● **She-wee** AKA the Miss Piss, this is for ladies who want to wee without the bother of removing layers or getting out of the tent at night. According to some, the 'female urinal' is cheaper and better. Blokes, by the way, usually make do with an empty mineral water bottle.

Luxuries

● **Mobile phone** You can get reception on much of the mountain now – including, so it is said, on the summit. What better place could there be from which to phone friends stuck behind their desks at work on a rainy day in Europe? We point out where you can get reception on the trails in Part 8 on p241.
● **Hot water bottle** Several people have suggested this, and indeed a number of trekking companies now supply them as standard. Get your crew to fill it with hot water before bedtime, and use the water in the morning to drink or wash with.
● **Pillow** One luxury that I have never used on the mountain but would love to is a pillow; and not one of those inflatable travel ones either but a proper, plump, goose-down number. Bulky and a pain to carry, of course – but so much nicer than resting one's weary head on a scrunched-up fleece at the end of the day.
● **MP3 players** and **iPods** While some find the idea abhorrent, many trekkers bring their music on the trek with them. There is nothing wrong with a little mountainside music, of course, but do remember that while you may think you've found the perfect soundtrack for climbing up Kili, others on the mountain may disagree: bring headphones, so as not to disturb.
● **Diary/reading material** A list of appropriate reading matter can be found in *Appendix D* on p345. Note that more than one client has said that books and other forms of entertainment are essential on Kili to while away the hours in camp, while others say it's all unnecessary; it depends who you're climbing with, I suppose, and how well you're all getting along.
● **Champagne** For celebrating, of course, though don't try to take it up and open it at the summit – the combination of champagne and altitude sickness could lead to tragedy and, besides, the glass could well crack with the cold.

❏ What to put in your daypack

Normally you will not see your backpack from the moment you hand it to the porter in the morning until lunchtime at least, and maybe not until the end of the day. It's therefore necessary to pack everything that you may need during the day in your bag that you carry with you. Some suggestions, in no particular order:

- sweets
- water
- water purifiers
- toilet paper and plastic bag for packing used paper to the next camp; see p226 for toilet etiquette
- trowel

- this book/maps
- camera and spare film/batteries
- sunhat/sunglasses and suncream
- rainwear
- walking sticks/knee supports
- medical kit, including chapstick
- lunch (supplied by your crew)

WHAT TO PACK IT IN

You'll need two bags: a **rucksack** and a smaller, lighter **daypack**. While trekkers usually spend a long time finding the rucksack that's most comfortable for them, few bother to spend as long when choosing a daypack. However, on Kili it is the porters who traditionally carry your rucksack for you (usually on their heads, and often inside a rice sack or similar outer layer to protect it from getting wet or damaged), while you will carry your daypack yourself. So make sure you **choose your daypack with care** and that it is both comfortable and durable. It also needs to be big enough to hold everything you may need with you when walking, as it is unlikely that you will see your main rucksack from morning until evening. See box above for a possible list of these things.

Two more points. Firstly, don't leave valuables in your rucksack. Though porters are very trustworthy, it's only fair that you do not put temptation in their path. Secondly, put everything in **plastic bags** (or **bin bags**) inside your backpack and daypack to keep everything dry.

❏ High altitude health

The illness you are most likely to suffer from is altitude sickness; indeed, it's a rare trekker on Kilimanjaro who doesn't to some degree. Altitude sickness is caused by the body's inability to adapt quickly enough to the thinner mountain air present at high altitudes. It can be fatal if ignored or left untreated but is also often preventable. For a run-down on the causes, symptoms and treatments of altitude sickness, read the section on pp217-223 carefully.

Before you go, if you suffer from heart or lung problems, high blood pressure or are pregnant, you must visit your doctor to get advice on the wisdom of climbing up Africa's highest mountain; many of the deaths on the mountain are due to pre-existing conditions that have gone undetected before.

Health precautions, inoculations and insurance

FITNESS

I ascribe the almost perfect health I have always enjoyed in Africa to the fact that I have made every step of my journey on foot, the constant exercise keeping my bodily organs in good order.   **Hans Meyer** *Across East African Glaciers* (1891)

There's no need to go overboard with fitness preparations for climbing Kili. The main reason why people fail to reach the summit is altitude sickness rather than lack of necessary strength or stamina. That said, the trek will obviously be more enjoyable for you the fitter you are, so anything you can do in the way of train-ing can only help (see box p72). A weekend of walking would be a good thing to do; it won't improve your fitness to a great degree but it will at least confirm that you can walk for more than a few hours at a time, and for more than one day at a time too. Wear the clothes you plan to bring to Kilimanjaro with you – particularly your boots and socks – and carry the daypack that you hope to be carrying all the way to the top of Kibo too.

One more thing: if you're planning on relying on it on the mountain, try Diamox (see p223) before you go to make sure you have no severe adverse reaction to it.

INOCULATIONS

Sort out your vaccinations a few months before you're due to fly. Note that it is once again **compulsory to have a yellow-fever vaccination in order to enter Tanzania**; see p83 for further details. In the UK the jab can cost anywhere from £25-45 (US$42.50-76.50). Remember to collect a health card or some other written evidence from your doctor to prove you've been vaccinated.

Other recommended inoculations include:

● **Typhoid** This disease is caught from contaminated food and water. A single injection lasts for three years.

● **Polio** The polio vaccine used to be administered by sugar-lump, making it one of the more pleasant inoculations, though these days it's more commonly injected. Lasts for ten years.

● **Hepatitis A** This debilitating disease of the liver is spread by contaminated water, or even by using cutlery that has been washed in this water. The latest inoculation involves two injections; the first will protect you for three years, the second, taken six to twelve months later, will cover you for ten years.

PLANNING YOUR TRIP

A FITNESS REGIME

Though altitude sickness is the main reason why people fail to reach the summit – and this can strike you regardless of whether you are fit or not – there's no doubt that you *do* need to be in reasonable condition to tackle Kilimanjaro, and will have a much more pleasant time on the mountain if you are fit and healthy.

For this reason, and to answer the many emails we get from people who want to undertake some sort of fitness regime before their trek, here is a typical daily exercise programme for Kilimanjaro. It should be started about four months (three minimum) before the climb itself. This should help to reduce body fat, improve aerobic fitness and also strengthen the muscles in the places where it really matters: the legs.

We think it helps to concentrate on aerobic exercises one day (say three times a week) alternating with leg strengthening exercises for the other three days – then follow God's example and rest on the seventh day.

Aerobic exercise

Aerobic exercise is designed to improve oxygen consumption in the body. Thirty minutes to an hour of jogging, cycling, climbing stairs or even just brisk walking are all good aerobic exercise. Aim to exercise at 70% of your maximum heart rate for the best results.

Leg strengthening

Go to any gym and you'll come across plenty of contraptions designed to increase the strength of your calves, thighs, hamstrings and buttocks. These are fine though the usual warnings apply: always read the instructions carefully before using any machine and never be too ambitious and overload the machine with too much weight. Either course of action could lead to serious injury and the cancellation of your trek altogether.

If you don't have access to gym equipment, however, don't worry: there are exercises that you can do without the need for machines. **Lunges**, where you take an exaggerated step forward with one leg, dropping your hips as low as possible while keeping your torso upright, are great for thighs, hamstrings and buttocks. A **reverse lunge**, which is the same as a regular lunge only you take a step *backwards*, until your forward thigh (ie the one you didn't take a step backwards with) is parallel to the floor, is also good, particularly for the hamstring. **Calf raises**, where you position yourself with the front half of your feet on a platform, then gently raise and lower yourself on your toes so that your heel is alternately higher and lower than the toes, is also useful.

Smoking and other preparations

While the above exercises certainly provide many benefits, we still maintain that nothing is better preparation than **going for a long walk**! A walk provides excellent aerobic exercise, is great for strengthening leg muscles and if the walk is long enough and involves plenty of uphills, can be great for improving stamina too. Find walks in your area, or take a walking weekend or holiday. You never know, you may even enjoy it too.

Finally, you can always take up **smoking**. I'd long heard the rumour that smokers have a better chance of reaching the summit, apparently due to the fact that their bodies are used to less oxygen due to the reduced functioning of their lungs – and certainly my experiences of taking smokers up the mountain bear this bizarre idea out. While those of my clients who've led a blameless, tobacco-free life frequently struggle with the altitude, long-term smokers tend to saunter up. Breathless, certainly, and often wheezing – but headache-free and happy. Of course, we're not seriously suggesting you take up smoking – but it's interesting, isn't it?

● **Tetanus** Tetanus vaccinations last for ten years and are absolutely vital for visitors to Tanzania. The vaccination is usually given in combination with one for **diphtheria**. Once you've had five injections, you're covered for life.

● **Meningococcal meningitis** This disease of the brain is often fatal though the vaccination, while not free, is safe, effective and lasts for three to five years.

● **Rabies** If you're spending some time with animals or in the wilderness, it's also worth considering having a course of **rabies** injections, though it isn't pleasant, consisting of three injections spread over one month.

Malaria

Malaria is a problem in Tanzania, which is considered one of the highest risk countries in the world. While you are highly unlikely to contract malaria on Kilimanjaro, which is too high and cold for the anopheles mosquito (the species that carries malaria but which is rarely seen above 1200m – much lower than your starting point on Kili), it is rife in coastal areas and on Zanzibar. It's also present in Moshi and, despite an altitude above 1200m, in Arusha too. When beginning a course of **anti-malarials**, it is very important to begin taking them before you go; that way the drug is established in your system by the time you set foot on Tanzanian soil and it will give you a chance to see if the drug is going to cause a reaction or allergy. Once started, complete the full course, which usually runs for several weeks after you return home.

Which anti-malarial you will need depends on which parts of Africa you are visiting and your previous medical history. Your doctor will be able to advise you on what drug is best for you. With Tanzania in the highest risk category, the chances are you will be recommended either Lariam (the brand name for mefloquine), Doxycycline or the new drug Malarone, which is supposedly free of side effects but very expensive. Stories of Lariam causing hallucinations, nightmares, blindness and even death have been doing the rounds in travellers' circles for years now but if you feel no adverse reaction – and millions don't – carry on taking it and don't worry.

Of course the best way to combat malaria is not to get bitten at all. A **repellent** with 30% Diethyltoluamide (DEET) worn in the evenings when the malarial anopheles mosquito is active should be effective in preventing bites. Some use it during the day too, when the mosquitoes that carry yellow and dengue fevers are active. Alternatively, you could just keep covered up with long sleeve shirts and long trousers, sleep under a **mosquito net** and burn **mosquito coils**; these are available within Tanzania.

Travellers' medical clinics (UK)

For all your jabs, malaria advice and anything else you need to know regarding health abroad, visit your doctor or one of the following clinics:

● **Trailfinders Travel Clinic** (☎ 020-7938 3999; 💻 www.trailfinders.com/travelessentials/travelclinic.htm) 194 Kensington High Street, London.

● **Nomad Travellers Store and Medical Centre** (☎ 020-7833 4114; 💻 www.nomadtravel.co.uk) in London at 40 Bernard Street, Russell Square, near

Victoria Station at 52 Grosvenor Gardens, and at Turnpike Lane (☎ 020-8889 7014); also has branches at Bristol (☎ 0117-922 6567), Manchester (☎ 0161 832 2134) and Southampton (☎ 02380-234 920).

● **MASTA** (Medical Advisory Services for Travellers Abroad; 🖳 www.masta-travel-health.com, ☎ 0845 600 2236), close to Oxford Circus at 52 Margaret Street.

Also worth looking at is the informative website of the **US Center for Disease Control** (🖳 www.cdc.gov), packed full of advice and the latest news.

INSURANCE

When buying insurance you must make clear to the insurer that you'll be trekking on a very big mountain. If you are taking an unusual route and will be using ropes then you need to tell them that too. This will probably increase your premium (it usually doubles it), and may even exclude you from being covered altogether. But if you don't make this clear and pay the lower premium you'll probably find, should you try to make a claim, that you aren't actually covered at all.

Remember to read the small print of any insurance policy before buying, and shop around, too, for each insurance policy varies slightly from company to company. Details to consider include:

● How much is deductible if you have to make a claim?
● Can the insurers pay for your hospital bills etc immediately, while you are still in Tanzania, or do you have to wait until you get home?
● How long do you have before making a claim and what evidence do you require (hospital bills, police reports etc)?

Remember the premium for the entire trip will probably double when you mention that you are climbing Kilimanjaro, even though you will actually be on the mountain for only a few days. However, you will need to be covered for your entire trip: there are just as many nasty things that can happen to you – indeed more – when off the mountain than on it, and theft becomes a much bigger issue too.

For UK residents, the following companies offer insurance up to 6000m.
● **British Mountaineering Council** (🖳 www.thebmc.co.uk; ☎ 0161 445 6111)
● **Columbus Direct** (🖳 www.columbusdirect.com; ☎ 0870 033 9988)
● **Insure and Go** (🖳 www.insureandgo.com; ☎ 0844 888 2787)
● **Insurancewide** (🖳 www.insurewide.com; ☎ 0870 112 8245)

PART 2: TANZANIA

'Strange country isn't it?'
'Yes. It seems so cruel one moment, then suddenly kind and very beautiful. Maybe there are parts God forgot about – he meant it all to be like this.'
  Robert Taylor and Anne Aubrey discuss the land we now call Tanzania in the 1959
  swashbuckling classic *Killers of Kilimanjaro*

Although this book concentrates specifically on Kilimanjaro, some background knowledge of the country in which it stands, Tanzania, is necessary. For the chances are that climbing Kilimanjaro forms only one part of your trip to Tanzania, and as such you are going to need to know what this beautiful country is like and how you are going to negotiate travelling around it. With this in mind, the following chapter is split into two halves. The first provides a background of the country by looking at the history, economy, culture etc. This should both increase your enjoyment of visiting Tanzania and serve to put Kilimanjaro in its national context. The second half of this chapter deals with the more practical side of things, offering advice and tips to help the visitor.

Facts about the country

GEOGRAPHY

Tanzania occupies an area of 945,087 sq km – a little over twice the size of California – made up of 886,037 sq km of land (including the offshore islands of Pemba, Mafia and Zanzibar) and 59,050 sq km of water. This makes it the largest country in the geo-political region of East Africa. It is bounded to the north by Uganda and Kenya, to the west by the Democratic Republic of Congo (DRC), Burundi and Rwanda, to the south by Mozambique, Malawi and Zambia, and to the east by the Indian Ocean. The terrain in that 886,037 sq km of land includes a wide, lush coastal plain and a large and dusty central plateau flanked by the eastern and western branches of the **Great Rift Valley** (see p94). There are highlands in both the north and south of the country, and in the centre of the plateau are some volcanic peaks which again owe their existence to the Rift Valley. Interestingly, over a quarter of the country is given over to national parks or nature reserves.

Tanzania is also a land of extremes, housing Africa's largest game reserve, the **Selous** (covering approximately 55,000 sq km, and with an approximately equal number of elephants), and the Serengeti, the park with the greatest concentration of migratory game in the world. Its borders also encompass a share in the continent's largest lake, **Lake Victoria**, and part of **Lake Tanganyika**, the longest and, after Lake Baikal in Siberia, deepest freshwater lake in the world. The third largest lake in Africa, **Lake Malawi**, also forms one of Tanzania's borders. These lakes were formed when the Great Rift Valley, which runs through the heart of the country, opened up about 30 million years ago. As a direct result of the formation of this valley, Tanzania contains Africa's lowest point, the floor of Lake Tanganyika, some 350m below sea level. It is also, of course, the proud owner of Africa's highest...

Beautiful as this country undoubtedly is, it is also beset by enormous environmental problems, from deforestation to desertification, soil degradation, erosion and reef bombing. Significant damage has already occurred, and is still occurring, with added pressures on the land caused by the meteoric rise in tourism over the past couple of decades. For details of how you can minimize your impact on the environment of Kilimanjaro, see p226.

CLIMATE

Tanzania's climate varies greatly, and you'll be encountering just about all of the variations in the four or five days it takes you to walk to the top of Kilimanjaro. For more about this, see the Kilimanjaro climate section on p98. Away from the mountain, the narrow coastal strip tends to be the most hot, humid and tropical part of the country, with the inland plateau being of sufficient elevation to offer some cooler temperatures and respite from the heat. On the coast the average temperature during the day is a sticky 27°C; luckily the sea breezes temper this heat and make it bearable. On the inland plateau you're looking at an average temperature of around 20-26.5°C during the cooler months of June to August, up to a roasting 30°C between December and March. The **rainy seasons** extend from November to early January (the short rains), and from mid-March to May (the long rains). On the coast the average annual rainfall is around 1400mm; inland it is a much drier 250mm, though in mountainous areas it can be a magnificent 2000mm; unsurprisingly, flooding can be a problem at this time.

HISTORY

We, the people of Tanganyika, would like to light a candle and put it on the top of Mount Kilimanjaro, which would shine beyond our borders, giving hope where there was despair, love where there was hate, and dignity where before there was only humiliation.
   Julius Nyerere in a speech to the Tanganyika Legislative Assembly in 1959. Following
      independence in 1961, his wish was granted and a torch was placed on Kili's summit.

The discovery of the 1,750,000-year-old remains of an early hominid, **Australopithecus Zinjanthropus Boisei**, at Olduvai Gorge in the Ngorongoro Crater (near hominid footprints that could be as much as three and a half million years old), suggest that Tanzania has one of the longest histories in the world. We are now going to cram these three and a half million years into the next three and a half pages – a task made considerably simpler by the fact that this history has been, until the last 200 years or so, unrecorded. (By the way, for a detailed history of Kilimanjaro, see p101.)

We know that **Khoisan speakers** (from southern Africa) moved into the area of modern Tanzania around 10,000 years ago, to be joined between 3000BC and 1000BC by Cushitic speakers from the Horn of Africa (Ethiopia and Eritrea), who brought with them more advanced agricultural techniques. Over the next few hundred years **Bantu speakers** from West Africa's Niger Delta and Nilotic peoples from the north and Sudan also migrated to the area we now know as Tanzania.

By 400BC merchants from Classical Greece knew about and traded with the coast of East Africa, which they called **Azania**. Some of them eventually settled here to take advantage of the trading opportunities, to be joined later by **traders from Persia** and, by the end of the first millennium AD as trade routes stretched into China, merchants from **India**. The majority of immigrants, however, proved to be the seafaring **traders from Arabia**, and soon the Swahili language and culture, an amalgamation of the cultures of Arabia and the Bantu speakers who had also settled on the coast, began to emerge there.

Portuguese, Arabs, Germans and British

Life on the coastal strip of what is now Tanzania continued, as far as we know, pleasantly enough for a number of centuries, a fairly idyllic existence that was rudely shattered by the arrival of the **Portuguese** following Vasco da Gama's legendary expedition at the end of the fifteenth century. As greedy as they were intrepid, they built the coastal village of Kilwa Kisiwani into a major trading port which, in typical Portuguese style, they later sacked. Understandably unpopular, the Portuguese nevertheless held on grimly and gamely to their East African possessions for almost 200 years until the end of the seventeenth century; that they managed to survive for so long is largely due to a lack of a united opposition, which didn't arrive until 1698 in the form of **Omani Arabs**, summoned to help by the long-suffering traders of Kilwa Kisiwani. Unlike the Portuguese, the Omani Arabs were keen to forge trading links with the interior. They pushed new routes across the plains to Lake Tanganyika, thereby facilitating the extraction of gold, **slaves** and ivory from deep within the continent. The Arabs grew inordinately wealthy from the fat of Africa's land to the extent that the Omani sultan decided to pull up his tent pegs from the desert sands of Arabia and relocate, establishing his new capital at Stonetown on Zanzibar.

While this was going on, the Europeans returned to Africa. Initially it was just a trickle of **missionaries** and **explorers**, hell-bent (if that's the right term) on making converts and mapping continents respectively. Indeed, one man who famously combined both vocations, Dr David Livingstone, spent a while in Tanzania as part of his efforts to find the source of the Nile, and it was at the village of Ujiji, on the Tanzanian side of Lake Tanganyika, that HM Stanley is believed to have finally caught up with him and uttered those immortal words 'Dr Livingstone, I presume'.

With intrepid, independent Europeans now roaming all over the continent, it could only be a matter of time before one European country or another would come up with the idea of full-scale colonization. By the late **1880s** Britain had already secured a dominant role on Zanzibar. But over on the mainland it was Germany who was making the most progress.

TANZANIA

Or rather, one German, for it was **Carl Peters** who, acting independently of his government, established German influence on the mainland at this time, negotiating treaties with local chiefs in order to secure a charter for his **Deutsch-Ostafrikanische Gesellschaft** (DOAG, the German East Africa Company). A few years later and with his homeland's government now supporting his work, Peters' DOAG was formally given the task of administering the mainland. This left the British on Zanzibar fuming – and not a little scared – at the German's impertinence, and war was averted between the two superpowers only with the signing of an accord in 1890 in which Britain was formally allowed to establish a protectorate over her Zanzibar territories. One year and further negotiations later and the land we now know as Tanzania (Zanzibar excluded) officially came under direct German control as **German East Africa**.

The Germans brought a Western education, a rail network, and a higher level of healthcare with them to Africa. They also brought harsh taxes, suppression, humiliation and no small amount of unrest. They were eventually replaced as colonial overlords after World War One by the **British** following a League of Nations mandate. The territory was renamed Tanganyika at this time. After World War Two a near bankrupt Britain clung on to administrative control, though officially Tanganyika was now a 'trust territory' of the fledgling United Nations.

Independence

Life under the British was marginally better than under the Germans, with greater political freedom and an improved economy thanks to the cultivation of export crops; but it was only marginal and soon political groups were springing up all over the country with each campaigning for the same thing: independence. The most important of these was the Dar es Salaam-based Tanganyika Africa Association which, in 1953, elected teacher **Julius Nyerere** as its president. Pressure from Nyerere and his party (now known as TANU, or the Tanganyika African National Union) forced Britain to agree to the formation of an internal self-government. Indeed, so impressed was Britain with Nyerere that the only condition they placed on the establishment of this new regime of self-government was that he should be its first chief minister.

Now a mere formality, **independence** for Tanganyika was eventually declared on the 9 December 1961. Exactly one year later it was formally established as a **republic**, with Nyerere, as Britain had hoped, as the first president.

On **Zanzibar**, meanwhile, things were going less smoothly. Whilst the Zanzibaris won their independence not long afterwards (December 1963), the two parties that formed the first government did not enjoy popular support but instead had been thrust into power by the departing British because of their pro-British leanings. With a tenure that was decidedly shaky, it came as no surprise when they were toppled in a revolution just a month later. In their place came the popular, radical Afro Shirazi Party (ASP). Less than a year after independence, on 26 April 1964 the ASP leader, Abeid Karume, was signing an act of union with his mainland neighbours and the **United Republic of Tanganyika** was formed.

In October of the same year the name was changed to the **United Republic of Tanzania**, the name being a neat combination of the two former territories.

The two maintained separate governments, however, even after 1977 when ASP and TANU were combined by Nyerere to form **Chama Cha Mapinduzi** (Party of the Revolution), or **CCM**, the party which maintains political control of Tanzania to this day.

Modern history

From 1967 to the late 1980s Nyerere and his party followed a socialist course; the economy was nationalized, the tax regime was deliberately aimed at redistributing wealth and new villages were established in order to modernize the agricultural sector and give the rural poor greater access to social services. Unfortunately, the twenty-year experiment was eventually deemed a flop, with the economy in seemingly perpetual decline. By 1992 things had got so desperate that the CCM took the unprecedented step of legalizing opposition parties after pressure from Western donors for more democracy in the country.

Curiously, this move seems to have done little to achieve this. Three years after the legalization of political opponents, the first democratic elections were held and the CCM, now under the leadership of **Benjamin Mkapa** following Nyerere's resignation in 1985, emerged once again as the major force in Tanzanian politics. The elections in late 2000 confirmed their dominance with over 95% of parliamentary seats won by CCM candidates. While they undoubtedly remain Tanzania's most creditable political party, the scale of the victory suggests that proper political debate is all but impossible, a prediction that the election of **Jakaya Kikwete** in 2005, another CCM candidate, did little to dispel.

On semi-autonomous **Zanzibar**, things, as usual, have been a little more explosive. In 1995 the incumbent CCM president, Salmin Amour, was returned to office after an election that many believe was rigged. Fresh elections in 2000 resulted in yet more controversy, with widespread reports of ballot rigging and intimidation of opposition leaders. In January 2001, 27 protesters were shot dead in Pemba as they marched through the streets protesting against these voting irregularities. And though the situation has quietened a little since then, following the latest bout of elections in late 2005 the Zanzibaris once more rioted. **Jakaya Kikwete** admitted that the unrest on Zanzibar would be his biggest problem in his first term as president, and it continues to simmer to this day.

The future

In some ways Tanzania is a model African nation, garnering international acclaim for its fight against corruption and its efforts to reform itself peacefully – as exemplified by the move towards democracy in the 1990s. The government of President Jakaya Kikwete, who was brought to power with over 80% of the vote in 2005, provided further evidence that Tanzania is one of the more enlightened nations with his promotion of female ministers to key finance and foreign posts. He has also attempted to rid his government of the malaise of corruption and in 2008 even dissolved his cabinet, forcing two members to resign following a scandal. It is, however, still a nation beset by problems. The usual African ailments – poverty, AIDS, and a lack of clean water, basic healthcare and decent education – are as prevalent in Tanzania as they are over much of the continent. In addition, Tanzania has other local problems to contend with, from a lack of credible opposition to the main autocratic CCM party to the secessionist grumblings of many on Zanzibar who were never happy with the union with the mainland – a dissatisfaction that four subsequent decades and more of turmoil have done little to dispel. The influx of refugees from neighbouring Burundi and Congo has also put added pressure on the country, particularly in the west around lakes Victoria and Tanganyika. It remains to be seen whether the moderate line that Tanzania has taken throughout its independence will continue into the future; and whether this thoughtful, conservative (with a small 'c') attitude will be enough to help it to overcome these difficulties.

ECONOMIC AND POPULATION STATISTICS

Tanzania is one of the world's poorest countries, in the bottom 10% of nations in terms of per capita income. Its per capita GDP stands at a modest US$1300 and just over 36% live below the poverty line. Nevertheless, these are significant improvements on the figures recorded in the first edition of this book, when GDP per capita was US$264 and over 50% lived below the poverty line. Other statistics also suggest that Tanzanians are better off than they were in 2001 when this book was first published. Infant mortality stands at a level of 69.28 per 1000 births (down from 85 per 1000 in 2001 and from 98 in 2005), and life expectancy is now 52.01, up from 45.2 in 2005 and 49 in 2001. Presumably some of this improvement can be put down to the decrease in HIV infection, with 6.2% of the population now estimated to be infected, down from 8.8% of the population in 2005 (though that 6.2% still represents over 1.4 million people).

It's early days yet but the economy is starting to show some positive signs too. Growth in real GDP, for example, was 7.1% in 2008, though this has in turn led to inflationary pressures, with the Consumer Price Index rising to 9.3% in 2008. These figures are a bit surprising given that Tanzania is still largely an **agricultural** country. The style of agriculture is mainly traditional, the large collective farms introduced under Nyerere's socialist experiment having been rejected on the whole in favour of the age-old system whereby each farmer cultivates a small plot of land called a *shamba*. The most popular home-grown crops are cotton, rice, sorghum, sugar, bananas and coconuts; sisal, coffee and tea are produced principally for the export market, while cloves and other spices are still grown on Zanzibar and the coast. Agriculture accounts for around a quarter of Tanzania's GDP and employs 80% of the workforce.

Tanzania also has a solid **mining** base with oil, tin, iron, salt, coal, gypsum, phosphate, natural gas, nickel, diamonds and, of course, tanzanite all extracted in the country. Tourism is now a major contributor to the GDP of the country and is a vital source of much-needed foreign currency, particularly in the north.

THE PEOPLE

With 41,048,532 people (CIA world factbook estimate 2009) split into more than a hundred different ethnic groups, numerous local languages and dialects and three main religions, Tanzania is something of an ethnic and cultural hotchpotch, and it is a credit to the country that they exist largely in harmony, without succumbing to the sort of ethnic hatred that has riven many other countries around these parts. Native Africans make up 99% of the population; of these, the vast majority (estimated at 95%) are of Bantu origin, though even here there are over 130 tribes. The other 1% are of European, Arabian or Indian origin. Around Kilimanjaro it is the Chagga people, one of the more wealthy and powerful groups in Tanzania, who dominate.

The **religious** division is a lot more equal. The slight majority (35%) are now Muslim (in the last edition it was Christian), with 30% now professing the Christian faith and traditional indigenous beliefs accounting for the other 35%. These figures exclude Zanzibar, which is 99% Muslim. Presumably adherents of the Hindu and Sikh faiths are too small in number to register in the statistics, though they are undoubtedly a highly visible presence in Tanzania with some large, ostentatious Hindu temples in Dar, Arusha and Moshi. The Chagga people around Kilimanjaro are largely Christian; you can read more about them, their culture and their beliefs on p134.

Language

The first and most common language in Tanzania is **Swahili**, the language originally used by traders on the coast and thus based on Arabic and various Bantu dialects. Zanzibar is still known as the home of Swahili, where the purest form of the language is spoken. A few words of Swahili will go a long way in Tanzania and although the prefixes and suffixes used in the language can be a little tricky to grasp, any efforts to speak a few words will endear you to the local people. *Appendix A* on p338 provides an introduction to Swahili.

Around Kilimanjaro, however, it is not Swahili but the language of the Chagga people, a tongue sometimes known as Kichagga, that predominates, though there are several different dialects. See the box on p135 for a brief introduction.

TANZANIA

Practical information for the visitor

DOCUMENTS AND VISAS

Visas for Tanzania are required by visitors from the following countries:

Afghanistan, Albania, Algeria, Angola, Argentina, Armenia, Australia, Austria, Azerbaijan, Bahrain, Belarus, Belgium, Benin, Bhutan, Bolivia, Bosnia, Brazil, Bulgaria, Burkina Faso, Burma, Burundi, Cambodia, Canada, Cape Verde, Central African Republic, Chad, Chile, China, Colombia, Comoros, Congo, Democratic Republic of Congo, Costa Rica, Cote D'Ivoire, Croatia, Cuba, Czech Republic, Denmark, Djibouti, Dominican Republic, Ecuador, Egypt, El-Salvador, Equatorial Guinea, Eritrea, Estonia, Fiji, Finland, France, Gabon, Georgia, Germany, Gibraltar, Greece, Guatemala, Guinea, Guinea-Bissau, Guyana, Haiti, Holy See, Honduras, Hungary, Iceland, Independent State of Samoa, India, Israel, Italy, Japan, Jordan, Kazakhstan, Korea (North & South), Kuwait, Kurdistan, Laos, Latvia, Liberia, Lithuania, Libya, Luxembourg, Macedonia, Malagasy, Maldives, Mauritania, Mauritius, Mexico, Moldova, Monaco, Mongolia, Morocco, Mozambique, Nepal, Netherlands, New Zealand, Niger, Norway, Oman, Panama, Papua New Guinea, Paraguay, Peru, Philippines, Poland, Republic of Ireland, Portugal, Qatar, Romania, Russia, Rwanda, Sao Tome & Principe, Saudi Arabia, Senegal, Slovak Republic, Slovenia, South Africa, Spain, Suriname, Sweden, Switzerland, Syria, Taiwan, Tajikistan, Thailand, Togo, Tunisia, Turkey, Turkmenistan, Ukraine, United Arab Emirates, United Kingdom, United States of America, Uruguay, Uzbekistan, Venezuela, Vietnam and Yemen.

A single-entry visa costs £38 for UK citizens, US$100 for US citizens, €50 for most European nations and US$50 for most other nations. A visa is typically valid for 90 days from the **date of issue** (and not the day you arrive in Tanzania, though I have to say many officials don't seem to recognize this!). It used to be the case that, unless you were coming from a country without Tanzanian representation, officially you had to buy your visa at the consulate/embassy beforehand. That law was never really enforced, however, and the latest news we have is that citizens of all EU countries can now buy their visa at the airport; and I expect the rule to apply to other nations soon. A list of the addresses of some of the more popular Tanzanian embassies and consulates is given in *Appendix C* on p343, for those who need or want to buy their visa beforehand. With all applications you will need to present a passport that's valid for at least six months together with two passport photos. If applying in person, some consulates/high commissions (including the ones in London and Washington) insist that you pay in cash.

You can pick up a visa at one of the **four border controls**: Dar-es-Salaam International Airport, Kilimanjaro International Airport, Zanzibar

International Airport and the Namanga border crossing between Tanzania and Kenya. (Note that at Kilimanjaro International Airport the fee that's charged for a visa currently seems to be US$50 for all nations bar Americans, who have to pay double).

Remember that, if you're flying in and out of Kenya rather than Tanzania you will need a **Kenyan visa** too (typically £30 for UK citizens, though a transit visa is only £10). If you plan to fly to Kenya and cross into Tanzania from there, you can return to Kenya using the same single-entry visa you arrived with *providing* your visit to Tanzania lasted for less than two weeks and that your Kenyan visa has not expired. Apparently, you can do this only once (ie it's a double-entry visa, not a multiple-entry one), or so we were told at the Kenyan border. Otherwise, you will need to buy a multiple-entry visa (UK£30). See *Appendix C* (p343) for a list of addresses of Kenyan embassies abroad.

Yellow-fever vaccination certificate

It seems that once again it is compulsory for visitors to Tanzania to show evidence that they have been vaccinated against yellow fever. Though this rule seems to change every few months, given that airport staff often ask to see proof of inoculation whether you require it or not it's probably best to play it safe and get one anyway. The certificate itself can be picked up from your doctor after you have received the jab and is usually free – though the inoculation itself is not.

AIRPORT TAX

Airport tax is currently US$30 for international flights (US$25 from Zanzibar) though this I believe is always included in the price of your ticket. Internal flights are subject to airport taxes of (usually) US$6.

MONEY

Currency

The Tanzanian shilling (Ts) is the national currency. It's fairly stable. The local currency cannot be imported except by residents of Tanzania, Kenya and Uganda and cannot be exported.

Foreign currency

Foreign currency can be imported and exported without limit. **Dollars** and, to a lesser extent, **sterling** and **euros** are the best currencies to bring.

The question therefore is: in what form should you carry your money to Tanzania, ie: should you bring travellers' cheques? Cash? Or rely solely on your credit card and use that to get money out of cashpoints in Tanzania? Well, the first option, **travellers' cheques**, is the worst

> ❑ **Exchange rates**
> To get the latest rates visit www.xe.com. At the time of writing they were:
>
> UK£1 = Ts2185
> €1 = Ts1952
> US$1 = Ts1324
> Can$1 = Ts1224
> A$1 = Ts1021
> NZ$1 = Ts961
> SwissFr1 = Ts1290
> KenyaS1 = Ts17.60
> Japan Y1 = Ts14.52

option. Few banks and bureaux accept them these days and if they do the rate tends to be lousy. Nowadays, Tanzanian banks prefer **cash** (US dollars are the only widely accepted currency). Dollars are also very useful for those occasions when the Tanzanian shilling is not accepted, such as when paying for upmarket hotel rooms and air tickets, both of which, officially at least, must be paid for in hard currency. The downside of cash is, of course, that it is also the riskiest way to carry money.

The third option, **credit/debit cards**, is now also the most popular. Though few places take them except for upmarket hotels and shops, they are the easiest to carry around and do give you the chance of withdrawing cash from an ATM. Of course, you do run the risk that the cash machines will reject them or, worse, swallow them, leaving you stuck in Africa with no means of support. But ATMs are not only getting more numerous, they are also becoming more reliable and most people have no trouble finding a machine that they can rely on with their cards.

Overall, then, we advocate **bringing** credit/debit cards (preferably one Visa and one MasterCard, to increase your chances of being able to withdraw cash from an ATM), with a few hundred dollars in cash as back-up in case you can't find a cashpoint that will take your card. How many dollars you bring, of course, depends on how much you've paid for in advance, how long you are staying in the region, and what you hope to do while you are there.

One more thing: when it comes to bringing dollars, **make sure they are new notes**. Notes printed before 2001 are seldom accepted and sometimes even those printed before 2003 are refused.

Banks and moneychangers

Banking hours are typically 8.30am-4pm Monday to Friday, and 8.30am-1pm on Saturday. As a general rule, you get a better rate for large denomination bills (US\$50 and \$100 bills) than small ones. Keep your **exchange receipts** so that when you leave the country you can change your spare shillings back into hard currency. They rarely check, but you never know.

There are **ATMs** ('**cashpoints**') in every town in Tanzania and Kenya.

Credit cards

Credit cards are useful in major tourist hotels, restaurants, gift shops and airline offices and their usefulness is growing every day. Visa is probably the more useful card in that you can withdraw money from more ATMs than with MasterCard.

TOURIST OFFICES

Dar es Salaam and Arusha have tourist offices (see p143 and p166) though they're the only cities that do. Outside Tanzania, there's a tourist office in New York (☎ +1-212-972 9160), 8th Floor, 205 East 42nd Street, New York 10017. Consulates and embassies around the world also have the odd brochure, or you can look at the online information services.

GETTING AROUND

Public transport in Tanzania is unreliable, uncomfortable, slow, and not recommended for those with either long legs or haemorrhoids. It is also dangerous. A little-known but highly pertinent fact about Tanzania's transport system is that 8% of deaths in Tanzanian hospitals are road-accident victims. According to one source, Tanzania suffers an average of 13,684 road accidents annually, resulting in the loss of 1619 lives; and these are just the ones the authorities know about. (Reckless driving is by far and away the biggest cause of most of these accidents.)

That said, Tanzanian transport is also cheap, convenient and, it must be said, cheerful: conversation usually flows pretty easily on a train, bus or dalla-dalla (providing you can make yourself heard above the noise of the stereo). And while the average road is little more than a necklace of potholes strung together with tyre tracks, the main roads between towns are splendid, well-maintained tarmac strips – with speed ramps to deter the bus drivers from going too fast.

The most luxurious form of ground transport is provided by the **express bus** companies; a few of them, such as Dar Express, deserve their reputation for safety and comfort; you may want to ask your hotel or a local which bus company is currently the most reliable. These express buses run to a fixed timetable and will leave without you if you're late. Buy your tickets in advance. The cheaper alternative is the ordinary buses or **Coasters** – minibuses which leave when full. These are cheap but you definitely get what you pay for. As with all forms of local transport, ask your fellow passengers what the correct fare is before handing any money over to the 'conductor'; rip-offs are the rule rather than the exception on many journeys.

In addition to the buses there are the indigenous **dalla-dallas**: minibuses (smaller than Coasters) plying routes around and between neighbouring towns. They're usually a tight squeeze as the drivers pile in the customers to maximize their takings. If you're being pushed into one that looks full-to-bursting, simply refuse to enter; there'll be another along in a minute. In Kenya these minibuses are known as **matatus**.

It is possible to **hire a car** in Tanzania. You can hire cars from many of the bigger tour and trekking agencies in Moshi and Arusha. Make sure you choose a vehicle that is suitable for your requirements. Don't, for example, be tempted to conduct your own off-road safari in a two-wheel drive.

You can **hitch** around the country, though payment will often be expected from a Western tourist; it is, of course, wiser not to hitch alone.

Tanzania has only a skeleton **train** service; services to Arusha and Moshi have long since stopped, though the stations and tracks are still there in both towns and are interesting places to look around if you're very bored.

Flying is an efficient way to cover the vast distances of Tanzania, and there are a number of small chartered and scheduled airlines serving visitors, including Coastal Air, Precision Air, Air Excel, Zantasair and ZanAir. For details of airlines flying to Kilimanjaro, see p340.

ACCOMMODATION

Tanzania's guesthouses and hotels can be split into three sorts: those that welcome tourists, those that accept them, and those that refuse them altogether. The latter are usually the cheapest, double as brothels, have minimum security, minimal advertising and can safely be ignored. Room rates for the other two start at about Ts7000 per night; dorms are a rarity.

Always take your time when choosing a hotel, particularly in the towns featured here where there are lots of options. Standards vary widely but you'll probably be surprised at how pleasant some of them can be, with mosquito nets and attached bathrooms and maybe even a telly. Bear in mind that most hotels have two tariffs, one for locals and people living in Tanzania (commonly known as the '**residents' rate**') and a more expensive one for foreigners. If business is slow, it doesn't take much effort to persuade some of the smaller hotels to charge you the residents' rate, regardless of whether you live in Tanzania or not.

In Nairobi, safety is a concern in some of the hotels, though the ones we have chosen to recommend in this book were fine. Accommodation on Zanzibar, incidentally, is generally much more expensive. Note, too, that in Swahili *hotel* or *hoteli* means restaurant rather than accommodation.

For details of **accommodation on the mountain**, see p244.

ELECTRICITY

Tanzania is powered by 250V, 50 cycles, AC network. Those bringing electrical items from home may wish to invest in a power breaker: Tanzania's electricity supply can be erratic on occasions and power surges could seriously impair the efficacy of your electrical instruments, if not melt them altogether. Plugs and sockets vary in style, though by far the most common are the British three-square-pin or, less common, European two-round-pin style.

TIME

Tanzania is **three hours ahead of GMT** and thus two hours ahead of Western Europe, eight ahead of New York, eleven ahead of San Francisco, one ahead of Johannesburg, seven hours behind Sydney and nine behind Wellington.

❏ **Abbreviations**
Throughout this book we have used the following abbreviations when writing about accommodation: **s/c** is short for self-contained, a local term meaning that the room comes with a bathroom (ie the room is en suite or attached); while **sgl/dbl/tpl** means single/double/triple rooms. So, for example, where we have written 's/c sgl/dbl/tpl US$35/40/45', we mean that a self-contained single room costs US$35 per night, a self-contained double costs US$40, and a self-contained triple costs US$45.

HOLIDAYS AND FESTIVALS

The following are public holidays in Tanzania; note that some, (eg Zanzibar's Revolutionary Day) are not held nationwide but are celebrated locally only.

1 Jan	New Year	**7 July**	Industrial Day
12 Jan	Zanzibar Revolutionary Day	**8 Aug**	Farmers' Day
April	Good Friday/Easter	**9 Dec**	Independence/Republic Days
26 April	Union Day (National Day)	**25 Dec**	Christmas Day
1 May	International Labour Day	**26 Dec**	Boxing Day

Islamic holy days

The dates of the following holidays are determined according to the Islamic lunar calendar and as such do not fall on the same date each year. Their **approximate** dates for the next few years are given. The extent to which these days are celebrated and whether these celebrations will impact on your holiday depends to a great extent on where you are in Tanzania; remember that around Kilimanjaro the people are largely Christian and so the impact tends to be minimal, though there will be some shops and businesses closed.

Idul Fitri (End of Ramadan – a two-day celebration)
approx dates: 10 September 2010; 31 August 2011; 19 August 2012
Eid El-Hajj (also known as Eid El-Adha or Eid Al-Kebir)
approx dates: 16 November 2010; 6 November 2011; October 26 2012.

A point of endless confusion for travellers, and with the potential to cause major problems for the uninitiated, is the concept known as **Swahili time**, used throughout much of East Africa where Swahili is the *lingua franca*. Swahili time begins at dawn, or more precisely at 6am. In other words, 6am is their hour zero (and thus equivalent to our midnight), 7am in our time is actually one o'clock in Swahili and so on.

To add further confusion, this system for telling the time is not prevalent everywhere in Tanzania, with most offices, timetables etc using the standard style for telling the time. Whenever you're quoted a time it should be obvious which clock they are using but always double check.

BUSINESS HOURS

These are typically 8am-noon and 2-4.30pm Monday to Friday, and 8am-12.30pm for some private businesses on Saturdays.

POST AND TELECOMMUNICATIONS

Telephone and fax

Yellow TTCL **cardphones** have been installed in the larger Tanzanian towns but they are seldom used and frequently vandalized. Furthermore, often the only place where you can buy the cards themselves is from a Telecom building any-

❏ The telephone country access code for Tanzania is ☎ 255.

way. The cards cost Ts10,000, plus you need to put credit on the card in order to call anywhere.

If you're staying in Tanzania for some time you'll find it far easier and often cheaper to invest in a Tanzanian mobile phone, or at least a **Tanzanian SIM card** (Ts2000) and a pay-as-you-go voucher (available just about everywhere). If your existing phone is unlocked you can put the SIM card straight in there; if not, you can pick a phone up cheaply in Tanzania. This method can save you a small fortune in bills compared to using a mobile and SIM from your home country.

That said, telephoning in Tanzania has always been a hit-and-miss affair, and sometimes it's an illogical one too. Phone a Tanzanian landline from a Tanzanian mobile, for example, and you still have to dial Tanzania's international dialling code (+255). Furthermore, if you are having trouble ringing home, try tacking an extra '0' on to the front of the international dialling code: for example, if you wish to ring the UK but the phone continues to bar your call, dial ☎ 00044 (or ☎ 000144) rather than just ☎ 0044 (or ☎ 00144). But even if you follow these rules, there are still occasions when it's impossible to get any sort of connection.

If you aren't in the country long, the best and cheapest way of ringing abroad is **via the internet**: The Patisserie in Arusha (see p166) is one place offering this service, currently charging Ts300 per minute to the UK.

Another option is to use the phone service at the **TTCL building**, of which there is one in every major town (including Moshi and Arusha). Note, however, that with the soaring popularity of the mobile phone the telephone service at these TTCL buildings has declined recently and may differ from that described here. But this is how the procedure should go: pick up a scrap of paper from the counter; if the office is posh you will have a form to fill out, but if it's not then you'll just have to write the name and number of the person you wish to call and how long you wish the call to last. Hand it over and the operator will dial the number and direct you to a booth where you can take the call. If you did not speak for your allotted time, the operators are usually scrupulously fair in giving back the correct change; if you do speak for the full number of minutes, the operator will come on the line to tell you when your time is up. Most Telecom offices open Mondays to Fridays 8am–4.30pm, Saturdays 9am–noon.

Email
In contrast to the phones, Tanzania's internet cafés are havens of efficiency and value, charging about Ts1500 per hour. Some of the equipment is a little dated, as you'd probably expect, and the speed of the connection can be a little slow. (That said, in July 2009 East Africa finally became connected to Broadband technology – so we can presumably expect connection speeds to increase rapid-

ly in the future.) If you've already tried to make a phone call or post a letter here, you'll come to regard the internet cafés with something approaching affection: they're your best chance of keeping in regular touch with home while you're in East Africa. In the city guides we have picked out some of the better cafés.

Post

Thanks to the presence of the English missionaries, matters have already advanced so far in Jagga that the Europeans stationed there get their letters and newspapers not more than a month old.
    Hans Meyer *Across East African Glaciers* (1891)

The postal system in Tanzania has improved since Meyer's day but not massively. Reasonably reliable and reliably sluggish, things do occasionally get 'lost in the post' but most gets through... eventually. You should allow about two weeks for letters to reach their destinations from Dar, a day or two longer from regional post offices. The much-loved **poste restante** system has all but disappeared though some of the larger post offices still hold mail for those of 'no fixed abode', usually in a shoebox in a dusty corner somewhere.

Media

You'll find that **BBC World** and **CNN** are both popular in Tanzania and often fill air-time on the national channels during the day (ITV, for example, switches to BBC at 8am every morning). **Channel O** is Africa's MTV equivalent and a favourite with waitresses who often have it blaring out in the restaurant while you're trying to eat. **EA TV** is the latest and trendiest station, broadcasting all over East Africa. **Radio Tanzania** is the most popular radio station, with some broadcasts in English.

The *Guardian* is the pick of the **English-language newspapers** for world events, while the *Daily News* is more Tanzania-centric and the weekly *Arusha Times* covers local news stories in its own inimitable fashion. There are a couple of Kenyan newspapers such as the *East African* which feel more professional and sophisticated and are worth checking out.

FOOD

The native foods do not offer much variety, though they do differ widely in different districts; but if the traveller is not too dainty and is prepared to make the best of what is to be had, it is wonderful what can be done. **Hans Meyer** *Across East African Glaciers* (1891)

Tanzanian food is, on the whole, unsubtle but tasty and filling. If there's one dish that could be described as quintessentially East African, it would be **nyama choma** – plain and simple grilled meat. If the restaurant is any good they'll add some sauces – often curry and usually fiery – to accompany your meat and the whole lot will usually come with rice, chips, plantains or the ubiquitous **ugali**. This is a stodgy cornmeal or cassava mush. Usually served in a single cricket-ball sized lump that you can pick up with your fork in one go, ugali has the consistency of plasticine and gives the impression of being not so much cooked as congealed. A bit bland, it nevertheless performs a vital role as a plate-filler and acts as a soothing balm when eating some of the country's more thermogenic curries.

The food of the dominant tribe of the Kilimanjaro region, the Chagga, is dominated by bananas, which you'll see growing all over the lower slopes of the mountain. Not only do they brew their own beer from them (see below) but the fruit (and its cousin the plantain) crop up in dishes such as *mchemsho*, a kind of banana and meat stew.

Aside from the Chagga's bias for the banana, however, the indigenous cuisine of Tanzania caters mainly for carnivores, allowing the country's significant Indian minority to corner the market for vegetarian fare. Indian restaurants abound in Dar, Moshi, Arusha and Nairobi, catering mainly for the budget end of the market; that said, the cuisine at a top-notch Indian restaurant in Tanzania is amongst the best served outside Britain or India.

For details about food on the trail, see p245.

DRINKS

The usual world-brand **soft drinks** are on sale in Tanzania. Juices are widely available and pretty cheap, though be warned: a lot of upset stomachs are caused by insanitary juice stalls. Far safer, coconuts are ubiquitous on the coast and Zanzibar. **Alcoholic** drinks include a range of beers including the tasty Serengeti (our favourite), Ndovu (a pretty close second), Safari and Kilimanjaro from Tanzania, Tusker from Kenya, and the potent Chagga home-

brew *mbege*, or banana beer. You'll usually be offered this if you take a stroll around Marangu (or indeed any Chagga village), particularly if it's market day when the world (or at least the male half of it) seems to be intent on obliterating itself by imbibing vast quantities of the stuff from jerrycans.

THINGS TO BUY

kíRìmíyà – A Chagga term meaning a treat brought home by mother to kids upon completion of a successful day at market From **University of Oregon**'s *Word of the Week* website

Tanzania has the usual supply of weavings and woodcarvings, T-shirts, textiles and trinkets. The shops in Arusha in particular are becoming more sophisticated and expert at appealing to Western tastes. Amongst the T-shirts, at least in Moshi, are a number of variations on the 'I climbed Kili' motif. Witchcraft items, battle shields, Masai beads and necklaces and bows and arrows are all up for grabs in the high streets of Moshi and Arusha. Kilimanjaro coffee makes for a good and inexpensive present for the person who's been feeding your cat while you've been away; buy it in a wooden box or velvet bag in a souvenir store, or pick a simple bag of it up for a third of the price in a supermarket. Though not grown on the slopes of Kilimanjaro, the organic Africafe has been described by one enthusiastic reader as the best instant coffee in the world and an affordable souvenir. Another popular souvenir is the *kanga*, the typical Tanzanian woman's dress that usually has a message or motto running through the print, or the similar but smarter and message-less *kitenge*.

In the afternoon I bought some small capes made of hyrax skins, of a style formerly much in vogue, and two long spears of the most modern narrow-bladed pattern, which were quite works of art. **Hans Meyer** *Across East African Glaciers* (1891)

It depends on your taste, of course, but Zanzibar is widely reckoned to have a better selection and higher quality of souvenirs (though I really think the shops of Arusha are catching up; check out the Blue Heron Café, for example, or the souvenir/furniture outlets by Shoprite in the TFA complex). Some of the stuff in Zanzibar, particularly the carved door jambs and furniture, are lovely, though difficult to get home; furthermore, these people are extremely tough negotiators, know the true price of everything and bargains are few.

SECURITY

Tanzania is a pretty safe country, at least by the standards of its neighbours. That said, the standards of its neighbours are very, very low indeed – as anybody who has already been to Kenya's capital, known to many travellers as 'Nairobberi', will testify – so do take care. Violent crime is relatively rare during the day but not unknown, especially in Dar es Salaam and Arusha, while pickpockets are common throughout the country and reach epidemic proportions in busy areas such as markets and stations. The best (if somewhat contradictory) advice is:

● Keep a close eye on your things.
● Don't walk around after dark but take a taxi (particularly in Arusha, and particularly by the bridges over the Themi River along the Nairobi–Moshi Highway, Sokoine Road where it crosses the Goliondoi River and Nyerere Road just east of the clock tower, all of which are notorious hotspots for muggers)
● Wear a moneybelt and don't flaunt your wealth
● Be on your guard against scams and con merchants...

... but at the same time don't let a sense of paranoia ruin your holiday and remember that the vast majority of travellers in East Africa spend their time here suffering no great loss beyond the occasional and inevitable overcharging. If you are unfortunate enough to become the victim of a mugging, remember that it's your *money* that they're after, so hand it over – you should be insured against such eventualities anyway. Report the crime as soon as possible to the police, who are generally quite helpful, particularly when the victim is a tourist. This will help to back up your claim from the insurers and may prevent further crimes against tourists in the future.

HEALTH

Diarrhoea is often symptomatic of nothing more than a change of diet rather than any malignant bacteria, so if you get a vicious dose of the runs and your sphincter feels like a cat flap in the Aswan Dam, don't panic and assume you've got food poisoning. That said, there are problems with hygiene in Tanzania, so it's wise to take certain precautions. Take heed of that old adage about patronizing only places that are popular – so food doesn't have a chance to sit around for long – as well as that other one about eating only food that has been cooked, boiled or peeled. Stick to **bottled**, **purified** or **filtered water** and avoid ice unless you're certain it has been made from treated water. Washing fruit, vegetables and your hands and ensuring food is thoroughly cooked can all prevent food poisoning. Shellfish, ice cream from street vendors and under-cooked meat should all be avoided like the plague, or you could end up feeling like you've got it. Slathering yourself in an **insect repellent** to prevent you from being eaten alive by the smaller members of Tanzania's animal kingdom is a good idea too.

We could go into a detailed examination here of all the dreadful diseases you could catch in Tanzania. But the truth is that for most of the worst ones you should have already had an inoculation or be taking some sort of prophylactic. Besides, it's unlikely that you'll suffer anything more in Tanzania than a dose of **the runs**, some **altitude sickness** or, if you're careless, a touch of **sunstroke**. If you've got the former, just rest up and take plenty of fluids until you recover; to protect against the latter wear a high-factor sun lotion and a hat and drink a lot of fluids – maintaining a reasonable salt intake will also help to prevent dehydration. As for altitude sickness, which the majority of trekkers on Kili suffer from to some extent, as well as other ailments that you may contract on the trail, read the detailed discussion on p217-225.

PART 3: KILIMANJARO

Geology

Our geological work was especially delightful.... Every rock seemed to differ from another, not only in form but in substance. In half-an-hour it was no uncommon thing for us to pick up specimens of as many as two-and-twenty different kinds.
Hans Meyer *Across East African Glaciers* (1891)

Rising 4800m above the East African plains, 270km from the shores of the Indian Ocean and measuring up to 40km across, Kilimanjaro is a bizarre geological oddity, the tallest freestanding mountain in the world and one formed, shaped, eroded and scarred by the twin forces of fire and ice. It is actually a volcano, or rather three volcanoes, with the two main peaks, **Kibo** and **Mawenzi**, the summits of two of those volcanoes. The story of its creation goes like this:

About three-quarters of a million years ago (making Kilimanjaro a veritable youngster in geological terms) molten lava burst through the fractured surface of the **Great Rift Valley**, a giant fault in the earth's crust that runs through East Africa (see box p94; actually, Kilimanjaro lies 50 miles from the East African Rift Valley along a splinter running off it, but that need not concern us here). The huge pressures behind this eruption pushed part of the Earth's crust skywards, creating the **Shira volcano**, the oldest of the volcanoes forming the Kilimanjaro massif. Shira eventually ceased erupting around 500,000 years ago, collapsing as it did so to form a huge caldera (the deep cauldron-like cavity on the summit of a volcano) many times the size of its original crater.

Soon after Shira's extinction, **Mawenzi** started to form following a further eruption within the Shira caldera. Though much eroded, Mawenzi has at least kept some of its volcanic shape to this day. Then, 460,000 years ago, an enormous eruption just west of Mawenzi caused the formation of **Kibo**. Continual subterranean pressure forced Kibo to erupt several times more, forcing the summit ever higher until reaching a maximum height of about 5900m. A further huge eruption from Kibo 100,000 years later led to the formation of Kilimanjaro's characteristic shiny black stone – which in reality is just solidified black lava, or **obsidian**. This spilled over from Kibo's crater into the Shira caldera and around to the base of the Mawenzi peak, forming the so-called Saddle. Later eruptions created a series of distinctive mini-cones, or **parasitic craters**, that run in a chain south-east and north-west across the mountain, as well as the smaller **Reusch Crater** inside the main Kibo summit. The last volcanic activity of note, just over 200 years ago, left a symmetrical inverted cone of ash in the Reusch Crater, known as the **Ash Pit**, that can still be seen today.

Today, **Uhuru Peak**, the highest part of Kibo's crater rim and the goal of most trekkers, stands at around 5895m. The fact that the summit is around five metres shorter today than it was 450,000 years ago can be ascribed to the simple progress of time and the insidious glacial erosion down the millennia. These glaciers, advancing and retreating across the summit, created a series of concentric rings like **terraces** near the top of this volcanic massif on the western side. The Kibo peak has also subsided slightly over time, and about one hundred thousand years ago a landslide took away part of the external crater, creating **Kibo Barranco** or the **Barranco Valley** (see p271). The glaciers were also behind the formation of the valleys and canyons, eroding and smoothing the earth into gentle undulations all around the mountain, though less so on the northern side where the glaciers on the whole failed to reach, leaving the valleys sharper and more defined.

While eruptions are unheard of in recent times, Kibo is classified as being dormant rather than extinct, as anybody who visits the inner **Reusch Crater** can testify. A strong sulphur smell still rises from the crater, the earth is hot to touch, preventing ice from forming, while occasionally fumaroles escape from the Ash Pit that lies at its heart. Indeed, according to the 2003 Nova documentary *Volcano Above the Clouds*, scientists say that Kibo is actually becoming active again and that, using estimates based on the temperature of some of the fumaroles, magma lies only 400m below the surface and a cataclysmic landslide, similar in magnitude to the one that led to the formation of the Western Breach, could happen any day!

The Great Rift Valley

According to the theory of plate tectonics, the Earth's exterior is made up of six enormous plates that 'float' across the surface. Occasionally they collide, causing much buckling and crumpling and the creation of huge mountain ranges such as the Himalayas. At other times, these plates deteriorate and break up because of the massive forces bubbling away in the earth's interior. When this happens, valleys are formed where the Earth fractures.

The Great Rift Valley, whose origins are in Mozambique but which extends right across East Africa to Jordan, is a classic example of a fracture in the Earth's surface caused by the movement of these plates. The same monstrous internal forces that two million years ago caused the disintegration of the tectonic plate and the formation of the Rift Valley are also responsible for the appearance of volcanoes along the valley, as these forces explode through the surface, pushing the Earth's crust skywards and forming – in the case of Kilimanjaro – one huge, 5895m-high geological pimple.

Of Africa's sixteen active volcanoes, all but three belong to the Rift Valley. Kili was just one of a number of volcanic eruptions to hit the valley; others included Ol Molog (to the north-west of Kilimanjaro) and Kilema (to the south-east).

By the way, don't be misled into thinking that these kind of major tectonic shifts happened millions of years ago and have little relevance to the present day: the earthquake in Arusha in 2007 shows that this 'active rifting' is still occurring, and even minor movements can have major repercussions.

THE GLACIERS

It is now time to consider the discovery on which Mr Rebmann particularly prides himself, namely, that of perpetual snow. **W D Cooley** *Inner Africa Laid Open* (see box p108)

At first glance, Kilimanjaro's glaciers look like nothing more than big smooth piles of slightly monotonous ice. On second glance they pretty much look like this too. Yet there's much more to Kili's glaciers than meets the eye, for these cathedrals of gleaming blue-white ice are dynamic repositories of climatic history – and they could also be providing us with a portent for impending natural disaster.

You would think that with the intensely strong equatorial sun, glaciers wouldn't exist at all on Kilimanjaro. In fact, it is the brilliant white colour of the ice that allows it to survive as it reflects most of the heat. The dull black lava rock on which the glacier rests, on the other hand, *does* absorb the heat; so while the glacier's surface is relatively unaffected by the sun's rays, the heat generated by the sun-baked rocks underneath leads to glacial melting.

As a result, the glaciers on Kilimanjaro are inherently unstable: the ice at the bottom of the glacier touching the rocks melts, the glaciers lose their 'grip' on the mountain and 'overhangs' occur where the ice at the base has melted away, leaving just the ice at the top to survive. As the process continues the ice fractures and breaks away, exposing more of the rock to the sun... and so the cycle begins again. The sun's effect on the glaciers is also responsible for the spectacular structures – the ice columns and pillars, towers and cathedrals – that are the most fascinating part of the upper slopes of Kibo.

You would have thought that, after 11,700 years of this melting process, (according to recent research, the current glaciers began to form in 9700BC) very little ice would remain on Kilimanjaro. The fact that there are still glaciers is due to the prolonged 'cold snaps', or ice ages, that have occurred down the centuries, allowing the glaciers to regroup and reappear on the mountain. According to estimates, there have been at least eight of these ice ages, the last a rather minor one in the fifteenth and sixteenth centuries, a time when the Thames frequently froze over and winters were severe. At these times the ice on Kilimanjaro would in places have reached right down to the tree line and both Mawenzi and Kibo would have been covered. At the other extreme, before 9700BC there have been periods when Kilimanjaro was completely free of ice, perhaps for up to 20,000 years.

The slush of Kilimanjaro – where have all the glaciers gone?

Of the 19 square kilometres of glacial ice to be found on Africa, only 2.2 square kilometres can be found on Kilimanjaro. Unfortunately, both figures used to be much higher: Kili's famous white mantle has shrunk by a whopping 82% since the first survey of the summit in 1912. Even since 1989, when there were 3.3 square kilometres, there has been a decline of 33%. At that rate, say the experts, Kili will be completely ice-free within the next decade or two.

'We found that the summit of the ice fields has lowered by at least 17 metres since 1962,' said Professor Lonnie Thompson of Ohio State University. 'That's an average loss of about a half-metre (a foot and a half) in height each year.'

So how high is it then?

Ever since Hans Meyer ambled down from the summit of Kibo and told anybody who'd listen that he'd reached 19,833ft above sea level (6010m), an argument has been raging over just how high Africa's highest mountain really is. For though Meyer's estimate is now unanimously agreed to be a wild over-estimate (an inaccuracy that can be ascribed to a combination of the imprecise nineteenth-century instruments that he had at his disposal, and perhaps a touch of hubris,) finding a figure for the height of Kili that meets with a similar consensus of opinion has proved altogether more difficult.

For years the accepted height of Kilimanjaro was 5892m, that being the figure set by the colonial German authorities some five years after Meyer's ascent. You'll see this figure crop up time and again in many a twentieth-century travelogue as well as on pre-World War Two maps of the Kilimanjaro region. Not many people at the time bothered to question this estimate; the few dissenting voices almost invariably belonged to climbers whose own estimates (which were, perhaps unsurprisingly, nearly always over-estimates, ranging from 5930m to 5965m) are today regarded as even more inaccurate than the Germans' figure.

Under British rule the figure was revised to 5895m following the work of the cartographers of the Ordnance Survey, who mapped Kilimanjaro in 1952; and it is this figure that those trekkers who reach the summit will find written on the sign at the top, as well as on the certificates they receive from KINAPA and on the souvenir T-shirts on sale back in Moshi.

The trouble was, of course, that whereas the Ordnance Survey's techniques and equipment may have been state of the art in the 1950s, so were vinyl records and the Ford Edsel. Technology has moved on a couple of light years since then. The Ordnance Survey's readings for Kilimanjaro had been taken from a distance of over 55km away from the mountain; as such, the probability that the OS's figure was not entirely accurate was rather high.

So in 1999 a team of specialists at the University College of Land and Architectural Studies in Arusha together with experts from Karlsruhe University in Germany set out to measure the precise altitude using a technique involving GPS (Global Positioning Satellites) that had previously been used on Everest, and which resulted in that mountain shrinking by a couple of metres to 8846.10m.

The result of their findings in Africa? Kilimanjaro was now a full 2.45 metres shorter than the traditionally accepted figure, at **5892.55m**.

That wasn't the end of the story, however, for in 2008 a team of 19 boffins from six countries decided that even this measurement wasn't accurate enough, for reasons too complicated for a layman to understand (and I include myself in this category), and by combining GPS data with gravimetric observations (where variations in a gravitational field are measured) they came up with a figure of **5889.51m** for the orthometric height (ie the distance above the mean sea level).

So is Kilimanjaro shrinking? Or was the old estimate of 5895m just plain inaccurate? Unfortunately, the scientists have yet to tell us that. And while they have every confidence in the accuracy of their latest readings, the old figure of 5895m is still the official figure and the one you'll hear bandied about by tour operators, guides, porters and anybody else you care to speak to; and until we are told otherwise, 5895m is the one we're using in this book too.

The big question, therefore, is not whether they are shrinking, but why – and should we be concerned? Certainly glacial retreats are nothing new: Hans Meyer, the first man to conquer Kilimanjaro, returned in 1898, nine years after his ascent, and was horrified by the extent to which the glaciers had shrunk. The ice on Kibo's slopes had retreated by 100m on all sides, while one of the notches he had used to gain access to the crater in 1889 – and now called the Hans Meyer Notch – was twice as wide, with the ice only half as thick. Nor are warnings of the complete disappearance of the glaciers anything new: in 1899 Meyer himself predicted that they would be gone within three decades, and the top of Kili would be decorated with nothing but bare rock.

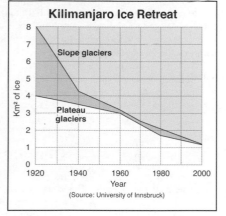

Kilimanjaro Ice Retreat

Km² of ice

Slope glaciers

Plateau glaciers

Year

(Source: University of Innsbruck)

What concerns today's scientists, however, is that this current reduction in size of Kili's ice-cap does seem to be more rapid and more extensive than previous shrinkages. But is it really something to worry about, or merely the latest in a series of glacial retreats experienced by Kili over the last few hundred years?

Professor Thompson and his team attempted to find answers to all these questions. In January and February 2000 they drilled six ice cores through three of Kibo's glaciers in order to research the history of the mountain's climate over the centuries. A weather station was also placed on the Northern Icefield to see how the current climate affects the build-up or destruction of glaciers.

Their conclusions were not good. In a speech made at the annual meeting of the American Association for the Advancement of Science in February 2001, the professor declared that while he cannot be sure why the ice is melting away so quickly, what is certain is that if the glaciers continue to shrink at current rates, the summit could be completely ice-free by 2015. Other, later calculations have extended this figure to 2040 or so: Austrian scientist Georg Kaser, who together with Thomas Moelg has been studying new glacial data, says 'We have done different kinds of modelling and we expect the plateau glaciers to be gone roughly within 30 or 40 years from now, but we have a certain expectation that the slope glaciers may last longer.'

But whatever estimates you believe, there can be no doubt that the glaciers are in serious trouble. This doesn't surprise locals who live in the shadow of Kilimanjaro, some of whom believe they know why the ice is disappearing.

KILIMANJARO

According to an AllAfrica.com news report, a 50-year-old native of Old Moshi, Mama Judith Iyatuu, reckons that it's the evil eyes of the white tourists which are melting the ice, while 65-year old Mzee Ruaici Thomas from Meela village believes that the ice is disappearing because God is unhappy with mankind.

Whatever the reasons, if Kilimanjaro were to lose its snowy top, the repercussions would be extremely serious: Kilimanjaro's glaciers are essential to the survival of the local villages, supplying their drinking water, the water to irrigate their crops and, through hydroelectric production, their power; never mind the blow the loss of the snow-cap would deal to tourism.

And these are just the local consequences. If the scientists are to be believed, what is happening on Kilimanjaro is a microcosm of what could face the entire world in future. Even more worryingly, more and more scientists are now starting to think that this future is probably already upon us.

Climate

Kilimanjaro is big enough to have its own weather pattern. The theory behind this pattern is essentially very simple. Strong winds travel across the oceans, drawing moisture up as they go. Eventually they collide with a large object – such as a mountain like Kilimanjaro. The winds are pushed upwards as they hit the mountain slopes, and the fall in temperature and atmospheric pressure leads to precipitation or, as it's more commonly called, snow and rain.

In one year there are two rain-bearing seasonal winds buffeting Kilimanjaro. The south-east trade wind bringing rain from the Indian Ocean arrives between March and May. Because the mountain is the first main obstacle to the wind's progress, and by far the largest, a lot of rain falls on Kili at this time and for this reason the March-to-May season is known as the **long rains**. This is the main wet season on Kilimanjaro. As the south-east trade winds run into the southern side of Kili, so the southern slopes tend to be damper and as a consequence more fertile, with the forest zone much broader than on the northern slopes.

Then there are the dry **'anti-trade' winds** from the north-east which carry no rain and hit the mountain between May and October. These anti-trade winds, which blow, usually very strongly, across the Saddle (the broad valley between Kilimanjaro's two peaks), also serve to keep the south-east trade winds off the upper reaches of Kilimanjaro, ensuring that the rain from the long monsoon season stays largely on the southern side below 3000m, with little falling above this. Which is why, at this time of year, the first day's walk for trekkers on the Marangu, Umbwe or Machame routes is usually conducted under a canopy of cloud, while from the second day onwards they enjoy unadulterated sunshine.

A second seasonal rain-bearing wind, the north-east monsoon, having already lost much of its moisture after travelling overland for a longer period, brings a **short rainy season** between November and February. While the northern side receives most of the rain to fall in this season, it is far less than the rain brought

Another inconvenient truth

In 2007 Kilimanjaro's disappearing glaciers became *the* symbol of global warming when it featured in Al Gore's film *An Inconvenient Truth*. His use of Africa's highest mountain seemed both an obvious and potent choice: everybody marvels at Kilimanjaro's snowy summit, and the thought of it being bare by 2020 is a distressing one. Indeed, Al Gore wasn't the only one to use Kilimanjaro's glaciers as a microcosm of man's deleterious effect on the environment: Greenpeace even held a satellite news conference from the summit in order to highlight the decline of Africa's largest collection of glaciers due to climate change.

However, there are several groups who think that it was wrong to use Kilimanjaro as a poster-child for global warming. Among their number are those who deny altogether that anything is wrong. It may not surprise you to find that the minister in charge of tourism in Tanzania, Ms Shamsa Mwangunga, is amongst their number, when she claimed in July 2008 that the snows of Kilimanjaro will be with us in perpetuity, citing eyewitness evidence that the glaciers were, contrary to all scientific opinion, actually growing. Nor was she the first minister to hold these opinions: one of her predecessors, Ms Zakhia Meghji, expressed similar sentiments when she held office in 2002.

While most will dismiss Ms Mwangunga's sentiments as those of someone who clearly has a vested interest in telling the world that the snows aren't melting, there are others who remain uneasy at Kilimanjaro being used by the green lobby in this way.

The main concern is that Kilimanjaro is a bad example to use when discussing global warming. As we said earlier in the chapter, Kilimanjaro's glaciers have been shrinking for the best part of a century, long before humans began pumping large amounts of carbon dioxide into the atmosphere. Indeed, it is believed that they have been expanding and contracting regularly over the past few thousand years – and separating this natural contraction from the reduction caused by man's effect on the climate is no simple matter. Furthermore, recent data from Kilimanjaro show temperatures never rise above freezing on the summit – so how can a warmer climate be responsible for melting glaciers?

The Austrian Georg Kaser, who has studied the glacial decline on Kilimanjaro for several years (see p97), is one who believes that global warming is *not* melting the ice on Kilimanjaro. Instead, he concluded that the loss of ice was driven by a lack of snowfall and sublimation (this is when ice essentially skips the melting step and simply evaporates, and is caused by exposure to sunlight and dry air), with melting having only a negligible effect. And while climate change could have led to a decline in precipitation (snowfall) that replenishes the glaciers – after all, there have been droughts in much of Tanzania in the past few years – contrary to popular wisdom the glaciers, while undoubted shrinking by about a metre a year, aren't actually melting. Indeed, if the current climate models are correct, global warming should actually *increase* rainfall in Eastern Africa. This should mean greater snowfall on the summit of Kilimanjaro, and thus, perversely, could be the thing that saves Kilimanjaro's snows!

And it is this last point that worries those who believe in the reality of global warming but are uneasy about Kilimanjaro being used by Al Gore and his supporters in this way: that global warming *is* responsible for the decline of many other glaciers in the world – but *not* on Kilimanjaro. And that by citing Kilimanjaro's shrinking glaciers as an example of the effects of global warming, they are allowing climate-change sceptics the chance to prove, justifiably, that it isn't so – which could then open the door to them dismissing other climate-change trends that *are* true, thereby diluting the climate change lobby's arguments.

KILIMANJARO

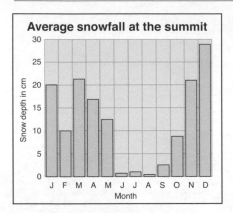

Average snowfall at the summit

Adapted from DR Hardy's *Kilimanjaro snow*
in: AM Waple & JH Lawrimore (eds.)
State of the Climate in 2002,
Bull. Am. Meteorol. Soc., 84, S48

by the south-east trade winds and as a result the northern side of Kili, though the main recipient at this time, remains drier and more barren than the southern side. Once again, the rain falls mainly below 3000m.

This theory seems fine in principle but it does pose a tricky question: if the precipitation falls below 3000m, how did the snows on the summit of Kibo get there in the first place? The answer, my friend, is blowing in the (anti-trade) wind: though these winds normally blow very strongly, as those who walk north across the Saddle will testify, they occasionally drop in force, allowing the south-east trade winds that run beneath them to climb up the southern slopes to the Saddle and on to the summit. Huge banks of clouds then develop and snow falls.

This, at least, is the theory of Kilimanjaro's climate. In practice, the only predictable thing about the weather is its unpredictability. What is certain is that, with rain more abundant the further one travels down the mountain slopes, life, too, becomes more abundant – as the *Fauna & Flora* section on p124 illustrates.

The temperature at the summit: bikinis – or brass monkeys?

It's a question many trekkers want to know the answer to – just how cold is it on the summit of Kilimanjaro? Well, there is an old mountaineer's saw that says that, above 4000m, for every 150 metres you ascend the temperature drops by 1°C. Given that the average temperature at around 4000m is 0°C, by the time you reach the summit you would have ascended through about 13 lots of 150m. In other words, the temperature would be around -13°C. Pretty chilly you may think, but bearable. But this, of course, fails to take into consideration the windchill factor which can push that figure even further downwards to around -30°C – and sometimes even lower.

For a more scientific look at the summit temperature of Kilimanjaro than the back-of-an-envelope calculations above, visit the University of Massachusetts' geoscience website 🖳 www.geo.umass.edu/climate/kibo.html which summarizes data from their summit weather station. The graph shows the average monthly air temperatures over the year at weather stations at 2340m, 3630m, 4570m and 5800m. It gives you an idea of how much the temperature drops as you ascend through the various vegetation zones: montane rainforest (2340m), heathland (3630m), Alpine desert (4570m) and on an icefield at

5800m, just 95m below Uhuru Peak. You can see that even in the warmest month the mean temperature doesn't rise above -5°C at the top; the mean temperature at the summit, by the way, is -7.1°C. We have also mapped on the graph mean precipitation (ie rain – or, at this altitude, snow) at this higher weather station. (Our source for this information is *General Characteristics of Air Temperature and Humidity Variability on Kilimanjaro, Tanzania* by WJ Duane, NC Pepin, ML Losleben and DR Hardy. Visit the University of Massachusetts' website to view the whole paper.)

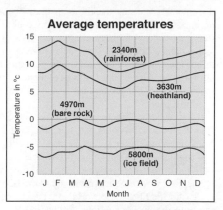

Temperature graph adapted from *General Characteristics of Air Temperature and Humidity Variability on Kilimanjaro, Tanzania* by WJ Duane, NC Pepin, ML Losleben and DR Hardy

The history of Kilimanjaro

EARLY HISTORY

Thanks to several primitive **stone bowls** found on the lower slopes of Kilimanjaro, we know that man has lived on or around the mountain since at least 1000BC. We also know that, over the last 500 years, the mountain has at various times acted as a navigational aid for traders travelling between the interior and the coast, a magnet for Victorian explorers, a political pawn to be traded between European superpowers who carved up East Africa, a battlefield for these same superpowers, and a potent symbol of independence for those who wished to rid themselves of these colonial interlopers. Unfortunately, little is known about the history of the mountain during the intervening 2500 years.

It's a fair bet that Kilimanjaro's first inhabitants, when they weren't fashioning bowls out of the local terrain, would have spent much of their time hunting and gathering the local flora and fauna, Kilimanjaro being a fecund source of both. Add to this its reputation as a reliable region both for fresh drinking water and materials – wood, stones, mud, vines etc – for building, and it seems reasonable to suppose that Kilimanjaro would have been a highly desirable location for primitive man and would have played a central role in the lives of those who chose to take up residence on its slopes.

Unfortunately, those looking to piece together a comprehensive history of the first inhabitants of Kilimanjaro rather have their work cut out. There are no

KILIMANJARO

documents recording the life and times of the people who once lived on the mountain; not much in the way of any oral history that has been passed down through the generations; and, stone bowls apart, little in the way of archaeological evidence from which to draw any inferences. So while we can *assume* many things about the lives of Kilimanjaro's first inhabitants, we can be certain about nothing and if Kilimanjaro did have a part to play in the pre-colonial history of the region, that history, and the mountain's significance within it, has, alas, now been lost to us.

And so it is to the notes of foreign travellers that we must turn in order to find the earliest accounts of Kilimanjaro. These descriptions are usually rather brief, often inaccurate and more often than not based on little more than hearsay and rumour rather than actual firsthand evidence.

One of the first ever descriptions of East Africa is provided by the *Periplus of the Erythraean Sea*, written anonymously in AD45. The *Periplus* – a contender for the title of the world's first ever travel guide – is a handbook for seafarers to the ports of Africa, Arabia and India and includes details of the sea

Kilimanjaro – the name

The meaning of the name Kilíma Njáro, if it have any meaning, is unknown to the Swáhili... To be analysed, it must first be corrupted. This has been done by Mr Rebmann, who converts Kilíma Njáro into Kilíma dja-aro, which he tells us signifies, "Mountain of Greatness." This etymology... is wholly inadmissable for the following reasons: 1st. It is mere nonsense....

So said **WD Cooley** (see p108), leading British geographer during the mid-nineteenth century in his book *Inner Africa Laid Open*. Nonsense Rebmann's suggestion may have been, but in the absence of better alternatives the translation is as valid as any other. For the fact of the matter is that despite extensive studies into the etymology of the name Kilimanjaro, nobody is sure where it comes from or exactly what it means.

When looking for the name's origin, it seems only sensible to begin such a search in one of the local Tanzanian dialects, and more specifically, in the language spoken by those who live in its shadow, namely the Chagga people. True, the name Kilimanjaro bears no resemblance to any word in the Chagga vocabulary; but if we divide it into two parts then a few possibilities present themselves. One is that Kilima is derived from the Chagga term *kilelema*, meaning 'difficult or impossible', while *jaro* could come from the Chagga terms *njaare* ('bird') or *jyaro* ('caravan'). In other words, the name Kilimanjaro means something like 'That which is impossible for the bird', or 'That which defeats the caravan' – names which, if this interpretation is correct, are clear references to the sheer enormity of the mountain.

Whilst this is perhaps the most likely translation, it is not, in itself, particularly convincing, especially when one considers that while the Chagga language would seem the most logical source for the name, the Chagga people themselves do not actually have one single name for the mountain! Instead, they don't see Kilimanjaro as a single entity but as two distinct, separate peaks, namely Mawenzi and Kibo. (These two names, incidentally, are definitely Chagga in origin, coming from the Chagga terms *kimawenzi* – 'having a broken top or summit' – and *kipoo* – 'snow' – respectively.)

routes to China. In it the author tells of a land called Azania, in which one could find a prosperous market town, Rhapta, where 'hatchets and daggers and awls ... a great quantity of ivory and rhinoceros horn and tortoise shell' were all traded. Yet interestingly, there is no mention of any snow-capped mountain lying nearby; indeed, reading the *Periplus* one gets the impression that the author considered Rhapta to be just about the end of the world:

Beyond Opone [modern day Ras Harun on the Somalian coast] *there are the small and great bluffs of Azania ... twenty-three days sail beyond there lies the very last market town of the continent of Azania, Rhapta ...*

Less than a hundred years later, however, **Ptolemy of Alexandria**, astronomer and the founder of scientific cartography, wrote of lands lying to the south of Rhapta where barbaric cannibals lived near a wide shallow bay and where, inland, one could find a '**great snow mountain**'. Mountains that wear a mantle of snow are pretty thin on the ground in Africa; indeed, there is only one candidate that is permanently adorned in snow, and that, of course, is Kilimanjaro.

Assuming Kilimanjaro isn't Chagga in origin, therefore, the most likely source for the name Kilimanjaro would seem to be Swahili, the majority language of the Tanzanians. Rebmann's good friend and fellow missionary, Johann Ludwig Krapf, wrote that Kilimanjaro could either be a Swahili word meaning 'Mountain of Greatness' – though he is noticeably silent when it comes to explaining how he arrived at such a translation – or a composite Swahili/Chagga name meaning 'Mountain of Caravans'; *jaro*, as we have previously explained, being the Chagga term for 'caravans'. Thus the name could be a reference to the many trading caravans that would stop at the mountain for water. The major flaw with both these theories, however, is that the Swahili term for mountain is not *kilima* but *mlima* – *kilima* is actually the Swahili word for 'hill'!

The third and least likely dialect from which Kilimanjaro could have been derived is Masai, the major tribe across the border in Kenya. But while the Masai word for spring or water is *njore*, which could conceivably have been corrupted down the centuries to *njaro*, there is no relevant Masai word similar to *kilima*. Furthermore, the Masai call the mountain *Oldoinyo Oibor*, which means 'White Mountain', with Kibo known as the 'House of God', as Hemingway has already told us at the beginning of his – and this – book. Few experts, therefore, believe the name is Masai in origin.

Other theories include the possibility that *njaro* means 'whiteness', referring to the snow cap that Kilimanjaro permanently wears, or that Njaro is the name of the evil spirit who lives on the mountain, causing discomfort and even death to those who climb it. Certainly the folklore of the Chagga people is rich in tales of evil spirits who dwell on the higher reaches of the mountain and Rebmann himself refers to 'Njaro, the guardian spirit of the mountain'; however, it must also be noted that the Chagga's legends make no mention of any spirit going by that name.

And so we are none the wiser. But in one sense at least, it's not important: what the mountain means to the 40,000-plus who walk up it every year is far more meaningful than any name we ascribe to it.

KILIMANJARO

How exactly Ptolemy came by his information is unknown, for he almost certainly never saw Kilimanjaro for himself. Nevertheless, based on hearsay though it may have been, this is the earliest surviving written mention of Africa's greatest mountain. It therefore seems logical to conclude that the outside world first became aware of Africa's tallest mountain in the years between the publication of the Periplus in AD45, and that of Ptolemy's work, sometime during the latter half of the second century AD.

THE OUTSIDERS ARRIVE

Arabs, an anonymous Chinaman and some Portuguese

Following Ptolemy's description, almost nothing more is written about Kilimanjaro for over a thousand years. The Arabs, arriving on the East African coast in the sixth century, must have heard something about it from the local people with whom they traded. Indeed, the mountain would have proved essential to the natives as they travelled from the interior to the markets on the East African shore: as one of the few unmissable landmarks in a largely featureless expanse of savannah and scrub, and with its abundant streams and springs, the mountain would have been both an invaluable navigational tool and a reliable source of drinking water for the trading caravans. But whether the merchants from the Middle East actually ventured beyond their trading posts on the coast to see the mountain for themselves seems doubtful, and from their records of this time only one possible reference to Kilimanjaro has been uncovered, written by a thirteenth-century geographer, **Abu'l Fida**, who speaks of a mountain in the interior that was 'white in colour'.

The Chinese, who traded on the East African coast during the same period, also seemed either ignorant or uninterested in the land that lay beyond the coastline and in all their records from this time once again just one scant reference to Kili has been found, this time by an anonymous chronicler who states that the country to the west of Zanzibar 'reaches to a great mountain'.

After 1500 and the exploration and subsequent conquest of the African east coast by Vasco da Gama and those who followed in his wake, the Arabs were replaced as the major trading power in the region by the Portuguese. They proved to be slightly more curious about what lay beyond the coast than their predecessors, perhaps because their primary motive for being there was as much colonial as commercial. A vague but once again unmistakable reference to Kilimanjaro can be found in a book, *Suma de Geographia*, published in 1519, an account of a journey to Mombasa by the Spanish cartographer, astronomer and ship's pilot **Fernandes de Encisco**:

West of Mombasa is the Ethiopian Mount Olympus, which is very high, and further off are the Mountains of the Moon in which are the sources of the Nile.

Amazingly, in the fourteen hundred years since Ptolemy this is only the third reference to Kilimanjaro that has been found; with the return of the Arabs in 1699, it was also to be the last for another hundred years or so. Then, just as the eighteenth century was drawing to a close, the Europeans once more cast an avaricious eye towards East Africa.

THE 1800s: PIONEERS . . .

With British merchants firmly established on Zanzibar by the 1840s, frequent rumours of a vast mountain situated on the mainland just a few hundred miles from the coast now began to reach their ears. British geographers were especially intrigued by these reports, particularly as it provided a possible solution to one of the oldest riddles of Africa: namely, the precise whereabouts of the source of the Nile. Enciso's sixteenth-century reference to *the Mountains of the Moon in which are the sources of the Nile* (see p104) is in fact a mere echo of the work of Ptolemy, writing fourteen hundred years before Enciso, who also cites the Mountains of the Moon as the true origin of the Nile.

But while these Mountains of the Moon were, for more than a millennium, widely accepted in European academia as the place where the Nile rises, nobody had actually bothered to go and find out if this was so – nor, indeed, if these mountains actually existed at all.

Interest in the 'dark continent' was further aroused by the arrival in London in 1834 of one Khamis bin Uthman. Slave dealer, caravan leader and envoy of the then-ruler of East Africa, Seyyid Said, Uthman met many of Britain's leading dignitaries, including the prime minister, Lord Palmerston. He also met and talked at length with the leading African scholar, **William Desborough Cooley**. A decade after this meeting, Cooley wrote his lengthy essay *The Geography of N'yassi, or the Great Lake of Southern Africa Investigated,* in which he not only provides us with another reference to Kilimanjaro – only the fifth in 1700 years – but also becomes the first author to put a name to the mountain:

The most famous mountain of Eastern Africa is Kirimanjara, which we suppose, from a number of circumstances to be the highest ridge crossed on the road to Monomoezi.

Suddenly Africa, long viewed by the West almost exclusively in terms of the lucrative slave trade, became the centre of a flurry of academic interest and the quest to find the true origins of the Nile became something of a *cause célèbre* amongst scholars. Long-forgotten manuscripts and journals from Arab traders and Portuguese adventurers were dusted off and scrutinized for clues to the whereabouts of this most enigmatic river source. Most scholars preferred to conduct their research from the comfort of their leather armchairs; there were others, however, who took a more active approach, and pioneering explorers such as Richard Burton and John Hanning Speke set off to find for themselves the source of the Nile, crossing the entire country we now know as Tanzania in 1857. This was also the age of Livingstone and Stanley, the former venturing deep into the heart of Africa in search of both knowledge and potential converts to Christianity; and the latter in search of the former.

. . . AND PREACHERS

Yet for all their brave endeavours, it was not these Victorian action men but one of the humble Christian missionaries who arrived in Africa at about the same time who became the first European to set eyes on Kilimanjaro. **Johannes Rebmann** was a young Swiss-German missionary who arrived in Mombasa in 1846 with an

David Livingstone preaching near Lake Tanganyika. (HG Adams, 1873)

umbrella, a suitcase and a heart full of Christian zeal. His brief was to help **Dr Johann Ludwig Krapf**, a doctor of divinity from Tubingen, in his efforts to spread the Christian faith among East Africa's heathen. Krapf was something of a veteran in the missionary field, having previously worked for the London-based Church Missionary Society in Abyssinia. Following the closure of that mission, Krapf sailed down the East African coast to Zanzibar and from there to Mombasa, where he hoped to found a new mission and continue his evangelical work.

Instead, his life fell apart. His wife succumbed to malaria and died on the 9 July 1844. His daughter, born just three days previously, died five days after her mother from the same disease, while Krapf too fell gravely ill with the same; and though he alone recovered, throughout the rest of his life he suffered from sporadic attacks that would lay him low for weeks at a time.

But though his body grew weak with malaria, his spirit remained strong, and over the next six months following the death of his wife, Krapf both translated the New Testament into Swahili and devised a plan for spreading the gospel throughout the interior of Africa. Estimating that the continent could be crossed on foot from east to west in a matter of 900 hours, Krapf believed that establishing a chain of missions at intervals of one hundred hours right across the continent, each staffed by six 'messengers of peace', would be the best way to promulgate the Christian religion on the dark continent.

Unfortunately for Krapf, Islam had got there first, which made his job rather tougher; indeed, in the six months following his arrival in Mombasa, the total number of successful conversions made by Krapf stood at zero. Clearly, if the faith was to make any inroads in Africa, fresh impetus was required. That impetus was provided by the arrival of Rebmann in 1846. Having recovered from the obligatory bout of malaria that all but wiped him out for his first month in Africa, Rebmann set about helping Krapf to establish a new mission at Rabaimpia (New Rabai), just outside Mombasa. The station lay in the heart of Wanika territory, a tribe who from the first had proved resistant to conversion. Even the founding of a mission in their midst did little to persuade the Wanika to listen to their preaching: by 1859, 14 years after Krapf first arrived, just seven converts had been made.

It was clear early on that they would have little success in persuading the Wanika to convert. So from almost the start the proselyting pair began to look to pastures new to find potential members for their flock. In 1847 they founded a second mission station at Mt Kasigau, three days' walk from Rabai-mpia – the first in their proposed chain of such stations across the African continent – and later that same year they began to plan the establishment of the next link, at a place called **Jagga** (now spelt Chagga). Rebmann and Krapf had already heard a lot about Jagga from the caravan leaders who earned their money transferring goods between the interior and the markets on the eastern shore, and who often called into Rabai-mpia on the way. A source of and market for slaves, Jagga was renowned locally for suffering from extremely cold temperatures at times, a reputation that led Krapf to deduce that Jagga was probably at a much higher altitude than the lands that surrounded it. This hypothesis was confirmed by renowned caravan leader Bwana Kheri, who spoke to Krapf of a great mountain called 'Kilimansharo' (this, incidentally, being the sixth definite reference to Kilimanjaro). From other sources, Krapf and Rebmann also learned that the mountain was protected by evil spirits (known in the Islamic faith as *djinns*) who had been responsible for many deaths, and that it was crowned with a strange white substance that resembled silver, but which the locals simply called 'cold'.

Following protracted negotiations, Bwana Kheri was eventually persuaded to take Rebmann to Chagga in 1848 (Krapf, being too ill to travel, remained in Rabai-mpia). The parting caused great distress to both parties, as detailed in Krapf's diary:

Here we are in the midst of African heathenism, among wilful liars and trickish men, who desire only our property... The only earthly friend whom I have, and whom he has, does at once disappear, each of us setting our face towards our respective destinations while our friends at home do not know where we are, whither we go and what we are doing.

Rebmann's journey and the discovery of snow
And so, armed with only his trusty umbrella – along a route where caravans typically travelled under armed escort – Rebmann, accompanied by Bwana Kheri and eight porters, set out for Chagga on 27 April 1848. A fortnight later, on the morning of 11 May, he came across the most marvellous sight:

*At about ten o'clock, (I had no watch with me) I observed something remarkably white on the top of a high mountain, and first supposed that it was a very white cloud, in which supposition my guide also confirmed me, but having gone a few paces more I could no more rest satisfied with that explanation; and while I was asking my guide a second time whether that white thing was indeed a cloud and scarcely listening to his answer that **yonder** was a cloud but what that white was he did not know, but supposed it was **coldness** – the most delightful recognition took place in my mind, of an old well-known European guest called **snow**. All the strange stories we had so often heard about the gold and silver mountain Kilimandjaro in Jagga, supposed to be inaccessible on account of evil spirits, which had killed a great many of those who had attempted to ascend it, were now at once rendered intelligible to me, as of course the extreme cold, to which poor Natives are perfect strangers, would soon chill and kill the half-naked visitors. I endeavoured to explain to my people the nature of that 'white thing' for which no name exists even in the language of Jagga itself...* **Johannes Rebmann** from his account of his journey, published in Volume I of the *Church Missionary Intelligencer*, May 1849

KILIMANJARO

An extract from the next edition of the same journal continues the theme:

The cold temperature of the higher regions constituted a limit beyond which they dared not venture. This natural disinclination, existing most strongly in the case of the great mountain, on account of its intenser cold, and the popular traditions respecting the fate of the only expedition which had ever attempted to ascend its heights, had of course prevented them from exploring it, and left them in utter ignorance of such a thing as 'snow', although not in ignorance of that which they so greatly dreaded, 'coldness'.

Still bent on spreading Christianity, and undeterred (indeed ignorant) of the scepticism with which his reports in the *Intelligencer* were about to be met back in Europe (about which, see the box below), Rebmann returned to Rabai-mpia but continued to visit and write about Kilimanjaro and the Chagga region for a few more years. His second trip, made in November of the same year, was blessed by favourable weather conditions, providing Rebmann with his clearest

WD Faulty? – The great snow debate

The most relentless critic was a redoubtable person, for long years a terror to real explorers, Mr Desborough Cooley, a kind of geographical ogre, who used to sit in his study in England, shaping and planning out the map of Africa (basing his arrangements of rivers, lakes and mountains on ridiculous and fantastic linguistic coincidences and resemblances of his own imagination), and who rushed out and tore in pieces all unheeding explorers in the field who brought to light actual facts which upset his elaborate schemes. **HH Johnston** *The Kilima-njaro Expedition – A Record of Scientific Exploration in Eastern Equatorial Africa* (1886)

Though Rebmann's accounts of Kilimanjaro caused a minor sensation amongst the wider reading public when first published in the *Church Missionary Intelligencer* of May 1849, the response it elicited from academic circles back in Europe was initially as cool as the top of Kibo itself. Leading the sceptics was one **William Desborough (WD) Cooley**. Cooley was widely regarded in his day as one of Britain's leading geographers and something of an expert on Africa (though he never actually ventured near the continent throughout his entire life). Indeed, Cooley had already added to the stock of knowledge about the mountain way back in 1845, a full four years before Rebmann's essay was published, by providing the world with a description of Kilimanjaro that he had managed to construct from details furnished to him by the slave dealer-cum-ambassador Khamis bin Uthman (see p105). But if he is remembered at all today it is as the man who refused to believe that Kilimanjaro could be topped with snow, as this response to Rebmann's first account (see p107) makes clear:

I deny altogether the existence of snow on Mount Kilimanjaro. It rests entirely on the testimony of Mr Rebmann... and he ascertained it, not with his eyes, but by inference and in the visions of his imagination. *Athenaeum, May 1849*

Absurd as it seems now, Cooley's reputation in intellectual circles at that time was as high as Kili itself, and such was the reverence with which his every pronouncement was received in the mid-nineteenth century that it was his version of reality that was the more widely accepted: as far as people in Europe were concerned, if Cooley said Kilimanjaro did not have snow on it, then it did not have snow on it.

view of Kilimanjaro, and the outside world with the most accurate and comprehensive description of the mountain that had yet been written:

There are two main peaks which arise from a common base measuring some twenty-five miles long by as many broad. They are separated by a saddle-shaped depression, running east and west for a distance of about eight or ten miles. The eastern peak is the lower of the two, and is conical in shape. The western and higher presents the appearance of a magnificent dome, and is covered with snow throughout the year, unlike its eastern neighbour, which loses its snowy mantle during the hot season.

On this second trip Rebmann was also able to correct an error made in his first account of Kilimanjaro: that the local 'Jagga' tribe were indeed familiar with snow and did have a name for it – that name being 'Kibo'!

A third and much more organized expedition in April 1849 – at the same time as the account of his earlier visits to Kilimanjaro was rolling off the presses in

A second report by Rebmann, following his trip to the Chagga lands in November 1848, did little to stem the scepticism, even though he – perhaps now aware of the controversy his first account had caused back home – went to great lengths to back up his earlier report:

.. during the night, I felt the cold as severely as in Europe in November; and had I been obliged to remain in the open-air, I could not have fallen to sleep for a single moment: neither was this to be wondered at, for so near was I now to the snow-mountain Kilimandjaro (Kilima dja-aro, mountain of greatness), that even at night, by only the dim light of the moon, I could perfectly well distinguish it.

If Rebmann hoped to persuade his critics, however, he was sadly mistaken: if he was capable of making a mistake once, they countered, then surely he could be wrong a second and third time too. And so for much of the next two years Rebmann's account of his time on Kili was treated with equal parts suspicion and derision. Indeed, it wasn't until 1850 and the publication of an account by Rebmann's friend and mentor, Dr Krapf, that doubts began to be cast on Cooley's ideas. In an edition of the *Church Missionary Intelligencer* in which he recounts his own experiences working in the Ukamba region immediately to the north of Kilimanjaro, Krapf baldly states that:

All the arguments which Mr Cooley has adduced against the existence of such a snow mountain, and against the accuracy of Rebmann's report, dwindle into nothing when one has the evidence of one's own eyes before one; so that they are scarcely worth refuting.

Suddenly it became that much harder to deny the existence of snow on Kili: after all, there were now two Europeans who had seen the mountain for themselves – and both of them had insisted that they'd seen snow there. Yet Cooley remained adamant in his convictions and, thanks to the support of some pretty influential friends to back up his arguments, enjoyed popular public support. No less a figure than the President of the Royal Geographical Society, **Sir Roderick Murchison**, said that the idea of a snow-capped mountain under the equator was to *'a great degree incredulous'*, (even though there are other snow-capped mountains in the Andes and Papua New Guinea that fall 'under the equator', and which were already known about by the mid-nineteenth century). *(Continued on p110)*

KILIMANJARO

Europe – enabled Rebmann, accompanied by a caravan of 30 porters (and, of course, his trusty umbrella), to ascend to such a height that he was later to boast that he had come 'so close to the snow-line that, supposing no impassable abyss to intervene, I could have reached it in three or four hours'.

After Rebmann's pioneering work it was the turn of his friend Krapf, now risen from his sickbed, to see the snowy mountain his friend had described in such detail. In November 1849 he visited the Ukamba district to the north of Kilimanjaro and during a protracted stay in the area Krapf became the first white man to see Mount Kenya. Perhaps more importantly, he was also afforded wonderful views of Kilimanjaro, and was able to back up Rebmann's assertion that the mountain really was adorned with snow (see box p109 for quote).

❏ **WD Faulty? – The great snow debate**   *(Continued from p109)*

Even those who *had* been to Africa for themselves had serious reservations about the missionaries' claims. The esteemed Irish explorer **Richard Burton**, for example, having listened to Krapf give a talk on Kilimanjaro in Cairo, declared that *'These stories reminded one of a de Lunatico'*; while **David Livingstone**, recently returned from his latest adventures in Africa, lent further weight to Cooley's arguments during an address to the Royal Geographical Society. In it, Livingstone related a story about some mountains in the Zambezi Valley which were described to him by locals as being of a *'glistening whiteness'*. Livingstone initially believed that these mountains must be covered by snow, until, having seen the mountains for himself, he realized that they were in fact composed of *'masses of white rock, somewhat like quartz'*.

As if to drum home the point of the tale, Sir Roderick Murchison later declared at the same meeting that Livingstone's account

... may prove that the missionaries, who believed that they saw snowy mountains under the equator, have been deceived by the glittering aspect of rocks under a tropical sun.

The next broadside fired by either side occurred in 1852 and the publication of Cooley's grandly (but inaccurately) titled *Inner Africa Laid Open*. This, Cooley clearly hoped, was to be his masterpiece: the culmination of a lifetime's armchair studying, this was the opus that would secure his reputation during his lifetime and ensure his name lived on in perpetuity as one of the great intellectual heavyweights of the nineteenth century. As it transpired, the book did indeed serve to preserve Cooley's name for posterity – though presumably not in the way that he had hoped.

To read the book now, it is clear that Cooley hoped it would once and for all dismiss all this nonsense about snow on Kilimanjaro. Within the first few pages almost every part of Rebmann's account is called into question, with the claim of snow on Kilimanjaro being treated with particularly vehement derision:

... it is obvious that the discovery of snow rests much more on 'a delightful mental recognition' than on the evidence of the senses..... But in his mind the wish was father to the thought, the 'delightful recognition' developed with amazing rapidity, and in a few minutes the cloudy object, or 'something white,' became a 'beautiful snow mountain', so near to the equator.

Later in the book Cooley forgets the conduct becoming of an English gentleman and the attacks on Rebmann border on the personal, starting with an attack on his eyesight:

FIRST ATTEMPTS ON THE SUMMIT

Baron von der Decken and Charles New

After the missionaries came the mountaineers. In August 1861 Baron Carl Claus von der Decken, a Hanoverian naturalist and traveller who had been residing in Zanzibar, accompanied by young English geologist Richard Thornton, himself an explorer of some renown who had accompanied (and been sacked by) Livingstone during the latter's exploration of the Zambezi, made the first serious attempt on Kilimanjaro's summit. Initially, despite an entourage of over fifty porters, a manservant for von der Decken and a personal slave for Thornton, their efforts proved to be rather dismal and they had to turn back after

Various and inconsistent reasons have been assigned for this failure [by Rebmann to see Kilimanjaro from a nearby hill], *but the only true explanation of it is contained in Mr Rebmann's confession that he is very short-sighted. He was unable to perceive, with the aid of a small telescope, Lake Ibe, three days distant to the south, which his followers could discern with the naked eye; nor could he even see the rhinoceroses in his path.*

And he goes on to finish his onslaught with this rather uncompromising, hysterical summary of Rebmann's accounts:

... betraying weak powers of observation, strong fancy, an eager craving for wonders, and childish reasoning, could not fail to awaken mistrust by their intrinsic demerits, even if there were no testimony opposed to them.

To further back up his argument, Cooley was able to point out a number of inconsistencies between Rebmann's and Krapf's accounts, such as the postulation by Krapf that the mountain is 12,500 feet (3800m) high – this after Rebmann had estimated the height to be closer to 20,000 feet (6000m, a remarkable guess by the myopic Rebmann).

Cooley's desire to prove Rebmann wrong was fuelled by more than just a desire to crush a young upstart in a field in which he considered himself the ultimate authority. He was also frightened that the existence of snow on Kilimanjaro would provide support for his rivals' theories at the expense of his own. In the big debate that raged in academic circles in the mid-1800s on the exact location of the source of the Nile, Cooley was firmly of the opinion that the river started from a large lake in Central Africa called Lake N'yassi. (Indeed, in the 1830s he even organized an expedition to prove his theory, though unfortunately it failed abysmally for reasons that remain rather obscure.)

Aligned against him, Cooley's opponents such as the geographer **Charles Beke**, preferred the idea that the Nile had its source in a mountain range in the interior – possibly, as Encisco had stated in the sixteenth century, the legendary Mountains of the Moon – and looked upon the discovery of snow on an East African mountain as evidence to back up their theories. Indeed, when Rebmann and Krapf's accounts first reached Britain, Beke was only too keen to accept their every word as gospel and even went so far as to suggest that Kilimanjaro was now the most likely source of the Nile.

And that, for the next decade or so, was that: Rebmann and Krapf continued to visit Kilimanjaro and continued to see snow, while Cooley and the gang back in England continued to refute their every utterance and enjoy the majority of public opinion.

(Continued on p112)

KILIMANJARO

❏ WD Faulty? – The great snow debate *(Continued from p111)*

Then in 1862, **Baron Carl von der Decken** made his second and more successful attempt on Kilimanjaro (see opposite), this time with his friend Dr Otto Kersten who had replaced Thornton for this second expedition to the region. In reaching a reported 14,200ft, von der Decken and Kersten came as close to the snow as any European ever had, and the brave baron's subsequent account of the expedition exploded Cooley's theories once and for all:

During the night it snowed heavily and next morning the ground lay white all around us. Surely the obstinate Cooley will be satisfied now.

There was now a third eyewitness claiming to have seen snow on Kilimanjaro, and a baron at that; Cooley's position as a result began to look increasingly untenable, and his support began to ebb quietly away.

If the baron really believed his testimony alone would persuade Cooley, however, he was much mistaken:

So the Baron says it snowed during the night....In December with the sun standing vertically overhead! The Baron is to be congratulated on the opportuneness of the storm. But it is easier to believe in the misrepresentations of man than in such an unheard-of eccentricity on the part of nature. This description of a snowstorm at the equator during the hottest season of the year, and at an elevation of only 13,000 feet, is too obviously a 'traveller's tale', invented to support Krapf's marvellous story of a mountain 12,500 feet high covered with perpetual snow.

But the redoubtable Cooley was fighting a lonely battle now. The Royal Geographical Society withdrew their backing, with Sir Roderick Murchison – presumably between mouthfuls of humble pie – finally admitting that Rebmann and Krapf were probably right after all. As if to add insult to Cooley's injured pride, the Society even awarded their Gold Medal in 1863 to von der Decken for his contributions to the sum of geographical knowledge of Africa. (Incidentally, in addition to his account of Kilimanjaro, von der Decken was also the first European to see and describe Mount Meru.)

Fourteen years after Rebmann had first announced that there was snow on the equator, the world was finally listening to him. Cooley meanwhile, resolutely refused to believe in the existence of snow on Kilimanjaro, carrying his scepticism with him to the grave and leaving behind a reputation for stubbornness and ignorance that has survived to this day.

In Cooley's defence, one has to remember just how little was known about the continent at that time: few people from Europe had ever visited Africa; fewer still had penetrated beyond the coast; and of those who had, even fewer had survived to tell the tale. So the armchair scholars of Europe were forced to rely upon the sketchy mentions of Kili in historical records for their information; and of those descriptions, none since Ptolemy mentions anything about snow.

As some compensation, perhaps, Cooley at least had the satisfaction of knowing that, while defeated in this particular battle, he gained at least a partial victory in the wider war: in 1858 a large body of water in the heart of central Africa was discovered, and was named **Lake Victoria** after Britain's sovereign. This lake would later be proved to be one of the sources of the Nile. Cooley may have got the name and location of this body of water wrong, but his supposition that the Nile had a lake as its source, and not a mountain, had been proved correct after all.

just three days due to bad weather, having reached the rather puny height of just 8200ft (2460m). Proceeding to the west side of the mountain, however, the pioneering baron did at least enjoy an unobstructed view of Kibo peak on the way:

Bathed in a flood of rosy light, the cap that crowns the mountain's noble brow gleamed in the dazzling glory of the setting sun... Beyond appeared the jagged outlines of the eastern peak, which rises abruptly from a gently inclined plain, forming, as it were, a rough, almost horizontal platform. Three thousand feet lower, like the trough between two mighty waves, is the saddle which separates the sister peaks one from the other.

Von der Decken also provided the most accurate estimate yet for the height of both Kibo – which he guessed was between 19,812 and 20,655 feet (5943.6m to 6196.5m) – and Mawenzi (17,257-17,453 feet, or 5177.1-5235.9m). Thornton, for his part, correctly surmised that the mountain was volcanic, with Kibo the youngest and Shira the oldest part of the mountain.

The following year von der Decken, now accompanied by Dr Otto Kersten who had replaced Thornton as the baron's travelling and climbing companion, reached a much more respectable 14,200ft (4260m) and furthermore reported being caught up in a snowstorm (see box opposite). On his return to Europe, the baron described Kibo as a 'mighty dome, rising to a height of about 20,000 feet, of which the last three thousand are covered in snow'.

Following this second attempt, von der Decken urged **Charles New** (1840-75), a London-born missionary with the United Free Methodist Church in Mombasa, to tackle the mountain, and in 1871 New made a laudable attempt to reach the summit. That attempt failed, as did a second attempt in August of the same year; nevertheless, by choosing on the latter occasion to climb on the south-eastern face of Kibo where the ice cap at that time stretched almost to the base of the cone, New inadvertently wrote himself into the history books as the first European to cross the snow-line at the African Equator:

The gulf was all that now lay between myself and it, but what an all! The snow was on a level with my eye, but my arm was too short to reach it. My heart sank, but before I had time fairly to scan the position my eyes rested upon snows at my very feet! There it lay upon the rocks below me in shining masses, looking like newly washed and sleeping sheep! Hurrah! I cannot describe the sensations that thrilled my heart at that moment. Hurrah!

On this second expedition New also discovered the crater lake of Jala, the mountain's only volcanic lake, at Kilimanjaro's foot to the south-east of Mawenzi.

New's experiences on Kilimanjaro fanned his passion for the mountain and two years later he was back preparing for another assault on the still-unconquered peak. Unfortunately, the volatile tribes living at the foot of the mountain had other ideas and before New had even reached Kilimanjaro he was forced to return to the coast, having been stripped of all his possessions by the followers of the Chief of 'Moji' (Moshi), a highly unpleasant man by the name of Mandara (see p250). Broken in both health and spirits, the unfortunate New died soon after the attack.

As rumours of New's demise trickled back to Europe, enthusiasm among explorers for the still unconquered Kilimanjaro understandably waned, and for

KILIMANJARO

the next dozen years the mountain saw few foreign faces. Those that did visit usually did so on their way to somewhere else; people such as **Dr Gustav A Fischer** in 1883, who stopped in Arusha and visited Mount Meru on his journey to Lake Naivasha and declared Kilimanjaro to be fit for 'European settlement', a statement that would have greater resonance later on in the century; and the Scottish geologist, **Joseph Thompson**, who became one of the first to examine properly the northern side of the mountain during an attempt to cross the Masai territories. He also attempted a climb of Kili, though having allowed himself only one day in which to complete the task his attempt was always doomed to failure, and in the end he reached no higher than the tree-line at about 2700m. (Failure though he may have been in this instance, his name lives on as a species of gazelle.)

The first European to venture back to the region with the specific intention of visiting Kilimanjaro arrived in the same year, 1883. In an expedition organized by the Royal Geographical Society, **Harry Johnston** arrived in East Africa with the aim of discovering and documenting the flora and fauna of Kilimanjaro. Though his work did little to further our understanding of the mountain, Johnston's trip is of anecdotal interest in that he later claimed in his biography that he was actually working undercover for the British Secret Service. No documentary evidence has ever turned up to back this claim (though there is a letter written by him to the foreign office in which he asks for 40 men and £5000 for the purpose of colonizing Kilimanjaro). Much doubt has been cast, too, upon his boast that he reached almost 5000m during his time on the mountain; while his suggestion that Kilimanjaro was 'a mountain that can be climbed even without the aid of a walking stick' was widely ridiculed when first broadcast later that year. But whatever the inaccuracies and falsehoods of Johnston's recollections, his journey did at least assure other would-be Kilimanjaro visitors from Europe that the region was once again safe to visit. His visit also served to bring the mountain to the attention of European powers...

COLONIZATION

... a country as large as Switzerland enjoying a singularly fertile soil and healthy climate, ... within a few years it must be either English, French or German ... I am on the spot, the first in the field, and able to make Kilima-njaro as completely English as Ceylon.
HH Johnston *The Kilima-njaro Expedition – A Record of Scientific Exploration in Eastern Equatorial Africa* (1886)

In describing the mountain thus, HH Johnston brought Kilimanjaro to the attention of the world's leading powers. Soon the two great colonizers in East Africa, Germany and Britain, were jockeying for position in the region. British missionaries were accused of putting the temporal interests of their country over the spiritual affairs of their flock, while for their part certain German nationals made no secret of the fact they wished to colonize Kilimanjaro. In 1884, the **Gesellschaft für Deutsche Kolonisation** (GDK), a political party founded by the 28-year old **Dr Carl Peters** with the ultimate goal of colonizing East Africa, persuaded a dozen local chiefs to throw off the rule of the (British controlled)

Sultan of Zanzibar and, furthermore, to cede large sections of their territory to the German cause; one of Dr Peters' envoys, Dr Juhlke, even managed to establish a protectorate over Kilimanjaro in 1885. The British fought fire with fire in response, forcing two dozen chiefs (including some of those who had sided with the Germans) to swear allegiance to the sultan – and therefore indirectly to them. The situation was becoming dangerously volatile, with war looking increasingly likely. After further bouts of political manoeuvring, in October 1886 the two sides met in London and Berlin to define once and for all the boundary between British- and German-controlled East Africa and head off the possibility of war: the border between British-ruled Kenya and German East Africa was now in place.

The first period of German rule over Kilimanjaro proved to be exceptionally harsh, and many Germans soon felt uneasy about the excesses of Dr Peters and his followers. In 1906 an enquiry opened in the Reichstag into the conduct of the doctor and his men, in which an open letter was read out to the court. Its contents give an idea of the hatred that the doctor and his men aroused in the locals:

What have you achieved by perpetual fights, by acts of violence and oppression? You have achieved, Herr Doctor, I have it from your own mouth in the presence of witnesses – that you and the gentlemen of your staff cannot go five minutes' distance from the fort without military escort. My policy enables me to make extensive journeys and shooting trips in Kilimanjaro and the whole surrounding country with never more than four soldiers. You have cut the knot with the sword and achieved that this most beautiful country has become a scene of war. Before God and man you are responsible for the devastation of flourishing districts, you are responsible for the deaths of our comrades Bulow and Wolfram, of our brave soldiers and of hundreds of Wachagga. And now I bring a supreme charge against you: Necessity did not compel you to this. You required deeds only in order that your name might not be forgotten in Europe.

Soon German soldiers were being attacked and killed and, with opposition to their rule growing stronger and more organized, they suffered a massive defeat

---

The biggest present ever?

There is a widely held belief that the kink in the border between Kenya and Tanzania near Kilimanjaro was created to satisfy the whim of Queen Victoria, Britain's reigning monarch at the time the border was first defined. According to the story, she magnanimously decided to give Kilimanjaro to her grandson, the future Wilhelm II, as a birthday present, following a complaint from him that while Britain had two snowy mountains in her East African territories (Mounts Kili and Kenya), Germany was left with none. In order to effect the transfer of such a generous gift, the border had to be redrawn so that Kili fell to the south of the boundary in German territory, which is why the border has a strange kink to the east of the mountain.

Alas, however romantic the story, it is simply not true. The kink is there not because of Victoria's largesse, but as part of the agreement struck between Germany and Britain, and it exists not because of Kili, but Mombasa. Britain's territories in East Africa needed a port: the Germans already had Dar, and if the border between the two was to continue on the same bearing as it had taken to the west of Kilimanjaro, the Germans were going to end up with Mombasa too. So a kink was placed in the border to allow Mombasa to fall in British territory.

KILIMANJARO

at Moshi at the hands of the Chagga, led by Meli, Mandara's son (see p250).

Though the Germans regained control, it was clear to them that a more benevolent style of government was required if they were to continue ruling over their East African territories. This new 'caring colonialism' paid off and for the last few years of their rule the Germans lived largely at peace with their subjects and even forged a useful alliance with the Chaggas during the Germans' push against rebellious Masai tribes. The Germans also started the practice of building public huts on Kilimanjaro, establishing one at 8500ft (2550m), called **Bismarck Hut**, and one at 11,500ft (3450m) known as **Peters' Hut**, after Dr Karl.

KILIMANJARO CONQUERED

While all this was going on, attempts to be the first to conquer Kilimanjaro continued apace. In 1887, **Count Samuel Teleki** of the Austro-Hungarian Empire made the most serious assault on Kibo so far, before 'a certain straining of the membrane of the tympanum of the ear' forced him to turn back. Then the American naturalist, **Dr Abbott**, who had come primarily to investigate the fauna and flora of the mountain slopes, made a rather reckless attempt. Abbott was struck down by illness fairly early on in the climb but his companion, Otto Ehlers of the German East African Company, pushed on, reaching (according to him) 19,680ft (5904m). Not for the first time in the history of climbing Kilimanjaro, however, this figure has been sceptically received by others – particularly as it is at least 8m above the highest point on the mountain!

Both Teleki and Abbott, however, played a part in the success of the eventual conqueror of Kilimanjaro, **Dr Hans Meyer**: Teleki, by providing information about the ascent to Meyer in a chance encounter during Meyer's first trip to the region in 1887; Abbott, by providing accommodation in Moshi for Meyer and his party during their successful expedition of 1889. Hans Meyer was a geology professor and the son of a wealthy editor from Leipzig (he himself later joined the editorial board and became its director, retiring in 1888, one year before the conquest of Kili, to become professor of Colonial Geography at Leipzig University). In all he made four trips to Kilimanjaro. Following the partial success of his first attempt in 1887, when he managed to reach 18,000ft (5400m), Meyer returned the following year for a second assault with experienced African traveller and friend Dr Oscar Baumann. Unfortunately, his timing couldn't have been worse: the **Abushiri War**, an Arab-led revolt against German traders on the East African coast, had just broken out and Meyer and his friend Baumann were captured, clapped into chains and held hostage by Sheikh Abushiri himself, the leader of the insurgency. In the end both escaped with their lives, but only after a ransom of ten thousand rupees was paid.

However, on his third attempt, in 1889, Meyer finally covered himself in glory. Though no doubt a skilful and determined climber, Meyer's success can largely be attributed to his recognition that the biggest obstacle to a successful assault was the lack of food available at the top. Meyer solved this by establishing camps at various points along the route that he had chosen for his attempt, including one at 12,980ft (3894m; Abbott's camp); one, Kibo camp, 'by a con-

spicuous rock' at 14,210ft (4263m); and, finally, a small encampment by a lava cave and just
below the glacier line at 15,260ft (4578m).
Thanks to these intermediary camps, Meyer
was able to conduct a number of attempts on
the summit without having to return to the foot
of Kili to replenish supplies after each; instead,
food was brought to the camps by the porters
every few days.

He also had a considerable back-up party
with him, including his friend and climbing
companion, Herr Ludwig Purtscheller – a gym-
nastics teacher and alpine expert from Salzburg
– two local headmen, nine porters, three other
locals who would act as supervisors, one cook
and one guide supplied by the local chief,
Mareale, whom he had befriended during his
first trip to the region. These men would help
to carry the equipment and man the camps,
with each kept in order by Meyer's strict code
of discipline, where minor miscreants received
ten lashes, and serious wrongdoers twenty.

The conquest of Kilimanjaro
*Taking out a small German flag,
which I had brought with me for the
purpose in my knapsack, I planted
it on the weather-beaten lava summit with three ringing cheers, and
in virtue of my right as its discover-
er christened this hitherto unknown
and unnamed mountain peak – the
loftiest spot in Africa and the
German Empire – Kaiser Wilhelm's
Peak* [now known as Uhuru Peak].
*Then we gave three cheers more for
the Emperor, and shook hands in
mutual congratulation.* **Hans
Meyer** *Across East African Glaciers*

The size of his entourage, however,
shouldn't detract from the magnitude of Meyer's achievement: as well as the usual hardships associated with climbing Kilimanjaro,
he also had to contend with deserters from his
party, a lack of a clear path, elephant traps
(large pits dug by locals and concealed by
ferns to trap the unwary pachyderm), as well
as the unpleasant, rapacious chief of Moshi,
Mandara (see p250). Furthermore, Meyer did
not begin his walk *on* the mountain, as today's visitors do, but in Mombasa, 14
days by foot, according to Meyer, from the Kilimanjaro town of Taveta!

Then there was the snow and ice, so much more prevalent in the late 1800s
on Kili than it is today. Above 4500m Meyer had to trek upon snow for virtually the whole day, even though his route up Kibo from the Saddle is not too dissimilar to that taken by thousands of trekkers every year – and today there is no
snow on the route. The added difficulties caused by the snow are well described
in Meyer's book *Across East African Glaciers*. Rising at 2.30am for their first
assault on the summit, Meyer and Purtscheller spent most of the morning carv-
ing a stairway out of a sheer ice-cliff, every stair laboriously hewn with an average of twenty blows of the ice axe. (The cliff formed part of the Ratzel Glacier,
named by Meyer after a geography professor in his native Leipzig.) As a result,
by the time they reached the eastern lip of the crater, the light was fading fast

KILIMANJARO

and the approach of inclement weather forced them to return before they could reach the highest point of that lip.

On their second attempt, however, three days later on 6 October 1889, and with the stairs in the ice still intact from the first ascent, they were able to gain the eastern side of the rim by mid-morning; from there it was but a straight-forward march to the three small tumescences situated on the higher, southern lip of the crater, the middle one of which was also the highest point of the mountain.

Meyer's route to the top and the modern trails: a comparison

While no modern path precisely retraces Hans Meyer's original route to the summit, some of today's paths do occasionally coincide with the trail he blazed. For instance, Meyer and his climbing partner, Purtscheller, began their assault on Kilimanjaro, on 28 September, 1889, from **Marangu** village. From there they headed due north up through the trees, arriving two days later at the very upper limits of the forest, where they made camp. Trekkers on the Marangu trail follow a similar itinerary today, though their starting point is a good deal higher than Meyer's at Marangu Gate, rather than Marangu village – which explains why trekkers today need only one day to reach the edge of the forest, while Meyer took two. It is also worth noting that, according to the beautifully drawn maps by Dr Bruno Hassenstein in Meyer's book *Across East African Glaciers*, his camp on this second night lay to the south-west of Kifunika Hill at an altitude of 8710ft (2613m), whereas the Mandara Huts lie a couple of hours' walk to the east of Kifunika, at a loftier 2743m.

On the third day, Meyer struck a westerly course, crossing the Mdogo (lesser) and Mkuba (greater) streams before making camp at an altitude of 9480ft (2844m). This was the all-important **Halfway Camp**, the intermediate station that Meyer would use as his base for tackling Kibo. In the history of climbing Kibo, no single spot on the entire mountain, save Uhuru Peak itself, has played a more prominent role: Harry Johnston had built some huts nearby during his reconnaissance mission of 1883; Meyer himself had camped here during his first expedition on the mountain, with Baron von Eberstein in 1887, and Abbott and Ehlers had also camped nearby in 1889, just a few months before Meyer and Purtscheller arrived. There's even evidence to suggest Count Teleki had also stopped here in 1887; in his account of their attempt on Kili in *Discovery by Count Teleki of Lakes Rudolf and Stefanie*, Lieutenant Ludwig von Höhnel speaks of making camp at 9390ft by a brook, near some old huts built originally by HH Johnston.

So where is this spot? There are plenty of clues. It is no coincidence, for example, that all these different parties chose to make camp at this site. Then, as now, campsites would have been chosen largely for their proximity to water and other amenities, so we can guess that a mountain stream or brook must run nearby. We also know that Meyer headed almost due west from his camp of the night before, and that the spot lies at around 2844m, above the tree-line. No modern campsite exactly fits this description – the Horombo Huts, the second night's accommodation on the Marangu trail, are too high up at 3657m. Rau Campsite, however, on the sadly now defunct Alternative Mweka/Kidia Route, seems a more plausible candidate: though this campsite is too high at 3260m, just below it is a glorious stretch of grasslands bordering the forest and near a mountain stream that would appear to fit the description given by Meyer. If the nineteenth-century explorers really did camp around there, they are to be congratulated on choosing one of the most beautiful places on the mountain.

AFTER MEYER

Mawenzi, Pastor Reusch and a frozen leopard

In the decades following Meyer's successful assault on Kili, few followed in his footsteps. Meyer himself climbed again in 1898, though this time he got only as far as the crater rim. In 1909 surveyor M Lange climbed all the way to Uhuru Peak, and in doing so became only the second to reach the summit of Kilimanjaro – a full twenty years after the first.

Leaving most of his porters behind at this site – it would be their duty from now on to ferry supplies up to the camp from Marangu – Meyer then struck due north up to the Saddle, past the **Spring in the Snow**, or Schneequell (12,910ft, 3873m) and on to **Abbott's Camp** at 12,980ft (3894m), so-called by Meyer because he found an empty Irish stew tin and a sheet of the Salvation Army newspaper *En Avant* at this spot, and guessed that this must have been where his missionary friend Dr Abbott had camped a few months previously. As to their location, according to the maps in Meyer's book the Schneequell lies almost exactly due south of the East Lava Hill, the easternmost of the parasitic cones on the Saddle, and would seem to tie in fairly neatly with the Last Water Point, the Mua River, that lies below the Zebra Rocks on the Marangu Route (see p255). Abbott's Camp, meanwhile, lies to the north-north-west of here, at a point between the two Marangu Route paths to the Saddle.

From here, Meyer's path and the Marangu Route diverge for good. Where Marangu trekkers head roughly north across the Saddle, keeping Kibo to their left, in 1889 Meyer and his two companions, the alpine expert Purtscheller and Mwini Amani, their guide, set off directly for the summit in a more westerly direction, stopping for the night by a prominent rock at 14,200ft (4260m). This is **Viermannstein**, the Rock of Four Men, a place popular with Kili explorers in the nineteenth century. Unfortunately, because it lies far from any trail today, the site rarely features on modern trekking maps; for an approximate location, draw a line running east from the Barafu Campsite, and a second due south from the easternmost Triplet: the rock stands near to where they coincide.

Meyer's aim in 1889 was the **Ratzel Glacier**, on the south-eastern rim of Kibo. The glacier has now, alas, disappeared, though we know from maps where it was: if walking up to the summit from the Barafu Campsite, it would have been on your right when approaching Stella Point. In Meyer's day the glacier covered the entire south-eastern lip of Kibo, and it was into this glacier that Meyer and Purtscheller, on 3 October, carved a series of steps that led all the way to the crater rim and a height of 19,260ft (5778m).

On this occasion, considerations of time and weather forced them to withdraw back down to camp, having seen – but not scaled – the highest point on Kibo. After a day's rest and contemplation, however, and having decided to bivouac at **Lava Cave** on the slopes of Kibo at 15,960ft (4788m), the duo were ready for another assault on the summit. From there, at 3am on a cold October morning, they set off. At dawn they were at the foot of the glacier where, to their delight, they found the glacial stairway that they'd built two days previously was still there. By 8am they had reached and crossed a large crevasse, the only serious obstacle on the way to the summit. Just 45 minutes later they were back standing on the crater rim, the limit of their achievements two days previously. On this occasion, however, both time and weather were on their side. Walking around the southern rim of Kibo, they climbed three small hillocks, the middle of which they found by aneroid to be the highest by some 40 feet or more. *(Continued on p120)*

The conquest of the last remaining peak on Kilimanjaro, that of the summit of Mawenzi (called, somewhat perversely, Hans Meyer Peak), was achieved by the climbers **Edward Oehler** and **Fritz Klute** on 29 July 1912. Thus, 64 years after the first European had clapped eyes on Kilimanjaro, both of its main peaks had been successfully climbed. As an encore, Oehler and Klute made the third successful attempt on Kibo and the first from the western side. In the same year, **Walter Furtwangler** and **Ziegfried Koenig** achieved the fourth successful climb, and became the first to use skis to descend. Two more successful assaults occurred before the outbreak of World War One, and **Frau von Ruckteschell** kept up the German's impressive record on Kilimanjaro by becoming the first woman to reach Gillman's Point.

Fresh attempts on Kilimanjaro were suspended for a while during World War One. The countryside around Kilimanjaro became the scene of some vicious fighting, including Moshi itself, which was attacked by British forces in March 1916. Paul von Lettow Vorbeck, the German commander, went down in military history at this time as the man who led the longest tactical retreat ever. With the German's defeat, however, Kilimanjaro, along with the rest of German East Africa, reverted to British rule.

After the war, attention turned away from Kibo to the lesser-known Mawenzi. In 1924 **George Londt** of South Africa became, by accident, the first to climb

---

❏ **Meyer's route to the top and the modern trails: a comparison**
(Continued from p119) Thus at 10.30am on 6 October 1889, Meyer and Purtscheller wrote themselves into the history books as the first to make it to the highest point in Africa.

So where exactly did they gain **access to the crater**? According to Dr Hassenstein's maps, the Lava Cave lies at the northern end of the large South-East Valley, due west of the middle of the three triplets. That puts it somewhere to the north-east of the Barafu Campsite, and more than 150m higher, on one of the rocky spurs that run south-east down from Kibo. Where it certainly is *not*, though many a guide will tell you otherwise, is the Hans Meyer Cave on the Marangu Route, which at 5151m is simply too high and too far north.

The notch by which they gained access to the crater lay almost exactly north-west of this Lava Cave Camp. Though again this is pure guesswork, all the evidence does seem to point to the fact that Meyer and Purtscheller on this particular occasion passed into the crater rim from a spot very near to **Stella Point** (5745m); the difference in height (Meyer estimated the height at this point on the crater to be 5778m) can possibly be ascribed to the fact that Meyer's estimates tend to be over-estimates (his height for Uhuru Peak, for example, is over 6000m) – perhaps because in Meyer's day there was a lot more ice at the summit, which would have raised the altitudes.

Having christened the summit after their Kaiser and taken the topmost stone from the summit as a souvenir (a stone that Meyer later gave to the Kaiser, who used it as a paperweight), the pair then hurried back to Abbott's camp on the Saddle. The next few days were spent trying to conquer **Mawenzi** but with no success, the mountain peak defeating them wholly on the first occasion on 13 October, and an attack of colic brought on by some over-ripe bananas stalling their second attempt two days later. Before returning to civilization, however, they spent five more days revisiting Kibo:

South Peak (he was aiming for Hans Meyer Peak but got lost); the peak (4958m), was named after him. Three years later three English mountaineers climbed Mawenzi, including **Sheila MacDonald**, the first woman to do so; the trio then climbed Kibo, with Ms MacDonald writing her name into the record books again as the first woman to complete the ascent to Uhuru Peak. In 1930 two British mountaineers, HW Tilman and Eric Shipton, names more usually associated with Everest, climbed Mawenzi's Nordecke Peak – again, like Londt, by accident.

While all this was happening on Mawenzi, over on Kibo another man was writing himself into the history of Kili: **Pastor Richard Reusch**. Missionary for the Lutheran Church, former officer in the Cossack army and long-time Marangu resident, Reusch climbed the mountain on no less than 40 different occasions. During his first assault on the summit in 1926 he found the frozen leopard on the crater rim that would later inspire Hemingway (Reusch cut off part of an ear as a souvenir), while on another sortie the following year he became the first to gaze down into the inner crater, a crater that he was later to give his name to. Later work by mountaineer **HW Tilman** and vulcanologist **JJ Richard** led to confirmation, in 1942, that Kilimanjaro was still active, and while this led to some local panic, in 1957 the Tanganyika Geological Survey and the University of Sheffield were able to allay fears by declaring the volcano to be dormant and almost extinct.

on 17 October they headed to the crater's northern side. There they reached 5572m before confronting a sheer wall of ice that forced them to retreat; and then finally, on the 18th, they approached the crater from the east.

The path Meyer took up to the crater on this occasion is not too dissimilar to the trail up to Gillman's from the Kibo Huts. Meyer and Purtscheller on this final climb bivouacked at a location they called **Old Fireplace** because, to their considerable surprise, they found the remains of a recent campfire there, along with the bones of an eland and some pieces of banana matting. This camp, according to Meyer, sat at an altitude of 15,390ft (4617m). It's just possible, therefore, that the Old Fireplace is in fact the site that we now call **Jiwe La Ukoyo**, which many local mountain guides insist was once a popular hunters' campsite. From the Old Fireplace, Meyer and Purtscheller climbed up the snow-clad slopes of Kibo once more, gaining access into the crater via a cleft in the rim that is now known as **Hans Meyer Notch**, and which lies just a few hundred metres to the north of Gillman's Point. Though they failed in their attempts to reach the inner cone of the volcano, they were at least able to confirm that the floor of the crater was made up of a mixture of mud and ashes. They were also startled when, peering into the first cone, they came across the carcass of an antelope (which possibly explains what the leopard, whose frozen body was found up here many years later, was doing at this altitude).

After one more unsuccessful attempt on Mawenzi, Meyer and Purtscheller finally decided to call it a day, and on 22 October they said goodbye to the Saddle for the last time. The pair had spent 16 days between 15,000 and 20,000 feet. During this time they had made four ascents of Kibo, reaching the crater three times and the summit once, and three sorties on Mawenzi, reaching the 5049m summit of Purtscheller's Spitze but failing to reach the very top.

KILIMANJARO

KILIMANJARO TODAY

The twentieth century witnessed the inevitable but gradual shift away from exploration towards tourism. The most significant change occurred in 1932 with the building of Kibo Hut; name plates and signs were put up too, as the mountain was gradually made more tourist-friendly. With a ready base for summit assaults now established, tourists began to trickle into Tanzania to make their own attempt on Africa's greatest mountain.

In 1959 the mountain became the focus for nationalist feelings and a symbol of the Tanganyikans' independence aspirations following Julius Nyerere's speech to the Tanganyika Legislative Assembly (see p76 for quote). Nyerere eventually got his wish and, after independence was granted in 1961, a torch was indeed placed on the summit of Kilimanjaro. Independence also provided Tanganyika with the chance to rename many of the features of the mountain; in particular, the very summit, dubbed Kaiser Wilhelm Peak by Hans Meyer, was renamed Uhuru Peak – Uhuru meaning, appropriately, 'Freedom' in Swahili.

Since this mountain's moment of patriotic glory, the story of Kilimanjaro has largely been about tourism. The early trickle of tourists of seventy years ago is nowadays more akin to a flood, with visitor numbers increasing exponentially from less than 1000 in the late 1950s to 11,000 in the 1990s, to the 40,000-plus we see today. What has been an economic boon to the people of Kilimanjaro, however, has brought little benefit to the mountain itself. With the increase in the number of trekkers comes commensurately greater numbers of pressures and problems. Its soil is being eroded, its vegetation is being burnt or chopped, its wildlife is disappearing and its glaciers are melting. Along with these environmental pressures come challenges to its dignity, as climbers dream up ever more bizarre ways of climbing to the top, whether driving up by motorcycle or walking in fancy dress, as discussed in the introduction to this book.

Then there's the problem of **fire**. In February 1999, fires raged for five days and 70 hectares were destroyed, the blaze finally being brought under control thanks to the combined efforts of 347 villagers, park rangers and 40 soldiers of the 39th Squadron of the Tanzanian People's Defence Force. Further fires on the Shira Plateau in 2001, on the Rongai Route before Kikelelwa Campsite in 2007 and, most obviously, in October 2008 on the Marangu Route, between Mandara and Horombo Huts, have caused yet more damage.

Depressingly but unsurprisingly, human activity is believed to have been behind the fires. Twenty-two men from the Kamwanga and Rongai districts were arrested for the 1999 fire, having been identified as the culprits by six hundred villagers in a secret ballot. The men were all squatters living illegally in the protected areas of the national park; according to one minister who visited the scene of the devastation, there were up to 10,000 such squatters living in Kilimanjaro's forests. It is believed that a cigarette butt discarded by one of them started the blaze, though others have pointed an accusing finger at local farmers who like to clear their farms by fire before the start of the annual rains. Other possible culprits include honey collectors, who make fires to smoke out the bees, and we've even heard accusations that those in charge of the park,

For the record

● **Fastest ascent of Kilimanjaro** On 26 October 2007 Gérard Bavato of France ran the 35.5km from base to summit in an incredible 5 hours, 26 minutes and 40 seconds. We are grateful to Gérard for his achievement, as it clears up the mess that has surrounded this particular record for the past few years, with Italian Bruno Brunod's old record of 5 hours, 38 minutes and 40 seconds, achieved in 2001, being constantly challenged by a couple of unverified claims from Sean Burch of Virginia (5 hours 28 minutes, achieved on 7 June 2005) and Christian Stangl of Austria (5 hours 36 minutes, recorded in October 2004).

● **Fastest ascent and descent** This belongs to Simon Mtuy (Tanzania), who runs the Summit Expeditions and Nomadic Experience trekking agency in Moshi (see p209). On 26 December, 2004, Simon achieved the incredible time of 8 hours 27 minutes. Apparently, it took Simon 6 hours exactly to reach the summit via the Umbwe Route, and after 7 minutes to catch his breath, just 2 hours 20 minutes to complete the descent to Mweka Gate. In fact, it's likely that Simon will be the holder for a while. His ultra-running background combined with the fact that he climbs the mountain regularly mean that even if his rivals do beat his time, their reign is likely to be shortlived.

Nor is that the end of Simon's record-breaking exploits, for on the 22 February 2006 Simon climbed from Umbwe Gate to the summit and back again in a time of 9 hours and 19 minutes and, in doing so, achieved the **fastest ever unaided ascent and descent** (by unaided, they mean that Simon carried his own food, water and clothing). This despite suffering from a nasty bout of diarrhoea, as well as a three-minute break at the top to video himself, plus two further breaks to vomit!

● **Fastest ascent (female)** Rebecca Rees-Evans (UK) achieved a time of 13 hours 16 minutes and 37 seconds in reaching Uhuru Peak via the Marangu Route, 21 May 2005.

● **Youngest person to reach the summit** On 21 January 2008 Keats Boyd from Los Angeles successfully hauled his seven-year-old body to the very summit of Africa's highest mountain - and in doing so became the youngest person ever to reach the top of Kilimanjaro. An impressive feat, not least because in breaking the record Keats must also have broken all sorts of rules, including the one that says you have to be at least ten to climb Kili! The youngest person to climb Kilimanjaro who was above the minimum age was Jordan Romero of Big Bear Lake, California, who achieved the summit on the 23rd July 2006 at the tender age of 10 years and 11 days.

● **Oldest person to reach the summit** Curiously, according to a previous edition of *Guinness Book of World Records* American Carl Haupt holds the record for the oldest man to summit Kilimanjaro, being 79 when he reached the top in 2004. This must have come as something of a surprise to Frenchman Valtée Daniel, who has long been regarded as the oldest man ever to reach Africa's highest point – and considering he was 87 when he made it to the top, we can see no reason why he's not still the record holder. One can assume only that Monsieur Daniel's expedition could not be verified according to the regulations governing Guinness records – though it seems a bit rough on the old fella to have his record snatched away by such a whippersnapper. However, Valtée's achievement hasn't been entirely forgotten and most people, including us, consider Valtée the main man. So come back when you're older, Carl, and try again.

Incidentally, while we have no information on who is officially the **world's oldest woman** to reach the summit, *The Oakville Beaver* carried a story of Canadian Ann Windh, from Bronte, Ontario, who in 2007 reached the summit aged 77. Ms Windh cited the break-up of her marriage as the reason why she had waited until her 78th year, as before that she led a sheltered existence as a housewife, raising three children.

KINAPA, start fires in order to extract more money from TANAPA, the body that oversees the administration of all of the country's reserves and parks – though we think this has more to do with the Tanzanians' love of a good conspiracy theory than any basis in reality. Needless to say, we don't endorse any of these accusations.

Yet no matter what indignities are heaped upon it, Kilimanjaro continues to inspire both awe and respect in those who gaze upon it. And while man will continue to visit in droves and in his clumsy way will carry on defacing and demeaning it, setting it ablaze and covering it with litter, the mountain itself remains essentially the same powerful, ineffably beautiful sight it always was; perhaps because, while we throw all that we can at it, the Roof of Africa does what it always has done – and what it does best: it simply rises above it all.

Fauna and flora

Kilimanjaro is often called 'The Island Above the Clouds' because it boasts more unique species than many small countries. Many happy years could be spent studying and writing about this mountain's fascinating flora and fauna. The following, therefore, is but a small introduction to the nature of Kilimanjaro.

FAUNA

'URGENT MESSAGE:
Location: Amboseli Game Park, Kenya
Human population: 150
Baboon population: 90,000
Meteorological conditions: Severe drought
Water supplies: Nil
Situation: Mutilated bodies discovered. Baboons have turned into man-eating primates –
POSITION DESPERATE!'
Taken from the back cover of terrible 1980s' horror film *In the Shadow of Kilimanjaro*, supposedly based on a true story. You may like to consider this when walking past a troop of them on your Meru climb.

In order to see much in the way of fauna, you have to be either very lucky or, it would seem, an author of a book on Kilimanjaro. When Hans Meyer was coming down from the mountain in 1889 he spotted an elephant on the slopes. In 1926 a leopard was found frozen in the ice at a place we now call Leopard Point – providing Hemingway with the inspiration for *The Snows of Kilimanjaro*. The mountaineer, HW Tilman, saw 27 eland on the Saddle when he passed this way in 1937, with each, according to him, especially adapted for the freezing conditions with thicker fur. In 1962, renowned travel writer Wilfred Thesiger and two companions were accompanied to the summit by five wild dogs (aka African hunting dogs). Though the dogs then turned round and disappeared after the three men made the summit, paw-prints in the ice proved that this wasn't the first time they had climbed to the top. More recently, Rick Ridgeway claimed he saw a leopard on his ascent, as did Geoffrey Salisbury while leading his group of blind climbers to the summit; and in 1979 a local guide called David was savaged by a pack of wild dogs above the Mandara Huts and lost a finger.

We mention these stories to demonstrate that the more exotic fauna of East Africa does occasionally venture onto the mountain. It just doesn't happen very often, with most animals preferring to be somewhere where there aren't 40,000-plus people (plus their crews) marching around every year.

The decline of fauna on Kilimanjaro is perhaps best illustrated by these random quotes I have drawn from *Tanganyika Notes and Records: Kilimanjaro*, an excellently informative book published in March 1965. It's depressing to see how abundant the wildlife appeared even then, just over forty years ago.

'Millard considers that the elephant population of Kilimanjaro is of the order of 1,500 and from personal observation this appears to be a very reasonable estimate.'
'Giraffe have been seen by Millard in heavy forest within the montane forest belt.'
'Up to about 1950, Rhinoceros were often encountered in the forest above Marangu...They are still to be found from West Kilimanjaro where their position is fairly good around to Kitenden where their numbers have been considerably reduced.'
'Wild Dogs have been seen in the Mandera [sic] *(Bismark) hut area and in the country to the south of Mawenzi (Forest Division).'*

Just for the record, elephants do still wander up the slopes of Kilimanjaro, particularly from Amboseli and from the West Kilimanjaro corridor, though in nothing like the numbers recorded above; giraffe are seldom if ever recorded on the mountain now, though it's feasible that they too may wander up the northern and western slopes; the total population of rhino in Tanzania is now less than fifty, with the nearest to Kilimanjaro now well over 100km away in Ngorongoro Crater to the west or Mkomazi National Park to the south-east; while wild dogs are so rare now in Tanzania that a website has even been set up so that those fortunate enough to spot one can tell the world about it!

So in all probability you will see virtually nothing during your time on the mountain beyond the occasional monkey or mouse. Nevertheless, keep your mouth shut and your eyes open and you never know...

Forest and cultivated zones

Animals are more numerous down in the forest zone than anywhere else on the mountain; unfortunately, so is the cover provided by trees and bushes, so sightings remain rare. As with the four-striped grass mice of Horombo (see p254), it tends to be those few species for whom the arrival of man has been a boon rather than a curse that are the easiest to spot, including the **blue monkeys**, which appear daily near the Mandara Huts and which are not actually blue but grey or black with a white throat. These are the plainer relatives of the beautiful **colobus monkey**, which has the most enviable tail in the animal kingdom; you can see a troop of these at the start of the forest zone on the Rongai and Lemosho routes, and near the Mandara Huts, where a couple are semi-tame. Strangely, despite their beauty, their name is actually derived from the Greek for 'mutilated' as unlike other primates they don't have a proper opposable thumb but a mere stump. This 'deformity' is even more bizarre when one considers that they are amongst the most arboreal of monkeys; in other words, they very rarely drop down to the ground, preferring instead to spend their time in the trees – where you would have thought a proper opposable thumb would be an advantage for grabbing hold of branches etc. Indeed, so rarely does it drop down to the ground that it would normally be rather difficult to spot were it not for its flamboyant coat and its strange, frog-like croak.

Olive baboons, **civets**, **leopards**, **mongooses** and **servals** are said to live in the mountain's forest as well, though sightings are extremely rare; here, too, lives the **bush pig** with its distinctive white stripe running along its back from head to tail.

Baboons in the branches of a Dum palm
(from *Across East African Glaciers,* Hans Meyer, 1891)

Then there's the **honey badger**. Don't be fooled by the rather cute name. As well as being blessed with a face only its mother could love, these are the most powerful and fearless carnivores for their size in Africa. Even lions give them a wide berth. You should too: not only can they cause a lot of damage to your person, but the thought of having to tell your friends that, of all the bloodthirsty creatures that roam the African plains, you got savaged by a badger, is too shaming to contemplate. Of a similar size, the **aardvark** has enormous claws but unlike the honey badger this nocturnal, long-snouted anteater is entirely benign. So fear not: as the old adage goes, aardvark never killed anyone. Both aardvarks and honey badgers are rarely, if ever, seen on the mountain. Nor are **porcupines**, Africa's largest rodents. Though also present in this zone, they are both shy and nocturnal and your best chances of seeing one is as roadkill on the way to Nairobi.

Further down, near or just above the cultivated zone, **bushbabies** or galagos are more easily heard than seen as they come out at night and jump on the roofs of the huts. Here, too, is the **small-spotted genet** with its distinctive black-and-white tail, and the noisy, chipmunk-like **tree hyrax**.

One creature you definitely won't see at any altitude is the rhinoceros. Over-hunting has finally taken its toll of this most majestic of creatures – Count Teleki (see p116), for example, is said to have shot 89 of them during his time in East Africa, including four in one day – and there are none on or anywhere near Kilimanjaro today.

KILIMANJARO

Heath, moorland and above

Just as plant-life struggles to survive much above 2800m, so animals too find it difficult to live on the barren upper slopes. Yet though we may see little, there are a few creatures living on Kilimanjaro's higher reaches.

Above the treeline you'll be lucky to see much. The one obvious exception to this rule is the **four-striped grass mouse**, which clearly doesn't find it a problem eking (or should that be eeking?) out an existence at high altitude; indeed, if you're staying in the Horombo Huts on the Marangu Route, one is probably running under your table while you read this, and if you stand outside for more than a few seconds at any campsite you should see them scurrying from rock to rock. Other rodents present at this level include the **harsh-furred** and **climbing mouse** and the **mole rat**, though all are far more difficult to spot. (Your best chance of seeing the harsh-furred mouse is probably on the Shira Plateau, particularly amongst the heather by the toilets near the caves at Shira Caves Campsite and, less often, at Shira 1 Camp on the Lemosho Route too.)

For anything bigger than a mouse, your best chance above 2800m is either on the Shira Plateau, where **buffaloes and other grazers** are said to roam occasionally, or on the northern side of the mountain on the Rongai Route. Kenya's Amboseli National Park lies at the foot of the mountain on this side and many animals, particularly **elephants**, amble up the slopes from time to time. **Grey** and **red duikers**, **elands** and **bushbucks** are perhaps the most commonly seen animals at this altitude, though sightings are still extremely rare. None of these larger creatures live above the tree-line of Kilimanjaro permanently, however, and as with the **leopards**, **giraffes** and **buffaloes** that occasionally make their way up the slopes, they are, like us, no more than day-trippers.

On **Kibo** itself the entomologist George Salt found a species of **spider** that was living in the **alpine zone** at altitudes of up to 5500m. What exactly these high-altitude arachnids live on up there is unknown – though Salt himself reckoned it was probably the flies that blew in on the wind, of which he found a few, and which appeared to be unwilling or unable to fly. What is known is that the spiders live underground, better to escape the rigours of the weather. We've also seen a white butterfly on the way up to Mawenzi Tarn Huts at 4122m; once again, we can only assume that it has been blown up the slopes from the moorland or forest zone.

AVIFAUNA

Kilimanjaro is great for birdlife. The cultivated fields on the lower slopes provide plenty of food, the forest zone provides shelter and plenty of nesting sites, while the barren upper slopes are ideal hunting grounds for raptors.

In the **forest**, one of the easier birds to spot is the dark green **Hartlaub's turaco**, partly because of its noisy, monkey-like call, and partly because when it flies, viewers are treated to flashes of bright red under-wings. If you're lucky you may also come across **silvery-cheeked hornbills**, though to be honest you're more likely to see them on Meru and even in Arusha near the Jacaranda Hotel

Tropical boubou

than on Kilimanjaro. **Montane white-eyes** – small green birds with distinctive white circles around their eyes – can be found around Machame Huts and occasionally elsewhere on the mountain, and another habitué of the Machame Hut is the **common stonechat**, a relative of the more common alpine chat but slightly more striking in appearance, with a white stripe on its black wings and a chestnut patch on its breast.

Other small birds said to live in the forest include the **speckled mousebird**, that hang around the fruit trees in the forest; the **trogon** which, despite a red belly, is difficult to see because it remains motionless in the branches. Smaller birds include the **Ruppell's robin chat** (black and white head, grey top, orange lower half) and the **common bulbul**, with a black crest and yellow beneath the tail.

Further up the slopes, the noisy, scavenging, garrulous **white-necked raven** is a constant presence on the mountain during the day, eternally hovering on the breeze around the huts and lunch-stops on the lookout for any scraps. Smaller but just as ubiquitous is the **alpine chat**, a small brown bird with white side feathers in its tail, and the **streaky seed-eater**, another brown bird (this time with streaks on its back) that often hangs around the huts. The **alpine swift** also enjoys these misty, cold conditions. The prize for the most beautiful bird on the mountain, however, goes to the dazzling **scarlet-tufted malachite sunbird**. Metallic green save for a small scarlet patch on either side of its chest, this delightful bird can often be seen hovering above the grass, hooking its long beak in to reach the flies sheltering in the lobelias.

Hartlaub's Turaco

Climbing further, we come to raptor territory. You'll rarely see these birds up close as they spend most of the day gliding on the currents looking for prey. **Augur buzzards** are very occasionally spotted hovering in the breeze; these are impressive birds in themselves – especially if you're lucky enough to see one up close – though neither is as large as the enormous **crowned eagle** and the rare **lammergeyer**, a giant vulture with long wings, a wedge tail and a tufty beard beneath the beak; currently a juvenile often hangs around the Kibo Huts.

Speckled mousebird

KILIMANJARO

Streaky seed-eater

Alpine chat

Malachite sunbird

White-necked raven

Skink or grey lizard

Four-striped grass mouse

Colobus monkey

Vervet monkey (Meru)

Two-horned chameleon

Lammergeyer

Bearded lichen

Protea kilimandsharica
(with malachite sunbird)

Bidens
kilimandsharica

Gladiolus
watsonides

Trifolium
usambarensis

Anenome thomsonii

Carduus
keniensis

Leonotis
nepetifolia

Disa stairsii
(orchid)

Adenocarpus mannii

Dierama
pendulum

Artemisia afra
African wormwood

Euryops dacrydioides

Ranunculus oreophylus

Hypericum revolutum
St John's Wort

Kniphofia thomsonii
Red hot poker

Arabis alpina
Alpine rock cress

Lobelia deckenii
(flowers)

Lobelia deckenii

*Dendrosenecio kiliman-
jari (*tree groundsel)
ssp kilimanjarii*

*Helichrysum meyeri-
johannis*

*Dendrosenecio kiliman-
jari (*tree groundsel)
ssp cottonii*

Fireball lily

Thunbergia alata

Polystachyus
(orchid)

*Impatiens
pseudoviola*

*Impatiens
kilimanjari*

*Impatiens
digitata*

*Desmodium
repandum*

*Begonia
meyeri-johannis*

Dracaena afromontana

Fragraria
Wild strawberry

*Parochaetus
communis*

Plectranthus sylvestris

FLORA

It is said that to climb up Kilimanjaro is to walk through **four seasons in four days**. It is true, of course, and nowhere is this phenomenon more apparent than in its flora. The variety of flora found on Kilimanjaro can be ascribed in part to the mountain's tremendous height and in part to its proximity to both the equator and the Indian Ocean. Add to this the variations in climate, solar radiation and temperature from the top of the mountain to the bottom (temperatures are estimated to drop by 1°C for every 150m gain in altitude), and you end up with the ideal conditions for highly differentiated and distinctive vegetation zones. In all, **Kilimanjaro is said to have between four and six distinctive zones** depending on what you read. A description of each follows; a picture chart of the more common species of flower can be found in the colour section opposite.

Cultivated zone and forest (800m-2800m)

The forest zone, along with the cultivated zone that lies below it, together receive the most rainfall – about 2300mm per year – of any part of the mountain. The forest also houses the greatest variety of both fauna (see p124) and flora.

For the layman, it may be difficult at first to identify the individual species of **tree**, though some do stand out. On the Marangu Route the first trees you'll notice – and Antipodeans should recognize – are actually non-native: the grey-barked **eucalyptus** was planted by the first park warden of Kilimanjaro, though it is now a tree that his successors are trying to eradicate as it takes so much water from the land. Enormous **camphorwoods** also flourish at this altitude, as do **fig** trees and *talamontana*, or **wild mango**. Further up the slopes towards the upper limit of the zone, the smooth grey **African holly** (*Ilex mitis*), with its characteristic red and yellow fruit, becomes the dominant tree. **African redwood** (*Hagenia abyssinica*), though nothing like as common, is perhaps more recognizable with its enormous, blousy, pink-flowered panicles – it's quite the most camp tree on the mountain. Another instantly recognizable species is the giant fern, *Cyathea sp*, which clearly enjoys the damp conditions, as does *Usnea sp* or **old man's beard**, which lies draped over most of the branches at the upper limit of the forest zone. At about the same altitude is the **podocarpus**, with its slender-finger leaves, and the **juniper** whose leaves, at least when gazing up at the canopy, look similar; put examples of each side by side, however, and you can clearly see the difference between them. Incidentally, with the drier climate the trees of the northern slopes are slightly different, with **olive trees** now abundant and one species, *Olea kilimandscharica*, indigenous to the mountain.

Podocarpus (left) and juniper (right)

What catches the eyes of most trekkers is not these giants, however, but the small splashes of colour that grow in their shade: the **flowers**. The star of the montane forest zone is the beautiful flower *Impatiens kilimanjari*, an endemic fleck of dazzling red and yellow in the shape of an inch-long tuba. You'll see them by the side of the path on the southern side of the mountain. Vying for the prime piece of real estate that exists between the roots of the trees are other, equally elegant flowers including its relatives, *Impatiens pseudoviola* and *Impatiens digitata*, and the beautiful **African violet**, *Viola eminii*. Hanging from the trees is the ***Begonia meyeri johannis***, with sweet smelling white and pink flowers that often litter the path like confetti. There's a **lobelia**, too, with blue or pink, distinctive, three-lobed flowers, that thrives in both the forest and the heath zone above. It's very similar to the ones you'll find in the hanging baskets of Europe, (though it bears very little resemblance to the lobelias that you will see further up the mountain). For that matter, it also bears little resemblance to *Lobelia gibberoa*, a giant lobelia almost 10m tall with a whorl of large leaves at its top and a very tall flower spike; these tend to love water and you'll usually find them growing on the banks of streams. **Orchids** also enjoy the dark moist conditions of the montane forest, in particular *Polystachyus*, with flowers that always resemble, to me at least, insects in flight.

Perhaps the most unusual aspect of Kilimanjaro's forest zone, however, is not the plants and trees that it *does* have but one that it doesn't. Kili is almost unique in East Africa in not having any bamboo at the upper limit of the forest zone, possibly because it is one of the driest mountains and cannot support bamboo stands the way other African mountains can. As a result, the forest zone ends suddenly, with little warning, throwing us immediately into the less shady trails of the ...

Heath and moorland (2800m-4000m)

These two zones overlap, and together occupy the area immediately above the forest from around 2800m to 4000m – known as the **low alpine zone**. Temperatures can drop below 0°C up here and most of the precipitation that does fall comes from the mist that is prevalent at this height.

Immediately above the forest zone is the **alpine heath**. Rainfall here is around 1300mm per year. The **giant heather** *Erica excelsa* and the similar but less bushy *Erica arborea* both grow in abundance. The latter also exists in the upper part of the forest zone, where it can grow to ten metres or more; the higher you go, however, the less impressive the specimens, with many refusing to grow beyond 2.5-3m. **St John's wort**, *Hypericum revolutum*, with its distinctive yellow flowers, also grows at this level, and occasionally at the upper reaches of the forest too. Most people will know this flower thanks to its anti-depressant properties.

Grasses now dominate the mountain slopes, picked out here and there with some splendid wild flowers including the yellow-flowered *Protea kilimandscharica*, an indigenous rarity that can be seen on the Mweka and Marangu trails and, so we've been told, around Maundi Crater – the best place for botanists to spot wild flowers. A whole raft of *Helichrysum* species make their first appearance here too, though certainly not their last; see box opposite for a study of these.

Identifying helichrysums (everlastings)

Perhaps the most prolific plants on the mountain, and ones that make their appearance just above the forest and continue up to the foot of Kibo (and even, on occasions, on it), are the **helichrysums**, also known as everlastings; those dry-looking flowers that resemble living pot pourri and grow in clumps all over the moorland (as well as above and below it). Members of the daisy family, the identification of individual helichrysums is complicated by three factors: 1) There are many different subspecies; 2) They change their appearance the further up the mountain they go in order to adapt to the conditions; 3) They all look much the same.

So how do you distinguish between different types of helichrysums? Well, the easiest one to recognize is *Helichrysum meyeri-johanis*, named after the first man to climb Kilimanjaro, which has a pinkish tinge to its petals. The others, however, require a little more detective work. *Helichrysum kilimanjari* differs from *H meyeri-johanis* in that its flowers are yellowy/brown, and when you crush its leaves they give off a distinctive lemon smell.

Helichrysum meyeri-johanis
(pink)

Helichrysum kilimanjari
(yellow)

Helichrysum cymosum
(yellow)

Those two tend to remain in the moorland zone, but as you move up to the high desert other species appear. *Helichrysum cymosum* and *Helichrysum splendidum* both bear tight clusters of small yellow flowers, the former being distinguishable by its leaves that hug the main stem tightly in order to protect it from the cold. *Helichrysum citrispinum* also has leaves that perform this function, though its flowers are larger, white, dry, and don't grow in tight clusters. Also present at this altitude is *Helichrysum newii*, named after Charles New, the first man to reach the snowline on Kilimanjaro. A truly remarkable plant, this was the helichrysum that was found surviving at 5670m near the eastern fumarole in the crater – a record on the mountain. It is believed that the heat from the fumarole allowed this plant to survive the extreme cold.

Helichrysum splendidum
(yellow)

Helichrysum citrispinum
(white)

Helichrysum newii
(yellow)

Another favourite, and one most readers will recognize instantly, is the back-garden favourite *Kniphofia thomsonii*, better known to most as the **red-hot poker**. Climbing higher, you'll begin to come across **sedges** such as *Mariscus kerstenii* with, like most sedges, a triangular stalk. Keep your eyes peeled and if you're extremely lucky you may also spot an orchid, *Disa stairsii*, a short flower with a spike of small pink flowers. Also growing in the grass here is a pretty, delicate **anenome**, *Anenome thomsonii*, with white flowers; a **scabious**, *Scabiosa columbaria*; and, occasionally, a vivid red **gladiolus** that's simply gorgeous, *Gladiolus watsonides*, which you an also find living in the upper reaches of the forest belt.

The shrubs are shrinking now: *Philippia trimera* is the most common of them, along with the gorse-like *Adenocarpus* beside which it often grows; the prettiest shrub in the upper reaches of the heath zone is the pink-flowered *Blaeria filago*. Growing in abundance in patches at this altitude is **African wormwood** (*Artemisia afra*), a waist-high plant that is more easily distinguished by its pungent aroma (that perfumes the air for entire sections of the trail) than by its rather dreary grey-green leaves. Known to the Chagga as *kichachayia* (my spelling), the wormwood, when placed in hot water and drunk as tea, is said to have medicinal properties and is a good cure for a bad stomach.

Climbing ever further, you'll soon reach the imperceptible boundary of the moorland zone, which tends to have clearer skies but an even cooler climate. Average per annum precipitation is now down to 525mm. At this altitude, perhaps the weirdest plant on the mountain is the strange *lobelia deckenii*, another endemic species. These curious, phallic- and cabbage-shaped plants take eight years to flower (the blue flowers are hidden inside the leaves to protect them from frost), and enjoy a symbiotic relationship with the *Nectarinia johnstoni*, the dazzling green malachite sunbird. It is said that any insects at this altitude are attracted by the purple flowers of the lobelia, and by the warmth and shelter that the velvet leaves supply. This in turn attracts the sunbirds who feed on the flies – and in doing so pollinate the flower. The lobelias are at their best in February and March.

Sharing the same cold, bleak environment are most distinctive plants on the entire mountain: the giant **tree groundsel**, or **dendrosenecio** (until recently called simply 'senecio', a name that you will see crop up in most books and is used by all the guides too). Even without the name change the literature on these plants is

❏ **Protecting Kilimanjaro**

Kilimanjaro has enjoyed some form of protection since the early years of the twentieth century under German rule, when the mountain and surrounding area were designated as a game preserve. In 1921 this status was upgraded to become a forest and game preserve, thereby protecting the precious cloud forest that beards Kili's lower slopes. Another change in 1957 saw the Tanganyika National Parks Authority propose that the mountain become a national park, though this wasn't actually realized until 1973, when Kilimanjaro National Park (KINAPA) was formed; a park that, for simplicity's sake, the authorities decided would include all land above 2700m. KINAPA didn't actually officially open until 1977; twelve years later, in 1989, the park was declared a World Heritage Site by UNESCO.

most confusing so I am grateful to Mr Eric Knox, director of the Indiana University Herbarium and the leading authority on these plants, for helping me.

There are two main dendrosenecio species on Kilimanjaro. The first is *Dendrosenecio kilimanjari*, which has two subspecies: *D. kilimanjari ssp cottonii* is found only above 3600m and has dull, mustard-coloured flowers. They cleverly protect themselves from the cold by using their dead leaves (which are like felt) to insulate their trunk. These groundsels are slow growers; according to some guides, you can estimate the age of a groundsel by counting the number of 'cabbages' or rosettes, with each 'cabbage' representing about 25 years growth. They tend to favour the damper, more sheltered parts of the mountain, which is why you'll see them in abundance near the Barranco Campsite as well as other, smaller valleys and ravines. The second subspecies, *D. kilimanjari ssp kilimanjarii*, thrives further down the slopes, can grow up to 5m high, and on the rare occasion it flowers the petals themselves are yellow and grow from a one-metre-long spike. Even further down, at a range of between 2750 and 3350 metres at the fringes of the montane forest, we get the second dendrosenecio species, *Dendrosenecio johnstonii*. Your best chance of seeing these giants is along the Machame Route where they form surprisingly big trees.

Alpine desert (4000m-5000m)

By the time you reach this sort of altitude, only three species of tussock grass and a few everlastings can withstand the extreme conditions. This is the **alpine desert**, where plants have to survive in drought conditions (precipitation here is less than 200mm per year), and put up with both inordinate cold and intense sun, usually in the same day. The everlastings continue to dominate, though they are shorter and stumpier now, presumably huddling nearer to the ground to protect themselves from the wind that whips across the mountain at this altitude.

By the time you get to this altitude flowers need special strategies to cope. The striking yellow star, *Ranunculus oreophylus*, and *Haplocarpha rueppellii* both do so by hugging the ground, better to avoid the wind and feed on what little warmth the ground can provide. The other yellow flowers at this altitude are the straggly senecio species, usually found surviving – if not exactly thriving – in the lee of the rocks and boulders. The shy white *Arabis alpina* or **Alpine rock cress** also clings on to survival at this chilly altitude by sheltering behind rocks.

Ice cap (5000m-5895m)

On Kibo, almost nothing lives. There is virtually no water. On the rare occasions that precipitation occurs, most of the moisture instantly disappears into the porous rock or is locked away in the glaciers. That said, specimens of *Helichrysum newii* – an everlasting that truly deserves its name – have been found in the crater (see p131), and moss and lichen are said to exist almost up to the summit. While these lichens may not be the most spectacular of plants, it may interest you to know that their growth rate on the upper reaches of Kilimanjaro is estimated to be just 0.5mm in diameter per year; for this reason, scientists have concluded that the larger lichens on Kilimanjaro could be amongst the oldest living things on earth, being hundreds and possibly thousands of years old!

The People of Kilimanjaro: the Chagga

With regard to the Chagga people, they are a fine, well-built race. Their full development of bone and muscle being probably due to the exercise they all have to take in moving about on steep hills: they seem intellectually superior to the general run of coast Natives, and despite their objectionable traits (almost always present in the uneducated Native), such as lying, dirty habits, thieving, &c., they are certainly a very nice and attractive race.
Rev A Downes Shaw *To Chagga and Back – An Account of a Journey to Moshi, the Capital of Chagga, Eastern Equatorial Africa,* 1924

Mount Kilimanjaro is the homeland of the **Chagga** people, one of Tanzania's largest ethnic groups. It is fair to say that when you are in Moshi, Marangu or Machame, there is little indication that you are in a 'Chagga town'. Yet in the smaller villages, though waning year by year, traditional Chagga culture remains fairly strong and occasionally a reminder of the past is uncovered by today's tourist, particularly when passing through the smaller villages on the little-visited eastern and western sides of Kilimanjaro. Such finds make visits to these villages truly fascinating.

Do not, however, come to Kilimanjaro expecting to witness some of the more extreme practices described in this section. This point needs emphasizing: the Chaggas' traditional way of life has been eroded by the depredations of Western culture and, as far as we know, is now largely extinct. Indeed, much of the material on which the following account is based is provided by the reports of the nineteenth- and early twentieth-century Europeans who visited the area; in particular, Charles Dundas' comprehensive tome, *Kilimanjaro and its People*, which was first published way back in 1924.

This, of course, begs the question: why have we included in a modern guide to Kilimanjaro descriptions of obsolete Chagga practices and beliefs that were largely wiped out almost 100 years ago? Well, research revealed the relevance of this inclusion since there are still faint echoes of their traditional way of life that have survived into the present day. Reading this admittedly brief account of the Chagga and how they lived and thought could provide you with a better understanding – and thereby some insight – into the mind, beliefs and behaviour of the people who live in Kilimanjaro's shadow today. In addition to these two reasons for including this section, it was a fascinating subject to research and we hope that at least some readers will find it as interesting to read.

ORIGINS

The Chagga are believed to have arrived between 250 and 400 years ago from the north-east, following local upheaval in that area. Logically, therefore, the eastern side of the mountain would have been the first to have been settled. Upon their arrival these new immigrants would have found that the mountain was already inhabited. An aboriginal people known as the Wakonyingo, who were possibly pygmies, were already living here, as indeed were the Wangassa, a tribe similar to the Masai, and the Umbo of the Usambara mountains. All of these groups were either driven out or absorbed by the Chagga.

Initially, these new immigrants were a disparate bunch, with different beliefs, customs and even languages. With no feelings of kinship or loyalty to their neighbour, they instead settled into family groups, or **clans**. According to Dundas, in his day some 732 clans existed on Kilimanjaro; by 1924, however, when his book was published, some of these clans were already down to just a single member.

These family ties were gradually cut and lost over time as people moved away to settle on other parts of the mountain. Thus, in place of these blood ties, people developed new loyalties to the region in which they were living and to the

---

Chagga language – a quick introduction

The language of the Chagga, Kichagga, is classified as a Niger-Congo language and has various dialects including Vunjo, Rombo, Machame, Huru and Old Moshi. The following is a very brief introduction to that dialect spoken in Marangu. As Chagga is rarely written down, compiling this 'phrasebook' wasn't easy; indeed, many of the spellings below are nothing more than phonetic guesswork. For their help with this box I am indebted to my Chagga chums Amina Malya and Vincent Munuo; and especially Frank Mtei, who came up with the first draft of the translations below, and Alex Minja for his expert help too.

1	kimu	2	shiwi	3	shiraru	4	shina	5	shitanu
6	shirandaru	7	mfungare	8	nyanya	9	kenda	10	ikumi

Yes	Ye'e
No	Ote
Please	Ngakuterewa
Thank you	Aika
How are you?	Shimbonyi shapfo?
Very well, thank you	Nashicha kapisa, aika
How old are you?	Nuore maka inga?
I am British	Inyi nyimwingeresa
I am American	Inyi nyimwamerikany
Don't mind	Molaswe
How far is it to the camp?	Ngeshika masaa yenga handun gendelaa?
How many times have you climbed the mountain?	Ni mara tsinga ulemro msari?
I have a headache	Ngiwawiyo mrue
I feel sick	Ngiwawiyo
I am very cold	Ngiichoo mbeo
Will you carry me?	Ochirima ingiira
I do not like porridge	Ngikundi msopfo
I cannot feel my fingers	Ngiichue shimnue shewaawaa
There is an elephant sleeping in my tent	Kuwore njofu eela itentiny lyako
There is a leopard biting my leg	Kuwore rung'we ilya kurende koko
We are together!	Luilose!

neighbours with whom they shared the land. Out of this emerged twenty or so states or chiefdoms, most of them on a permanent war footing with the other nineteen. Wars between the tribes and indeed between villages in the same tribe were commonplace, though they usually took the form of organized raids by one village on another rather than actual pitched battles. Slaves would be taken during these raids, cattle rustled and huts burned down, though there was often little bloodshed – the weaker party would merely withdraw at the first sign of approaching hostilities and might even try to negotiate a price for peace.

Eventually the number of different groups was whittled down to just six tribes, or states, with each named after one of the mountain's rivers. So, for example, there are the Wamoshi Chaggas (after the Moshi River) and the Wamachame Chaggas who settled near the Machame River. With all this intermingling going on, a few words inevitably became used by all the people living on the mountain – and from this unlikely start grew a common language, of which each tribe had its own dialect. Similar customs developed between the tribes, though as with the language they differed in the detail. However, it was only when the Germans took control of the region during the latter part of the nineteenth century and the local people put aside their differences to present a united front in disputes with their colonial overlords that a single ethnic group was identified and named the Chagga. From this evolved a single, collective Chagga consciousness.

Today the Chaggas, despite their diverse origins, are renowned for having a strong sense of identity and pride. They are also amongst the richest and most powerful people in Tanzania, thanks in part to the fertile soils of Kilimanjaro, and in part to the Western education that they have been receiving for longer than almost any other tribe in East Africa, Kilimanjaro being one of the first places to accept missionaries from Europe. Take a tour around Tanzania and you will also find the Chagga people to be one of the most widespread of all the tribes, seemingly able to settle in even the furthest-flung corners of the land, and – thanks to their talent for trade and politics – to thrive and prosper too.

SOCIAL STRUCTURE AND VILLAGE LIFE

Hans Meyer notes in his book that the biggest Chagga settlement when he visited in 1889 was Machame, with 8000 people. 'Moji' (Moshi) had 3000, as did Marangu. Each family unit, according to him, lived in two or three extremely simple thatched huts in the shape of beehives, with a granary and small courtyard attached. There are several examples of these **'beehive' huts** still dotted around Kilimanjaro's slopes. Only the **chief**, the head of village society and its lawmaker, lived in anything more extensive. The chief of every village was often venerated by his subjects and to meet him required going through an elaborate ceremony first. According to his report in the *Church Missionary Intelligencer*, Johannes Rebmann, the first white man to see Kilimanjaro, had to be sprinkled with goat's blood and the juice of a plant and was then left waiting for four days before being granted an audience with Masaki, the chief of Moshi. While modern society has reduced his role to a largely ceremonial one, the chief

THE CHAGGA VIEW OF KILIMANJARO

The summit of Kilimanjaro is and always has been as enchanting to the Chagga as it has been to visitors. According to Dundas, the Chagga view the Kibo summit as something beautiful, eternal and strengthening, its snows providing streams that support life, while the clouds that gather on its slopes provide precious rainfall. By comparison, the plains that lie in the opposite direction are seen as oppressively hot, where famine stalks, drought and malaria are rife and large creatures such as crocodiles and leopards prey on man. Indeed, so venerated is Kilimanjaro that the Chagga dead are traditionally buried facing towards Kibo, and the side of the village facing the summit is known to be the honourable side, where meetings and feasts are held and chiefs are buried. Furthermore, when meeting somebody, he who comes from higher up the slopes of Kilimanjaro should traditionally greet the other first, for it is he who is coming from the lucky side.

Intriguingly, some Chagga myths about Kilimanjaro are remarkably accurate. In particular, the Chagga traditionally believed that the mountain was formed by a volcano – even though the main eruption that formed Kibo occurred around half a million years ago, way before the arrival of man. What's more, there is a story in Chagga folklore concerning the twin peaks of Mawenzi and Kibo, in which Mawenzi's fire burns out first, and the Mawenzi peak is forced to go to Kibo, whose fire was still burning. Parallels between this story and what scientists now believe really happened – with Kibo continuing to erupt long after Mawenzi expired – are remarkable.

Did the Chagga climb to the top of Kilimanjaro before the Europeans?

The answer is: probably not. The quote on p108 by Rebmann in which he talks about '*the popular traditions respecting the fate of the only expedition which had ever attempted to ascend its heights*' suggests that he had information that they had tried only once – and failed. True, they definitely seem to have reached the snowline before the *mzungu* (white man) arrived: their belief that Kibo was covered in a magic silver which melted on the way down suggests as much. Furthermore, Rebmann's guide refers to the snow on the summit of Kilimanjaro as 'coldness' (see p107 and p108), and later on Rebmann discovers the Chagga have a word for snow: Kibo. What's more, Meyer found traces of a hunting expedition on the Saddle. All of which seem to confirm that they had climbed Kilimanjaro and had some experience of snow. But the fact that Charles New's entourage of porters and guides were buck naked when they climbed up to the snow-line suggests that they were, on the whole, unused to the conditions on Kibo; that, and the fact that the name Kilimanjaro, if it is of Chagga origin (about which, see p102), roughly translates as 'That which is impossible for birds', suggests that they thought that it was therefore impossible for man to reach the top.

Charles Dundas is equally sceptical of the notion that the Chagga climbed Kilimanjaro before Meyer:

It is inconceivable that natives can ever have ascended to the crater rim, for apart from cold, altitude and superstitious fears, it is a sheer impossibility that they could have negotiated the ice. Nor is there any tradition among the natives that anyone went up as high.... Rebmann tells us that Rengwa, great-grandfather of the present chief of Machame, sent an expedition to investigate the nature of the ice, which descends very low above Machame, but is impossible to scale. Only one of the party survived, his hands and feet frozen and crippled for life; all the rest were destroyed by the cold, or by evil spirits, as the survivor reported.

KILIMANJARO

is still a widely respected person in village life today – though thankfully there is now less ceremony involved when paying him a visit.

There are other similarities between the Chagga society of yesterday and today. The economy was, then as now, largely agricultural, using the environmentally destructive slash-and-burn technique for clearing land. **Bananas** were once the most common crop, and though banana bushes were largely replaced by **coffee** plantations in the early twentieth century, both are still grown today.

When it came to trading these bananas and coffee in former times, instead of the Tanzanian shilling people used red and blue glass beads as currency, or lengths of cloth known as *doti*. One hundred beads were equal to one *doti*, with which you could buy, for example, twenty unripe bananas; twelve *doti* would get you a cow.

Traditional Chagga beehive hut
(from *The Kilima-njaro Expedition*, HH Johnston, 1886)

RELIGION AND CEREMONIES

Unsurprisingly for a people that has been subjected to some pretty relentless missionary work for over a century, most Chagga are today **Christian**. Traditional beliefs are still held by some, though the intensity of the beliefs and the excesses of many of the rituals have largely disappeared. Superstition played a central role in traditional Chagga religion: witchcraft (*wusari* in Chagga) formed a major part, **rainmakers** and rain-preventers were important members of society and dreams were infallible oracles of the future; indeed, many Chagga were said to have dreamt of the coming of the white man to Kilimanjaro.

The traditional faith was based around belief in a god called **Ruwa**. Ruwa was a tolerant deity who, though neither the creator of the universe nor of man, nevertheless set the latter free from some sort of unspecified incarceration. Ruwa had little to do with mankind following this episode, however, so the Chagga instead **worshipped their ancestors**, whom they believed could influence events on Earth. Chagga mythology had many parallels with stories from the Bible, including one concerning the fall of man (though in the Chagga version, a sweet potato was the forbidden fruit, and it was a stranger rather than a serpent that persuaded the first man to take a bite); there are also stories that bear a resemblance to the tales of Cain and Abel, and the great flood.

The Chagga faith also had its own **concept of sin** and their own version of the Catholic practice of confession. In the Chagga religion, however, it is not the sinner but the person who is sinned against who must be purified, in order that the negative force does not remain with him or her. This purification would be performed by the local medicine man, with the victim bringing along the necessary ingredients for performing the 'cleansing'. These included the skin, dung and stomach contents of a hyrax (the small tree-dwelling mammals that live on Kilimanjaro); the shell and blood of a snail; the rainwater from a hollow tree and, as with all Chagga ceremonies, a large quantity of banana beer for the medicine man. All of this would then be put into a hole in the ground lined with banana leaves and with a gate or archway built above, which the victim would then have to pass through. This done, the victim would be painted by the medicine man using the mixture in the hole. This entire ceremony would be performed twice daily over four days.

Medicine men did more than care for one's spiritual health; they looked after one's physical well-being too. For the price of a goat and, of course, more banana beer, the medicine man would be able to cure any affliction using a whole host of methods – including spitting. If you were suffering from a fever, for instance, you could expect to be spat upon up to 80 times by the medicine man, who would finish off his performance by expectorating up your nostrils and then blowing hard up each to ensure the saliva reached its target. For this particular method, the traditional payment was one pot of honey – and probably some more banana beer.

Traditional Chagga society also practised preventative medicine, and not just in matters of health. If, for example, a prominent man in the village was for some reason worried about his own safety, the medicine man would order him to lie with his 'favourite wife' in a pit dug in the ground. With the man and wife still inside, the hole would be decked with poles and covered with banana leaves. They would remain there until evening, while the man's friends above cooked food.

Medicine men also performed the vital role of **removing curses**. Curses took many forms: a cheated wife, for example, might curse her husband by turning her back on him, bowing four times and praying for his death. The most feared curse, however, was that of the deathbed curse, issued by somebody shortly before they expired. These were widely held to be the most difficult to reverse, for to have any hope of removing it the medicine man would require the victim to get hold of a piece of the curser's corpse.

Funerals

If the medicine man's efforts at lifting the curse proved to be in vain, a funeral would be the most likely outcome. As with most Chagga ceremonies, this would vary slightly from place to place and from tribe to tribe, and also depended on the status of the deceased. Only married people with children, for example, would be buried: dead youths and girls would be wrapped in banana leaves and left in a banana grove, while babies were merely covered in cow dung and left out for jackals and hyaenas. (It is said that this practice was stopped after a jackal dropped the severed head of a small baby at the feet of a local chief.)

For married adults, the corpse would be stripped and bent double, with the head and legs tied together. **Animal sacrifices** would take place on the day of the burial, with the hide of a sacrificed bull used to cover the grave. Interestingly, the corpse would face Kibo in the grave – as if the Chagga believed that the summit of Kilimanjaro was in some way connected with the afterlife. A lot of beer-drinking was also involved. Sacrifices would continue for the next nine days until, it was believed, the soul had finally crossed the harsh desert separating the earthly world from the spirit world. The afterlife, incidentally, was said to be very like our temporal world, only not as good, with food less tasty and the scenery less majestic.

The Ngasi

One of the occasions in which children frequently died was during the initiation ceremony known as **Ngasi**. This was a brutal rite-of-passage ceremony to mark the passing of boys into adulthood. The ceremony was presided over by the so-

Chagga warriors
(from *Across East African Glaciers*, **Hans Meyer**, 1891)

called King of Ngasi, a man who had the authority to viciously flog any boy taking part in the ceremony who displeased him.

Before the Ngasi started, the boys who were to take part were summoned from their houses by the singing of lugubrious songs at the gate of their homes. From there they were taken to the place of ceremony deep in the forest and the proceedings began. **Hunting** formed a large part of the Ngasi; boys were tested on their ability to track down and kill game, the animals caught being smeared with the novices' excrement. Another test they had to undergo was to climb a tree on the riverbank and cross the river by clambering along its branches to where they intertwined with the branches of the trees on the other side. After this, a chicken would be sacrificed and the boys ordered to lick the blood.

The final part of the initial stage was the most brutal, however: orders were secretly given to the boys to slay a crippled or deformed youth amongst their number. Traditionally, the victim was killed in the night. The parents were never actually told what had happened to their son and, as all present at the Ngasi ceremony were sworn to silence, they rarely found out the whole story. The boys then moved to a new camp. They were now called Mbora, and were free to collect the old clothes that they had shed at the start of the Ngasi (one set of boy's clothes, of course, was left unclaimed). They then repaired to the chief's house for a feast, from where they headed home.

After the tribulations of the ceremony, the boys were allowed a month's holiday, before they returned to the chief's house to participate in the sacrificing of a bull. They were then free to head back to their homes, raping any young women they chanced to meet on the way; the poor women themselves had no redress. The Ngasi was now at an end, and the boys who successfully completed the ceremony were now men.

Matrimony

Ver hard on Wachaga to get wife, but when he get her she can make do plant corn, she make wash and cook and make do work for him. Ingreza [English] *man very much money to spend. She wife no can wash, no plant corn, herd goats or cook. All money, much merkani (cloth), heap money, big dinner. She eat much posho. She no can cook dinner. She only make 'Safari' and look. Porr, porr Ingreza man.*

A local's view of matrimony as recorded in **Peter MacQueen**'s book
In Wildest Africa, published in 1910

After the Ngasi, boys were free to marry. **Marriage** was arranged by the parents, though the boy and girl involved were allowed to voice their opinions – and unless the parents were particularly inflexible, these opinions would count for something. Furthermore, in order for the boy to stand a chance with his potential suitor, he had to woo her. The Chaggas' courtship process involved, as elsewhere in the world, a lot of gift-giving, though the gifts followed a strict set of rules: spontaneity played little part in this process. The first gift, for example, from the man to the woman, was always a necklace. The Chagga male would be well rewarded for his generosity, for traditionally in return the girl would dance naked all day with bells attached to her legs by her mother. Over the following days other gifts were exchanged until the time came when the girl, having visited all her relatives, would be shut away for three months. No work would be done by the girl during this time but instead she would be given fattening food and would be kept in a cage. At the end of this period a **dowry** would be paid, the marriage ceremony performed and the bride would be carried on the back of the Mkara (the traditional Chagga equivalent of the best man) to her new husband's house.

KILIMANJARO ECONOMY

Tourism is the biggest earner in the region, though agriculture is still very much part of the local economy. The volcanic soil of the mountain slopes, so rich with nutrients, is amongst the most fertile in East Africa. Thanks to the regular and reliable rainfall blown in from the Indian Ocean (see p98) and the proliferation of springs trickling forth from the bare rock, Kilimanjaro is also one of the damper parts of the region, and the south-eastern slopes particularly so, thus increasing still further the agricultural fecundity of the mountain.

On the lower slopes of Kilimanjaro annual staple crops such as beans, maize and millet are grown, while cash-crops such as Arabica coffee are planted in the *kihamba* land further up the mountainside. Bananas are also grown at this altitude, their leaves and stems providing both a nutrient-rich mulch for the coffee trees and fodder for the livestock that are traditionally grazed at this height. In Chagga society it is customary for a farmer's land to be divided between his sons on his death; whilst this may seem a fair way of dividing land, it also means that farmer's landholdings diminish in size with every generation, and many farms are now less than a hectare in size.

The Chagga are also keen bee-keepers, the hives being hollow sections of a tree trunk closed at both ends and left to hang in trees; you may see these hives placed (illegally) in Kilimanjaro's forests. Once the swarm has taken possession and completed the combs the bees are smoked out and the honey collected.

The following chapter is devoted to helping you take your first few steps in East Africa. It contains guides to the two cities that you are most likely to fly into — namely **Dar es Salaam** and **Nairobi**. The guides to the two cities are deliberately rather brief but they should be adequate for finding your way around and for choosing somewhere to sleep and eat, as well as to experience something of metropolitan East Africa. We also explain, at the end of each description, how to get to Kilimanjaro.

Kilimanjaro International Airport is, of course, the most convenient airport for the mountain; details about it can be found on p161.

Dar es Salaam

Dar es Salaam is a city with an identity crisis: a large metropolis (population 2.2 million) which behaves as if it were a small and sleepy seaside town; a city that was at the forefront of the country's struggle for independence in the 1950s and yet still contains the finest collection of dusty old colonial buildings in possibly the whole of East Africa; and a place that everybody thinks is the administrative capital of Tanzania – but isn't.

It *is* the commercial heart of the country, however, and has been almost since its inception in the 1860s by Sultan Sayyid Majid of Zanzibar. Intended as a mainland port for many of the goods and spices being traded on his island, the sultan, a man of poetic bent, named his new city Dar es Salaam (Haven of Peace). And peacefully was how it spent its first few years, too, as the sultan died soon after founding the city, allowing Bagamoyo, a dhow port to the north, to emerge as the pre-eminent harbour on this particular stretch of the east coast. Missionaries from Europe added fresh impetus to Dar with their arrival in the 1880s but it was the coming of the Germans in 1891 that really gave this city a fillip, the colonials feeling that the harbour here was more suitable to their steam-powered craft than Bagamoyo. Having made Dar their seat of power, it remained the capital until 1973 when the Tanzanian government decided to move the legislature to Dodoma, smack in the geometric heart of the country – which probably seemed like a good idea at the time, until somebody pointed out the shortage of water and other basic amenities there.

So while the capital may be Dodoma, much of the politicking and indeed everything else of importance takes place here in Dar. For tourists, there's nothing particularly special to warrant a long stay in this city; but by the same token, don't fret too much if you do have to spend some time in Dar: it's pleasant, it's laidback and, compared to Nairobi, it's a whole lot saner too.

ARRIVAL

Though safer than arriving in Nairobi, it still pays to be on your guard when landing in Dar: like a recently hatched turtle taking to the ocean for the first time, you are at your most vulnerable when you land in a new country – and even in The Haven of Peace there are still plenty of sharks out there. There are two terminals at Dar airport, about 700m apart from each other. Whether arriving from overseas or within Tanzania, the chances are you will land at **Terminal Two**, the busier of the two, about 12km out from the town centre to the west. The taxi counter has a set rate of Ts25,000 to take you into the centre, or you could try to negotiate a lower rate with the drivers themselves. You could also walk to the main road (around 500m) and take a **dalla-dalla** into town for Ts300, though this is not really practical if you have a lot of luggage. **Going to the airport**, look for the dalla-dalla signed either 'airport' or U/Ndege (short for Uwanja wa Ndege, Ts400) that departs from the seafront; leave in plenty of time – it can take well over an hour and drops you a ten-minute walk away. From town a taxi's a little cheaper at Ts15,000-20,000.

Arriving by bus you'll be dropped either at the Ubungo Bus Station or, if you're very lucky, in the city centre at Kisutu Bus Station. If arriving at Ubungo, a taxi will cost around Ts8000 to the centre.

ORIENTATION AND GETTING AROUND

Navigating your way around central Dar is no easy task. Things are fairly straightforward on the coast, where Kivukoni Road/Ocean Road follows the shore from the train station to the Ocean Road Hospital and beyond. But step back from the shore and you find yourself in a labyrinth of small streets, many of which curve imperceptibly but dramatically enough to confuse and disorientate. Keep the map on p147 with you, using it first to help you find your way to the tourist office (see below) where they have a more detailed and extensive map of the city. They will also be able to help you out with the city's **public transport** system, which can also be rather confusing. Buses and dalla-dallas ply all the main routes, though finding where they start and stop can be difficult. Ask locals, your hotel, or take a cab. Fortunately, central Dar is compact enough to walk around.

SERVICES

Tourist office

There's a tourist office in the Matasalamat Building on Samora Avenue (Mon-Fri 8am-4pm, Sat 8.30am-12.30pm; ☎ 022-213 1555, 🖳 ttb2@ud.co.tz). It depends on who is working there when you call in but we found the staff to be helpful, knowledgeable and patient. They may well have a copy of the free bi-monthly *Dar Guide* magazine, too, the most useful run-down of the city.

Banks

There are **cashpoints** at Standard Chartered on Garden Avenue (just up from the museum) and Sokoine Drive, and a Barclays **ATM** opposite the Mövenpick Hotel. Of the local banks, Bank Exim has Mastercard cashpoints (there's one on Sokoine opposite the Azania Front Lutheran Church), while the NBC also has Visa ATMs; their main branch is on the corner opposite the Lutheran Church and the New Africa Hotel. For later opening hours, try the moneychangers down Samora Avenue. The AMEX rep is Rickshaw Travels in Peugeot House on Mwinyi Road.

❏ **Diplomatic missions in Dar es Salaam**

Belgium 5 Ocean Rd; ☎ 022-211 2688

Burundi Lugalo Rd, Plot No.1007, Upanga East, PO Box 2752;
  ☎ 022-212 6827/ 211 3710

Canada 38 Mirambo St, Garden Ave; ☎ 022-211 2837

Democratic Republic of Congo 438 Malik Rd, Upanga; ☎ 022-215 0282

Denmark Ghana Ave, PO Box 9171; ☎ 022-211 3887/90

Egypt 24 Garden Ave; ☎ 022-211 3591/211 7622

Finland Mirambo St, Garden Ave; ☎ 022-211 9170/211 8788

France Ali Hassan Mwinyi Rd, Angle Kulimani Rd; ☎ 022-266 6021/3

Germany NIC Life Building, 10th Floor, Samora Ave; ☎ 022-211 7409/15

Ireland 353 Toure Drive, Oysterbay; ☎ 022-260 2355

Italy Lugalo Rd (Upanga), PO Box 2106; ☎ 022-211 5935/6

Japan Plot 1018 Upanga Rd, PO Box 2577; ☎ 022-211 5827/29

Kenya 14th floor, NIC Investment House, PO Box 5231; ☎ 022-211 2955

Malawi NIC Life Building, 6th Floor, PO Box 7616; ☎ 022-211 3240/41

Norway Mirambo St/Garden Ave junction, PO Box 2646; ☎ 022-211 3366

Poland 63 Ali Khan Rd, Upanga, PO Box 2188; ☎ 022-211 5271

Russian Federation Plot 73 Kenyatta Drive, PO Box 1905; ☎ 022-266 6005/6

Rwanda Plot 32 Ali Hassan Mwinyi Rd, PO Box 2918; ☎ 022-213 0119

South Africa Plot 1338/39 Mwaya Rd, Masaki, PO Box 10723; ☎ 022-260 1800

South Korea Plot 1349, Haile Selassie Rd, Msasani Peninsula, PO Box 1154;
  ☎ 022-266 2000/260 0496/260 0499

Spain Plot 99B Kinondoni Rd, PO Box 842; ☎ 022-266 6018/266 6936

Sudan 64 Upanga Rd, PO Box 2266; ☎ 022-513 2022

Sweden Mirambo St, Garden Ave, PO Box 9274; ☎ 022-211 1265/68/211 1235/40

Switzerland 17 Kenyatta Drive, PO Box 2454; ☎ 022-266 6008/9

Uganda Extelcoms Building, Floor 7, Samora Machel Ave, PO Box 6237;
  ☎ 022-266 7391

UK Umoja House, PO Box 9200; ☎ 022-211 0101

United States 686 Old Bagamoyo Rd, Msasani, PO Box 9123; ☎ 022-266 8001

Zambia Plot 5, Junction of Ohio/Sokoine Drive, PO Box 2525; ☎ 022-512 7261

Zimbabwe 6th floor, NIC Life Building, Sokoine Drive, PO Box 20762;
  ☎ 022-211 6789

❏ Dar's area code is ☎ 022. If phoning from outside Tanzania dial ☎ +255-22. We have included the area code in the phone numbers of this chapter.

Communications

The main **post office** is on Maktaba/Azikiwe Street (Mon-Fri 8am-4.30pm, Sat 9am-noon). The **telephone office** is on Bridge Street. You won't have any trouble finding an **internet** café in Dar; they are everywhere. Most tourists head for the one in the Safari Inn (see below), probably just because of its convenient location, though it does offer an efficient service.

Trekking agencies

You *can* organize your Kili trek from here, though unless there are mitigating circumstances you'd be daft to do so, it being far easier, safer and cheaper to travel to Moshi and arrange it from there. The following travel agents are the most well known, and two have branches in Arusha too.

● **Coastal Travels** Upanga Road, (PO Box 3052, ☎ 022-2117959; 🖳 safari @coastal.cc, aviation@coastal.cc). The most established agent in the city with offices in both Dar es Salaam and Zanzibar airports, as well as Arusha.

● **Rickshaw Travels** (PO Box 1889, ☎ 022-211 4094), Peugeot House, AH Mwinyi Road. Expensive but reliable.

WHERE TO STAY   (see map p147)

The following are listed in **price order**, with the **cheapest first**. For details of the abbreviations, see overleaf.

● *YWCA* (☎ 022-213 5457) Ghana Ave; sgl/dbl Ts13,000/17,000. Perhaps the most popular budget hostel currently operating, the YWCA (men are allowed too) has pretty basic accommodation but it's clean, cheap and has a good location by the post office.

● *Safari Inn* (☎ 022-213 8101; 🖳 safari-inn@lycos.com) Band St, off Libya Street; s/c sgl/dbl Ts18,000/24,000, or Ts20,000/26,000 with TV; with air-con Ts26,500 s/c dbl. Still a popular budget choice, despite the best efforts of the miserable staff to frighten travellers away. All the rooms are en suite, though some are a bit gloomy with many lacking windows. There's a small but popular internet café here too. The room rates include something that resembles a breakfast, only smaller.

● *Jambo Inn* (☎ 022-211 0711) Libya St; s/c sgl/dbl with fan Ts20,000/30,000. Just a few doors down from the Safari (see above) on Libya Street, the Jambo is more welcoming, cleaner, all the rooms have windows and the people are way friendlier. The restaurant serves Indian, English and Chinese and very tasty it is too, even if a lot of the items on the menu often aren't available. Also has an internet café. Recommended.

> ❏ **Abbreviations**
> Throughout this book we have used the following abbreviations when writing about
> accommodation: **s/c** means self-contained, as in en suite (ie the room comes with a
> bathroom); **sgl/dbl/tpl** means single/double/triple rooms. For example, where we
> have written 'sgl/dbl/tpl US$35/40/45', we mean that a single room costs US$35 per
> night, a double US$40, and a triple US$45.

● *Econolodge* (☎ 022-211 6048; 💻 www.econohotel.8m.com), Libya St; s/c
sgl/dbl/tpl Ts20,000/27,000/35,000, or Ts33,000/38,000/45,000 with air-con.
Not quite as 'Econo' as it makes out, this is the smartest in the huddle of hotels
around Libya St. Singles, doubles and triples are spacious and all come with
bathroom. Some tourists have complained about the hassle from touts, however.
● *Starlight Hotel* (☎ 022-211 9387) Bibi Titi Mohamed St; US$51/60 s/c sgl/dbl.
Catering mainly for local businessmen and warranting a mention largely due to
its position in the mid-range price bracket, the Starlight looks impersonal but is
friendly, central and – with all 150 rooms equipped with air-con, hot water, TV
and fridge – fair value too.
● *Peacock Hotel* (☎ 022-212 0334; 💻 www.peacock-hotel.co.tz) Bibi Titi
Mohamed St; s/c sgl/dbl US$100/120; bigger s/c sgl/dbl rooms (with sofas!)
US$125/145. Refreshingly free of any pretension, this ugly but friendly establishment
is seeing more and more tourists. It's OK, with all the facilities you'd
expect from a hotel of this class, and it's so nice to be welcomed by receptionists
who seem genuinely glad you've dropped in.
● *New Africa Hotel* (☎ 022-211 7050; 💻 www.newafricahotel.com) corner of
Azikiwe/Sokoine Drive; s/c US$190, US$200 for sea view, up to US$300 in the
executive suite. In a better location than the Mövenpick Hotel (see p148), its
nearest rival, though not with quite the same level of sophistication, the New
Africa stands on the site of the Germans' original Kaiserhof. Home to Dar's
main casino as well as a host of bars and restaurants, the New Africa's rooms
have everything you'd expect from a hotel of this calibre, including mini-bar,
satellite TV, telephones with internet hook-up and so on. If you're willing to pay

Town plan key

🏠	Where to stay	ⓘ	Tourist Information	🕇	Church/cathedral
○	Where to eat	📖	Library/bookstore	🕓🕙	Bus station/stop
Λ	Campsite	Ⓢ	Internet	Ⓣ	Telephone office
⊠	Post office	🏛	Museum/gallery	—▭—	Rail line & station
Ⓢ	Bank/ATM	Ⓒ	Mosque	●	Other

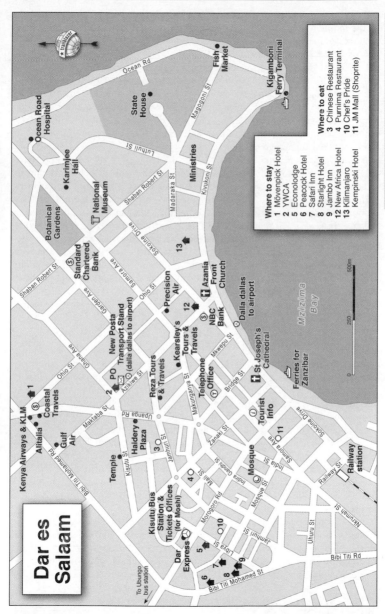

Dar es Salaam

Where to stay
1 Mövenpick Hotel
2 YWCA
5 Econolodge
6 Peacock Hotel
7 Safari Inn
8 Starlight Hotel
9 Jambo Inn
12 New Africa Hotel
13 Kilimanjaro
Kempinski Hotel

Where to eat
3 Chinese Restaurant
4 Purnima Restaurant
10 Chef's Pride
11 JM Mall (Shoprite)

over a hundred dollars for all this, you may as well pay the extra US$10 for one of the rooms with a sea view. A courtesy airport shuttle is available to passengers on certain flights.

● *Mövenpick Royal Palm Hotel* (☎ 022-211 2416, 🖥 www.moevenpick-dares salaam.com) Ohio Street; s/c rooms US$330 up to US$3900 for the presidential suite. This used to be the top place in the town centre before the arrival of the Kempinski and boasts a swimming pool, gym and all mod-cons, as well as being the base for Hertz, British Airways, Rickshaw Travels and a Bureau de Change that stays open from 8am to 8pm. Even if you're not staying here, do call in to have a peek at the photos of Kili that adorn the shopping walkway, or simply to take advantage of their fierce air-con.

● *Kilimanjaro Kempinski Hotel* (☎ 022-213 1111; 🖥 www.kempinski-dares salaam.com) Kivukoni St; rooms €240 up to, wait for it, €3080 for the presidential suite. If you've got a rucksack full of money you won't find a more refined or, given its name, *appropriate* place to stay. Actually, the hotel's association with the mountain is tenuous, other than the fact that you need a bank balance the size of Kilimanjaro to be able to stay here. However, it *is* gorgeous, glitzy, sophisticated and shiny and the rooms feature what they describe as 'elegantly tropical' interiors, wood floors, high-speed and wireless internet access, international satellite LCD TV with movie channels, multilingual telephone voicemail and all the other bits 'n' bobs you'd expect of a hotel of this standard. The location overlooking the Indian Ocean is great, too.

WHERE TO EAT

Many eateries in Dar close on Sundays. One that doesn't, and which has for many years been the most popular place in town amongst travellers – and indeed amongst many locals too – is *Chef's Pride* on Chagga Street. It is a popularity that is well deserved: tasty, huge portions of food, fair prices, a location close to the cheaper hotels and English football on the telly is a combination that for some is hard to resist, and many travellers, having eaten here once, venture nowhere else in the city. Nearby is the restaurant at the Jambo Inn (see p145) which is pleasant and a good option if you want a change from Chef's Pride.

For alternative cheap-eats the Indian quarter of central Dar, particularly around the junction of Indira Gandhi and Zanaki streets, is as good a place as any to start looking. *Purnima* on Zanaki Street is a great little place, where a plate of bhajias with various sauces and curds will make you poorer by only Ts1000 or so. There are other similar places around here – follow your nose to find them.

For more refined cuisine in plusher surroundings, try the restaurants in the upmarket hotels, including the *Sawasdee Thai* or the Indian *Bandari Grill*, both at the New Africa (see p146), and the *Serengeti Buffet Restaurant* at the Mövenpick (see above). Your bank manager won't thank you for dining here, but your stomach certainly will.

A TOUR OF THE CITY

None of Dar's attractions is going to make your eyes pop out on springs from their sockets, but the following tour is fine for those with time to kill in the city and a cursory interest in the place. For those in a hurry, the National Museum at least is worth seeing (see box below), being the most absorbing and, for Kili-bound trekkers, the most relevant attraction in Dar.

One word of warning: if any of the streets listed below seem unhealthily deserted – the lanes around State House and Ocean Road in particular can be a little *too* quiet at times – consider taking an alternative and safer route.

Your tour begins around the back of the **Azania Front Lutheran Church**, built on the seafront at the turn of the century by German missionaries. Heading east along the promenade past many old colonial buildings now used by the Tanzanian authorities to house various ministries, walk round the south-eastern tip of the peninsula and on to the **fish market**, Dar's most vibrant attraction. Having ensured all money and valuables are securely tucked away, feel free to take a wander around – it's at its best early in the morning – and see what the

---

 National Museum

(Open 9.30am-6pm daily; Ts6500, Ts2600 for students.) Please note that Tanzania's National Museum is currently undergoing a major overhaul and **the following description may well be out of date** by the time you arrive. Nevertheless, we hope some of the exhibits remain. It's true that the museum fares badly when compared to Kenya's version but is still mildly diverting at times and a cool escape from the heat of the day. And if you manage to avoid the marauding school parties you may well have the entire complex to yourself, with only the cleaner for occasional company.

Begin your tour by walking through the back door to a small courtyard, home to a small **memorial garden** dedicated to the twelve victims who perished in the US Embassy bombing in Dar on 7 August 1998. Similar in style to the one in Nairobi (see p158), the **sculpture** here includes twisted metal and a window pane shattered by the blast, as well as a face emerging from concrete, presumably recalling those who were buried in the rubble.

The original museum building that stands beyond is of only minor interest with its displays of zoological and ethnographic items. If you hunt around in the latter you'll find a couple of old Chagga storage baskets and some interesting old photos of tribal customs, but nothing to keep you in the musty old building for too long.

The main building, however, is a different story. Here you'll find a number of absorbing displays including the **Hall of Man**, which describes our evolution with the help of some apposite objects from Leakey's discoveries at **Olduvai Gorge**, as well as a few items of particular interest to those climbing Kili in the **History Gallery** upstairs, which maps out in concise and thorough detail the story of Tanzania. Take your time wandering around – it's fascinating. Indeed, our only gripe is that the letter from Hans Meyer (the original conqueror of Kilimanjaro) to the German representative in Zanzibar, in which he begs for a ransom of 10,000 rupees to be paid to Chief Abushiri, by whom he had been taken hostage during his second expedition to Kilimanjaro (see p116), has been removed for some reason.

local fishermen have managed to catch overnight. Retracing your steps for a few metres, take the first turning on the right (west) up Magogoni Street. Surrounded by spacious grounds, **State House**, built by the British in the years following World War One, stands to your right; you will get your best view of the house itself at the very end of the road at the junction with Luthuli St. Crossing this junction and continuing straight on along Shaban Robert St, to your right is the **National Museum** (see the box on p149); a right turn after that will land you on one of the prettier roads in central Dar, the eastern end of Samora Avenue, with the **botanical gardens** to your left and, on the opposite side towards the end of the street, steeple-topped **Karimjee Hall**, where Nyerere (see p78) was sworn in as Tanzania's first president. Facing the end of the street and hidden behind high walls is the now-defunct **Ocean Road Hospital**, another German building dating back to the last years of the nineteenth century. Stroll round to the sea-facing front of the hospital to study the rather curious architecture, a hybrid of Arabic and European styles, and to view the curious spiked mace that sits atop the hospital roof.

From here you have two choices: one is to continue your walk along the coast road back to the fish market and on to the church; the other is to return to the junction behind the hospital, press on for another hundred metres or so southwards, then take a right and amble along attractive, tree-shaded Sokoine Drive back to the Lutheran church.

MOVING ON – TO KILIMANJARO

Buses

Some ticket offices are located in the Kisutu terminal in the heart of downtown on Libya Street, including Dar Express, currently the best of the coach operators travelling to Moshi and Arusha. Unfortunately, the buses do not depart from there but from Ubungo, a new terminal a fair distance out of town. A taxi from Kisutu to Ubungo will set you back about Ts8000; you can try to catch a dalla dalla from outside the Peacock on Bibi Titi Mohammed Road but it's not easy.

Choose your bus company carefully: despite the presence of speed ramps and traffic police, the Dar to Moshi highway is notorious for accidents and often it's the same few bus companies that are involved. Unfortunately, the number of touts operating at both of Dar's stations means that it can be difficult to buy the ticket you want. Be persistent and insistent and take anything the touts say with a pinch – no, make that a huge bucket – of salt. The buses associated with the hotels in Moshi, namely Buffalo and Kindoroko, have the worst reputations.

Flights

Air Tanzania still operate local flights, with one service a day to Kilimanjaro Airport from Dar. The flight takes about an hour and 20 minutes. Precision Air fly three times daily to Kilimanjaro from Dar, as well as twice or three times a day to Arusha Airport. Air Excel have a daily flight to **Arusha Airport** at 4.20pm (2hr 5min; US$210 plus US$11 tax), while Coastal Aviation on Upanga Road have daily flights from Dar to Arusha at 9am, arriving at 11am.

Nairobi

As rough as a lion's tongue, East Africa's largest city has come quite a long way since its inception in May 1899 as a humble railway supply depot on the Mombasa to Kampala line. It is a city that has suffered much from plagues, fire and reconstruction – and that was just in its first ten years – yet it has obstinately continued to prosper and grow, rising from a population of exactly zero in 1898 to around 3 million today. Official recognition of the city's increasing importance arrived in 1907 when the British made it the capital of their East African territories, and you can still find the occasional colonial relic in the city today, from the Indian-influenced architecture of a few downtown buildings (shipped over from the subcontinent, the Indians supplied much of the labour force used in building the railway) to some distinctly elegant hotels and orderly public gardens (including one, just to the north of Kenyatta Avenue, which still bears a statue of Queen Victoria). But if you came with the specific purpose of seeing a faded colonial city you'll be disappointed: because as the capital of the Kenyan republic and the UN's fourth official 'World Centre', Nairobi is East Africa's most modern, prosperous and glamorous metropolis. It is also, first and foremost, black Africa at its loudest and proudest.

SECURITY

A few years back some genius dubbed Kenya's capital 'Nairobberi', and lesser geniuses have been retreading that joke ever since. Tired as the gag may be, however, it does still have relevance, for Nairobi's reputation as East Africa's Capital of Crime is well founded.

To be fair, the authorities are trying to improve matters, at least in the centre, blocking off many of the darker backstreets. There seem to be fewer beggars and touts populating the centre too. There is also a 'beautification' programme going on, which seems to involve a lot of tree-planting.

Nevertheless, the need to be wary when out on the streets of Nairobi remains paramount. The most notorious hotspot is the area immediately to the **east of Moi Avenue**, including **River Road** and the bus stations, a popular location with travellers because of the cheap hotels there. During the daytime violent robbery is rare though certainly not unheard of, simply because it's so packed with people; pickpocketing, on the other hand, is rife at this time, probably for the same reason. At night, both techniques are common.

To avoid becoming another victim, be vigilant, leave valuables with the hotel (having first checked their security procedures) and make sure that they give you a receipt for any goods deposited too. Furthermore, tuck moneybelts under your clothing and don't walk around at night but take a taxi, even if it's for just a few hundred metres.

It can only be to your advantage if you are over-cautious for your first couple of days in the capital. After that, if you're still staying here, you can begin to appreciate Nairobi's charms – which do exist, and are not entirely inconsiderable – and can begin to moan, like the rest of the travellers here, about how unfair guidebook writers are about Kenya's capital.

ARRIVAL

If you haven't got a **visa** you should get one before passing through passport control. Payment is accepted in US dollars, euros or pounds sterling only.

Passing through **immigration**, **luggage collection** is straight down the stairs. Once again be vigilant and, having retrieved your bags, check that nothing is missing: when climbing Kilimanjaro, there are few things more annoying than finding that your thermally insulated mountain hat that you thought was safely tucked away in the side-pocket of your rucksack had in fact been taken by a light-fingered baggage handler and is now being used as a makeshift tea cosy in the staffroom of Jomo Kenyatta Airport.

Entering the arrivals' hall after customs, to your right is a **moneychanger** offering, as moneychangers are wont to do at airports worldwide, dismal rates, and an **ATM** that accepts Visa cards – your best bet for a fair rate at the airport, though you could pay for your cab in dollars and wait to change money in town.

You have a number of choices in tackling the 15km from the airport to the centre of Nairobi. Taxis cost about Ks1300 with bargaining, or before 8pm you can take the number 34 bus that runs down River Road (Ks50). Remember to be careful of pickpockets on this route.

Arrive in Nairobi by shuttle bus and, if they don't drop you off at your hotel, you'll probably be dropped off by Jevanjee Gardens right in the heart of the action (the exception being passengers on the Impala Shuttle who will be dropped off first at the Silver Springs Hotel). **Arrive by bus**, on the other hand, and you could well be dropped off near infamous River Road – take care!

ORIENTATION AND GETTING AROUND

Despite decades of unplanned growth, a mass of sprawling suburbs and a wholesale aversion to street numbers, central Nairobi is actually very easy to navigate, with nearly everything of interest to the traveller within walking distance of Kenyatta Avenue. A couple of obvious landmarks are the enormous **KANU Tower**, to the south of City Hall, and the even more enormous **Nation Centre**, a red Meccano-type structure nestling between two giant cylindrical towers just off the eastern end of the avenue. Central Nairobi is fairly compact and the fit will be able to walk everywhere. Buses and matatus (Kenyan minibuses) run from early morning to late at night, though **we strongly advise you to take taxis after dark**. During the day things are much safer, though keep your wits about you. In the text we give the numbers of some of the buses you may need.

SERVICES

Banks

Banks are usually open Mon-Fri 9am-3pm, Sat 9-11am; foreign exchange bureaux open later though on Saturday often they too close early (usually noon). Many of the banks have **ATM**s (cash machines) too, with most accepting Visa cards. Be on your guard for onlookers when withdrawing money from an ATM.

Communications

Big, bright and gleaming, the new **post office** (Mon-Fri 7.30am-6pm) occupies a fairly large slice of valuable real estate at the western end of Kenyatta Avenue. Registered, recorded and normal deliveries can be made here and there's a poste restante counter (number 15). Upstairs on the second floor is one of the town's main **telephone** exchanges: to phone abroad the cheapest method is to pick up a Telcom Card (they come in denominations of Ks100, 200, 500, 1000 and 2000) from the counter, then use one of the phones to dial 888, then the country code and then the number in the normal way. The rates to the UK are Ks15 per minute.

You'll have no trouble finding an **internet** café in the centre. Surf City, just off Jevanjee Gardens (Ks0.50 per minute), is reliable though there are doubtless others closer to you that are just as competent and speedy. **Wireless** internet is only just starting to become popular though the Wildebeest Campsite (see p156) has it (Ks300 per day for guests).

❏ Nine useful things to know about Nairobi

● Citizens of most countries need a **visa** for Kenya, including Britain and the US. Get your visa before leaving home. You can buy one at Nairobi's Jomo Kenyatta Airport, though this takes time.

● One thing to remember: as long as you remain in East Africa there is no need to buy a multiple-entry Kenyan visa if you are flying into Kenya but wish to visit Tanzania or Uganda too, as long as you stay in those countries for less than two weeks and providing, of course, your Kenyan visa has not expired by the time you return to Kenya.

● The official **language** of Kenya is Swahili. For a quick guide to Swahili, see p338. In addition, many Kenyans speak both their own tribal language and English, which is widely spoken everywhere.

● As with Tanzania, Kenya is **three hours ahead of GMT**. Note that, in addition to standard time, many locals use **Swahili time**, which runs from dawn to dusk (or 6am to 6pm to be precise). See p87 for details on how to convert between East African time and Swahili time.

● The Kenyan **currency** is the shilling (Ks). At the time of writing, €1=Ks111, US$1=Ks75, UK£1=Ks124. Don't change money on the street.

● Kenya's **electricity supply** uses the British-style three-pin plugs on 220-240V.

● The **international dialling code** for Kenya is ☎ 254.

● The **emergency telephone number** is ☎ 999.

● The **opening hours** in Kenya are typically 8am to 5 or 6pm.

❏ **Diplomatic missions in Nairobi**

Australia Riverside Drive, 400m off Chiromo Rd (PO Box 39341;
☎ 020-445 035)
Belgium Limuru Rd, Muthaiga (PO Box 30461; ☎ 020-741 564)
Canada Comcraft House, Haile Selassie Ave (PO Box 43778; ☎ 020-214 804)
Denmark HFCK Building, 11th floor, Kenyatta Ave/Koinange St (PO Box 40412;
☎ 020-331 088)
France Barclays Plaza, 9th floor, Loita St (PO Box 41784; ☎ 020-339 978)
Japan 15th floor, ICEA Building, Kenyatta Ave (PO Box 60202; ☎ 020-332 956)
Thailand Rose Ave, off Denis Pritt Rd (PO Box 58349; ☎ 020-715 800)
UK Upper Hill Rd (PO Box 30465; ☎ 020-714 699)
United States United States Information Service, Barclays Plaza, Loita St
(PO Box 30137; ☎ 020-334 141).

Camping equipment

Remember that you can probably rent everything you need from your trekking
agency, or Gladys Adventure in Moshi (p193) or from the stall at Marangu Gate;
see p246. But if you're not going there, **Atul's** (☎ 020-228064; Mon-Fri 9am-
noon, 2-5pm, Sat 9am-noon, 2.30-4pm) on Biashara St, which is more a haber-
dashery than anything else, is the only place in the city that rents out camping
gear. However, they're not cheap: Ks250 per day for a down sleeping bag for
example (plus Ks3000 returnable deposit); they also have smaller items such as
water bottles and purifiers for rent. To be fair, they've not raised their prices since
the first edition of this guide was published.

Trekking agencies

It's a lot cheaper to book your trek in Tanzania. Still, many like to see what's on
offer here and there is a good company operating out of Nairobi. **Kibo Slopes
Safaris** (PO Box 58064; ☎ 020-3861 509; 🖳 www.kiboslopessafaris.com) are
a smart and professionally run agent offering Kilimanjaro treks combined with
a Kenyan safari. Using their own climbing outfit in Tanzania, Kibo Slopes
Tanzania, in Arusha, they are a KPAP partner. Prices for a safari and Kili climb
combination are steep, however, at US$5194 for 11 days for one person,
US$3837 each for two people. The trek itself is conducted on the Lemosho Route,
before diverging off to head round the Kili's northern side, while the safari takes
you to Kenya's Amboseli National Park. You can find a branch of their office in
the compound of the Silver Springs Hotel where the Impala Shuttle pulls up.

WHERE TO STAY

The following list of hostels and hotels is arranged with the cheapest first. Those
intending to **camp** should check out Wildebeest Campsite (Ks500 per person),
listed below – currently the best-value place for backpackers to stay in Nairobi.
River Road remains the cheapest area, though tourist-friendly hostels are slowly
disappearing from the area and those that remain are distinctly scruffy. If you can

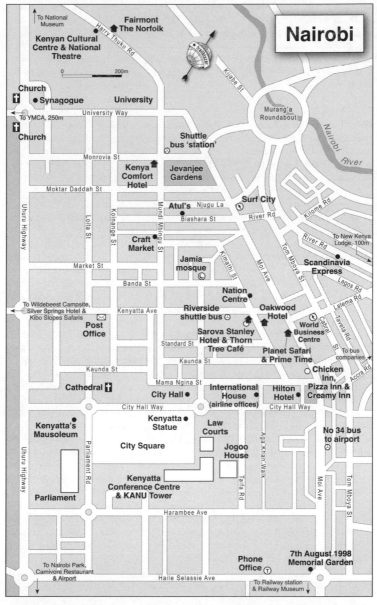

Nairobi

To National Museum

Fairmont The Norfolk

Kenyan Cultural Centre & National Theatre

Harry Thuku Rd

Kjabe St

Church

Synagogue

University

To YMCA, 250m

University Way

Murang'a Roundabout

Nairobi River

Church

Shuttle bus 'station'

Monrovia St

Kenya Comfort Hotel

Jevanjee Gardens

Moktar Daddah St

Mundi Mbingu St

Atul's

Njugu La

Surf City

River Rd

Kilome Rd

Biashara St

River Rd

To New Kenya Lodge, 100m

Loita St

Koinange St

Craft Market

Jamia mosque

Kimathi St

Mol Ave

Tom Mboya St

Scandinavia Express

Lagos Rd

Market St

Banda St

Nation Centre

Oakwood Hotel

Lalema Rd

Taveta Rd

To Wildebeest Campsite, Silver Springs Hotel & Kibo Slopes Safaris

Kenyatta Ave

Riverside shuttle bus

Post Office

Standard St

Sarova Stanley Hotel & Thorn Tree Café

World Business Centre

Cabral St

To bus companies

Planet Safari & Prime Time

Accra Rd

Kaunda St

Kaunda St

Chicken Inn, Pizza Inn & Creamy Inn

Cathedral

Mama Ngina St

International House (airline offices)

Hilton Hotel

City Hall

City Hall Way

City Hall Way

Kenyatta's Mausoleum

Kenyatta Statue

Law Courts

No 34 bus to airport

City Square

Jogoo House

Aga-Khan Walk

Mol Ave

Tom Mboya St

Parliament Rd

Uhuru Highway

Parliament

Kenyatta Conference Centre & KANU Tower

Taifa Rd

Harambee Ave

To Nairobi Park, Carnivore Restaurant & Airport

Phone Office

7th August 1998 Memorial Garden

Haile Selassie Ave

To Railway station & Railway Museum

0   200m

afford the extra few shillings, you'll be grateful you stayed in the Wildebeest.

● *Wildebeest Campsite* (☎ 020-210 3505; 🖳 www.wildebeesttravels.com) Kibera Road, off Ngong Road; rates are Ks800 in a dorm, Ks1500-2000 single, Ks1800-2500 double; deluxe tents Ks4000/5000 sgl/dbl. Simply put, this is a wonderful place and proves that sleeping cheap in Nairobi doesn't have to mean bedding down in a fleapit on River Road. Housed in a lovely old colonial building to the west of Uhuru Park, the Wildebeest is efficiently run by an Australian family. The rooms are clean and surprisingly pleasant but it's the fragrant, bird-filled tropical grounds that truly steal the show, bordered as they are by deluxe en-suite safari tents that provide some of the most appealing accommodation in the capital, with cotton sheets and full electricity. Food and wi-fi internet are also available. All in all, definitely worth the trip out of town, whatever your budget.

● *New Kenya Lodge* (☎ 020-222 2202; 🖳 www.nksafari.com) River Road opposite the end of Latema Road; rates are Ks300 in a dorm, Ks500 sgl, Ks700 dbl. Another scruffy, old-style backpacker place that's friendly enough. It does have a few private rooms but the chances are they'll be full and you'll be forced to share a dorm. Might be an idea to ring ahead. Like most such places, New Kenya also has a safari operation.

● *YMCA* (☎ 020-272 4116/7; 🖳 www.kenyaymca.net) University Way; non s/c dorm/sgl/dbl Ks800/920/1500; s/c dorm/sgl/dbl Ks900/1200/1800; add Ks400-half-board, Ks800 full-board. Despite the name, women, atheists and the elderly are all welcome at this friendly, secure hostel, a fair choice for those on a budget who don't fancy their chances in the hurly-burly of the River Road area but still want to be reasonably close to town. The real clincher, however, is the pool (Ks100 for non-residents).

● *Kenya Comfort Hotel* (☎ 020-317 605; 🖳 www.kenyacomfort.com) Jevanjee Gardens. Superbly situated just five minutes north of Kenyatta Avenue – and, more importantly, right next to where the shuttle buses pull in, which could be very handy if you've taken the afternoon shuttle and arrived after dark. Though it looks fairly petit, features include a sauna and steam room, internet and 91 bedrooms. With rates starting at US$38/56/70 for s/c sgl/dbl/tpl rising to US$42/60/74 if you want a TV and wardrobe thrown in, this is not a bad deal for central Nairobi and one of the better mid-range choices.

● *Oakwood Hotel* (☎ 020-220 592/3; 🖳 www.madahotels.com/oakwood/) Kimathi Street; s/c sgl/dbl/tpl US$50/60/80 including breakfast. Wooden floors, wooden walls, wooden ceiling and wooden doors – spending a night at the Oakwood can make you feel like Charles II hiding from Parliament. The Oakwood's strengths are its location opposite the Thorn Tree Café, its elegant antique lift, the digital satellite TV and video in each room and the vague whiff of colonial charm. It's main drawback is the casino that occupies much of the ground floor of the building, desecrating the once-charming façade. Nevertheless, though not spectacular this 1940s' hotel is convenient and reasonable enough value.

● *Silver Springs Hotel* (☎ 020-272 2451; 🖳 www.silversprings-hotel.com) Out of town near the hospital, this is nevertheless a fine choice, popular in particular with tour groups and the main stop for the Impala shuttle bus. Facilities include a pool, gym and hot-stone massages – perfect post-Kili therapy. Rates start at sgl/dbl Ks12,000/14,000, rising to Ks98,000, all inclusive of breakfast.

● **The Sarova Stanley** (☎ 020-228 830; 🖳 www.sarovahotels.com) corner of Kenyatta Avenue and Kimathi Street; s/c sgl/dbl US$360/400 up to US$970 for presidential suite; breakfast US$24 extra for the cheaper rooms. A luxury hotel with a bit of character, the Stanley first opened its doors to the very well-heeled in 1902 – making it just a few years younger than the city itself. Edward, Prince of Wales, Ernest Hemingway and Hollywood's finest from Ava Gardner to Clark Gable have all rested their eminent heads on the Stanley's sumptuously stuffed pillows. Victorian elegance still abounds, though the demands of the modern client have led to the introduction of a shopping arcade, swimming pool and gymnasium. Also plays host to the Thorn Tree Café (see below).

● **Fairmont The Norfolk** (☎ 020-221 6940; 🖳 www.fairmont.com) Harry Thuku Road; room-only prices start at US$355, rising up to US$515 for the 'Acacia Deluxe' suite; add to these figures around 30% in taxes, and breakfast is an extra US$25. Nairobi's *other* historic hotel, and younger by two years, the Norfolk has been oozing class from its premises since it first opened its doors on Christmas Day 1904. Boasts the same facilities as The Stanley plus a fine collection of carriages and classic cars in the central courtyard and a more peaceful, out-of-town feel.

WHERE TO EAT

Kenya's cuisine is virtually indistinguishable from Tanzania's, being hearty, meaty and with an emphasis firmly on quantity rather than quality. Embodying this description is the legendary tourist-attraction-cum-restaurant, *Carnivore* (Langata Road, near the Nairobi National Park; take a taxi from the town centre), designed specifically for those people whose thoughts upon seeing the playful gambolling of a young impala for the first time is to wonder what it would taste like coated in a spicy barbecue sauce. Actually, the menu has had to be severely reduced in recent years though you can still find ostrich and antelope migrating across the pages most nights, and there are even a few vegetarian options too.

Vying with the celebrity of Carnivore is the *Thorn Tree Café*, something of a Mecca for travellers. Now on its third acacia, the original idea behind planting a tree in the middle of the courtyard was so that travellers could leave messages for other travellers on its thorns. Unfortunately, trees being trees, the roots of the previous two eventually started to undermine the building itself and had to be destroyed. As for the food here, it's a great place for a post-climb breakfast feed-up, while at other times of day it's an Italian restaurant.

For cheaper and more mundane fare, there are any number of fast-food places around River Road and Tom Mboya St, where lunch shouldn't cost more than Ks150 or so (though be warned, 'kebab' is usually a battered sausage containing meat of unknown origin, and not the kind of kebab you'd enjoy on a Friday night after the pubs have closed back in your home country). More upmarket fast-food restaurants include Pizza Inn, Chicken Inn and Creamy Inn, branches of which can be found throughout the city, including near the Hilton Hotel. If you're down near the station, do call in at the restaurant there – with liveried staff and a genteel, restrained atmosphere, it's ideal for those who enjoy a touch of colonial nostalgia, and the prices are good too, with huge meals costing no more than Ks230.

A TOUR OF THE CITY

The number one sight in Nairobi is the National Museum, now reopened following its two-year renovation; details of it can be found opposite.

As for Nairobi's other sights, they can be seen as part of a half- to full-day walking tour. This is best done on a Sunday morning, when the hassle from safari touts is at its lowest and the gospel choirs are out in force on the streets and in the parks. It begins at the the **Railway Museum** (daily 8am-6pm; Ks400). To reach it, from the railway station head west for 5-10 minutes along the road running parallel to the tracks. The museum is a gem. If it's possible to feel nostalgia for a time that one never knew and a place that one has never visited before, then this is the museum that will prompt those feelings with its fading photos of British royalty riding in the cow-catcher seats and its old posters advertising the newly-opened Uganda railway. This is an endearing little museum and the rusty locomotive graveyard out front is a diverting place for a nose around too.

Returning to the station, head north along Moi Avenue. At the junction with Haile Selassie Avenue is the **former site of the American Embassy**, blown up on 7 August, 1998 by Al-Qaeda. The site has now been landscaped into a very small **remembrance garden** (entry Ks20; Mon-Sat 9am-6pm, Sun 1-6pm), at the back of which is a **Visitor Centre** (Ks400) which explains in greater detail what happened that day. They also show a video, *Seconds From Disaster*, daily at 10am, 1pm and 3pm. Though some may deem the centre overpriced, the garden itself is worth a visit. Here you'll find a memorial bearing the names of the Kenyan victims (who constituted all but 12 of the 263 who died), while at the back of the enclosure is a glass pyramid sculpture containing some of the debris from that day, namely some twisted metal, a lump or two of concrete and a door handle. It's a busy junction, and the Co-op building behind – also badly damaged in the blast – is from the eyesore school of architecture; yet still the park is suffused with an atmosphere of the deepest poignancy.

Continuing north along Moi, City Hall Way runs parallel to Haile Selassie, two blocks north. The **hall** itself lies about 400m along the road on the right (north). Opposite, to your left, is a **statue** of first president Jomo Kenyatta, sitting regally overlooking the city square with his back to the **law courts**. To Kenyatta's left, rising imperiously from fountains, are the **Kenyatta International Conference Centre**, like a giant water-lily bud on the verge of opening, and the vertiginous **KANU Tower**, formerly the tallest building in the city and still one of the ugliest – though most locals would probably take issue with this opinion. (KANU, incidentally, are the most powerful party in Kenya and have dominated the political arena since independence.)

Strolling along City Hall Way – past the **Holy Family Cathedral**, neatly juxtaposed with the casino directly opposite – you'll find to the left of the road, lined with flags and guarded by two black lion statues and several bored-looking guards in neo-colonial ceremonial livery, the object of the Kenyatta statue's gaze: his own **mausoleum**. Next door and adorned with a rather quaint clock tower is the Kenyan **Parliament**, which can be visited; entry is gained through the entrance on Harambee Avenue.

Heading back north along the Uhuru Highway, ten minutes later you'll come to a large roundabout and the centre of worship in the city, surrounded as it is by a **synagogue** (to the north-east) and no less than **four churches** (St Paul's Catholic Chapel to the north-west, with St Andrews behind it up the hill, the First Church of Christ Scientist further along the same road and the city's main Lutheran church on the roundabout's south-western edge). From the roundabout you can continue north for fifteen hot, dusty minutes along the highway to the National Museum (see below), or turn east along University Way, taking a right turn south through the business heart of Nairobi along Muindi Mbingu Street. On the way you might wish to take a short detour to see the craft market or **Jamia Mosque** (Nairobi's most impressive mosque but closed to infidels), before rejoining Kenyatta Avenue. Take a left here, pausing on the way at one of the street vendors to pick up some reading material to peruse at your table, and after a couple of hundred metres you'll come to the final port of call on this walk, the Thorn Tree Café with its overpriced but wonderfully cold beer.

National Museum

(Off Museum Hill, near the Uhuru Highway; daily 7.30am-8pm; Ks800). If you have time to see only one sight in Nairobi, this is definitely the one to head for, an institution that is not only almost as old as the city itself (having been established way back in 1910) but which effortlessly manages the difficult feat of justifying the whopping great entrance fee.

The recent renovation which saw the museum closed for two years has undoubtedly been a blessing. From the diverting Hall of Kenya, which celebrates the nation's cultural and natural wealth, to the bird hall – where a member of every species of Kenya's avifauna has been stuffed and put on display – there is much here to keep you absorbed for hours. Other highlights include a model, faithfully cast in fibreglass, of the **nation's favourite pachyderm**, Ahmed, an elephant so huge its tusks alone weighed a whopping 65kg each; the evolution room, which studies in great detail (but never tediously so) the different theories as to the evolution of man; and even a section on the history of the museum itself. Heading upstairs, photographers will find much to enjoy on the first floor, where two rooms have been given over to the work of local photographer Masud Quraishy and the superb black-and-white work of photojournalist Guillaume Bonn. Hopefully the powers that be will also reconsider the status of the African Rock Art exhibition and make this a permanent feature of the museum too – it deserves to be.

MOVING ON – TO KILIMANJARO

Flights   Precision Air fly three to four times daily between Nairobi and Kilimanjaro International (first one 9am, last 6pm, or 9.30pm Thursdays to Sundays). Fly 540 have one flight daily, leaving at 11.30am and arriving at 12.15pm. Both have their offices at the airport.

   To get to Nairobi International Airport, bus No 34 leaves from virtually opposite the Hilton Hotel (Ks50). Leave plenty of time as this service frequently gets snarled in heavy traffic. Alternatively, a taxi will be about Ks1300.

Coach and shuttle bus   Though there are plenty of **coach** operators willing to take you to Arusha, only two can currently be recommended without hesitation. **Akamba** can be found on Lagos Road near the River Road bus terminus. They have one bus daily at 6.30am and charge Ks1000 to Arusha, Ks1050 to Moshi. Charging a similar amount and leaving at the same time is **Dar Express**, whose offices can be found on River Road upstairs in Veew Plaza (opposite Barclays).

   Far more convenient and comfortable than the coaches are the **shuttle buses**. There are three main companies operating shuttles to Arusha. **Riverside** (☎ 020-229 618) on the third floor of Pan African House, Kenyatta Avenue, is the most established. They have two buses, at 8am (which continues on to Moshi) and 2pm (though note that this will probably not arrive in Arusha until after dark). The fare for non-residents is US$30 to Arusha, or US$35 to Moshi. **Impala** (☎ 020-271 7373) also operates buses to Arusha at 8am and 2pm for US$30. Their offices are a little way from the centre in the Silver Springs Hotel but their service is the best; if you are staying at the Wildebeest (see p156) in Nairobi this is the company to use as their office is only a short taxi ride away. The third firm is **Bobby** (☎ 0722-763 818), on Muindi Mbingu Street very near where the shuttles terminate, which also operates two buses (8am to Moshi via Arusha and 2pm to Arusha only). Their shuttles, like Riverside's and Impala's, depart from Jevanjee Gardens.

Crossing the border between Kenya and Tanzania

The drive between Nairobi and Arusha is fascinating, not least because you may find yourself sharing the road with camels, zebras, impalas, giraffes and Masai tribesmen on bikes. Despite the chaos of hawkers, warriors and travellers that surrounds the Namanga crossing, the border formalities themselves are straightforward enough. On the Kenyan side you'll doubtless have to queue to have your passport stamped, and on the Tanzanian side there's usually a little wait while customs officials cast a cursory eye over your belongings and draw a little chalk cross on your bag. You can change money at the border though the crossing is renowned for its charlatans so you're better off waiting until Arusha.

PART 5: ARUSHA, MOSHI AND MARANGU

Kilimanjaro International Airport

Is Kilimanjaro the first mountain to have its own international airport? It is situated roughly equidistant between Moshi (42km away) and Arusha (50km away), 6km to the south of the main road running between the two.

Arriving
Arriving is straightforward: the terminal is small and you'll instantly be ushered into immigration and passport control where you fill out a Customs Declaration form (if you haven't already done so on the flight). The immigration formalities are easily negotiated – Kilimanjaro is one of only four places in the country where you can pick up a visa if your own country of residence does not have a Tanzanian consulate or embassy. They're currently being very strict about yellow-fever certificates (see p71), so make sure you have yours to hand.

Having collected your baggage, the only thing now separating you from Tanzania is customs from which, safely negotiated, you emerge into the Arrivals Hall, where you'll find a moneychanger offering fair rates for the dollar – though you're better off waiting until you get to town if you can. In a separate cubicle outside the entrance is a Barclays ATM. To get to Moshi or Arusha, about 40 or 50 minutes away respectively, costs US$50 in a taxi or you may be lucky enough to get a shuttle bus depending on which airline you flew in with. See p163 for more details. If you were expecting to be picked up and your lift hasn't arrived, there's a nice drinks stall outside where you can enjoy what, in this author's opinion, is some of the best birdwatching to be had in Tanzania outside of the national parks. The stall also serves up the odd samosa, though for something more substantial there's a reasonable canteen two minutes away just outside the airport grounds, with *kuku na chipsi* (chicken and chips) for Ts4000.

Departing
Leaving Tanzania, things are just as simple. Before heading to the Departure Lounge, if you have any Tanzanian money you want to change you can go and see if the bureau de change in the Arrivals Hall is open (the dollar and Kenyan shilling rates are reasonable, but the other rates are a bit stingy). Back at the Departure Lounge, there are X-ray machines right by the entrance before you've even reached the check-in desks.

Having checked in for your flight, don't be in too much of a hurry to get through to the departure lounge, for there's even less to do on that side of passport control than there is on this side. Instead, peruse the small string of shops, have a coffee from the café, check your email from the two computer terminals by the check-in desks (weirdly, there's also wi-fi from certain places, though I don't know whose this is or if they know they are supplying the public).

Arusha

Arusha may only be Tanzania's fourth largest town but it is, nevertheless, one of considerable consequence. During the days of British rule, Arusha was the symbolic halfway point between Cairo and Cape Town – the two termini of the old British Empire in Africa – and it maintains a central role in African affairs today. It was, for example, the obvious choice as headquarters of the East African Community when Tanzania, Kenya and Uganda were part of an economic union in the seventies; and latterly became the centre for recent attempts to revive this union by the Tripartite Commission for East African Collaboration. More recently it has become the venue for sorting out issues from all over Africa – including the Tanzanian-brokered peace talks on Burundi and, most famously, the Rwanda War Crimes Tribunal, still taking place in the Arusha International Conference Centre, or AICC.

(It should be noted, by the way, that the *actual* midpoint between Cape Town and Cairo lies not here but somewhere in central Congo.)

Time was when a visit to Arusha was a pretty excruciating affair. Relentless badgering from safari touts (known locally as 'flycatchers') would render one's time in the city tiring at best, and few fell in love with the place. The present Minister of Natural Resources and Tourism, Shamsa Mwangunga, has put an end to those bad old days, however. True, the ban she imposed on flycatchers wasn't entirely welcomed – with many of those who lost their jobs threatening to turn to crime as the only alternative way they knew of making a living – but on the whole it has served to make the entire Arusha experience a more enjoyable one for foreigners. Indeed, apart from the odd newspaper seller or somebody trying to sell you dope the place is much more hassle-free nowadays and with the touts gone it has become so much easier to spot and appreciate Arusha's charms. These include some decent restaurants and other tourist amenities, some pretty suburbs filled with jacaranda trees and other blossoms, and a chaotic and occasionally fascinating central market. Nevertheless, with the call of the wild from Kilimanjaro, Ngorongoro and the Serengeti beckoning from east and west, it's a rare tourist who stays long enough to savour them.

ARRIVAL

Arusha Airport (or 'the little airport' as it's commonly called locally to distinguish it from Kilimanjaro International) lies to the west of the city and serves internal flights only. There's not much to the place other than a tiny 'departure lounge', a great little bookshop crammed with English titles, a souvenir shop or two and a couple of cafés. A taxi into town will set you back about Ts12,000 (though they'll ask for almost double that), or you can walk to the main junction (about one hot, dusty kilometre) and wait for a dalla-dalla to pass by (Ts300).

Not to be confused with Arusha Airport, **Kilimanjaro International Airport** lies to the other (eastern) side of town, 44km along and 6km to the south of the road to Moshi. KLM passengers have the chance to catch a shuttle to Arusha with Impala (US$15), their minibuses leaving when full. Precision Air operate their own shuttle service (Ts10,000) for their flights from Dar, Zanzibar, or Shinyanga. Air Tanzania operate a free shuttle for their once-a-day flight to Dar via Zanzibar. Fly in with any other airline, however, such as Ethiopian, and you'll have to take a cab, there being no public transport to and from the airport. A hefty US$50 is charged for this. For details on **going to the airports**, see *Gettting around*, below, and the box on p190.

Arriving in Arusha by **public bus**, expect to be dumped (sometimes literally) at the terminus, reasonably close to the budget hostels at the southern end of Colonel Middleton Road in the western half of town. If you've reached Arusha by **shuttle bus**, on the other hand, hopefully you would have told the driver where you wish to jump out; if not, the chances are you'll be dropped off at the car park of the Bella Luna Hotel and Restaurant on Simeon Road (or the Impala Hotel car park if you took their shuttle). From here you'll have to catch a cab or walk to your destination.

ORIENTATION AND GETTING AROUND

Arusha is bisected by the Goliondoi River Valley, a narrow and shallow dip in the town's topography. The division is more than just geographical: to the west is downtown, the busier, noisier and more fun part of Arusha, where most of the cheap lodgings can be found. To the east of the valley lies the tourist centre, where most hotels, safari companies and better restaurants are located. This eastern section is further divided by a second river, the Themi, that runs along the back of such major landmarks as the Arusha Hotel and the AICC.

Arusha is not a big place, most things are within walking distance of each other and **getting around** is not a major hassle, though to get from one half of town to the other it's a good idea to take a **dalla-dalla**. They charge Ts250 for short trips around town or Ts300 for destinations further afield. To the west of the post office on Sokoine is the stop for dalla-dallas heading west towards **Arusha Airport** (listen out for the touts shouting 'Kisongo'), dropping off passengers by the junction a kilometre from the terminal for Ts300; if you're carrying all your luggage, you've got to be seriously tightfisted to opt for this rather than take a taxi from town (about Ts12,000, though they'll ask for more). Speaking of taxis, they are distinguishable by their white number plates (other vehicles have yellow ones). They charge around Ts2000 for a trip within the town centre – though expect to bargain pretty hard for this.

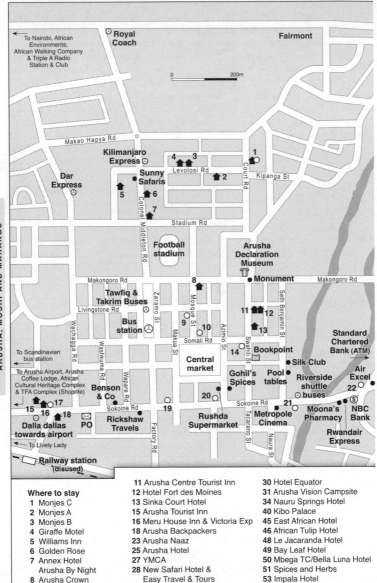

ARUSHA, MOSHI AND MARANGU

Where to stay
1 Monjes C
2 Monjes A
3 Monjes B
4 Giraffe Motel
5 Williams Inn
6 Golden Rose
7 Annex Hotel
  Arusha By Night
8 Arusha Crown

11 Arusha Centre Tourist Inn
12 Hotel Fort des Moines
13 Sinka Court Hotel
15 Arusha Tourist Inn
16 Meru House Inn & Victoria Exp
18 Arusha Backpackers
23 Arusha Naaz
25 Arusha Hotel
27 YMCA
28 New Safari Hotel &
   Easy Travel & Tours

30 Hotel Equator
31 Arusha Vision Campsite
34 Nauru Springs Hotel
40 Kibo Palace
45 East African Hotel
46 African Tulip Hotel
48 Le Jacaranda Hotel
49 Bay Leaf Hotel
50 Mbega TC/Bella Luna Hotel
51 Spices and Herbs
53 Impala Hotel

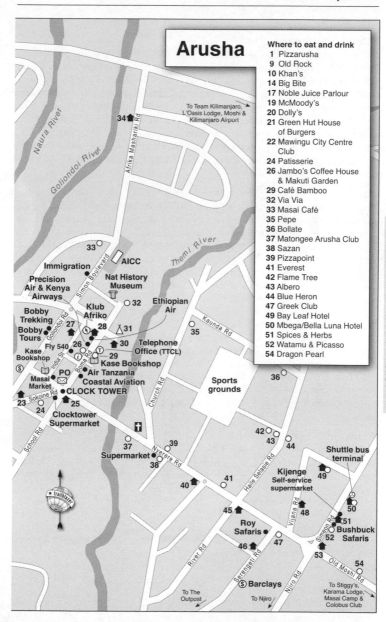

Arusha

Where to eat and drink
1 Pizzarusha
9 Old Rock
10 Khan's
14 Big Bite
17 Noble Juice Parlour
19 McMoody's
20 Dolly's
21 Green Hut House of Burgers
22 Mawingu City Centre Club
24 Patisserie
26 Jambo's Coffee House & Makuti Garden
29 Café Bamboo
32 Via Via
33 Masai Café
35 Pepe
36 Bollate
37 Matongee Arusha Club
38 Sazan
39 Pizzapoint
41 Everest
42 Flame Tree
43 Albero
44 Blue Heron
47 Greek Club
49 Bay Leaf Hotel
50 Mbega/Bella Luna Hotel
51 Spices & Herbs
52 Watamu & Picasso
54 Dragon Pearl

To Team Kilimanjaro, L'Oasis Lodge, Moshi & Kilimanjaro Airport

Naura River
Goliondoi River
Afrika Mashariki Rd
Themi River

33
AICC
Immigration
Nat History Museum
Simon Boulevard
Precision Air & Kenya Airways
Klub Afriko
32
Ethiopian Air
Bobby Trekking
Bobby Tours
Goliondoi Rd
27
28
31
Kaunda Rd
Fly 540
26
30
35
Kase Bookshop
India St
i
Boma Rd
29
Telephone Office (TTCL)
PO
Kase Bookshop
Air Tanzania
Coastal Aviation
Masai Market
CLOCK TOWER
36
25
Sokoine Rd
Church Rd
23
24
Clocktower Supermarket
Sports grounds
School Rd
37
39
42
43
Shuttle bus terminal
Supermarket
38
Nyerere Rd
44
Kijenge Self-service supermarket
49
40
41
Haile Selasie Rd
48
50
45
Vijana Rd
51
Bushbuck Safaris
Roy Safaris
Simeon Rd
52
46
47
53
54
River Rd
Serengeti Rd
Njiro Rd
Old Moshi Rd
Barclays
To The Outpost
To Njiro
To Stiggy's, Karama Lodge, Masai Camp & Colobus Club

★ trailblazer

SERVICES

Tourist information

The **tourist information** is on Boma Road (Mon-Fri 8am-4pm, Sat 8.30am-1pm). Full of brochures, the office has really improved over the last few years and depending on which person is serving you at the time (and what mood they're in) may well be the best source of information on the city and the safari circuit. They keep a list of licensed tour agencies in both Moshi and Arusha and a blacklist of those companies to avoid; have a photocopied map of the city that they provide to tourists for free; and even have a rundown of bus services from Arusha to East African destinations. They also have a noticeboard where some people advertise for trekking companions. In our opinion, it's the best tourist office in East Africa.

Banks

The emergence of numerous cashpoints (ATMs) means that you should be able to find at least one that takes your card. The most central cashpoint to take foreign bank cards, usually without complaint, is outside the NBC on Sokoine. The Standard Chartered cashpoint at the southern end of Goliondoi Road is temperamental, the Bank Exim over the road is often broken (though if it isn't it *usually* works OK with foreign cards) and the NMB Bank by the clock tower seldom accepts foreign cards (though is worth a try if you've exhausted other options). If you've got a vehicle or are staying in the area you may prefer to use Barclays' ATM on the way down to The Outpost on the Serengeti Road or their branch at the TFA Shopping Centre.

As for changing money, the Bureaux de Change are far more efficient than the banks, with the three Sanya outlets (all on Sokoine; daily 7am-6pm) reliable and usually offering close to the best rates in town. They are also just about the only bureaux to open on Sundays. You can find one about 50m down from the Patisserie, and one next to the Metropole Cinema.

The **AMEX** agent in Arusha is Rickshaw Travels in the Marshall Building on Sokoine (☎ 027-250 6655).

Communications

The **post office** is by the clock tower (Mon-Fri 8.30am-5pm, Sat 9am-noon). For phoning abroad, TTCL is on Boma Road (Mon-Fri 8am-4.30pm, Sat 9am-noon), though it is cheaper to use one of the discount phone services offered by internet cafés and other outlets such as the Patisserie (see p177; Ts400 per minute to the UK for example).

Finding an **internet** café in Arusha isn't difficult. All charge much the same with Ts1500 for an hour being the norm. The current favourite with most travellers is the Patisserie on Sokoine, though this is mainly because a) they have wi-fi facilities (for which they charge the same rate of Ts1500 per hour); and b) all the overland tours stop there. Klub Afriko, round the back of the New Safari Hotel (see p174), charges the same and offers a little more peace and privacy. TTCL now have internet, too, for which they charge Ts500 for 30 minutes.

Airline offices

● **Ethiopian Air** New Safari Hotel, Boma Road (PO Box 93; ☎ 027-250 4231/250 6167; 🖳 www.flyethiopian.com; Mon-Fri 8.30am-5pm, Sat 8.30am-1pm).

● **Air Excel** First floor, Subzali Building above Bank Exim on Goliondoi Rd (PO Box 12731; ☎ 027-254 8429; 🖳 reservations@airexcelonline.com).

● **Coastal Aviation** Boma Road (☎ 027-250 0087; 🖳 www.coastal.cc; closed Sat pm & Sun).

● **Kenya Airways** and **Precision Air** New Safari Hotel, Boma Road (PO Box 1636; ☎ 027-250 8589; Mon-Fri 8am-5pm, Sat and Sun 8am-2pm). If you have an e-ticket issued in your home country and want to change the dates, you may well be told to contact the offices in Dar or Nairobi.

● **KLM and Northwest Airlines** Boma Road. Office now closed.

● **Precision Air** (🖳 www.precisionairtz.com); see Kenya Airways, above.

● **Regional Air** (PO Box 14755; ☎ 027-250 4164; 🖳 www.regional.co.tz).

● **Air Tanzania** Boma Road (☎ 027-250 3201; 🖳 www.airtanzania.com).

● **Rwandair Express** Sokoine Rd (☎ 0732-978558; 🖳 www.rwandair.com).

Immigration

The immigration office (Mon-Fri 7.30am-3.30pm) is across the road from the AICC on Afrika Mashariki Rd.

Shopping

You can get most things in Arusha – it's just a question of knowing where to look. Some of the shops seem to have been deliberately set up with tourists and expats in mind, particularly those at the TFA ('Shoprite') complex at the western end of Sokoine, where you'll find upmarket souvenir shops including the excellent Travel Market, a couple of safari operators, a well-stocked camping/trekking shop, a DVD-hire outlet (Ts2000 a time, Ts25,000 joining fee), a photographic store and even a massage parlour (☎ 0754-925092; Ts35,000 for a one-hour full-body massage). This arcade may lack charm, being centred around a dusty parking lot next to a supermarket; nevertheless, if you're missing home, this place is unrivalled in Arusha.

● **Books** With the demise of the much-loved Bookmark, the book-buying public of Arusha are now poorly served, though Kase Bookshop on Boma Road by the Air Tanzania office and to west of the clock tower is OK, and Bookpoint, near the Big Bite curry house, is fair too. In either place, however, don't expect much in the way of fiction. Better, perhaps, is Travel Market in the TFA complex.

● **Electrical goods/cameras** Benson & Company, on Sokoine, should be your first port of call for electrical goods, camera batteries, repairs and so forth. This is also the first place to come if you need to have your phone unlocked (see p88).

● **Pharmacy** Moona's Pharmacy lies near the eastern end of Sokoine, below the NBC Bank. The staff speak good English.

● **Souvenirs** You won't have any trouble finding souvenirs in Arusha – indeed,

ARUSHA, MOSHI AND MARANGU

often they come and find you. Much of the stuff is poor quality, however. We recommend two places: the first is Travel Market, in the TFA by Shoprite, which has a quirky collection of locally made items including purses, bags and other stuff made out of recycled materials including tin cans and celebrity magazines, as well as some charming handmade cards and toys. They also have a fairly decent bookshop and photographic gallery out back.

Outdoing even this place in terms of the variety of goods on offer is the Blue Heron Café (see p179), which has a couple of rooms of souvenirs; note, however, that while much of their stuff is highly desirable, not all of it is locally made. Both of these places have fixed prices. One place that definitely hasn't, however, is the Masai market just to the west of the clock tower – the place for Masai beadwork and tyre sandals.

● **Supermarket** Shoprite, at the western end of Sokoine in the TFA Complex, is Arusha's first full-blown supermarket. Vast, and with plenty of choice, most of the customers at this latest branch of the pan-African chain unsurprisingly appear to be expats. If you can't be bothered to schlep all that way, Kijenge Self-Service Supermarket by the Spices and Herbs hotel/restaurant is good, though again a little out of the way for most people; the supermarket next to the Japanese restaurant Sazan is OK, though a little short of stock; Rushda, just off Sokoine on Azimio Street, has a fair selection; while most central of all is the clock tower Supermarket on the main roundabout (Mon-Sat 8am-10pm, Sun 9am-9pm).

WHERE TO STAY [see map pp164-5]

As with much of the rest of Tanzania, the hotels in Arusha officially charge different rates for locals and foreigners, particularly for mid-range and high-end hotels. For the prices listed below, we have usually opted to list the **non-residents' rate** only; the residents' rate is usually lower by 50% or more though not always; sometimes it's just the shilling equivalent of the non-resident price.

We have divided the hotels in approximate price order, and within each category have ordered them approximately from west to east (see map pp164-5).

Camping

The *Arusha Vision* (☎ 0754-040810) campsite on Boma Road, opposite the Hotel Equator, has improved safety-wise and if it wasn't for the presence of two safari companies based there who have been known to apply pressure to campers to join one of their safaris, it would be recommended. Rates are Ts3000 per person.

The *Masai Camp* (☎ 0754-507131, 🖳 www.masaicamp.com) lies 3km east from the centre on the Old Moshi Road and charges US$5 per person including hot showers. It's a great place (see under *Where to Eat* and *Nightlife* on p178 and p181 respectively) but it's not the quietest campsite (indeed, they actively discourage campers looking for peace and quiet from staying on Friday and Saturday nights while they host their Wild and Whacky weekenders). They also have a few private rooms (US$15 single) and a dorm (US$10).

Budget: under US$20 for a double

The focus for budget travellers these days is the western end of Sokoine Road, just a few hundred metres east of Shoprite. The *Arusha Backpackers* (☎ 027-250 4474, 🖳 www.arushabackpackers.co.tz) stands in an unpromising position in the forecourt of a petrol station by the Meru Post Office on Sokoine. The only backpacker place that is so popular that you have to book in advance in order to stand a chance of staying there, this is the sister of the Kindoroko and Backpacker hotels in Moshi. The rooms themselves are basic but clean and there's a small internet café on the ground floor. The highlight, however, is the rooftop restaurant with perhaps the best view of Meru. It's also a great place to stay if you have to catch an early flight in the morning: the noise of the traffic outside won't let you sleep beyond 6.30am. Rates, including breakfast, begin at just Ts7000 for a place in a four-bed dorm, rising to US$10/16 sgl/dbl, though there are no en suites.

Surviving largely on the overspill from Arusha Backpackers, *Meru House Inn* (☎ 027-250 7803; 🖳 meruhouseinn@hotmail.com; non-s/c sgl/dbl/tpl Ts8000/10,000/16,000, en suite Ts12,000/15,000/22,000) has been around for a while and is another hotel often patronized by foreign tourists, which is surprising given that it makes little effort to attract them. Still, it's pleasant, relaxed, the manager and his staff are friendly, there's a cheap café on the first floor and a good Indian restaurant (the Noble Juice Parlour – see p176) by the entrance. But do avoid the rooms overlooking either the central courtyard or the road if you want a good night's sleep.

If you want to get away from other tourists, then it's worth heading to Kaloleni, a small cluster of roads to the north of the bus station and a few metres east of Colonel Middleton Road. For years this was the backpackers' centre of Arusha and wandering around it today little has changed, with all the budget hotels still there – it's just the travellers who've disappeared. Places to stay include the three *Monjes Guest House* (☎ 0754-462308, 🖳 janemonjes@ yahoo.com), labelled A, B and C, all built on or just off Levolosi Road. While *Monjes A* is friendly but suffers from a surfeit of safari touts, and *Monjes B* has large rooms with mozzy nets but can be deathly quiet, the best is *Monjes C* (US$12 dbl, US$20 en-suite, the latter including free tea and coffee too) which not only boasts the brightest rooms but is also the new home of legendary eatery Pizzarusha (see p176).

Just outside Kaloleni, one place that does still see the occasional backpacker is the curiously named *Annex Hotel Arusha By Night* (☎ 027-250 1434), just north of the stadium at the corner of Colonel Middleton Road and Stadium Road. *(Continued on p172)*

❏ **Abbreviations**

Throughout this book we have used the following abbreviations when writing about accommodation: **s/c** means self-contained, as in en suite (ie the room comes with a bathroom); **sgl/dbl/tpl** means single/double/triple rooms. For example, where we have written 'sgl/dbl/tpl US$35/40/45', we mean that a single room costs US$35 per night, a double US$40, and a triple US$45.

Accommodation around Arusha

Whilst we have spent pages in this book describing the accommodation in Arusha, the fact of the matter is that most of you will have booked your trek before you arrive, and your agency in turn will have arranged your hotel for you; and it's more than likely that this accommodation won't even be in Arusha but outside of it, where several swish, smart and salubrious lodges are situated, surviving on the patronage of foreign travel companies and their local agents. It's hard to criticize these places except that they do tend to be in the middle of nowhere.

The following reviews are ordered from west to east.

A classic example is the **Arusha Coffee Lodge** (🖥 www.arushacoffee lodge.com), twenty-three luxury chalets that are just gorgeous. Unlike the other hotels in this section, it lies to the west of Arusha on the way to the local airport but is still being used by a couple of trekking companies, particularly those who combine their treks with a safari afterwards. There are 21 private chalets on the plantation, with plenty more being built, as well as a pool and massage service. Another thing in its favour is its renowned restaurant. Prices: low season sgl/dbl US$150 per person, high season sgl/dbl US$260/225 per person.

East of town, **Karama Lodge** lies 3km along Old Moshi Rd beyond Masai Camp (☎ 027-250 0359, 🖥 www.karama-lodge.com) who actually own the place. An unusual lodge, the Karama is tucked quietly on a hillside facing away from Arusha and boasts 22 stylish en-suite rooms housed in log cabins on stilts, with views of Meru from many. A sauna, massage and yoga room complete the facilities. Rates are sgl/dbl US$87/118.

Firmly in the luxury bracket, **Onsea** (☎ 0784-833207; 🖥 www.onseahouse.com), is a delight. If money was not a concern, this is where I would stay. Everything, from the locally made furniture to the outdoor pool and jacuzzi with views across to Meru, the friendly Belgian designer-manager and the tranquil setting on Namasi Hill, 7km east of Arusha, with views across to Meru, is spot on. I want to get married just so I can have my honeymoon here. And I haven't yet mentioned the food, prepared by the owner's talented cousin who's been working in Michelin-starred restaurants since he was 16. The downside? They have only four rooms and a guest cottage, all doubles, and availability can be hard to come by. Rates: sgl/dbl US$145-175/170-210; not cheap by Arusha's standards, but fair value.

There's another coffee-themed lodge tucked away at the end of a bumpy dirt track about 7km east of Arusha, 2km south of the road to Moshi. **Moivaro Coffee Plantation Lodge** (🖥 www.moivaro.com) consists of 40 cottages, each hidden away amongst the lush vegetation of the beautifully tended grounds. Each room has its own en-suite bathroom and veranda and the lodge also boasts a swimming pool and bar. A massage service is available, too, which will enable you to while away the hours when you're not on the mountain. Rates: sgl/dbl U$100/150 for B&B.

Kigongoni Lodge (☎ 027-255 3087, 🖥 www.kigongoni.net) is located about 11km from Arusha. I love this place. It occupies a beautiful hilltop location on an old coffee estate; the rustic cottages are simple but wonderful, with fireplaces, four-poster beds and lovely wooden verandas overlooking the monkey-filled forest below; the family who run it are jolly and helpful, the food is good, and, to top it all, part of the profit of the lodge goes to the nearby Sibusiso Foundation, a centre for mentally and physically handicapped children. Throw in the usual facilities, including wi-fi internet and a swimming pool, and you have a wonderful lodge. Unfortunately, I don't see many of the trekking agencies using them – I've no idea why. Rates: B&B US$80-120.

(see map p172)
Serena Mountain Village Inn (☎ 027-250 4158, 🖥 www.serenahotels.com) is one of many Serena properties in Tanzania and yet another lodge that is situated on a coffee plantation, though this time with the added attraction of Lake Duluti behind. This gorgeous location and the grand reception aren't quite matched by the concrete bungalows but nevertheless some have full sunken baths and lake views. Rates sgl/dbl US$125/185 low season, US$195/245 high season.

Arumeru River Lodge (☎ 027-255 3573, 🖥 www.arumerulodge.com) consists of ten large, comfortable chalets and a huge, high-roofed reception, all standing amongst the bushes of a coffee estate 15km east of town at Tengeru, 1km south of the road to Moshi. All the usual facilities are here, including internet, a small solar-heated pool, satellite TV and a highly regarded restaurant. Rates are sgl/dbl US$117/174.

The *Dik Dik* (PO Box 1499, Arusha; ☎ 027-255 3499; 🖥 www.dikdik.ch) is homely and in a good location north of the highway. Swiss-owned, the hotel is named after one of Africa's smallest antelopes and is appropriately petite, particularly when compared to the nearby Ngurdoto, save for the high-roofed reception. It boasts just nine bungalows, each with fireplace, veranda, hammock and mini-bar, and there's a small pool here too. It's a pleasant, cosy place. Rates: sgl/dbl US$150/200.

Rivertrees Country Inn (PO Box 235, Arusha; ☎ 027-255 3894; 🖥 www.river trees.com) sits on the banks of the Usa River, 22km east of Arusha, and boasts ten self-contained guestrooms and two cottages. It's a stylishly rustic place, the cosy reception and lounge making good use of old reclaimed wood and agricultural implements. It also has a pool, internet access and a kitchen that bakes its own bread; that and a lovely location with the river flowing through the grounds and some great old trees providing welcome shade. Overall, peaceful and serene. Rates: dbl US$178 B&B.

Opposite is another place that's full of character. *Mount Meru Game Lodge & Sanctuary* (☎ 027-255 3885, 🖥 www.intimate-places.com) was established back in 1959 although its colonial style harks back to an earlier era, with the founder's son now in charge. The 17 large, en-suite rooms in wooden bungalows are comfortable and the restaurant is renowned among expats who flee Arusha to dine here at weekends; but it's the animal sanctuary, with its rescued elands, ostriches, and even buffalo, that really sets this place apart. Rates are sgl/dbl US$105-175/US$160-240.

Situated by a golf course, the *Ngurdoto Mountain Lodge* (PO Box 7302; ☎ 027-255 5217; 🖥 www.thengurdotomountainlodge.com) is a massive place just off the Moshi Road on the way to Arusha National Park. The rooms and chalets are en-suite and come with TV and mini-bar – and some even have their own jacuzzi. With two restaurants, coffee shop, 'BBQ ranch', tennis and badminton courts, swimming pool, health club and even its own golf course, this is just about as good as it gets facility-wise – though it must be said that it's not so much a lodge as a full-on hotel. It's also geared more towards the business client than the tourist. Rates: sgl/dbl US$135/175 up to US$2000 for the presidential villa.

Right by the airport, the *KIA Lodge* (PO Box 43, KIA; ☎ 027-255 4194; 🖥 www. kialodge.com) has been recommended by more than one reader as a great place to spend your last night in Africa before flying out from the neighbouring Kilimanjaro International Airport. It's decorated in a smorgasbord of Tanzanian styles, too, from the Zanzibar-style reception, the Tinga-Tinga paintings in the restaurant and the Makonde woodcarvings in the rooms. Their hilltop location also allows you unequalled views of both Kili and Meru, as well as distant glimpses of the Blue Mountains and Maasai plains. Lovely. Rates: sgl/dbl US$114-168/171-264.

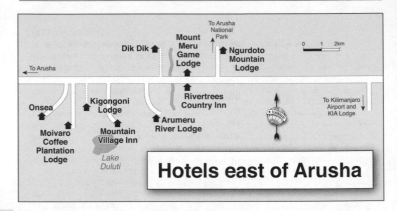

To Arusha National Park

Dik Dik

Mount Meru Game Lodge

Ngurdoto Mountain Lodge

0   1   2km

To Arusha

Rivertrees Country Inn

Onsea

Kigongoni Lodge

Arumeru River Lodge

To Kilimanjaro Airport and KIA Lodge

Moivaro Coffee Plantation Lodge

Mountain Village Inn

Lake Duluti

Hotels east of Arusha

(Continued from p169) With rooms built either side of a long corridor, at first Annex Hotel Arusha By Night feels a bit like an institution but actually the rooms themselves – large, self-contained and comfortably furnished with fans and mosquito nets – are quite pleasant. Rates are Ts15,000/17,000 s/c sgl/dbl including continental breakfast.

Also in this bracket, the *YMCA* on India St (☎ 027-254 4032; US$10/13/23 for non-self-contained sgl/dbl/tpl) is actually OK – quiet, tired but tidy and clean – and the fact that they haven't put up their prices in a few years makes it fair value, though the area is a favourite with flycatchers (see p162).

Mid-range: US$20-50 for a double
West of Col Middleton Road, *Williams Inn* (☎ 027-250 3578) is run like a boarding school with notices everywhere reminding people of the rules of the house, including orders barring guests from bringing in both alcohol and 'women of immoral turpitude'. Given its location at the seamier side of town, however, such severity is no bad thing and the rooms are comfortable, quiet and pleasant enough, and US$25 for s/c sgl/dbl with nets and hot water is fair value.

The smartest place in Kaloleni is the *Giraffe Motel* (☎ 027-250 4618 or 0754-817912) on Levolosi, with 13 impeccably scrubbed and tiled en-suite rooms each with box mosquito nets. If it wasn't for the sour faces that greet tourists this would be one to recommend. Prices of Ts25,000 per room are high for Kaloleni but reflect the better class of accommodation on offer.

Three new hotels have opened up in the last couple of years in the previously hotel-free area between the bus station and the Naura River. Of most interest to tourists are the two places standing side by side on Pangani Street, north-east of the bus station. The *Hotel Fort des Moines* (☎ 027-254 8523) is a 23-room affair and very comfy, with each room boasting fan, TV, telephone, mosquito nets and its own bathroom with hot water. Rates are a very reasonable at Ts25,000/30,000 s/c sgl/dbl including breakfast. It is probably a place that appeals more to the locals, at least when compared to the neighbouring *Arusha*

Centre Tourist Inn (☎ 027-250 0421; ✉ icerestaurant@yahoo.com) which has similar facilities, again with a TV (caged to prevent theft!) and mosquito net (though no fan) in every room, all of which are en suite. B&B rates are again reasonable at US$25/30 s/c sgl/dbl. Round the corner on Swahili Street is the third option, the *Sinka Court Hotel* (☎ 027-250 4961; ✉ sinka-court-hotel@hotmail.com) with much the same facilities (en suite, TV) though perhaps slightly smarter, brighter and airier, a difference that's reflected in the price (US$40/45 s/c sgl/dbl, US$50-55 for suites).

Heading right across town, *Le Jacaranda Hotel* (☎ 027-254 4945; ✉ www.chez.com/jacaranda/Default.html; US$45/50 sgl/dbl) is set to the east of town in a quiet street to the north of Nyerere Road. This is a characterful place, its exterior walls painted with cartoon animals, its communal seating areas comfy and laidback. There's even a mini-golf course in the garden. The downside, however, is the rooms, with some doubles tired and stark, while the singles, some of which are plain, uncosy and, tucked away from the main hotel proper, feel like a bit of an afterthought.

One block further east, Ethiopian *Spices and Herbs* restaurant (see p178; ☎ 0754-313162, 0784-281320; ✉ axum_spices@hotmail.com) has 20 en-suite rooms built around a central courtyard at the back of their premises. The rooms are clean and airy, with box nets, but a tad overpriced at US$35/45 s/c sgl/dbl (all prices inclusive of breakfast).

Upper-range: US$50-100 for a double

Arusha Tourist Inn on Sokoine Rd (☎ 027-254 7803, ✉ atihotel@habari.co.tz; dbl US$55-60) is a spanking new hotel hidden away behind the much tattier Meru House Inn. The twenty-nine en-suite rooms come with all the facilities including satellite TV but do lack views; indeed its location verges on the claustrophobic. Still, it's a safe, decent choice, though there are no singles.

On the western side of town, the major landmark on Col Middleton Road is the *Golden Rose* (☎ 027-250 7959; s/c sgl/dbl US$40/60 in the old wing, US$50/70 in the new wing, all including English breakfast), a popular place that's now dwarfed by its neighbouring conference centre. The hotel's name is apt too, for this is a hotel with something of a gilt complex, many of its rooms now being decorated in shiny golden hues.

A relative newcomer to the city's hotel scene is the *Arusha Crown Hotel* (☎ 027-250 8523; ✉ www.arushacrownhotel.com) on Makongoro Road by the south-eastern corner of the stadium. Very much a hotel for local businessmen, it's smart and comfy enough though a little bland and the walls cannot entirely block out the noise from the streets below. That said, you do at least get a grandstand view of the football across the road from some rooms. Rates start at US$60/75 s/c sgl/dbl, which in our opinion is fair.

Right in the centre of town, the *Arusha Naaz* (☎ 027-250 2087; ✉ www.arushanaaz.net; s/c sgl/dbl US$45/60) comes as a bit of a surprise. The façade looks unpromising and the staff's attitude to their guests can sometimes border on the disdainful. Nevertheless, the rooms are squeaky-clean and en-suite and all come with TV; there's also a (dazzlingly bright) roof terrace. Try to get a room away from the road if possible.

The Outpost (☎ 027-254 8405; 🖳 www.outposttanzania.com) lies down Serengeti Road to the south of Nyerere Road, a lane so exclusive that Arusha's usual noise of traffic and touts is replaced by the soothing sound of birdsong and the gentle rhythm of people brushing the dust from the street. Popular with tour groups, the Outpost has its own internet and laundry service and a lovely lounge area kitted out, as with the rooms, in a spartan but relaxed, comfy style. The rooms have TV, are all en suite and there's a small pool and attractive bar/restaurant area. B&B here costs US$48/US$66 s/c sgl/dbl: pretty good value and a nice place.

A few hundred metres away, the *Mbega Tourist Camp* (☎ 0732-978013, 🖳 mbegatourist camp@yahoo.com; rates US$45/60 sgl/dbl B&B), perhaps better known as the *Bella Luna Hotel*, is OK if you're stuck but there are some nicer and more popular choices around town.

L'Oasis Lodge (PO Box 1908; ☎ 027-250 7089) is located in an obscure location, a 15-minute walk north of the town, with accommodation in huts, rondavels and 'boma-style' rooms all hidden behind a high wall. The rooms themselves are fine, the food is said to be great and they've even got internet access and a small pool. The only quibble we have, in fact, is that more than one reader has written to say that they've failed to get any sleep due to the barking of the neighbourhood dogs. This is particularly true for those who've opted for the cheaper Backpackers Lodge, across the dirt track, which has shared amenities and lacks some of the charm of the main lodge. Rates: sgl/dbl US$72/90, Backpackers Lodge US$20 per person in one of the 12 twin-bedded rooms.

Expensive: US$100 and above for a double

Nauru Springs Hotel (☎ 027-205 0001; 🖳 www.nauraspringshotel.com; rates sgl/dbl US$120/160, rising to US$1200 for the Presidential Suite) is a soaring, shiny blue-glass landmark just north of the AICC. It's not a bad place – a bit dazzling, but the open-air reception is a nice touch and the rooms have all the features you'd expect of a hotel of this size (internet access, satellite TV, safes, bathrooms with jacuzzis); there can be no concealing the fact, however, that this hotel is aiming for businessmen rather than holidaymakers.

Moving south, the smart *Hotel Equator* (☎ 027-250 8409; 🖳 equator @bol.co.tz) is hidden away behind the phone office. With every room fitted out with a shower, private balcony, satellite TV and phone – some with internet connection – this is now one of the plushest places in the town centre, and the price is fair at s/c sgl/dbl US$80/100 including continental breakfast. Unfortunately, its obscure location and the prestige of the other hotels near here – the New Safari and Arusha – means that it's very much third choice in this price bracket.

Nearby, and occupying what it describes as a 'lavish location' on Boma Road, is its sister establishment the *New Safari Hotel* (☎ 027-250 3261/2, 🖳 www.the newsafarihotel.com; s/c sgl/dbl/tpl/suites US$85/105/135/170-180). Once the haunt of Hemingway (though it's doubtful he'd recognize the place) and now one of the smarter places in town, the gleaming, polished nature of the lobby is mirrored by the spotless en-suite rooms, all with TV, wireless internet and mini-bar.

No review of Arusha's hotels would be complete without mention of the oldest of the lot, the *Arusha Hotel* (☎ 027-250 7777; 💻 www.arushahotel. com), which is actually fairly anonymous despite its location in the very heart of the action by the clock tower. Formerly known as the *New* Arusha, the name has recently been changed which is only sensible really considering it opened in 1894 (though the current building dates 'only' from 1927). It remains amongst the swishest and plushest of all the town-centre hotels, with wood-pannelled walls and, to use that well-worn brochure phrase, a real 'atmosphere of yesteryear'. The restaurant is, of course, very good, the swimming pool heated and the rooms sumptuous and kitted out with television, internet ports and, of course, a bathroom. All this luxury doesn't come cheap, however, with rack rates starting at sgl/dbl US$200/240-440.

East of here, two new hotels sit close to each other on Nyerere Road: *Kibo Palace Hotel* (☎ 027-254 4472; 💻 www.kibopalacehotel.com), with rooms from sgl/dbl US$160/180 rising to US$400/450 for the suites; and the *East African* (☎ 027-205 0075; 💻 www.eastafricanhotel.com; rooms sgl/dbl US$140/170 rising to US$180/190). As with the Nauru, it's unlikely you'll end up here, the majority of their clients being local and Western businessmen.

Still further east, *African Tulip* (☎ 027-254 3004; 💻 www.theafrican tulip.com) is yet another fine hotel in this neck of the forest. Named after the bright orange flowers that grow on the trees along this lane, the Tulip is owned by Roy Safaris. The rooms are huge and kitted out with every possible modern convenience including flat-screen TVs, remote-controlled air-con and wireless internet. Aside from all this high-tech gadgetry, it's worth mentioning that it's also a very comfortable place in a shiny, glamorous sort of way. Rates are US$155/200, rising to US$450 for the two-bedroom suites.

One can only guess at the number of woodland creatures that were made homeless in order to furnish the *Impala Hotel* (☎ 027-250 8448/49/50/51; 💻 www.impalahotel.com) with its wood-heavy reception. Along with the new Nauru Springs Hotel, it's one of the main business centres in Arusha, with all the trimmings one would expect – a plethora of bars and restaurants (Indian, Chinese, Italian), a pool and conference facilities, and the rooms, all en suite, come equipped with colour televisions and hot water. Strangely they are all actually quite reasonably priced at sgl/dbl s/c US$80/100-210 with breakfast.

Finally, the Arusha Hotel's long-standing reputation as the best hotel in town is now being challenged by the arrival of *The Bay Leaf Hotel* (☎ 027-254 3055, 💻 www.thebayleafhotel.com), a 'boutique hotel' just round the corner from the Jacaranda. Currently boasting only six rooms (though with five more being constructed in an annex out the back), this is currently Arusha centre's classiest accommodation, with features including a pool that sits in landscaped grounds, extra king-size beds, flat-screen TVs, wi-fi broadband internet connection, and such little touches as bath gowns and slippers, complimentary daily newspapers and even a free laundry service. Such luxury comes at a price, however, and at the Bay Leaf that price is sgl/dbl US$110/200 – which is actually not bad value at all!

WHERE TO EAT AND DRINK   [see map pp164-5]

Arusha is a good place for foodies, with African, Oriental and Indian eateries abounding. Some also advertise Continental food, which basically means any dish that doesn't fit into one of the categories above. There are a couple of local hangouts specializing in Tanzania's hearty, cheap and simple brand of cuisine, of which **Khan's** stands out. Long a favourite with locals, it has also been winning a whole legion of foreign fans over the past decade or so and is now something of a tourist attraction, to the point where they even sell T-shirts. A garage by day, at around 5pm Khan's transforms itself into a barbecue to serve up their take on the chicken-in-a-basket theme, namely 'chicken-on-a-bonnet'. They also do mixed grills, including chips, naan bread and a serve-yourself table full of salads and spicy sauces. Expect to get change from Ts10,000 for your meal, including drink (their passion fruit juice is delicious). It's just to the north of the Central Market on Mosque Street; be careful around here after dark – take a cab.

Just to the north of Khan's is **Old Rock**, a pleasant little option proffering cheap burgers and sandwiches, steaks (Ts4800) and its own pizza oven. It's one of those hygienic places with an open kitchen so you can see what's going on with your food, which is reassuring, and you can't fault the value. Perfect for lunch after a morning's stroll around the market, do note that they don't serve alcohol.

At the eastern end of the Kaloleni district, north of the stadium, **Pizzarusha** is a real travellers' stalwart. Claiming to conjure up the 'finest damn pizzas' in Africa, this was once a real meeting place for budget travellers, though they've suffered from the fact that few travellers now stay in Kaloleni. Nevertheless, this is still a tout-free haven and a great place for budget-conscious backpackers. What's more, the pizzas are indeed very good and fine value at around Ts5000.

Down on Sokoine, if you thought Tanzanian fast food simply meant impala on the hoof then think again and pay a visit to **McMoody's** (closed Monday). The food's OK and, according to one expat, their milkshakes are unrivalled throughout Arusha. On the same section of Sokoine, **Dolly's** is a curious place, ostensibly a patisserie though with a vast array of Indian dishes on offer too, all served in spotlessly clean surroundings, making this a favourite for travellers with children.

There is no shortage of good Indian restaurants in the city. Two worth mentioning are **Big Bite**, one block east of the market, which has long been a favourite with expats; and **Noble Juice Parlour**, beneath the Meru House Inn at the western end of Sokoine. Be warned: some of the dishes are truly fiery at both of these places.

Across Sokoine from Noble Juice Parlour, and just south along Station Road (the street running alongside the Arusha Backpackers), Dutch-run **The Lively Lady** is a curious place. The food from their barbecue is first rate (with mains around Ts7000-10,000) but the subdued lighting, loud rock music and impressively comprehensive bar (the most complete in Arusha according to local barflies) suggest this should be considered primarily as a place for imbibing rather than scoffing, though the section out front is brighter and quieter.

Moving up Sokoine, the **Green Hut House of Burgers** is a bit of a misnomer, for burgers feature only twice on the menu. This is a great little place for lunchtimes, however, with cheap, simple but filling local fare the order of the day. Unfortunately, both locals and tourists have found out about this place so you may find yourself sharing a table with complete strangers.

Still further up Sokoine and entering into the tourist land surrounding the clock tower, the first place to catch the eye is *Patisserie*, possibly because of the huge overland trucks that stop outside so that their clients can use the internet there. Food-wise it's OK but nothing worth travelling across Africa for.

Moving up past the clock tower, on Boma Road by the tourist office is *Jambo's Coffee House* and *Makuti Garden*. The first is a little coffee house serving great coffee but pretty average food. The latter is more a bar/evening cocktail venue and, like so many places around here, it can be chock-a-block one night and deadly quiet the next. Opposite, the *Café Bamboo* is a busy place and in our opinion a better one than its rivals across the road. The African music and ethnic design on the walls can't quite eradicate the impression that this is actually a very English-style tearoom, but there's nothing wrong with that and the reasonably-priced food is served in large portions.

With branches in Honduras, Java and Zanzibar, *Via Via* is a chain of 14 travellers' cafés scattered around the globe which are renowned for the good work they do in introducing travellers to the local cultures (though most of the clients in the Arusha branch seem to be expats working at the Rwanda trials over at the nearby AICC). Situated in the grounds of the old German Boma, it offers live local music every Thursday (see p181) and an array of daytime activities, from drum-making and batik workshops to cookery and Swahili courses (see box p180). And if you don't give a cuss about the culture there's always the food, which includes such travellers' staples as banana pancakes and tuna sandwiches. The manager is a mine of information too.

A couple of hundred metres to the west, *Masai Café*, off Afrika Mashariki Road, opposite the AICC, is a part Italian-owned pizza and pasta joint (with a small art gallery attached to it too) that exists mainly to cater to the expats working across the road. For this reason it boasts a lively atmosphere during the day but come in the evening and you could be dining alone. Food-wise, the portions are big and the food tasty and, given the owners' background, authentic; it's also pretty reasonable value, with pizzas from Ts4500, and there's a fair wine list by Arusha standards too.

To the south on Nyerere Road and its continuation, Old Moshi Road, there are several large-scale restaurants that are perfect as venues for that post-Kili celebration (or commiseration) meal. These include two Chinese restaurants within a few hundred metres of each other. The first you'll come to is *Everest*, which is by far the more established, though it's *Dragon Pearl* that is currently attracting the customers. This can only be because of the service at Everest, which is occasionally a little slow, for the offerings in both places are enormous, authentic and first rate. Situated a few hundred metres to the north of Nyerere Road on Church Road, the spacious *Pepe* describes itself as an Indian-Italian restaurant. Though you'd be forgiven for thinking that they've taken the concept of fusion cuisine a step too far, thankfully the restaurant keeps the two cuisines apart, with each having their own separate menu. What they have in common, however, are the

ARUSHA, MOSHI AND MARANGU

same high standards of preparation and authenticity – and both are delicious too. The prices verge on the cheeky (Italian mains Ts16,000-17,500, though the pizzas are reasonable at Ts6000-9000, while Indian dishes go for Ts9000-12,000) and the service can, on occasion, be desultory, but otherwise it's a good choice for a large group looking for a post-trek celebration.

Back on the Old Moshi Road, past the Impala Hotel, *Stiggy's* advertises itself as a Pacific-Thai restaurant though everybody else knows it as the place to come for delicious pizzas (Ts6500-9500) – the best in Arusha, according to more than one expat – from a wood-fired oven. The service can border on the surly at times but otherwise this is a great place that also boasts a pool table, a stage for live music, a great cocktail list (Ts6000) and a decent bar. This is also the meeting point of the local Hash House Harriers; ask Stiggy himself (who's easy to spot: he's the Australian in apron and colourful trousers) for details. It's closed on Mondays, by the way. Stiggy also runs a café, *Stiggbucks*, in the TFA complex. Still on Old Moshi Road and further down, *Masai Camp* (see p168) is *the* campsite for the huge number of overland trucks that call in at Arusha. Their kitchen conjures up some pretty fair approximations of Mexican food as well as pizzas and other popular Western dishes, but for us the place itself is the main selling point, a fine open-sided wooden affair with pool tables and a comprehensive bar, all infused with a sociable, relaxed ambience.

For something out of the ordinary, a trip to *Spices and Herbs*, the blossom-laden Ethiopian restaurant in the hotel of the same name, could be in order. With vegetarian dishes ranging from Ts3500 to Ts8500 as well as meat dishes (around the Ts10,000 mark), this place has been garnering praise from hungry travellers for years. Try the *yebeg alitcha fit fit* – lamb cooked with curry, garlic, onions, fresh ginger and spicy butter (Ts7500) – and you'll see why.

Also on this stretch is *Bella Luna*, which can boast a huge menu, mainly European, and the food's not bad though a little overpriced in places (with steaks Ts15,000 and the mixed grill Ts18,000); the main reason people come here, however, is for the Saturday night live performances by acrobats and/or bands. Down the road is *Watamu*, a clean, tiled place serving up local food, including *chipsi mayai* (a sort of chip omelette) and a tasty – and at Ts2000, dirt cheap – banana and mutton soup. Open 7am-10pm, the menu is small and the place itself unexceptional but it's nice to see a decent-class restaurant that isn't afraid to serve local food. At the other extreme – yet only a couple of hundred metres away – is the restaurant at the *Bay Leaf*, a dining-room whose cuisine is as flamboyant and fancy as its rooms are stylish and comfy. Doing great business since its opening in late 2008, the menu

---

❏ **The top six places to celebrate a climb in Arusha**
● **Pepe** For large groups, with a sizeable dining area and a large and varied menu.
● **Spices and Herbs** Classy African food, good for sharing.
● **Bollate** Good food, reasonably priced.
● **Flame Tree** Posh nosh for the smarter summiter.
● **Stiggy's** Cocktails, beer and pizzas – for those who've had enough of Africa.
● **Masai Camp** For those wanting a party afterwards without changing venue.

here changes monthly so it's pointless my recommending anything to you, though at the time of writing there were such exotic dishes as snails for starters (Ts7900) and Persian duck with apricots (Ts15,000) for mains, which gives you a flavour of the flavours on offer here. Finally in this corner of Arusha, there's the *Picasso Café*, yet another smart café that, with its largely *mzungu* clientele, wouldn't look out of place back home.

To the north of Nyerere Road are several fine restaurants hidden amongst the jacaranda trees. *The Flame Tree* (☎ 0754-377359) on Kenyatta Road, one block west of the Jacaranda, is perhaps the smartest and most tasteful restaurant in town. There's no disputing the calibre of the food here, nor indeed the care taken to prepare it, with tomatoes carved to look like rosebuds and baskets that teem with fancy bread. Nor, for that matter, can the quality of the service be criticized, with the waitresses polite, attentive and good-natured. What stops the Flame Tree from being entirely satisfactory, however, is that their food, while undoubtedly tasty, is fancy rather than filling; and that, from the point of view of trekkers who, having spent the best part of a week suffering various deprivations and dreaming of being face down in a trough full of calorific nosh, is one large and definite drawback. Their puddings (Ts5000), with chocolate a main ingredient, provide some compensation – but overall, this is a place to bring your (rich) elderly aunt (or any ex-presidents you may know, as the picture of Bill Clinton on the wall can testify).

If it's lunch you're after, *Blue Heron* (closed eves and Sundays) occupies, in our opinion, the best grounds in Arusha, a sweet 1950s house set in the middle of some lovely manicured gardens, complete with fountain and some gorgeous blossom trees. This place is also notable for its fine souvenir emporium (see p168) as well as some of the comfiest sofas in East Africa. As for the food and drinks, well it's OK, with bruschettas and salads featuring prominently, but if you can live without the gardens and armchairs you'll find the same sort of stuff – and for half the price – in the TFA (Shoprite) Centre at *Ciao Gelati*, ostensibly an ice-cream parlour but one that also serves some of the biggest salads in Arusha.

Virtually opposite Blue Heron, *Albero* is yet another Italian restaurant, with Italian mains Ts7000-10,000, though it also boasts such exotic treats as lobster thermidor (or Lobuster Tellmidor as they put it) for Ts18,000. What sets this place apart, however, is the lovely outside bar built round a huge fig tree.

Bollate, one block north on Kaunda Road, is a bit of a find, a smart restaurant that actually manages to be good value too. Situated just off Haile Selassie Road, one block north of the Flame Tree (see above), it describes itself as a Mexican/Italian/Continental restaurant; and while we didn't sample everything on the menu (which, given its size, would have taken many months), we can vouch that the Mexican dishes are fine, filling and, given the fact we're a few thousand miles from Central America, fairly authentic too. A serious contender for those looking to celebrate – though you'll need to get a taxi to and from it at night as the streets around here are dark.

Back on Nyerere, as far as I am aware *Sazan* is Arusha's only Japanese restaurant, which is presumably looking to capitalize on the increasing numbers

Organized tours and courses around Arusha
The **Via Via Café** (see p177) organizes tours around the city and neigh-bouring hills. None of these sights will take your breath away, nor is that their intention: they are simply very pleasant escapes from the city and a refreshing way of discovering the country that exists outside the national parks. They also operate a number of courses including a **cookery course** (Ts10,000 plus ingre-dients), where you spend the morning shopping for ingredients at the local market and the afternoon making something tasty out of them. Or you can take a trip to a **batik workshop** to learn how to print batiks (Ts10,000 plus a further Ts10,000 for materials), take **African drumming lessons** (Ts9000), or even attend a three-day **drum-making** workshop (Ts50,000).

For local tours that take you further afield, the Tanzanian Tourist Board, with help from Dutch development organization SNV, have created **Cultural Tourism Programmes** where you can visit the rural areas of Tanzania and experience 'real' African life, with all profits going towards various development projects. These tend to be a bit more expensive than Via Via's at around U$30 per day, though the choice is larger and the service more professional. Amongst the many tours they organize country-wide are trips to **Machame** to see the environmentally sound 'agro-forestry' practices of the region, and **Marangu** to visit the waterfalls, caves and farms (see p215 for details of these sights). Perhaps of more interest to the Kili trekker, on this latter trip you also visit the home and memorial of Yohana Lauwo, one of Hans Meyer's guides and a man who lived to be over 118 (see quote on p51) and you get a chance to see his log books. For more information, visit the tourist office in Arusha on the Boma Road where you can pick up brochures, find out prices and book a trip.

of Japanese tourists flocking to Tanzania and who are reluctant to try the local cuisine. Whether there are enough of them coming to warrant a whole restaurant is a moot point, but it is nice to see a place that's willing to serve up something other than pizzas. The restaurant lies along from the Kibo Palace Hotel. Opposite, *Pizzapoint* is actually not bad and the service is quick; they also do a takeaway service. Pizzas are Ts6000-7000.

For the ultimate treat in Arusha head down to the Shoprite Complex and *Chocolate Temptation*, a bijou boutique that specializes in extracting every last milligram of pleasure from the humble cocoa bean. My advice? Come here before climbing to admire the mouthwatering beauty of the confectionery on offer, then promise yourself that, should you reach the summit, you can gorge on anything in the shop, be it a 100g box of the finest Belgian chocolates (Ts7900) or an entire cake (Ts22,000-60,000). You never know, such an incentive might just be the dif-ference between success and failure...

NIGHTLIFE

Arusha is the **nightclub** and **live music** capital of northern Tanzania, attracting rastas and ravers from far and wide. Unfortunately, as with any large city, the scene changes rapidly and what's recommended here may well be out of date by the time you arrive.

One place that's almost certain to remain, however, is ***Triple A*** (just north-west off the map on p164), the city's favourite radio station and also its favourite nightspot. If you're around when a gig is being held, don't miss it, for this place attracts the finest bands from all over East Africa. Also hosting live bands, though this time to a much more Western crowd, ***Via Via*** (see p177) has a live-music evening every Thursday and movie nights on Wednesdays. They also organize the Washarusha Music Festival in December. Visit them during the day to find out what they've got lined up.

Masai Camp (see p178), at the eastern end of Old Moshi Road, has a disco at weekends and is a pleasant place to visit at any time, with relaxed seating in a lovely open-sided building, a giant TV, two decent pool tables and, if one of the overland trucks is in town, maybe a live act too. It's rather a laidback place, save for Friday and Saturday when they host their Wild & Whacky club nights that are so noisy, they advise campers not to pitch a tent here at weekends!

On the same road but a little nearer to the town centre, the ***Colobus Club*** (Ts5000) is owned by the same guy who runs Via Via. It opens only on Fridays and Saturdays and has two rooms, one playing Western music, one African. There are more club nights at the ***Empire Sports Bar***, in the TFA Complex, which hosts regular reggae nights and occasional live acts – again, drawing a largely Western crowd. Finally, there's ***Silk*** on Seth Benjamin St (Ts1500), and the new ***Mawingu City Centre Club*** opposite Excel Bank – much more home-ly venues playing largely African tunes to a mainly African audience.

If all this sounds a bit too hectic, you can always opt to drink the night away in more relaxed surroundings, either in the gardens of the ***Matongee Arusha Club*** on Nyerere Road, 200m east of the clock tower; or you can play **pool**, either at Stiggy's, Matongee or Masai Campsite, or challenge the locals to a game in the hall next to the Silk Nightclub. There's also a **cinema**, Metropole, on Sokoine (tickets Ts1500), with a far superior one out at Njiro (Ts5000).

Finally, for those who can't live without their weekly dose of premier league football, the most atmospheric place to watch is the ***Greek Club***, at the junction with Serengeti Road and Nyerere Road.

WHAT TO DO

Very little is the short answer. There are a couple of museums that could con-ceivably be worth visiting but only if you're absolutely sure you've finished preparing for your trek, have written all your postcards, bought all your souvenirs, sent all your emails, cut all your toenails and done all your laundry. The better of the two is the **Natural History Museum** (Mon-Fri 9am–5.30pm, Sat & Sun 9.30am–5.30pm), housed in the old German fort, or Boma. For US$4 (or US$2 students) you can look at a few incomplete skulls of early hominids, one diorama of a neanderthal sitting in a cave and a fragment or two of a prehistoric rhinocer-os skeleton, while in a separate building the history of the Boma is examined.

There's also the Academy of Taxidermists round the back featuring the heads of a number of Tanzania's animal treasures, all taxidermically treated and mounted on a wall; and nearby a couple of cages occupied by rescued animals – namely a baboon, a monkey and an owl – which, given their proximity to the taxidermy room, must be wondering what the museum has in store for them.

By the Arusha Monument there's the **Arusha Declaration Museum** (US$4; 7.30am-6pm daily), which manages the rather difficult feat of making the Natural History Museum seem fascinating. Consisting in the main of a few photos and a number of traditional tools and weapons, perhaps the most interesting part is the building itself, which is where Nyerere and chums met to hammer out the details of the Arusha Declaration (26-29 January 1967); that, and a torch which is supposed to be carried around the country every year to promote unity and patriotism among folk (and which is a copy of the torch that was placed at the summit of Kili following independence). We suppose some might find this place provides a useful précis of Tanzanian history from pre-colonial times to the death of Nyerere, and the authorities are to be commended for trying. Overall it's worthy, if not exactly worthwhile.

The **African Cultural Heritage Complex** lies to the west of town on the way to Arusha Airport. Once again, perhaps the most interesting exhibit is the actual building, the roof of which is designed to resemble the Kibo summit. The complex itself, however, is little more than a market for woodcarvings with a couple of recreated Masai dwellings in the courtyard. While there's no denying the artistry that's gone into the sculptures, the designs themselves may be a bit too elaborate to appeal to Western tastes. Nearby, the **arts centre** will perhaps be of more interest when it is finally completed; it aims to be the biggest in East Africa. However, it was unfinished when the first edition of this book went to print and, despite work continuing on it, it's still a little way from completion now, so don't hold your breath.

With such a dearth of formal attractions, perhaps the most educational and entertaining thing you can do in Arusha is visit a **football game** (Ts1000); it will teach you more about Tanzanians (or at least the male half of the population) and what makes them tick than any papier maché diorama or reconstructed Masai dwelling. The next game is usually chalked up on the noticeboard outside the stadium's main entrance on Col Middleton Road. Some of the games are rather low-key but attend a big league match and you're in for a treat.

If football's not your game then you can always **play pool** (see p181) or go **swimming** (Ts5000) in the pool at the Impala Hotel (see p175).

TREKKING AGENCIES

There are around 125 local companies that offer climbs up Kilimanjaro. In terms of value for money and choice, many will say that you're better off organizing your trek in Moshi than Arusha. Agencies in Arusha tend to be more expensive than those in Moshi for three reasons: firstly, some Arusha agencies are just acting as middlemen for those in Moshi and add their commission on top; secondly, most of the larger and more expensive companies prefer to base themselves in Arusha and enjoy the greater facilities there; and thirdly, the transport costs to Kilimanjaro are that much higher than they are from Moshi.

That said, there are plenty of good quality, reliable companies, so it is well worth investigating what the Arusha agents have to offer – which is exactly what

How we researched this section

As with the previous two editions, for this third edition we once again did as much of our research as possible anonymously. In other words, the companies we contacted thought we were just regular customers and no idea that we were researching for the next edition of the book.

Since the first edition we have noticed some significant changes in the way people book their treks. Where once people would often just buy a ticket to Tanzania and sort out a trek when they arrived, these days almost everybody books their climb via the internet before they set foot on Tanzanian soil. So for this edition we, too, mimicked this process, and like most other would-be Kili climbers we began our research online.

Having first checked out each company's website, the next step was to email them in order to find out a bit more about the service they could provide, and what they would charge for it. To do this we invented a fictional couple, set up an email address for them, and then sent a standard email to each of the trekking agencies concerned. In it we asked them for their prices for two people for a) six days on Marangu, and b) seven days on Machame. We also asked them whether they ran treks up the Western Breach (see p294), and if so how much extra this would cost. Finally, we asked them why we should book with them above all the other agencies.

Our research didn't stop there, however. Where possible, we tried to visit their offices in Tanzania (though this was sometimes not possible, particularly with the bigger agencies in Arusha whose offices are buried deep in the suburbs and are not set up for customers walking in off the street). We also asked trekkers we met on Kilimanjaro or in Arusha/Moshi of their experiences; consulted all the letters and emails from climbers that we'd received over the years, in which recommendations and complaints about agencies often featured; and finally, we talked with KPAP (see box pp46-49) to find out how well or badly each company treated and paid their staff on the mountain.

Please bear in mind that **the reviews we compiled are our opinions only**. Remember, too, that things change very quickly in this part of the world, so some of the following will inevitably have altered by the time you begin your own research into the trekking agencies. If you have any advice, comments, praise or criticisms about any of the following agencies, or indeed any agencies that we haven't mentioned, please write to us at the email/postal address given at the front of this book.

we've done here. To find out how we researched this section, please see the box above. While for details of what to look for in an agency, and what questions to ask, see p37. And one other tip: don't be afraid to tell the tour operator that you're shopping around; it's the quickest way to get them to give you a good deal.

● **African Environments** (PO Box 2125; ☎ 027-254 8625; 🖳 www.africanen vironments.co.tz). Established in mid-1987, American-owned African Environments are at the very top end of the market, claiming a 98% success rate on the Lemosho Route – a route that they actually pioneered. They are also the only company to equip *all* their expeditions with Gamow hyperbaric bags and oxygen as safety precautions. No surprises, then, that they are widely regarded as just about the most luxurious operator on the mountain and are a favourite with many foreign film crews. That said, though their equipment is of good quality some of it is starting to look more than a little tatty now. They don't take bookings directly but only through agents; and their website offers no advice on how to contact these agents. As you'd expect they're expensive (the exact price depending on which of their agents you actually book with), but it's good to see that some of that money filters down to their staff, for they're also one of the best payers and a KPAP partner. In addition to Lemosho, they also run a Machame trail trek.

● **African Walking Company** (📧 awc-richard@habari.co.tz). Founded by Brit Jim Foster, despite the lack of a website this is one of the more ubiquitous companies on the mountain thanks to a reputation for reliability and a high standard of treks. As such, they're a favourite with overseas agencies (African Travel Resource being one, Peak Planet another). With so much custom from abroad they don't really need independent trekkers – hence the lack of publicity. But if you've booked with an overseas agency you may well end up with them; and congratulations if you do, for they're one of the best on the mountain. KPAP partner.

● **Arunga Expeditions** (PO Box 2560, ☎ 0732-971780, 📧 www.aruexpedition.com). Their website is a bit of a mess – it was impossible to call up the itineraries, for example – and their email to us was originally sent to someone else; so our initial impression was not good, which was disappointing given that they have several Kenyan companies as clients, including Wildebeest. When their reply to our email did finally arrive their prices were certainly cheap at US$1000 per person for six days on Marangu (US$50 less if joining a group), or US$1220 for seven days on Machame. Add US$250 if wanting to take the Western Breach. So you can't argue with the fees but if you do sign up, please check everything carefully, including the equipment, the guide that will take you – everything, in fact, to make sure that your trek is a safe and happy one.

● **Auram Safaris** (PO Box 15966; ☎ 0732-972 459; 📧 www.auramsafaris.com) This lot certainly talk a good trek when I met them and their list of clients is impressive, including Leopard (Tanzania's largest safari operator). We hesitate to recommend them as I've yet to meet anyone who's been on the mountain with them – and it would appear the wages they pay are not as good as they claim. Still they may be worth a look – just investigate every claim they make thoroughly.

● **Base Camp Tanzania** Golden Rose Arcade Building, Conference Centre, First Floor, Col Middleton Rd (PO Box 568; ☎ 027-250 0393; 📧 www.basecamptanzania.com). Half-British husband-and-wife team that's been operating a trekking/safari business for more than a dozen years now and offers a friendly and reliable service as befits their background: he's a former overland guide, she is from a family who've worked in tourism for decades. Prices seem reasonable at US$1525 for seven days on Machame, US$1325 for six days on Marangu, including accommodation at Marangu's Babylon Lodge. Uses Tanzania Journeys of Moshi.

● **Big Expeditions** Shule Road, Near Exim Bank (PO Box 13780; ☎ 027-254 8449; 📧 www.bigexpeditions.net). Around since 2002 but only now really grabbing a decent share of the Kili market thanks in large part to their adoption by US outfit Alpine Ascents, who in turn have encouraged them into becoming KPAP partners. Their itineraries seem fairly standard but they do try to make themselves slightly different by, for example, setting up a table and buffet at Mweka Gate for those finishing their trek and putting plastic flowers on the picnic tables. Prices: US$1380 for six days on Marangu or seven days on Machame for US$1490.

● **Bobby Trekking** Goliondoi Rd (PO Box 14794; ☎ 0754-317948; 🖳 www.bobbytrekking.com). Bobby Trekking is a small operator sitting alongside its much bigger namesake, Bobby Safaris, and offers tiny-budget treks for those who want no-frills whatsoever but just the joy of tackling Kilimanjaro. Be sure to ask how they manage to offer prices that are so low – and how much they pay their crew on the mountain. Prices: US$1090 per person for *five* days on Marangu, US$100 more for *six* days on Machame.

● **Bobby Tours** Goliondoi Rd (PO Box 2169; ☎ 027-250 3490; 🖳 www.bobbytours.com). Established way back in 1976, Bobby are a very slick and professional company with a whole fleet of 4WDs and the swishest offices on Goliondoi. One glance at their oh-so-thorough website before you arrive in Arusha will give you some idea of how seriously they take their work. They are also surprisingly cheap; indeed, it may be worth asking them how they can be so cheap, where they make their savings and how much they pay their crew. Prices: US$1250 for seven days on the Machame Route; US$1100 for six days on Marangu. Add another US$150 to the Machame price if climbing via the Western Breach.

● **Bushbuck Safaris** Simeon Rd (PO Box 1700; ☎ 027-254 4186; 🖳 www.bushbuckltd.com). Huge operator housed in a suitably large building north of the Impala Hotel. As with most of the big companies around here, Bushbuck rarely deals with individuals walking off the street. Kilimanjaro expeditions come very much second to safaris with this company, too, which may explain their lack of knowledge (they were one of the companies who stated that the Western Breach was shut). Their prices were US$1670 per person for a private trek for six days on Machame, US$1430 for five days on Marangu – though as I've yet to meet anyone who's actually climbed with them, it's hard to know whether this is good value or not. Uses Mountain Inn as their base.

● **Corto Safaris** Near Moivaro Coffee Lodge (PO Box 12267; ☎ 027-255 3153, 🖳 www.cortosafaris.com). Based outside Arusha, this French-Tanzanian company was founded in 1994 and is still run by its original owner. Concentrating mainly on the whole of Tanzania rather than just Kilimanjaro, they are a KPAP partner thanks in part to their high salaries – which provide compensation for the lack of gratuities they receive from the notoriously ungenerous French who form most of their customer base. Prices: Machame Route, seven days, US$1830; Marangu six days US$1500.

● **Crown Eagle** Joel Maeda St (PO Box 177; ☎ 027-254 5200, 0754-263085). A small outfit occupying second floor offices by the clock tower, Crown Eagle has been going for six years or so and its boss, Salehe Abdalah, has been in the business for more than 15. Unfortunately, we have received one very damning email from a customer about their service. As for prices: US$1060 per person for six days on Marangu, US$1170 per person for the seven-day Machame trek and, weirdly, they say they charge the same whether the trek goes via Barafu or the Western Breach. There's no doubting they're cheap, but do check *thorough-ly* before booking with them as to what exactly is included – and to satisfy yourself that they really are competent to take people up the Western Breach Route.

● **Dik Dik** Arusha-Moshi Rd (PO Box 2289; ☎ 027-255 3499; 🖥 www.dikdik.ch). You can tell a Dik Dik expedition on the mountain with their smart luggage crates and mountain gear emblazoned with the Dik Dik logo. No longer operating on the Western Breach but still offering other routes, they never mix groups together – so if you book a trek with them, you won't be lumped with another party (which may be a blessing, or may not). Efficient, reliable and well-run – as you'd expect from a company with significant Swiss input – their prices are: Marangu, six days, US$1850 each; Machame, seven days, US$2550.

● **Duma Explorer** PPF Oloirien Estate, Off #22, Njiro (PO Box 2289; ☎ 0787 -079127 🖥 www.dumaexplorer.com/). No relation to the Duma agency in Moshi, this outfit, established in 2004 with considerable American involvement, offers just Rongai, Machame and Lemosho treks. Prices: Machame, seven days, US$2099 per person; all ascents via Crater Camp incur an additional US$500 per person charge. A shower on your trek will be an extra US$300 (they are one of the very few to offer this). KPAP partner.

● **Easy Travel and Tours** Boma Road (PO Box 1912; ☎ 027-250 7322; 🖥 www.easytravel.co.tz). In a prestigious location sandwiched between the old KLM office and the New Safari Hotel, Easy Travel and Tours are an efficient and very busy safari company and the representatives for airlines such as Air Mauritius and Air Zimbabwe. Their service is thoroughly reliable, though with so much else going on one gets the feeling that Kilimanjaro treks aren't really their priority. Prices: six days on Marangu for US$1210; seven days on Machame US$1420 – with airport transfers and hotel accommodation extra in both cases.

● **Equatorial Safaris** Room 428, 4th floor, AICC bldg (PO Box 2156; ☎ 027-250 2617; 🖥 www.equatorialsafaris.com). Fairly well-established Kili operator with Austrian links who have now diversified into offering trips to Rwanda to see the gorillas, treks up Mount Kenya – and even a 68-day program to Everest! Regarding Kili, on their website they offer just Machame, Marangu and Lemosho. They also have their own campsite on the lower slopes of the mountain at 2000m, an hour out of Moshi, which they use as a base for 'ecotourism' excursions to Chagga villages etc. As for the treks themselves, alas I didn't meet anybody who had trekked with them when researching for this edition, though their reputation for safaris at least is one of competence. Prices: US$1450 for either seven days on the Machame Route or six days on Marangu.

● **F&S Kiliwarrior** (PO Box 12339; 🖥 www.go-kili.com). Co-owned by Wilbert Mollel – the original Kiliwarrior, so-called because of his Masai heritage – F&S are a KPAP partner (see box beginning p46) who also make their own DVDs of the mountain. For their Western Breach climb they like to use the Lemosho Route (climbing helmets are, as usual, essential). The company offers two levels of cost: a Platinum rate, in which almost everything – drinks, laundry, meals, even tips and a private car in Arusha (though not airfares) – is included, and a better-value Gold rate which offers a similar deal to the other trekking agencies. Sample prices: seven-day Machame US$3500 on the Gold Rate, or US$4800 for the Platinum Rate; nine days via the Western Breach US$4600 Gold Rate, US$5600 Platinum.

● **Good Earth** Arusha Municipality Road, Plot 1896 (PO Box 1115; ☎ 0732-902655; 🖳 www.goodearthtours.com). Established tour operator with offices in the AICC Building, and a second branch in Florida (see p34). Despite the overseas connections they are one of the Arusha companies that really do promote their tours around town, and you'll often see their posters on noticeboards advertising for trekkers to join their forthcoming trips. Their website also claims that they practise responsible tourism, providing scholarships, books, and supplies to local children and financial support to various environmental groups. They charge US$1490 per person on the Marangu Route (six days), US$1750 on Machame (seven days), both including two nights' accommodation at the Jacaranda and airport transfers. They also offer the Western Breach (though not with a night at Crater Camp), with seven days costing US$1970.

● **Maasai Wanderings** Njiro (PO Box 14035; ☎ 0755-984925; 🖳 www.maasai wanderings.com). Run by an Australian woman and her Tanzanian husband, this company have garnered good reviews thanks in part to their considerate treatment of porters. Laudably, they also use some of their profits to support a number of schools and community schemes around Arusha. Offer Rongai and Machame treks, as well as a 15-day safari and trek combination that takes in the Serengeti, Tarangire and Ngorongoro plus a saunter up the Machame Route (US$4190 per person). Prices: Marangu, six days, US$1650; Machame, seven days, US$1995 if joining a scheduled climb, or US$2820 if two people are booking a private trek. KPAP partner.

● **Nature Discovery** (PO Box 10574; ☎ 027-254 4063; 🖳 www.naturediscov ery.com). Upmarket company in operation since 1992 that specializes in tailor-made tours; perhaps best known as the company that arranges Thomson Safari's treks on the mountain. Sample prices: seven days on Machame US$2930 per person, six days on Marangu US$2461 per person. Note that climbers on the 'budget' option, even though it's not that cheap, are still asked to limit their baggage to 8kg. Some of that money goes towards paying the porters whom they claim receive the highest pay on the mountain. KPAP partner.

● **Roy Safaris** 44 Serengeti Rd (PO Box 50; ☎ 027-250 8010; 🖳 www.roysaf aris.com). One of the bigger safari operators and now boasting their very own sumptuous hotel in town too (see p175), I unfairly dismissed Roy last time as a company that doesn't take Kili too seriously. True, their reputation rests on their safaris, but they do seem to know what they're doing on Kili, too, with a good service provided including use of pulse oximeters (which, to put it simply, reads the amount of oxygen in a person's blood) on each trek, all of which are private (ie if you book with them you won't suddenly find yourself lumped with a larger group). Overall they seem pretty competent and charge US$1415 per person for six days on Marangu, US$1670 per person for seven days on Machame; add on another US$250 to the latter if climbing via the Western Breach.

● **Safari Makers** South of the AICC Club (PO Box 12902; ☎ 027-254 4446, 0754 300817; 💻 www.safarimakers.com). Claimed that the Western Breach was closed when we enquired but otherwise this is a reasonably efficient and helpful company, run jointly by a Tanzanian and an American, that also offers treks up Kilimanjaro on all the major routes. For Marangu, six days is US$1395 per person; Machame, seven days, US$1630 per person.

● **Shidolya** Room 218, at the end of the corridor on the second floor, Ngorongoro wing, AICC building (PO Box 1436, ☎ 027-254 8506, 💻 www.shidolya-safaris.com). Shidolya are undoubtedly one of the more professional outfits, with a busy office and a slick style, including computer print-outs of the day-to-day itineraries of each trek. They are also, somewhat surprisingly, pretty cheap by Arusha standards, with seven-day Machame treks for US$1330 per person, or US$1130 for six days on Marangu. They also run the Colobus Mountain Lodge in Arusha National Park (see p231) – a good base for exploring the park and climbing Meru. Worth investigating.

● **Summits Africa** (☎ 0732-972692 or 0787-130666; 💻 www.summits-africa.com). New company formed by the son of one of the founders of Hoopoe Adventure – one of the biggest names in climbing and safaris in recent years. Darlings of KPAP for the way they treat their porters, they are also very safety-conscious with oximetry tests for their clients as standard. Such service doesn't come cheap, however, at US$2500 for their Lightweight 'budget' trek, rising to US$3650 for a more comfortable trek that includes thicker mattresses, bigger tents, airport transfers and hotels for a night before and after the trek. Their response to our email was informative and considered, they offer all routes (though prefer Lemosho and Machame) and offer a 'Plains to Peak' tour (US$4655) which includes a couple of nights amongst the elephants of the West Kilimanjaro Corridor before a saunter up the Lemosho trail. You'll pay around an extra US$500 for a private trek.

● **Sunny Safaris** Col Middleton Rd (PO Box 7267; ☎ 027-250 7145; 💻 www.sunnysafaris.com). One of the busier budget companies in Arusha, now slightly less popular than in previous years – possibly because their office on Colonel Middleton Road sees far fewer budget travellers than in years gone by when this part of town was backpacker-central. The price they quoted us of US$1425 for seven days on Machame seems reasonable, though this includes neither hotel accommodation nor airport transfers (US$70 extra one way). Probably more a safari specialist than a Kili expert but they're OK.

● **Tanzania Serengeti Adventure** (PO Box 1742; ☎ 027-250 4069; 💻 www.abouttanzania.com). Quite an unknown quantity, we've yet to meet anyone who's climbed with them but their prices certainly seem OK – though do check that they pay a fair wage. Prices: for two people, Marangu six days is US$1212 each; Machame seven days US$1418 each. Add an extra US$150 to these prices for a private trek. Not a KPAP partner – yet – but according to sources the porters are happy and do receive the proper wage.

● **Tawisa** (☎ 0787-620611; 💻 www.tanganyika.com). Unusual company that goes under various different names: Mount Kilimanjaro Safari Club, Tawisa and also Tanganyika Expeditions (which I think is the name of their European representatives). Further investigation revealed them to be a largely French company. Hopefully that doesn't put you off, however, for the email I received from their British representative was helpful almost to the point of being servile, including offers to meet up beforehand with no obligation attached to such a meeting. They were a bit less forthcoming with the prices, however, though when they did it was OK at US$1890 for seven days on Machame including two nights in the very plush Sal Salinero Hotel in Moshi as well as transfers.

● **Team Kilimanjaro** Kundayo (PO Box 12023; ☎ 0787-503595; 🖳 www.teamkilimanjaro.com). Arusha office of recommended British-based company. The location is an obscure one but if you give them a ring they'll pick you up. See p29 for details of their treks.

● **Thomson Safaris** (PO Box 6074; ☎ US toll free 1-800-235 0289; 🖳 www.thomsontreks.com). Highly regarded outfit that's been running for more than 25 years and is the main operator on the Western Breach Route (for which they will ask you to wear a climbing helmet) – even though it is actually Nature Discovery (see p187) who run their treks these days. They tend to concentrate on the American market, even offering airfares from the US to Arusha as part of their package. When we contacted them to find out about their Machame and Marangu treks, they instead tried to push us to do an Umbwe trek (US$3990 including return flights from the US), concentrating on just this trail and the Lemosho Route now to avoid the crowds of Machame. However, they can organize a private trek on other routes, for which you pay a healthy US$4590 (with US flights) for a ten-day trip including seven days on the Machame Route. Nevertheless, they are extremely reliable and efficient, offering one of the best services on the mountain with good safety equipment (including Gamow bags) and 'gourmet' food. KPAP partner.

● **Victoria Expeditions** Meru House Inn, Sokoine Rd (PO Box 14875; ☎ 027-250 0444; 🖳 www.victoriatz.com) Run by a Norwegian lady and her husband, Victoria Expeditions appear to be a busy operation that's been going for over ten years now, a success that can be attributed in part to their location on the ground floor of one of the more popular and enduring budget hotels, and in part to a very cheap service. Their brochures have all their itineraries *and* tariffs listed, which is a relief for those with an aversion to haggling. Though with prices as cheap as this – Marangu six days US$1100, for example – you won't have to haggle much to get a low-cost trek; as always with budget operators, however, check where the savings are being made and if they are paying a fair wage.

GETTING AWAY

Buses

To Moshi Those heading towards Kili will find the local 'Coaster' buses are the most convenient way to travel the 80km to **Moshi**. They run throughout the day from the main bus station, with the last one at around 5pm (Ts3000, or Ts2500 if there are five of you in a four-seat row). This last option is the best way to get to know the locals, mainly because some of them will be sitting on your lap.)

It's not a particularly pleasant way to travel but other options are thin on the ground, with Moshi ill-served by the **shuttle bus** companies. Riverside (☎ 027-250 2639 or 250 3916; 🖳 www.riverside-shuttle.com), with its office in a chemists on Sokoine, have one bus per day at 2pm (US$10), as do Bobby Shuttle (☎ 027-250 3490; 🖳 www.bobbyshuttle.com), part of Bobby Tours on Goliondoi. Both these companies depart from the car park in front of Bella Luna Hotel (p174) on Simeon Road, though if you book in advance you should get picked up from your hotel. At the foot of Simeon Road is the Impala Hotel (p175), whose car park is home to Impala Shuttle (☎ 027-250 7197; 🖳 www.impalahotel.com). They, too, operate a daily bus to Moshi (US$10), that starts in Nairobi and calls in at Arusha at around 2pm – and may drive on to Marangu if the demand's there.

To Nairobi and Kampala Of the **bus** companies, Scandinavia, who are based at Kilombero, just north of Shoprite, remain popular despite the financial difficulties they have suffered over the past few years. They run buses on Mondays, Tuesdays, Thursdays and Saturdays at 4pm to Nairobi's Central Bus Station (Ts25,000), continuing on to Kampala (Ts60,000). Dar Express (3pm; Ts22,000), in new offices on Wachagga Road, and Akamba (☎ 027-250 9491), five minutes away in the Sango petrol station on the Nairobi Highway, are also good and safe.

As for the **shuttles**, Riverside (☎ 027-250 2639 or 250 3916; 🖳 www.riverside-shuttle.com/) on Sokoine Road run two shuttles daily to Nairobi, at 8am (arrive 2pm) and 2pm (it's the one from Moshi, and arrives in Nairobi at 6.30pm). They charge US$30 for foreign tourists. Bobby Shuttle, part of Bobby Tours, operate identical times and prices, as do Impala (☎ 0754-550 010), who have an office in the car park of the hotel (see p175) that shares their name. As with all shuttles, they should pick you up from your hotel, though you should press home this point when making the booking.

To Dar es Salaam The former travellers' favourite, Scandinavia, have **buses** daily to Dar at 8.30am and 11.30am for Ts20,000 and Ts24,000 respectively – the different prices reflecting the quality of the buses). Dar Express, in new offices, Kilimanjaro Express on Col Middleton Road, and Akamba (☎ 027-250 9491), ten minutes away in the Sango petrol station on the Nairobi–Moshi Highway, are all reliable though it pays to ask around for the latest information.

❏ **Getting to Kilimanjaro International Airport**

Impala (☎ 027-250 7197) run a shuttle from their base in the Impala Hotel car park, the shuttle leaving around three hours before the KLM flight – thus allowing passengers who are joining the KLM flight enough time to check-in – and returning when the bus is filled with KLM passengers who've just landed (US$15 each way). Precision Air also offer a shuttle service to and from KIA for their flights (Ts10,000). Air Tanzania have a free shuttle for their passengers, their buses leaving from their office on Boma Road two hours prior to the scheduled departure of their flights.

A **taxi** to the airport officially costs US$50, though with bargaining this can be reduced. For **transport to Arusha Airport**, see p163.

Flights

Arusha effectively has two airports, with **Kilimanjaro International Airport** being less than an hour away. See p167 for details of the airline offices in Arusha and p340 for details of flights. Remember that there is a **departure tax**, namely US$6 for domestic flights, US$35 for international destinations (the latter always, in our experience, already included in the price of the ticket); these figures do change, however, so do check when reconfirming your flight.

Moshi

Cheaper, quieter, nearer and prettier, Moshi sits in the shadow of Kilimanjaro and, for climbing the mountain, is perhaps a superior base to neighbouring Arusha, 80km away to the west. As the unofficial capital of the Chagga world, most visitors find Moshi a little more interesting too. The missionaries who followed in the wake of Rebmann gave the Chaggas the advantage of a Western education and this, combined with the agricultural fecundity of Kilimanjaro's southern slopes, has enabled the Chaggas to become one of the wealthiest, most influential and most securely self-aware groups in the country. Moshi has reaped the benefits too, prospering to the point where it is now one of the smartest towns in Tanzania (though grim poverty is still not difficult to find, as anybody who has walked around Moshi at night, stepping over the sleeping bodies of the dispossessed lying on the pavements as they do so, can testify).

While the Chaggas are the dominant force in town, Moshi is still a cosmopolitan place, with a highly visible Indian minority; this colourful ethnic mixture is reflected in the architecture, with a huge Hindu temple abutting an equally striking mosque and with dozens of small churches and chapels scattered in the streets thereabouts. There also seems to be more civic pride here in Moshi than in other parts of the country; check out the Kilimanjaro flower garden outside Kibo House, for example. Indeed, the only dark cloud for tourists in Moshi is the inordinate amount of hassle they suffer from trekking agency touts, 'artists' and the like. Look beyond this, however, and you're sure to find Moshi a charming place, with enough facilities to enable you to organize a trek – and enjoy some long nights of celebration at the end.

ARRIVAL

Precision Air operate a shuttle from Moshi to the airport, a twice-daily service (Ts10,000) that is supposed to coincide with their flights. Air Tanzania also offer a shuttle, this time free, for those arriving on their daily flight from Dar. Arriving on KLM you'll either have to catch a cab (US$50) or take the Impala shuttle to Arusha (US$15), and with Ethiopian Airlines a cab is the only option. Arrive by **bus** and you'll be dropped off at the terminal on Mawenzi Road, 200m south of the clock tower, within walking distance of most hotels.

ARUSHA, MOSHI AND MARANGU

ORIENTATION AND GETTING AROUND

According to Harry Johnston, Moshi could simply mean 'town' or 'settlement', though as with everything Johnston wrote, this could well be wrong. Indeed, Moshi also translates as 'smoke' – a reference, perhaps, to its situation at the foot of a volcano?

What is certain is that Moshi is compact, with almost everything of interest to the holidaying visitor lying on or near the main thoroughfare, **Mawenzi Road** (aka Nyerere Road, which is also, strangely, known as Double Road), and its northern extension, **Kibo Road** (the two names borrowed from the peaks of Kilimanjaro). Together they run all the way from the market situated down the hill at the southern end of town, to the roundabout at the northern end with the statue of a soldier facing north towards Kilimanjaro.

Separating Mawenzi Road from Kibo Road is a second roundabout adorned with a soft-drink sponsored clock tower, the centre of town. **Dalla-dallas** drive up and down the main Mawenzi and Market streets for Ts300, though it doesn't take long to walk anywhere, Moshi being compact. The one exception to this rule is the suburb of **Shanty Town**, north-west of the centre, home to a great Indian restaurant, a Chinese and a couple of fine hotels. A cab to Shanty Town will cost Ts3000 from the town centre.

Chagga Tours, just off Mawenzi Road on the road leading down to the Buffalo Hotel, offer the services of a **guide** to show you around town, though to be honest Moshi is compact enough that one isn't really necessary.

SERVICES

Banks

The banks don't change money now. In their place, **moneychangers** such as Executive in the Vodacom Building and its near neighbour, the wonderfully named God Hates Corruption – Join Him Executive Bureau de Change, stay open later, their rates are fine and they don't charge commission. The money-changer with the best rates is currently Trust (spelt 'Trast' on the sign), which also happens to be the most convenient for most of the tourist-friendly hotels.

Just as convenient, there's an **ATM** at Barclays that's on the main drag near most of the budget hotels, another at the NBC (though there have been occasions when tourists have used this machine, only to find their accounts drastically reduced upon returning home by a sum much greater than that which they withdrew); and one at Bank Exim on Boma Rd, opposite Abbas Ali's. The supermarket near the Leopard Hotel also has one.

Communications

The **post office** is by the clock tower, at the junction with Boma Road. Opening times are Mon-Fri 8am-4.30pm, Sat 9am-noon. The **Telecom office** (Mon-Fri 8am-4.30pm, Sat 9am-noon) next to the post office can sell you phonecards (Ts1000) which you can then load up with credit and use in the phone boxes outside. EasyCom, in the basement of Kahawa House near the clock tower, offers international phone calls at just Ts250 per minute to Europe, Australia and South Africa, and Ts200 per minute to America. Presumably the calls are made through the internet using Skype or something similar, so it's possible the phone calls could be subject to delays on the line or other problems; however, it's so cheap that it's definitely worth trying out. Their **internet** service has long been highly regarded (Ts500 for 15 minutes, Ts1500 per hour), though there are plenty of choices in this town including Duma Cybercafé (same prices as EasyCom), down the hill from the Coffee Shop; the Buffalo Hotel (cheaper than the others at Ts1000 per hour, with longer opening hours – 8am-9pm – and with a pretty fast connection too) and the friendly Dot Café, up from the Malindi Club on Rengua St, which is currently the only place in town with wi-fi facilities (though the Watering Hole, outside the centre, has them too, and charges just Ts1500 for as long as you like).

Airline offices
Precision Air are in the KNCU Building (☎ 027-275 3498; Mon-Fri 8am-5pm, Sat, Sun & hols 9am-2pm). **Air Tanzania** are on Rengua (☎ 027-275 5205). For other airlines, visit Emslies on Old Moshi Road, (☎ 027-275 2701).

Swimming pools
The YMCA, Impala, Sal Salinero and Key's Hotel all charge Ts3000 to use their pools, and Ameg Lodge charges Ts7000, the latter also including use of their gym; in all of these places hotel guests can use the facilities for free.

Shopping
● **Trekking provisions** Finally, Moshi can boast a decent trekking equipment supplier. Indeed, it's the best we've found in East Africa. **Gladys Adventure** is run by the enterprising, eponymous Gladys, who started out trading souvenirs from her curio shop in return for hard-to-come-by bits of trekking equipment with tourists coming off the mountain. Having built up an extensive collection over the past ten years, Gladys has now moved her operation from her former base 5km out of town to brand new premises on Hill St in the heart of Moshi. Her collection is extensive, her stuff is good quality and her rental prices are cheap: US$5 for a head torch, foam mattresses US$5, thermarests US$10, bottles US$4, and sleeping bags US$10 – all prices per trip and not per day! Perhaps most usefully of all, she also does a nice line in fleeces and base layers – items that can be really difficult to source in Tanzania. Just one word of caution: while Gladys is indubitably a godsend, do remember that your agency should be able to supply you with most major bits of equipment that you might have forgotten to bring with you and it may be included in the price.

Other items that you may well have overlooked but will find extremely useful include: chapsticks (along with mosquito repellent and most other pharmaceutical needs), which can be bought from the Third Millennium **Pharmacy** on Mawenzi Road, between the New Kindoroko and Backpacker Lodge; and bin liners (or large shopping bags), useful for keeping clothing within your rucksack dry and available from the market or one of the little supermarkets mentioned on p194. **Maps and books** about Kili can be bought from the Old Moshi

---

MOSHI MAP KEY

Where to stay
2 Key's Hotel
3 YMCA
6 Kilimanjaro Crane Hotel
8 New Coffee Tree Hotel
18 Park View Inn
19 Bristol Cottages
29 Zebra Hotels
33 Buffalo Hotel
34 Kindoroko Hotel
36 Moshi Leopard Hotel

41 Golden View Hotel
42 Big Mountain Inn
44 Kilimanjaro Backpackers
45 Umoja Lutheran Hostel

Where to eat & drink
8 New Coffee Tree Café
13 Pub Alberto & Chrisburger
14 Malindi Club
15 Corner Café
17 Aroma

21 Central Garden
24 Deli Chez
25 Coffee Shop
27 East African Pub
28 Milan's
31 Sikh Club
32 Indoitaliano
37 Tanzanian Coffee Lounge
38 Chagga Bar & Grill
39 Kili Attik
43 Salzburger

Bookshop on Rindi Lane at the junction with Kibo, the bookshop at the Kilimanjaro Crane Hotel or the souvenir shop by Marangu Gate.

● **Supermarkets and other possibly useful stores** Carina Supermarket, next to the Impala Shuttle office, is handy for those staying near the clock tower, while Safari, on Riadha St south of the market, has a slightly wider array of stock and is handy for those at the southern end of town. Another convenience store that truly deserves the description is Kilimanjaro D, just up from Barclays. Up the hill to the west of the clock tower, on Boma Road is *Abbas Ali's Hot Bread Shop*, a very pleasant place with great fresh bread.

● **Souvenirs** There are plenty of souvenirs to buy in Moshi, and plenty of places willing to flog them to you. Two in particular deserve special mention. **Shah Industries** is a leather-workshop-cum-aquarium housed in what used to be a flour mill. It's a strange combination but a beautiful place and a worthy one too: over a third of the workers at Shah Industries have some sort of disability. Definitely worth looking around, it lies to the south-east of town across the train tracks on the way to the Springlands Hotel. Much more central, **Tahea Kili** sits opposite the Coffee Shop and is another charitable concern, with the profits returning to local women's groups.

Of the 'regular' souvenir shops, the best in terms of choice and quality is iCurio, just round the corner from the Kindoroko Hotel, with the widest array of stock including a fine line in Kilimanjaro Beer T-shirts. **Our Heritage**, sharing the same building as the Coffee Shop, has a fair array of knick-knacks, while **Cranecraft**, in the Kilimanjaro Crane Hotel, has similar stock plus a decent selection of books about the country, its wildlife and, of course, the mountain. Worth a nose around. **Chui Traders**, near the New Castle Hotel on Nyerere Road, is the place to come for Masai clothes and implements.

The **Coffee Shop** on Hill St runs a profitable little trade in neatly wrapped Kilimanjaro coffee, though apparently you can get much the same sort of stuff for half the price at the supermarket.

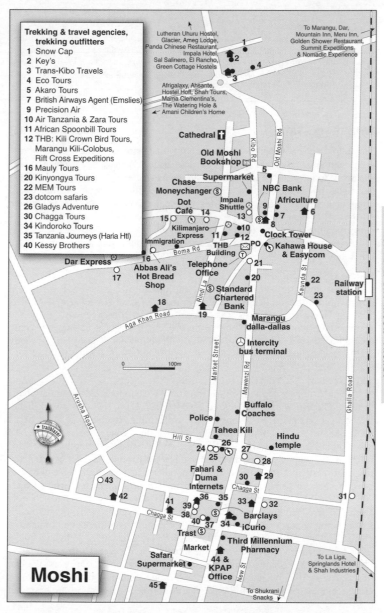

Trekking & travel agencies, trekking outfitters

1 Snow Cap
2 Key's
3 Trans-Kibo Travels
4 Eco Tours
5 Akaro Tours
7 British Airways Agent (Emslies)
9 Precision Air
10 Air Tanzania & Zara Tours
11 African Spoonbill Tours
12 THB: Kili Crown Bird Tours,
   Marangu Kili-Colobus,
   Rift Cross Expeditions
16 Mauly Tours
20 Kinyongya Tours
22 MEM Tours
23 dotcom safaris
26 Gladys Adventure
30 Chagga Tours
34 Kindoroko Tours
35 Tanzania Journeys (Haria Htl)
40 Kessy Brothers

Lutheran Uhuru Hostel,
Glacier, Ameg Lodge,
Panda Chinese Restaurant,
Impala Hotel,
Sal Salinero, El Rancho,
Green Cottage Hostels

To Marangu, Dar,
Mountain Inn, Meru Inn,
Golden Shower Restaurant,
Summit Expeditions
& Nomadic Experience

Afrigalaxy, Ahsante,
Hostel Hoff, Shah Tours,
Mama Clementina's,
The Watering Hole &
Amani Children's Home

Cathedral

Old Moshi
Bookshop

Old Moshi Rd
Kibo Rd

Supermarket

Chase
Moneychanger $

Dot
Café

15

Kilimanjaro
Express

Immigration

Boma Rd

16

Dar Express

17

Abbas Ali's
Hot Bread
Shop

Impala
Shuttle

13

14

11

10

12

THB
Building

Telephone
Office

20

Rind La

Standard
Chartered
Bank

19

Aga Khan Road

18

5

NBC Bank

Africulture

9

7

8

Clock Tower

PO

Kahawa House
& Easycom

21

22

23

Railway
station

Kaunda St

Marangu
dalla-dallas

Intercity
bus terminal

Market Street

Mawenzi Rd

Ghalla Road

Buffalo
Coaches

Police

Tahea Kili

Hindu
temple

24

26

25

27

28

Fahari &
Duma
Internets

30

29

Chagga St

43

42

41

39

38

40

36

35

33

37

34

32

Barclays

iCurio

31

Trast $

Market

Third Millennium
Pharmacy

Safari
Supermarket

44 &
KPAP
Office

45

Hill St

Chagga St

New St

To La Liga,
Springlands Hotel
& Shah Industries

To Shukrani
Snacks

Arusha Road

0   100m

trailblazer

Moshi

ARUSHA, MOSHI AND MARANGU

❏ **Abbreviations**
Throughout this book we have used the following abbreviations when writing about accommodation: **s/c** means self-contained, as in en suite (ie the room comes with a bathroom); **sgl/dbl/tpl** means single/double/triple rooms. For example, where we have written 'sgl/dbl/tpl US$35/40/45', we mean that a single room costs US$35 per night, a double US$40, and a triple US$45.

WHERE TO STAY   [see map p195]

The following is not an exhaustive list but whilst there are some cheaper places at the southern end of town, many refuse to accept Westerners. Manage to persuade one to let you stay for the night and you can expect to pay around Ts3000 per night, though the chances are it'll be assumed that you want bed and broad rather than bed and board. **Campsites** include the grounds of the *Green Cottage Hostels* (US$3 per person) and at the *Golden Shower Restaurant* (US$3 per person) on the main road to Marangu and Dar.

As for the hotels that definitely do welcome tourists, in approximate price order they are as follows:

Below US$20 per double

Moshi has hotels to suit every budget and the following review is written in **approximate price order**. To begin, we must mention *Hostel Hoff* (☎ 0787-225908; 🖳 www.hostelhoff.com). This place, situated between and just to the north of the two main roundabouts on the way out of Moshi, usually accepts only long-term guests and as such is popular with volunteers. Run by an Irish lady with a David Hasselhoff obsession, it's scruffy but clean and the price is very reasonable at US$15 per day including meals and laundry, which is one reason why it regularly receives rave reviews from its residents.

If you're not staying long in Moshi, you'll have to look at the regular hotels instead. The *Kilimanjaro Backpackers* (☎ 027-275 5159; 🖳 www.kiliman jarobackpackers.com) on Nyerere/Mawenzi/Double Road is a relative of its namesake in Arusha, but while it's around the same price at US$5/7/12 dorm/sgl/dbl for B&B (add US$4 per person for half-board, another US$4 for full board), it's nowhere near as smart and has poky rooms (though with fan and mosquito net); that said, it's certainly popular and you can't argue with the price. Nearby, just south of the market is the *Umoja Lutheran Hostel* (☎ 027-275 0902; 🖳 umohost07@yahoo.com); look for the sign 'KKKT Umoja Hostel'. There's nothing wrong with this place – it's clean, well-run and the *alfresco* eating area is certainly pleasant – but again it's a little lacking in atmosphere. Still, at US$7/12/18 sgl/dbl/tpl, all with breakfast, it's good value.

At the northern end of town by the roundabout, the *New Coffee Tree Hotel* (☎ 027-275 1382) is a place for those for whom every *shilingi* matters. We like this place: we like the staff, we like the location right next to the clock tower and we like the restaurant on the top floor. Admittedly, the rooms are basic but they do come with sink and mozzy net and are functional, fine and very fairly priced at only Ts8000 for a single with shared facilities, or Ts12,000-20,000 for en-suite doubles (the more expensive ones with TV), all including breakfast. Curiously, tourists rarely stay here. Continuing northwards, the *YMCA* (☎ 027-275 1754) on the main roundabout has always felt a little rundown. To be fair, the prices of US$10/13 sgl/dbl with shared bathroom for B&B are just about reasonable and guests say it's functional, fine and the pool is lovely.

The *Buffalo Hotel* (☎ 027-275 0270) on New Street has clean bright rooms, all en suite and with mosquito nets, and a fairly popular bar and restaurant downstairs. The hotel has installed cable TV into the en-suite rooms (Ts12,000/20,000-50,000 sgl/dbl) but there are also some fairly priced doubles with common facilities (Ts12,000), all rates including breakfast.

The Buffalo's nearest rival, both geographically and in terms of quality, is the *Kindoroko Hotel* (☎ 027-275 4054; 🖳 www.kindoroko.com), a busy place which boasts an internet café and even a massage service (Ts30,000 for the full body). Rates are US$15 per person, which is fair, as well as a couple of twin rooms with shared bathroom for just US$15 for the room, which is good value.

US$20-50 per double
The *Zebra Hotels* (☎ 027-275 0611; 🖳 www.zebhotelstz.com) is a large and swish affair. The tiger-print blankets, while not entirely appropriate for this part of the world, are just one of the features of their facility-heavy en-suite rooms; they also come with satellite TV, direct-dial telephone and room service. The prices are very fair, however, at US$30/35 s/c sgl/dbl or US$45 for executive rooms that come with mini-bar and air-con.

The *Moshi Leopard Hotel* on Market Street (☎ 027-275 0884; 🖳 www.leopardhotel.com) is an old favourite with tour groups and independent travellers alike. Boasting an excellent terrace bar (from where, if you peer through the branches of the nearby tree, you can see Kibo), an extravagantly liveried doorman and smiling staff, the rooms themselves are very comfy and as well as being en suite also include a fridge, TV, wardrobe, fan and balcony. The hotel now offers massages too – just the thing for that post-trek indulgence you promised yourself? Pay Ts8000 for back, Ts8000 each for front and back of legs – or Ts30,000 for the full body. As for the room rates, the non-residents' prices are US$40/50 s/c sgl/dbl, which is fair value but not exceptional.

While we're in this quarter, on Chagga St is *Golden View Hotel* (☎ 0757-365558 or 0754-775596; 🖳 www.goldenhotel.4t.com), which lacks for nothing except custom. Situated in the market area, it's a smart and polished establishment where all the rooms (which are a bit small) have their own balcony, bathroom and mosquito net and rates (US$15/25 s/c sgl/dbl) include breakfast. It's a good place if you want to avoid other Westerners – something that it is becoming increasingly difficult to do in this town. Moving further north onto Kiusa St is a new place: *Big Mountain Inn* (☎ 027-275 1862; 🖳 pmtitos@hotmail.com) has some very smart rooms squashed together around a small garden. It feels a bit cramped but it's nevertheless pleasant enough and the prices (US$30/45 s/c sgl/dbl) are very fair.

Moving to the other side of the clock tower but staying in the same price bracket, *Kilimanjaro Crane Hotel* (☎ 027-275 1114; 💻 www.kilimanjarocra nehotels.com) seems to be more of a local businessmen's hotel. It's a decent enough place, however, with 30 smart rooms, sauna, gym and even a very small pool. Singles, which have showers, TV and telephone, are US$40 each; doubles and triples have both bathtubs and showers and go for US$45/50, or it's US$50 for a double with air-con. These rates have stayed the same for a few years now and as a consequence the hotel is looking rather good value.

The *Moshi Hotel*, by the way, is currently closed for renovations, with the new management planning to reopen as the *New Livingstone Hotel* sometime in the future. So far the sign has gone up – and very impressive it is too – but every-thing else appears to have fallen into a state of dilapidation, disrepair and decay. It wasn't ready in time for the last edition and it won't be ready in time for the publication of this one; and we don't expect it to reopen anytime soon.

US$50 and above per double

The *Bristol Cottages* (☎ 027-275 5083; 💻 www.bristolcottages.com) describe themselves as 'The countryside hotel in the middle of town', and though the noise from the buses revving up the hill outside rather shatters that boast, it's true that this is a little blossom-filled haven and the most convenient upper-bracket hotel in Moshi. The smart cottages, all with large TV and mosquito net, go for US$60/72 s/c sgl/dbl; the new wing, a little noisier due to its proximity to the road, is consequently slightly cheaper at US$45/60 s/c sgl/dbl, while there are some rooms with mountain view that will set you back US$120/140 s/c sgl/dbl.

Just a few metres up the hill on Aga Khan Road is another smart place. The *Park View Inn* (☎ 027-275 0711; 💻 www.pvim.com) is only small, with a dozen rooms or so, though the rooms themselves have the kind of elegant uni-formity and features – TV, telephone, air-con and bath or shower – of a large chain hotel. Thankfully, however, it has a friendly informality commensurate with its size. The noise from the building site next door is unfortunate but hope-fully merely temporary too. Rates are US$45/55-65 for s/c sgl/dbl.

North again, this time on Uru Road, is the *Key's Hotel* (☎ 027-275 2250 or 275 1875; 💻 www.keys-hotel-tours.com), a traditional-looking family-run hotel and one of the smartest addresses in Moshi. In the main building it's doubles only (US$50), all coming with TV, telephone, mini-bar, toilet and a shower with hot/cold running water; air-con is US$20 extra. There are also 15 small thatch-and-cement cottages in the grounds which are quite fun. All rates include con-tinental breakfast.

However, for the top places in Moshi you have to go to a part of town per-haps misleadingly called Shanty Town – a smart area of jacaranda-lined boule-vards that's quite unlike any shanty town you've seen before. Even the hostels are smart in Shanty Town. The *Lutheran Uhuru Hostel* (☎ 027-275 4084; 💻 www.uhuruhostel.org), for example, sits in fairly vast grounds. It's a quiet, relaxed place, the only activity coming from the team of gardeners and cleaners maintaining the neat-and-tidyness of it all. Rooms are very pleasant – particu-larly those in the new Kibo or Kilimanjaro wings – and all are self-contained;

indeed, our only beef is its location, a bit too far out of town to walk and thus engendering a Ts2000 cab fare whenever you want to go anywhere. That and the tariff which, in our opinion, is a little high at US$45/55 s/c sgl/dbl in the Mawenzi Wing, US$40/50 in the Kilimanjaro and Kibo wings. Despite these moans, it maintains a healthy trickle of customers and if you've got your own transport – or are happy doing nothing all day except watch a battalion of gardeners watering the grass – it's fine.

Three of the finest hotels can be found in Shanty Town too. The first is something of a curiosity. Maybe it's the high concrete walls surrounding the place, maybe it's the uniform whitewashed, green-roofed chalets, or maybe the popular pool where everybody seems to congregate – whatever it is, there's something about the *Ameg Lodge* (☎ 027-275 0175, 0754-058268; 🖳 www.ameglodge.com), off Lema Road, that's reminiscent of a 1950s' British seaside holiday camp. Thankfully, the rather bland, shadeless exterior belies some rather stylish rooms, each with shower, satellite TV, fan, veranda and phone. Prices (all doubles) start at US$79, rising to US$110 for the junior suite. In addition to the pool, guests are also entitled to use the hotel gym.

Further north and on Lema Road, the *Impala* (☎ 027-275 3443/4 or 0757-725944; 🖳 impala@kilinet.co.tz) is from the same herd as the one in Arusha, though where that Impala is more of a business centre, this one is more homely and all the better for it. A lovely pool and friendly staff are just two of its selling points, along with stylish yet inviting en-suite rooms with TV and all mod-cons. For those of us who aren't living in Tanzania it's US$80/100 for s/c sgl/dbl B&B.

West off Lema Rd lies a flashier and more ornate hotel. *Sal Salinero* (☎ 027-275 2240; 🖳 salinerohotel@yahoo.com) is a shiny Italianate villa housing seven enormous en-suite rooms (with 17 more being built) each with TV and tea and coffee-making facilities. The sparkling sunkissed pool is very inviting, while those who seek shade can lean against the bar and watch English football every Saturday. With the prices at sgl/dbl US$75/95-130, this may be one of the more expensive places in town but it's also one of the smartest.

Finally, there are two places, both just a little out of town, that are owned and run by trekking agencies. Unless you have booked with one of these agencies it is highly unlikely you will stay here; if you *have* booked with these agencies, on the other hand, the chances are you will get a night or two free at the hotel before and after your trek. The first is the very comfortable *Mountain Inn*, four kilometres from town on the way to Marangu, which is owned and run by Shah Tours (see p209 for contact details). A pool, sauna and a pretty garden are just some of the attractions here. The second place is the Zara-run *Springlands Hotel* (☎ 027-2750011; 🖳 www.springlands.co.tz), 2km to the south of town. Most people who stay here are happy with what they find, the pool being the main attraction, though the buffet dinners are to be recommended too. It is, however, rather isolated, and the high walls and over-zealous security really give the place a kind of them-and-us atmosphere, with the have-nots crowding outside the hotel to peer through the gaps in the gates to gaze upon the blessed.

WHERE TO EAT AND DRINK   [see map p195]

As befits a town that grew wealthy on the back of the bean with the caffeine, Moshi has some rather decent little coffee houses. The *grande dame* of these establishments is the *Coffee Shop* on Hill Street. The travellers' number-one hangout, the food here, including salads, juices, cakes, pies and a wealth of Tanzanian coffees, is very good, the drinks are cold and there's heaps of local information on the noticeboards and in the invaluable Moshi guidebook that they have for sale. Perhaps the best thing about this café, however, is the wonderfully tranquil little garden out back.

Its position as the Westerners' number one hangout, however, is being challenged by the *Tanzanian Coffee Lounge* (Mon-Sat 8am-7pm, Sun noon-6pm; 🖥 www.coffeelounge.co.tz). This place hoovers up the tourist trade, probably because it seems to be going out of its way to supply everything a *mzungu* could want, from internet to ice cream. Despite the name the place feels distinctly 'un-African' – but then that's probably the idea. A third coffee lounge, *Aroma*, is in a similar vein to the Coffee Lounge but more peaceful and spacious and with bigger cups – and thus, in our opinion, a more attractive proposition.

Nearby, *Corner Café* is a newish place on Rengua St serving sandwiches and salads, all made by the older girls of the charity Kilimanjaro Young Girls in Need (🖥 www.kygn.org), with all profits going to the charity.

When the Tanzanian Coffee Lounge closes, the volunteer students migrate en masse to *Indoitaliano*, whose popularity can be ascribed to two factors, a) a great location amongst the hotels near the market, and b) some great food. The name may conjure up all sorts of unappealing fusions – spaghetti currybonara, perhaps, or chicken dopizza – but there's no need to fear; this is really just a straightforward Indian restaurant that happens to make some delightful pizzas too (from Ts5500). Unfortunately, if you are neither in your late teens nor visiting Moshi as a volunteer, you may feel out of place here. If this is the case, the *Sikh Club* provides welcome sanctuary. It's a lovely peaceful spot with some great Indian food and views across a hockey pitch to the hills beyond. They change the chef regularly so it's difficult to judge the food, though the standard is generally very high.

Nearby is our favourite place in Moshi. Half of *Milan's* is taken up with a typically scruffy snack café of the kind you find all over the country. The other half, however, is rather different: a cute little pink-painted eatery with hand-stitched place mats that boasts an extensive menu of cheap and delicious vegetarian food as well as a quick and friendly service. No dish is over Ts3800, and some, such as the Gujurati thali (Ts3500) or, my personal favourite, the wondrous masala dosa (Ts2500) are simply awesome. In my mind this is the best value-for-money place in East Africa.

Not far away, up the hill from the Coffee Shop, sits another new-ish place that is well worth a mention. Some people may be put off by the appearance of *Deli Chez*, which from the outside looks like a fast-food café and from the ground floor décor feels like a wedding reception before the guests have arrived. But upstairs you'll find a very pleasant shaded terrace, the food is fine and fair value – and with both a Japanese and Chinese menu, this place provides a welcome break from the pizzas and popadums offered by other eateries.

Most of the hotels in Moshi also have restaurants. Boasting terrific scenery and tardy service, the *New Coffee Tree Café*, on the top floor of the eponymous hotel, is a light and airy place with sumptuous views towards Moshi in one direction and Kili in the other – both of which you'll have plenty of time to enjoy while you wait the interminably long time for your food. When it does finally put in an appearance, it's tasty, hearty and very good value. The same cannot be said of the *Kindoroko*, alas, despite possessing similar views from its rooftop restaurant, with the worst pizza I've tasted in Africa emanating from its kitchen.

> ❏ **The top five places in Moshi to celebrate a climb**
> ● **El Rancho** Lovely Indian food, good atmosphere, well-stocked bar – enough said.
> ● **Indoitaliano** The old favourite and convenient for many hotels. Book in advance if you're a large group or plan to arrive after 8pm.
> ● **Panda** As good as Chinese food gets in the region.
> ● **Chrisburger** Well it's cheap and cheerful and you can always hang around for the nightclub next door to open.
> ● **Deli Chez** With a decent-sized upstairs area and a massive menu, this is a good spot for large groups.

Just north of the clock tower roundabout, *Chrisburger* offers very good-value dishes and if you can get a seat on its leafy veranda it's a good place to hide away and watch the world go by. Just across the roundabout, despite an inauspicious location near the clock tower and at the junction of two main streets *Central Garden* is actually a pleasant little spot to take the weight off your feet for a few minutes and enjoy a cold drink or snack.

On Kenyatta Street, *Salzburger* is perhaps Africa's most eccentric restaurant, a place that is clearly infatuated with the twee Austrian city after which it is named (and where the boss studied). Despite the obscure location – it calls itself Africa's best-kept secret – it's a great little eatery and a pleasant escape from all those pimply volunteering students that swarm like locusts on other restaurants. And where else can you can munch on Mandara beef kung po to the strains of Mozart, or devour *weinerschnitzel* while the Von Trapp kids smile down at you from the walls. Good value, and good fun.

All this Austrian-aping is fine, but for some real homegrown East African cooking there are several choices. The *Chagga Bar and Grill*, just south of the Leopard Hotel, is the place to come for authentic Chagga fare in authentic Chagga surroundings with authentic Chagga cutlery (ie: none). The menu is small but includes *mchemsho*, a kind of banana and meat stew, and other Chagga favourites. If you like your atmosphere lively, your fingers dirty and your bananas tasteless, this is the place for you. They also have a pool table and TV – useful when one considers how long the food can take to arrive. Another steadfastly African joint, situated behind a mosque, is *Shukrani Snacks*, a Somali-run establishment that's popular and cheap. Closed in the evenings, come here at lunch to try their 'Federation' dish – a silver platter filled with samples of their greatest hits (curry, boiled bananas etc), all served with rice and yours for just Ts1800.

ARUSHA, MOSHI AND MARANGU

Moving uptown and upmarket, for a bit of a treat there are a couple of fine places in chic Shanty Town. The first, *El Rancho*, clearly has an identity crisis, being an Indian restaurant with a Mexican name and a menu that includes dishes from all over the globe. Weirdly, it also has its own pool table and even a small crazy-golf course! Despite the confusion, the food can't be faulted and this is a lovely jacaranda-shaded spot. Try the mutton sheekh kebabs (Ts4500) with vegetable rice (Ts2500). They also have an extensive alcohol selection, making this

Amani Children's Home

When Hosea, aged 5, was brought to Amani he was living with his alcoholic mother, his father having died of AIDS. His friend at Amani, Andrea, 14, had been living on the streets, having fled from his abusive grandfather's house where he'd been forced to live following the death of both his parents. Then there's Oscar, aged 12, who has only just started speaking after years of begging on the streets, the only option left open to him after his grandmother refused to feed him. As for Daudi, found abandoned by the police at the central bus station, nobody knows how old he is: he's autistic, and apparently will never be able to speak.

Despite the Chaggas' reputation among Tanzanians for prosperity and power, the region is not immune to the problems afflicting the rest of the country, and that includes the malaise of street children. And while the stories of the children are unique, the general themes of neglect, poverty and desperation run like a common thread through all of them.

Whatever their reason for ending up on the streets, the gate is always open to them at the **Amani Children's Home**. Founded in 2001 by dedicated Tanzanians, the centre has grown to become the largest in the region, caring for around eighty children. Most of the children are boys, though around a dozen of the eighty are girls. Their ages range from 4-16, though most are between 8 and 14.

They've arrived at the centre in a number of ways. Most come with the social workers who are employed full time by the centre to meet and rescue children living on the streets. A few have been handed over to the centre by the Social Welfare Department which doesn't have the resources to help children who have come into their custody and who have no desire to return home – or, perhaps, no home to go to. Some of these kids are orphans who've lost both their parents, in many cases to AIDS, while others have run away from home because of the physical, mental or sexual abuse they face there. Once on the streets it's a precarious existence. The boys can try to graft a living by collecting scrap metal, begging or stealing; for the girls, a life on the streets is even more dangerous, with many ending up as prostitutes.

Once in the Amani centre, they are washed, fed and, if necessary, clothed. Eventually, once their circumstances are known and their suitability for joining the orphanage has been established, they are welcomed into the home and inducted into the **daily routine**. This begins with the morning clean, in which the rooms are swept and mopped by the children. After breakfast most of the kids are sent off to school or, if they have never been to school and are deemed too old to join the first grade, they are taught basic reading, writing and mathematics in Amani's own classrooms. School ends mid-afternoon and then is free-time, although there are duties the kids have to perform. Each must wash their own dishes and clothes, for example, as well as chop firewood, feed the orphanage's chickens or tend to the garden. After this, for many kids the highlight of the day follows: **the afternoon football match**.

perhaps the best place for a post-trek knees-up. Just south of El Rancho and also off Lema Road, *Panda Chinese* is, as you've probably already guessed from the name, a Chinese restaurant, and as you may have guessed from the Shanty Town location, a pretty smart one too. Some of their dishes, the sizzling beef in Chinese black bean sauce and pork à la Sichuan being but two, are a delight, and this is a wonderful place to sit with a jasmine tea – or something stronger – and reflect on your trek.

Despite the security and comparative normality provided by the home – at least compared to their life pre-Amani – the aim eventually is to return the children to their parents or another relative, having first checked that such a move would be appropriate. Indeed, at Amani they try to replicate family units, dividing the kids into *upendo* groups (*upendo* is Swahili for 'love'), with a member of staff acting as 'parent' to the group, supervising them and listening to their problems. Only one of the children has been at the orphanage since its foundation, with most staying for between 6 and 18 months.

It is both possible and worthwhile to visit the orphanage. One of the most heartwarming aspects of visiting the children is seeing how the older ones look after the newcomers and the more vulnerable. For example, Daudi, the autistic child, is looked after without complaint and treated with both kindness and respect by the other children.

In 2007 Amani made the move from the family house in which it began to a purpose-built centre. At one time in the old house, 65 children shared a bedroom; in the new facility, each child is given his or her own bunk bed. The growth of Amani is due to the dedication of the staff and careful management of funds. As an essentially secular organization (though many of the staff are motivated by Christian beliefs and values) the centre is not supported by any one church or organization but instead relies on donations. Companies such as the Australian travel agents Intrepid Travel and Brighton-based search-engine marketing agency iCrossing, Peace House Africa in the US and the Montreal Canadiens hockey team's Childrens Foundation have all helped to support and build upon the volunteers' hard work. The majority of Amani's support, though, comes from individuals and families who visit the centre or hear about its good work and want to help.

Amani welcomes new volunteers but needs those who have a good working knowledge of Swahili. If you don't have this then you need to be willing to commit to staying for six months or more (by which time the home reckons your Swahili will be of an acceptable level). But if you can't commit that kind of time, don't despair. The home welcomes foreigners to come and look around the centre and spend some time with the kids. (America's Tusker Safaris, Moshi-based Tanzania Journeys, as well as our own trekking company, Climb Mount Kilimanjaro, are three companies who recommend their clients take time to visit.) Many tourists find that turning up to join in the afternoon football game (around 3pm daily) is a good idea, being an easy way to mix and bond with the kids without the need for a common language. To tell them you're coming, make a donation or merely to ask about their work, give them a call on ☎ 0754-892456 or 0752-220637, or email ✉ info@amanikids.org. Or you can visit their website on 🖳 www.amanikids.org.

Trust us, if you've got a day to spare in Moshi, there's no more rewarding a way to spend it.

ARUSHA, MOSHI AND MARANGU

Heading out of Shanty Town and out of Moshi, around 2km west of town on the way to Arusha is *Mama Clementina's* (☎ 027-275 1746), a women's vocational training centre that makes some great food, too, but the highlight for most people is the lovely grounds in which you can sit and snack on three-course set menus or from an à la carte menu (full meals around Ts5000). Note that you have to order all food at least one hour prior to your arrival.

The Watering Hole (🖥 www.twhmoshi.com) sits just next door though you'd never know it. Under new (American) management, this place hardly goes out of its way to advertise itself, being hidden behind a car park for 4x4s with no signboard outside. Nevertheless, manage to find it and you're in for a treat. Open Wednesday to Sunday evenings (plus Sunday afternoon), the 'Hole', with its pleasant riverside setting, is one of nicest places to hang out. The menu is small and clearly designed to cater for its largely *mzungu* clientele, with burgers, fajitas and macaroni cheese all present, plus regular barbecues (Ts6000). But it's not the food but the comprehensive bar and the pleasant atmosphere that are the main reasons for coming. They also host film nights on Thursdays and Sundays (Ts3000 including a drink and popcorn). And don't worry too much about not being able to find it: give them a ring beforehand and you'll get a free taxi ride there (though you'll have to pay to get back again, the rate being about Ts6000).

Nightlife

In the centre of town, the *East African Pub* is a real rowdy locals' hangout that lovers of English football will adore: not only do they show premiership matches live but turn up just before kick-off on Saturday (5pm) and you can take advantage of their happy hour, when beers are buy-two-get-one-free. They also serve a decent nyama choma (grilled meat).

The *Pub Alberto*, aka *Cool Bar*, part of Chrisburger, has a couple of pool tables and a lively atmosphere and continues to gather a reasonable crowd at the weekends, though is now under serious pressure from the *Malindi Club*, a few metres west of Philip Hotel. Entrance is through a set of concrete elephant legs; inside you'll find a cavernous, friendly place serving food and beer and showing football on the telly. By the Leopard Hotel is *Kili Attik*, which is promoting itself as the place to be seen in Moshi with over 120 different cocktails available. Unfortunately, the promotion's not having any effect and currently it's a bit quiet.

If you don't mind the cost of a cab to Shanty Town, *El Rancho* (see p202), off Lema Road, comprises a fine restaurant and the best collection of booze in town. *Glacier*, another Shanty Town option, is, ironically, one of the hottest places in town. It sits on Sekou Toure Way, 200m past the Lutheran Hostel, and is open every night. Even further out, *The Watering Hole* (see above) is a largely mzungu establishment and more a restaurant than anything else, though it does have a good bar and twice-weekly film nights.

All of these options have now been eclipsed by the arrival of *La Liga*, a two-floor club out east of town beyond Shah Industries that even outdoes its rivals in Arusha. Open Tues-Sun 8pm-1am, entrance is Ts3000, jumping to Ts5000 on Fri and Sat. They even lay on a taxi for punters – just call ☎ 0767-770022.

TREKKING AGENCIES

Often cheaper than both Arusha and Marangu, Moshi captures the lion's share of the Kilimanjaro-trekking business, and some of the trekking companies in this town do a roaring trade. But beware: there is still a fair bit of monkey business going on here too, and you do need to be on your guard against cheetahs(!). For this reason we have compiled the following summary of some of the bigger agencies in town. Before booking with any of them, read the general advice given on pp37-40 about dealing with the trekking companies. Note, too, that often the agencies frequently lower their costs by hitting the wages of the crew; please, if you are going to book with one of these agencies, at the very least increase the amount in tips you pay to compensate for their lower wages.

For details on how we arrived at the following reviews, please see p183. And if you have any information or reviews on any agency, please send it to us – we'd love to hear from you.

● **Afrigalaxy** CCM Regional Building, Ground Floor, Taifa Road (PO Box 8340; ☎ 027-275 0268; ▱ www.afrigalaxytours.com). A company that does little to promote itself, yet maybe they should, especially as they organize cycling tours *around* Kili (US$400) as well as treks up it. Regarding treks, typical prices are: five/six days on the Marangu Route US$1150/1320; six/seven days on Machame for US$1370/1540; prices tumble quickly if there's more than one of you.

● **African Spoonbill Tours** (☎ 0713-408291, ▱ www.africanspoonbilltours.com) is a new operator located on the first floor of the NHC Building on Rindi Lane near Stanbic. We've received one recommendation from readers but have heard little else. Regarding their prices, they provided us only with a six-day Machame-with-Western-Breach quote for US$1200.

● **Ahsante Tours** New Street (PO Box 855; ☎ 027-275 3498; ▱ www.ahsantetours.com). Though no longer the rock-bottom cheapest – indeed, they're rapidly leaving the budget end of the market altogether – they're still one of our favourite operators and have been adopted by a number of overseas travel companies as their agents on Kili, including Explore, Gap Challenge and Discover Adventure. Very professional and deservedly popular, they have taken on board the lessons preached by KPAP concerning the welfare of porters and continue to improve in this and every other department. Overall: very good indeed. Let's just hope their prices don't continue to drift upwards or they would no longer be considered good value – which was always one of their strengths. Example prices: US$1620 Machame for seven days, Marangu six days US$1370 per person per trek; they also operate on the Western Breach, with a seven-day Machame climb via Western Breach US$1620 per person per trek, while an eight-day trek including a night at Crater Camp is US$2020 per person. KPAP partner.

● **Akaro Tours** National Social Security Fund Building, Old Moshi Road (PO Box 8578; ☎ 027-275 2986 or 0754-272124; ▱ www.akarotours.com). This company has been through a lot of upheaval over the past few years, from the tragic death of its owner to the loss of his former right-hand lady, Teddy, who went to set up her own company. These blows have been hard to bear and feedback has been mixed recently. Still they are cheap at US$1165 per person for seven days on Machame, US$995 for six days on Marangu. Again, you need to ask yourself how they can keep the price so low and pay their porters a living wage.

● **Chagga Tours** Off Mawenzi Road (PO Box 7746; ☎ 027-275 1318 or 0754-597109; 💻 www.chagga-tours.com). Occupying a prime location near the Buffalo and Indoitaliano, this outfit has been making a fairly big noise since their inception just a few years ago. Heavily involved in the Kilimarathon, this German-owned company (hence the euro price quotes below) are also, refreshingly, one of the few to run bicycle tours around Kilimanjaro. Regarding their climbs, they're slightly pricey at €1550 for seven days on Machame, €1350 for six days on Marangu, though these do include three nights half-board accommodation. The price for the bike tour is €1595 each for two people, a nine-day package that includes six days on the bike.

● **dotcom safaris** Kaunda Street (PO Box 38; ☎ 027-275 4104; 💻 www.dot comsafaris.com). Despite being in Tanzania for four months while researching this edition, we never managed to catch their offices on dusty, unmetalled Kaunda Street open. Their first reply to our enquiry by email bordered on the rude ('either book with us or stop wasting our time with questions' being the gist of their reply), but when we gave them a second chance they did eventually warm to the task and were polite and helpful. Prices: Machame Route, seven days, US$1400 per person; Marangu Route for six days US$1250 per person.

● **Eco Tours** Up by the roundabout near the YMCA (PO Box 7393; ☎ 027-275 1480; 💻 www.ectourism-tz.com). Situated in a big white house, Eco Tours are a fairly new company that's making a big noise on the trekking scene these days and is now the supplier for American agency Adventures Within Reach. Their prices seem reasonable – though do ask what sort of wage they are paying their staff on the mountain: a seven-day Machame trek and a six-day Marangu expedition for two people are US$1375 and US$1175 per person sharing respectively. Joining a group reduces these prices to US$1350 for Machame and US$1150 for Marangu. They also do the Western Breach Route; strangely, they say that there are no extra rules for this, though they do charge an extra US$250. These prices include two nights' accommodation in Moshi.

● **Evans** Memorial Stadium, 2km from Moshi (PO Box 114; ☎ 027-275 2612; 💻 www.evansadventuretours.com). Evans are a typical Moshi outfit, being a longstanding company that aims squarely at the cheaper end of the market. If you're in the market for a budget trek and aren't too concerned about the wages of your mountain crew, then they're worth investigating. Prices: US$1105 per person for six days on the Marangu Route; US$1345 for seven days on Machame, or US$1437 if going via the Western Breach. These prices also include two nights at the semi-swish Zebra Hotel and airport transfers.

● **Kessy Brothers** (PO Box 7502; ☎ 0754-803953; 💻 www.kessybrothers tours.com). There's little point in telling you where to find this company, for the truth is they'll come and find you if you stay in Moshi for more than a day or so. They're a friendly bunch but I'm afraid they do have a few negative reviews online and from readers. In response to our email they gave us just one price, for a weird six-day Machame/Western Breach/Umbwe-descent route, and while it didn't exactly answer our questions there's no doubting they are fairly cheap at US$1368 per person, including two nights in the Buffalo Hotel. The trouble is, I am pretty sure that the route they've described in their email is neither legitimate nor, indeed, the one that they would use. If you do decide to go with them, check everything very carefully and make sure it's all written down in a contract.

● **Key's** Key's Hotel (see p198 for contact details). Rather expensive by Moshi's standards, though you do get to stay in the Key's Hotel – which is a bonus. Fulfilling the criteria to become a KPAP partner, they are used by several overseas operators including International Mountain Guides, Tribes Travel (who pushed their efforts to become a KPAP partner) and Wild Frontiers. Example prices: Marangu US$1265 per person for two people for six days on Marangu; or it's US$1655 for seven days on Machame.

● **Kilimanjaro Crown Bird Tours & Safaris** THB/Vodacom Building, Room 113/114 (PO Box 9519; ☎ 027-275 1162; 🖳 www.kilicrown.com). Another small operator but one that's been going for a few years and, to be fair, seems to have improved greatly since the last edition. The prices are not rock bottom but their service – if the questionnaires they give to their clients at the end of the trek are anything to go by – has risen more than commensurately. This may have something to do with their adoption by a couple of German agencies. Using the Key's Hotel as the base for their clients, they now charge US$1350 for one person for seven days on the Machame Route (this price decreasing rapidly if more people join), or US$1100 for six days on Marangu; add US$150/200 for extra days on Machame/Marangu. When booking, do ask about how much they are paying their mountain crew.

● **Kindoroko Tours** Kindoroko Hotel (PO Box 8682; ☎ 027-275 4054; 🖳 www. kindorokotour.com). No-nonsense, up-front and offering a pretty good deal, Kindoroko Tours, part of the hotel empire that owns half a dozen hotels in northern Tanzania, aims squarely at the budget end of the market. To keep prices low they offer regular scheduled treks that climbers are encouraged to join. They're good value, too, at US$1238 per person for two people for six days on Marangu, or US$1452 for seven days on Machame, this latter price including two nights at the Kindoroko Hotel. Note that they no longer offer the Western Breach Route because of the risks involved.

● **Kinyonga Tours and Safaris** (☎ 027-275 2218, 🖳 www.kinyongasafaris. tz.com) Now installed in Shah Tour's old Moshi office, Kinyonga used to operate from the Kilimanjaro Guides' Cooperative hut at Marangu Gate, from where they still hire out equipment to trekkers. Their treks are fairly standard though if anything is distinctive about this team, it is the patient and kind attitude they show to their clients. Covering all routes, they are worth checking out for those seeking a budget but not bottom-dollar trek. Price-wise, they are similar to Zara (see p210).

● **Marangu Kili-Colobus Travels** THB/Vodacom Building, first floor (PO Box 8410; ☎ 027-275 3458, 🖳 www.kili-colobus.com). Despite their obscure location in the THB/Vodacom Building this company, founded by a group of ex-guides, has been around since 1997 without ever doing anything spectacular enough to merit a bigger write-up in the book than I've already given them. The quotes they gave us for Kilimanjaro – Machame for six days US$1400, Marangu for five days US$1200, add US$150 for each extra day – are in our opinion unexceptional, and offer a glimpse as to why this lot don't seem to have developed much over the years.

● **Mauly Tours** Near the Immigration Office on Boma Road (PO Box 1315; ☎ 027-275 0730; 🖳 www.mauly-tours.com). This lot have the honour of being the first company to virtually throw me out of their office because of what I wrote about them in the last edition. Threats were issued too. Clearly they take great exception to anyone criticizing their food and the small portions, which was the main complaint against them from trekkers a few years ago. I did also happen to mention that they were a well-run, professional agency, and they're reliable too – though they preferred to overlook this when I visited. Suffice to say that the above is still true, and the prices they quote are very reasonable given the service they provide, namely US$1350 for seven days on Machame, US$1150 for six days on Marangu – both prices including two nights' accommodation. Add another US$280 to the Machame Route for the Western Breach (plus they will ask you to write a letter to say that you are taking this route at your own risk). Not bad, overall – though if you do make an enquiry about trekking with them, ask how much they pay their porters. And don't, whatever you do, criticize the food!

● **Moshi Expedition and Mountaineering** Kaunda Street (aka **MEM Tours and Safaris**; PO Box 146; ☎ 027-275 4234; 🖳 www.memafrica.com). Their website is a study in hyperbole (claiming they use the best tents on the mountain, boast of having a 98% success rate and also saying they have the best safety equipment on Kili, 'including oxygen on special trips'), but to be fair to MEM they're a fairly slick and fairly professional agency that belies their location on dusty, dishevelled Kaunda Street. The online agency BootsnAll World Adventures use them. MEM Tours are unusual in that they offer three standards of treks. At the top is Class A, with smarter hotels and a service on the mountain that includes chemical toilets and a greater ratio of guides and porters per trekker. While at the other extreme there's Class C, with a luggage limit of just 10kg per person and accommodation in a cheaper (but still smart) hotel such as the Zebra. With oxygen available only on Class A treks, you'd be wise to consider this category only; luckily, the difference in price between the categories is actually quite small: six days on Marangu on a Class A trek, for example, is US$1690 for two people, while on a Class C trek it's US$1670. (For seven days on Machame, by the way, the prices are US$1760 and US$1620 respectively; add on US$200 if going via the Western Breach.) The information they finally provided in response to our email enquiry was comprehensive and useful. It's worth noting, too, that they also now offer a Rongai Route trek that culminates in a climb of Kibo using the Western Breach, which they reach via the Northern Circuit – interesting.

● **Real Life Adventure Travel** (PO Box 6902; ☎ 0732-972159; 🖳 www.real lifeadventuretravel.com). Fairly unknown quantity, though one glance at their website shows that they seem to have some sort of American connection, are knowledgeable when it comes to Kilimanjaro, support a number of charitable projects and are a KPAP partner too. Prices: US$2170 per person double occupancy for six days on Marangu including two nights 'moderate' accommodation in Moshi; US$2825 for the same deal on the Western Breach.

● **Rift Cross Expeditions** THB/Vodacom Building Room 213 – look for the Global Alliance for Africa advert on the door (PO Box 15260, ☎ 027-250 9396 🖳 http://riftcrossadventure.com/). Company tucked away in a dark corner of the THB building but which has contacts in both America and the US. A KPAP partner, the website is descriptive and overall they seem very helpful; impressions that are borne out by reviews from readers we've received, one of whom said they provided a detailed breakdown of prices that even included the tax they have to pay. Overall, though I haven't met anyone who's climbed with them they do seem OK. Prices: US$1422 for six days on Marangu, US$1572 for seven on Machame.

● **Shah Tours** Sekou Toure Way, Shanty Town (PO Box 1821; ☎ 027-275 2370; 🖳 www.kilimanjaro-shah.com). Owners of the Mountain Inn and now in new premises in Shanty Town, Shah are a long established firm and one of the biggest in Moshi. They're good value, especially as their rates usually include two nights at their Mountain Inn base (see p199) – though watch out for hidden charges: they are the only agency I know, for example, who said they charged extra for the rental of a tent. Costs: six days on Marangu US$1246 per person; seven days on Machame US$1476 per person. Their payment and treatment of porters has allegedly been a concern in the past.

● **Snow Cap Mountain Climbing Camp** Rau Road past Key's Hotel (PO Box 8358; ☎ 027-275 4826; 🖳 www.snowcap.co.tz). There's one reason to contact Snow Cap and one reason only: to do the Rongai Route, which they concentrate on more than any other company and which they have done more than any other company to help popularize; indeed, they renovated the School Hut, the final hut on the Rongai ascent, and built the rather smart cottages on the Kenyan border by the start of the trek (see p303). Their price for six days on the Rongai Route is US$1372 per person. They do operate on other routes, however: for Machame, they charge US$1994 for a nine-day Machame trip including seven days on the mountain; and for an eight-day Marangu trip, including six days on the mountain, they charge US$1394.

● **Summit Expeditions and Nomadic Experience** (PO Box 6491; ☎ 027-275 3233, US toll free 1-866-417-7661; 🖳 www.nomadicexperience.com). Run by the irrepressible force of personality that is Simon Mtuy – an ultra-racer and the holder of the record for the fastest ascent and descent of Kili (see p123) – Summit Expeditions (aka SENE) deserve mention for the respect and kindness they show to their porters, with the whole crew, porters included, invited to the post-trek celebratory meal with the trekkers at the end of every climb. Different from other companies in Moshi, SENE concentrate mainly on the Lemosho/Western Breach Route, for which they charge a steep US$3665, though this is for a total of 13 days and includes a stay at Simon's cottages and farm at Mbahe village, 15 minutes west of Marangu Gate, and at Simba Farm/Poverty Gulch near the start of the Lemosho Route. They can arrange a Machame climb too (US$2880 for a ten-day package including seven days on Kili and nights at Mbahe), though they do not touch the Marangu Route. Those who trek with this company are often effusive in their praise – I have received some truly glowing reports from delighted trekkers about this bunch – and they're also partners of KPAP (see pp46-49), who clearly love them too, mainly for the fact that they are one of the few wholly Tanzanian companies to follow KPAP's guidelines. Not cheap, but by all accounts worth it.

● **Tanzania Journeys** Haria Hotel (PO Box 1724; ☎ 027-275 0549; 🖳 www.tanzaniajourneys.com). Formed in 2006, this company has its heart in the right place according to KPAP. Tanzania Journeys boast a UK connection, are friendly and profess an ecological and humanitarian outlook. Unfortunately, they were the very last agency to reply to our emails (indeed, it took three emails before finally getting a response). Nevertheless, when they did respond they were reasonably priced (Marangu 6 days US$1445, Machame 7 days US$1720; add US$425 for the Western Breach), including two nights B&B in Moshi's Bristol Cottages and transfers from either Kilimanjaro Airport or, unusually, Nairobi. KPAP partner.

● **Trans-Kibo Travels Limited** YMCA Building, Kilimanjaro Road (PO Box 558; ☎ 027-275 2207; 🖳 www.transkibo.com). Trans-Kibo Travels are a strange company, still operating out of shabby offices in the YMCA and yet, weirdly, they boast a list of foreign agencies and tour operators that other companies must envy, including Outward Bound International. I have to say, however, I've never met anyone who's actually climbed with them and so cannot comment on their service. Example prices: Marangu route for five/six days: US$1100/1270; six/seven days on Machame US$1380/1550. Prices fall by US$50 if there are more than six of you.

● **Zara Tours** Rindi Lane (PO Box 1990; ☎ 027-275 0233; toll-free 1-866-550-4447; 🖳 www.zaratours.com). They may come last in the *Yellow Pages* but in terms of size this agency comes out on top. Zara continue to rule the trekking scene in Moshi, even though their presence in the town centre is limited to a small office near the clock tower. There's no doubting their competence; one look at the number of overseas agents who use them, together with the glowing testimonials on the website, should convince you of that, and I think it's fair to say that they put more people on the summit of Kilimanjaro than anyone else. That's not to say they're perfect, however, and there have been a few grumbles in the past about old equipment and what one trekker called a sense of 'complacency'. Furthermore, because of their popularity with overseas agents, independent trekkers calling into their Moshi office may find they are treated a little brusquely, as if they are too busy to deal with mere independent trekkers – which may in fact be the case. Still, they are competent, no doubt, and it's nice to see that they are becoming more interested in ecotourism and porter welfare. Published costs: Marangu US$1367 for six days; Machame US$1642 for seven days; take off US$50 if your group is greater than five. Note that they don't run treks on the Western Breach anymore owing to the potential dangers involved.

GETTING AWAY

Buses

Arusha and Marangu Heading to **Arusha**, 'Coaster' buses (the small thirty-seat minibuses) leave regularly throughout the day from the terminal on Mawenzi (Ts3000). Travellers wishing to journey to **Marangu** can catch one of the dalla-dallas from the adjacent terminal (Ts1500). The **shuttles** – Impala, Riverside, Bobby – charge US$10 for the two-hour journey to Arusha. Services tend to leave at 6.30am and 11am. (See below for details of their offices.)

Nairobi and Mombasa Shuttle buses leave from outside their respective offices. Riverside are in Room 122 on the first floor of the Vodacom Building (☎ 0755-996453); their buses to Nairobi leave at 6.30am and 11.30am (US$35). Impala (☎ 027-275 1786, 0754-293119), in the Impala Hotel and also in town next to the Pub Alberto, also operate two shuttles, at 6.30am and 11.30am, charging US$35 to Nairobi. Remember that, if you book in advance, you should get picked up from your hotel, though emphasize this when buying your ticket.

Cheaper are the big **buses**, though to Nairobi they're not recommended due to lack of comfort and the fact that they arrive at the bus terminal in Nairobi after dark. There is also a bus to **Mombasa**, operated by Doliphine via Taveta, leaving at 7am daily; tickets can be bought from Hiren's Café (☎ 0784-452500), opposite Kahawa House.

Dar es Salaam There are plenty of **bus** companies plying the route to Dar. Be careful, however: as we've already stated, this route is notorious for speeding and, as a result, horrific crashes. The cheaper companies are best avoided even though they could save you Ts5000 or more – it's simply not worth it. There are two that have managed to garner a reputation for safety, however: Dar Express have new offices on Boma Road and run to Dar no less than 8 times per day from 7.15am-noon. The cost is Ts23,000, or it's Ts 28,000 on the 'luxury' buses departing at 9.30am and 11am. Their only real rivals are Kilimanjaro Express, with buses at 8am, 8.30am and 9.30am (Ts20,000); their offices can be found near the Air Tanzania office on Rengua St.

Flights

For details of flights out of Kilimanjaro International, see *Appendix B*, p340. **Getting to Kilimanjaro airport** takes about 45 minutes from Moshi. There is no public transport and while you can take an Arusha-bound bus from Moshi and jump off at the junction, that still means you have to hitch the final 6km to the airport itself. Precision Air run a shuttle service (Ts10,000), though only to coincide with their domestic flights; the bus leaves from outside their office 2hrs prior to departure. A **taxi** costs US$50 and while bargaining can reduce this, you'll struggle to get much of a discount at night.

Marangu

According to legend, Marangu got its name when the first settlers in this part of Kilimanjaro, astonished by the lush vegetation, well-watered soils and the countless waterfalls they found here, cried out in delight 'Mora ngu! Mora ngu!' ('Much water! Much water!'). It remains a verdant and extremely attractive place today, at least once you move away from the small huddle of shops and hustlers by the bus stop (in a part of the town called Marangu Mtoni, or Lower Marangu) and start to climb up the hill towards Marangu Gate. The town, 14km along the Himo-Taveta highway, is extremely elongated but is in reality little more than two roads running up the mountain, with a filigree of dusty paths running off both.

ARRIVAL

Marangu is reached by **dalla-dalla** from Moshi (Ts1500), which takes about an hour. Passengers are normally dropped by the junction next to the bridge, though occasionally they will drive up the hill to drop you off on your doorstep. If not, a ride in the back of a pick-up truck up from the bridge to Marangu Gate costs Ts300 (Ts500 in a shared taxi), the pick-ups leaving when full.

SERVICES

There's a **post office** close to the bridge, a **telephone office** and round the back an **internet facility** (Mon-Sat 8.30am-5.30pm, Sun 10.30am-5pm) – though at Ts1500 for 15 minutes (Ts2500 on Sun), it's better to wait until you get back to Moshi if you can.

WHERE TO STAY

Accommodation in Marangu is fairly luxurious and survives by catering to the tour-group trade. Note that just about all of the hotels and campsites have some sort of trekking agency attached, and though they are not the cheapest, they are amongst the most reliable.

There are five **campsites** in Marangu, too, though three of these are also rather luxurious: *Coffee Tree Campsite* (PO Box 835; ☎ 027 -275 6604; 🖳 www.alpinesafari.com), is an immaculate, manicured place to the east of main road leading up to Marangu Gate where camping alone costs US$8 per person per day, or it's US$12 per person for a mattress in one of their dorms. Tents can be hired (US$10). Alpine Tours are based here, arranging trips to waterfalls and other beauty spots around Marangu. There's a second campsite near Kilasiya Falls; named *Gillman's Campsite* after the point where the Marangu Route reaches the crater rim, it's a very smart little place that exudes that lush, flower-filled charm that is Marangu's signature. As pleasant as these two places are, they pale in comparison to the grounds of the *Mountain Resort Hotel* (see below) where camping is also allowed. The grounds are gorgeous, the facilities spotless and huge and they charge US$12, or US$20 with tent hire included – plus you get to enjoy the bar/restaurant facilities of one of Marangu's most charming and luxurious hotels. Truly a lovely spot.

Camping is also available at *Kibo Hotel* (see below; US$5 per person including use of kitchen and pool) and at the *Bismark Hut Lodge* (US$5 per tent). This last place is also the nearest thing to budget **hotel accommodation** in Marangu, though at US$20/25 sgl/dbl it's neither cheap nor particularly good value. And that, alas, is it for 'cheap' accommodation in Marangu. Some of the other places in the village, however, while not 'budget', do at least offer some sort of value for money. Near the Coffee Tree Campsite is the friendly *Hotel Nakara* (PO Box 105; ☎ 027-275 6571), which is clearly aiming to grab its share of the tour-group trade, though independent trekkers are welcome if there's space and rates are negotiable (rack rates US$50 per person per night for B&B, US$60 half-board, or US$70 full board).

Further down the hill and on the main road, the *Capricorn Hotel* (☎ 027-275 1309; 🖳 www.thecapricornhotels.com) is made up of a number of different buildings, some older (and therefore cheaper) than others. If you don't mind spending the extra five dollars or so, try to get a room in the newer wing or, better still, the gorgeous Kisera House, up the hill behind the main reception building. More like a home than a hotel, and a particularly smart home at that, there's something decidedly colonial about the décor and furniture at Kisera House, from the plush carpets to the chandeliers and a four-poster bed that's so high it comes with its own set of steps. Then there's the splendid garden, too, a real labyrinth of flowers, birds and streams and with giant Chagga storage baskets outside reception. Rates: US$40-US$65 per double.

No hotel review of Marangu would be complete without mentioning the *Kibo Hotel* (☎ 027-275 1308; 🖳 www.kibohotel.com) which, whilst it cannot compete with most of the other hotels here in terms of luxury or comfort, cannot be beaten when it comes to character and history. A sign welcoming former US president Jimmy Carter still hangs above the door – it's a perfect symbol of the faded yet fascinating grandeur of the place, and of the time-warp it appears to be living in now. Indeed, rather comfortingly, the place hasn't changed one iota since we first visited in 2001, save for the ever-changing array of flags, T-shirts and banners from trekking groups that decorate the dining-room walls. Antique German maps and other paraphernalia from the last century (and the one before that) adorn reception, and while the rooms themselves are overpriced (sgl/dbl US$42/66), it remains an absorbing place to wander around even if you don't intend staying. Lunch (currently US$10) and dinner (US$14) are also available.

Further up the road, ten minutes past the market and right by the Chagga Museum, is a relatively new hotel that makes all the others in Marangu look a little tired. The *Mountain Resort* (☎ 027-275 8950; sgl/dbl US$70/120) is luxurious and lovely, with sumptuous rooms that boast huge bathrooms, digital TVs and their own balconies. The grounds are gorgeous, the bar is beautiful and the roof

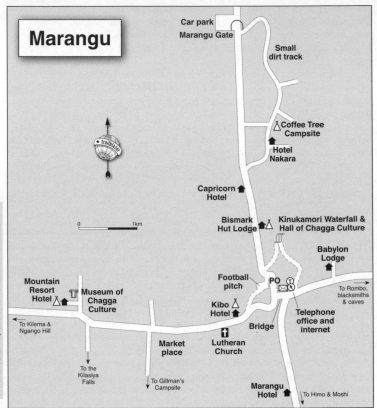

terrace terrific, with views of Kili to boot. A few foreign tour agencies have discovered this place but other than them there are very few people who make it here. If you have the time, energy and money, you won't be disappointed.

Finally, there are two places worth mentioning on the Himo-Taveta road: east of Marangu and just off the main road is the pleasant but slightly shabby ***Babylon Lodge*** (☎ 027-275 6355; 🖥 www.babylonlodge.com), a deceptively large place with many unusually shaped rooms, some of them sunnier and cleaner than others so check a few out before checking in (sgl/dbl US$30/50). Then there's the ***Marangu Hotel*** (☎ 027-275 6591/4; 🖥 www.maranguhotel. com), an established favourite, standing in 12 acres of gardens (with pool) a couple of kilometres south of town on the way to Himo. The building used to be a farmhouse and was built in the early 1900s. The food is great, and rates are sgl/dbl US$60/90 in the low season, US$85/120 in the high. Their main claim to fame, however, is not the hotel, as venerable and comfortable though it may be, but their treks – about which, see below.

Trekking agencies

● **Kibo Hotel** (PO Box 102; ☎ 027-275 1308; 💻 www.kibohotel.com). The most interesting hotel in Marangu also organizes treks – with the shirts, banners and flags of many of those who've completed the climb with them now decorating the dining hall. Reliable and experienced, the hotel currently charges US$1385 for one climber for six days on Marangu; on Machame it's US$1827 for seven days; the prices include two nights full-board at the hotel.

● **Marangu Hotel** (PO Box 40, Moshi, ☎ 027-275 6594; 💻 www.maranguho tel.com). Few companies can boast of the pedigree and experience of the Marangu Hotel, which has been sending climbers up Kilimanjaro since, wait for it, 1932! What's more, their reputation is one of the best too – superb guides who work *only* for them, and an endorsement from KPAP who reckon they are the best amongst the 'budget' agencies for their fair treatment of porters. Indeed, all of the porters are introduced to the clients at the beginning of the trek and at the end it's customary for everyone to share a celebratory meal together. As for their service, it's efficient without being exceptional, save for the wooden trekking poles that they give to each of their clients but which they're only allowed to keep if they make it to the summit! Current charges: US$1330 per person for six days on Marangu; US$2020 for seven days on Machame, with small reductions for larger groups. Note that these prices are exclusive of accommodation (for which they charge the low-season rates to their climbers of US$60/90 sgl/dbl), and airport transfers (US$70 from Kili Airport).

WHAT TO DO

Always one of the prettiest villages on Kili's slopes, for some reason over the past couple of years Marangu has become the unofficial centre of Chagga culture – and it's really fascinating. You can try to find many of the attractions yourself – they're all pretty well signed – but it's much nicer and easier to hire one of the local kids who'll doubtless come up to you to offer themselves as guides (give them around Ts7000-10,000 per day); they can also show you some shortcuts which will save you time. And while none of these 'Chagga' sights are going to have you rushing to the nearest phone booth in order to tell your nearest and dearest back home of the wonders you have seen, nevertheless it's good to see some sort of revival of a fascinating culture that would otherwise be confined largely to the history books. What's more, though your interest in Chagga culture may be slight, the chance to walk around one of the prettiest, homeliest parts of Tanzania should not be passed up; it's a lovely way to spend a day.

The first port of call is usually the **Kinukamori Falls** (7am-6.30pm; Ts3000), just ten minutes' walk up from the bridge. As lovely as these are, we feel that these falls are the one sight that maybe should have been left as it was, for the addition of a **Hall of Chagga Culture** – an open-air series of statues or dioramas lining the path down to the falls, each one depicting some aspect of Chagga culture or history – seems unnecessary and adds nothing to the beauty of the place. Indeed, with that God-awful statue of a woman about to plunge to her death that's now been installed at the top of the falls, this is one 'enhancement' that is anything but.

Still, some of the other sights are really absorbing. Falling into this category is the **Museum of Chagga Culture**. To reach it from the Kinukamori Falls, cross the school field, drop down to the road, turn right and continue walking for 25 minutes or so past the Kibo Hotel and the small market square (Friday is the market day here); the museum is right next to the Mountain Resort Hotel, ten minutes beyond this market square. Alternatively, you can catch a dalla-dalla (Ts250) from the bridge up to the market square. The first exhibit is a reconstruction of a thatched Chagga house complete with livestock inside. (We have been told by several people that the Chagga kept their livestock indoors not out of fear that they would be rustled by their neighbours but merely to save space.) The museum also has a display of traditional Chagga tools, farm implements, rope made from the bark of the mringaringa tree, a genealogical look at the history of the Chagga, some drums and a bugle made of kudu horn.

Just before the museum is a turn-off to many people's favourite attraction in Marangu, the delightful **Kilasiya Falls**. The waterfalls are just part of the attraction, for it's the local flora that really catches the eye and many of the plants have been labelled. Reached via a steep muddy path, the falls are exquisite and there are even a couple of natural swimming pools in the gorge for those who fancy a cold dip. It's a great place to have lunch.

Those who've really got a taste for all this Chagga culture may also like to venture east along the Himo-Taveta road to the village of Mamba Kua Makunde, (about Ts500 by dalla dalla from Marangu Mtoni). Walking up the hill from the main road, you'll soon hear the sound of the **Chagga blacksmiths**, making anything from weapons to farm implements, often with little children working the bellows to keep the fires hot. It's free, though they'll sting you if you want to take a photo. Nearby, there are some underground **caves** once inhabited by the Chagga. Claustrophobic, dark and difficult for anyone bigger than a smurf to negotiate, they're not the most pleasant of attractions though they are, in their own way, fascinating.

Finally, for modern-day Chagga culture look no further than the twice-weekly **markets** (Mondays and Thursdays) in the main village square by the junction, which are lively and, by the end of the day, often quite drunken too.

GETTING AWAY

Dalla dallas back to Moshi leave when full from the main junction at Marangu Mtoni; don't worry about finding one – they'll find you. There's also a bus straight from here to Dar es Salaam: every day at about 7am a Meridian bus drives through on its way from Rombo, further north; the total travel time to Dar is about six hours. The only other option is to catch a dalla-dalla to Moshi and reserve a seat there; it is in theory possible to stop a Dar-bound bus on the Moshi-Dar highway at Himo, though travellers who try this usually end up waiting for hours for one with a spare seat, and eventually most give up.

Safe trekking

Came to cave. Men cold. Passed two corpses of young men who died of exposure, a short time ago. The vultures had pecked out their eyes, the leopards had taken a leg from each.
    From the diary of **Peter MacQueen** as recorded in his book *In Wildest Africa* (1910)

Because of the number of trekkers who scale Kilimanjaro each year, and the odd ways in which some of them choose to do so, many people are under the mistaken impression that Africa's highest mountain is also a safe mountain. Unfortunately, as any mountaineer will tell you, there's no such thing as a safe mountain, particularly one nearly 6000m tall with extremes of climate near the summit and ferociously carnivorous animals roaming the lower slopes.

Your biggest enemy on Kilimanjaro, however, is likely to be neither the weather nor the wildlife but the altitude. KINAPA are shy about revealing how many trekkers die on Kili each year, though the most common estimate I've heard is ten. The main culprit behind these fatalities is nearly always the same: the altitude.

The authorities do try to minimize the number of deaths: guides are given some training in what to do if one of their group is showing signs of acute mountain sickness, or AMS, and trekkers are required to register each night upon arrival at the campsite and have to pay a US$20 'rescue fee' as part of their park fees. But you, too, can do your bit by avoiding AMS in the first place. The following few pages discuss in detail what AMS actually is, how it is caused, the symptoms and, finally, how to avoid it. Read this section carefully: it may well save your life. Following this, on p223 you'll find details of other ailments commonly suffered by trekkers on Kilimanjaro.

WHAT IS AMS?

In the first edition we stated that 'at Uhuru Peak, the summit of Kilimanjaro, the oxygen present in the atmosphere is only half that found at sea level'. This is not quite the case as reader Janet Bonnema pointed out for the second edition – and her explanation is worth repeating in this third edition too. As Janet explains, throughout the troposphere (ie from sea level to an altitude of approximately 10km), the air composition is, in fact, always the same, namely 20% oxygen and nearly 80% nitrogen. So it's not the lack of oxygen that's the problem but the lack of *air pressure*. As Ms Bonnema writes: 'The atmospheric pressure drops by about 1/10th for every 1000m of altitude. Thus the air pressure at the top of Kilimanjaro is approximately 40% of that found at sea level.' In other words, though each breath inhaled is still 20% oxygen, just as it is at sea level, it becomes much harder to fill your lungs since the atmosphere is not 'pushing' so much air into them. As a result, every time you breathe on Kibo you take in only about half as much air, and thus oxygen, as you would if you took the same breath in Dar es Salaam. This can, of course, be seriously detrimental to your health; oxygen is, after all, pretty essential to your physical well-being. All of your vital organs need it, as do your muscles. They receive their oxygen via red blood cells, which are loaded with oxygen by your lungs and then pumped around your body by your heart, delivering oxygen as they go. Problems arise at altitude when that most vital of organs, the brain, isn't getting enough oxygen and malfunctions as a result; because as the body's central control room, if the brain malfunctions, so does the rest of you, often with fatal consequences.

Fortunately, your body is an adaptable piece of machinery and can adjust to the lower levels of oxygen that you breathe in at altitude. Unconsciously you will start to breathe deeper and faster, your blood will thicken as your body produces more red blood cells and your heart will beat faster. As a result, your essential organs will receive the same amount of oxygen as they always did. But your body needs time before it can effect all these changes. Though the deeper, faster breathing and heart-quickening happen almost as soon as your body realizes that there is less oxygen available, it takes a few days for the blood to thicken. And with Kilimanjaro, of course, a few days is usually all you have on the mountain, and the changes may simply not happen in time. The result is **AMS**.

AMS, or acute mountain sickness (also known as **altitude sickness**), is what happens when the body fails to adapt in time to the lack of air pressure at altitude. There are three levels of AMS: mild, moderate and severe. On Kilimanjaro, it's fair to say that most people will get some symptoms of the illness and will fall into the mild-to-moderate categories. Having symptoms of mild AMS is not *necessarily* a sign that the sufferer should give up climbing Kili and descend immediately. Indeed, most or all of the symptoms suffered by those with **mild AMS** will disappear if the person rests and ascends no further; and assuming the recovery is complete, the assault on the summit can continue. The same goes for **moderate AMS** too, though here the poor individual and his or her symptoms should be monitored far more closely to ensure that they are not getting any worse and developing into **severe AMS**. This is a lot more serious and sufferers with severe AMS should always descend immediately, even if it means going down by torchlight in the middle of the night.

The following describes the symptoms of the various levels of AMS, while **there's a more comprehensive and more scientific summary of acute mountain sickness in Appendix E, p356**.

What are the symptoms?

The symptoms of **mild AMS** are not dissimilar to the symptoms of a particularly vicious hangover, namely a thumping headache, nausea and a general feeling of lousiness. An AMS headache is generally agreed to be one of the most dreadful headaches you can get, a blinding pain that thuds continuously at ever decreasing intervals; only those who have bungee-jumped from a 99ft building with a 100ft elasticated rope will know the intense, repetitive pain AMS can cause. Thankfully, the usual headache remedies should prove effective against a mild AMS headache though do be careful as they can also mask any worsening of symptoms. As with a hangover, mild AMS sufferers often have trouble sleeping and, when they do, that sleep can be light and intermittent. They can also suffer from a lack of appetite. Given the energy you've expended getting to altitude in the first place, both of these symptoms can seem surprising if you're not aware of AMS.

Moderate AMS is more serious and requires careful monitoring of the sufferer to ensure that it does not progress to severe AMS. With moderate AMS, the sufferer's nausea will lead to vomiting, the headache will not go away even after pain-relief remedies, and in addition the sufferer will appear to be permanently out of breath, even when doing nothing.

With moderate AMS, it is possible to continue to the summit, **but only after a prolonged period of relaxation** that will enable the sufferer to make a complete recovery. Unfortunately, treks run to tight schedules and cannot change their itineraries mid-trek. Whether you, as a victim of moderate AMS, will be given time to recover will depend largely upon how fortunate you are, and whether the onset of your illness happens to coincide with a scheduled rest day or not.

With **severe AMS**, on the other hand, there should be no debate about whether or not to continue: if anybody is showing symptoms of severe AMS it is imperative that they **descend immediately**. These symptoms include a lack of coordination and balance, a symptom known as **ataxia**. A quick and easy way to check for ataxia is to draw a 10m line in the ground and ask the person to walk along it. If they clearly struggle to complete this simple test, suspect ataxia and descend. (Note, however, that this lack of coordination can also be caused by hypothermia or extreme fatigue, so ensure that the sufferer is suitably dressed in warm clothing and has eaten well before ascertaining whether or not he or she is suffering from ataxia.) Other symptoms of severe AMS include mental confusion, slurred or incoherent speech, and an inability to stay awake. There may also be a gurgling, liquid sound in the lungs combined with a persistent watery cough which may produce a clear liquid, a pinky phlegm or possibly even blood. There may also be a marked blueness around the face and lips, and a heartbeat that, even at rest, may be over 130 beats per minute. These are the symptoms of either HACO and HAPO, as outlined below, while ways to treat somebody suffering from AMS are given on p222.

HACO and HAPO

Poor Mapandi, a carrier whom I had noticed shivering with fever for the last day or two, stiffened, grew cold and died beside me in the mud. **Peter MacQueen** *In Wildest Africa*

HACO (High Altitude Cerebral Oedema) is a build-up of fluid around the brain. It's as serious as it sounds. It is HACO that is causing the persistent headache, vomiting, ataxia and the lack of consciousness. If not treated, death could follow in as little as 24 hours, less if the victim continues ascending.

Just as serious, **HAPO** (High Altitude Pulmonary Oedema) is the accumulation of fluid around the lungs. It's this condition that is causing the persistent cough and pinkish phlegm. Again, the only option is to descend as fast as possible. In addition, one of the treatments outlined on p222 should also be considered.

GO *POLE POLE** IF YOU DON'T WANT TO FEEL POORLY POORLY – HOW TO AVOID AMS

Haraka haraka haina baraka 'Great haste has no blessing' – a common Swahili saying.

AMS can be avoided. The only surefire way to do so is to **take your time**. Opting to save money by climbing the mountain as quickly as possible is a false economy: the chances are you will have to turn back because of AMS and all your efforts (and money) will be wasted.

According to the Expedition Advisory Committee at the Royal Geographical Society, the recommended acclimatization period for any altitude greater than 2500m is to sleep no more than 300m higher than your previous night's camp, and to spend an extra night at every third camp. But if you were to follow this on Kilimanjaro's Marangu Route, for example, from Mandara Huts you would have to take a further *eight* nights in order to adjust safely to the Kibo Huts' altitude of 4713m – whereas most trekkers take just two days to walk between the two. The EAC realize that the short distances and high per diem cost of climbing Kilimanjaro make this lengthy itinerary impractical, so instead they recommend a pre-trek acclimatization walk on Mount Meru or Mount Kenya (4895m to Point Lenana, the third highest peak on the mountain and the highest point that 'trekkers' can reach). This is an excellent idea if you have the time and are feeling fit; and providing you do one of these walks *immediately* before you climb Kili, these treks can be beneficial – and the views towards Kilimanjaro from Meru are delightful too (see p229 onwards for a description of this route).

But what if you don't have the time or money to do other climbs? The answer is to plan your walk on Kilimanjaro as carefully as possible. If you've enough money for a 'rest day' or two, take them. These 'rest days' are not actually days of rest at all – on the Marangu trail, for example, guides usually lead their trekkers up from Horombo to the Mawenzi Hut at over 4500m before returning that same afternoon. But they do provide trekkers with the chance to experience a higher altitude before returning down the slopes again, thereby obeying the mountaineers' old maxim about the need to '**climb high**, **sleep low**' to avoid mountain sickness.

The route you take is also important. Some of the routes – the Machame, Lemosho and Shira trails via the Barafu Huts, for example – obey the mountaineers' maxim on the third or fourth days, when the trail climbs above 4500m (around Lava Tower) before plunging down to an altitude of 3986m at Barranco Camp where you spend the night. Some of the shorter trails, however, do not: for example, it is possible for a trekker walking at an average pace on the Marangu or Rongai trails to reach Kibo in three days and attempt an assault on the summit for that third night. This sort of schedule is entirely too rapid, allowing insufficient time for trekkers to adapt to the new conditions prevalent at the higher altitude. This is why so many people fail on these trails and it is also the reason why, particularly on these shorter trails, **it is**

* '*Pole pole*' is a phrase you'll probably hear more than any other on Kili. It's Swahili for 'slowly slowly' and is usually uttered by guides to dissuade their charges from ascending too fast.

imperative that you take a 'rest' or acclimatization day on the way up, to give your body more time to acclimatize.

How you approach the walk is important too. Statistically, men are more likely to suffer from AMS than women, with young men the most vulnerable. The reason is obvious. The competitive streak in most young men causes them to walk faster than the group; that, and the mistaken belief that greater fitness and strength (which most men, mistakenly or otherwise, believe they have) will protect them against AMS. But AMS is no respecter of fitness or health. Indeed, many experienced mountaineers believe the reverse is true: the less fit you are, the slower you will want to walk and thus the greater chance you have of acclimatizing properly. The best advice, then, is to **go as slowly as possible**. Let your guide be the pacemaker: do not be tempted to hare off ahead of him but stick with him. That way you can keep a sensible pace and, what's more, can ask him any questions about the mountain that occur to you along the way.

There are other things you can do that may or may not reduce the chance of getting AMS. One is to **eat well**: fatigue is said to be a major contributor to AMS, so try to keep energy levels up by eating as much as you can. Dehydration can

---

The table below shows the oximeter readings of five trekkers on the Machame Route.You can see how the amount of oxygen in the blood decreases as they ascend the mountain. Perhaps the most interesting feature of the graph, however, is the way that everybody's oxygen saturation declines and climbs at the same places. Despite the differences in each individual's readings, it may interest you to know that all of the climbers made it to the top.

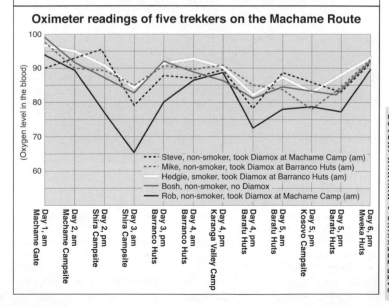

Oximeter readings of five trekkers on the Machame Route

exacerbate AMS too, so it is vital that you **drink every few minutes** when walk-ing; for this reason, one of the new platypus-style water bags (Camelbaks) which allow you to drink hands-free without breaking stride are invaluable (see p63). **Wearing warm clothes** is important too, allowing you to conserve energy that would otherwise be spent on maintaining a reasonable body temperature. Although there hasn't been a serious study on this subject, many people swear that carrying your own rucksack increases your chance of succumbing to AMS. Certainly, in our experience, this is true, so, finally, **hire a porter to carry your baggage** (the agencies will assume you want this unless you specify otherwise).

HOW TO TREAT IT

Sat down beside P.D. in the mud. Gave him one bottle of champagne. Revived him greatly.
Peter MacQueen *In Wildest Africa* (1910)

It is possible that on your trek you will see at least one poor sod being wheeled down Kili, surrounded by porters and strapped to the strange unicycle-cum-stretcher device that KINAPA uses for evacuating the sick and suffering from the mountain. Descent is the most effective cure for AMS but in some severe cases it is not enough. Diamox (see box opposite) is also usually given, though again, if the victim has been suffering for a while or Diamox is not available, some other treatment may be used such as:

Other drugs Nifedipine is useful in treating HAPO though is hard to source in Africa and thus is seldom seen on the mountain. To administer the drug, prick a 10mg capsule many times with a pin before giving to the sufferer who should then chew it thoroughly before swallowing. If the victim then shows signs of breathing more easily, this should then be repeated 15 minutes later. The drug has the side-effect of lowering blood pressure but can be most effective in help-ing treat victims of HAPO and some people even continue to ascend if they respond well to the drug – though we don't recommend this. **Dexamethasone** is useful for treating severe AMS and, in conjunction with other treatments, in treating HACO. Two 4mg tablets should be given to the HACO sufferer, fol-lowed by one tablet every 6 hours until the victim has recovered.

Gamow hyperbaric bag This is a man-sized plastic bag into which the victim is enclosed. The bag is then zipped up and inflated. As it is inflated, the pressure felt by the sufferer inside the bag is increased, thus mimicking the atmospheric conditions present at a lower altitude. The disadvantage with this method is that of inconvenience. The cumbersome bag has to be taken up the mountain and, worst of all, in order to work effectively once the patient is inside, the bag must be kept at a constant pressure. This means that somebody must pump up the bag every two or three minutes. This is tricky when at least two other people are try-ing to manoeuvre the bag with the body inside it down the slopes. Some of the upmarket trek operators carry one with them and KINAPA are trying to make this compulsory for all groups on the Western Breach. Certainly, while Gamow bags are essential in places where rapid descent is difficult, on Kilimanjaro some agencies now consider them to be gimmicky.

Diamox

Acetazolamide (traded under the brand name Diamox) is the wonder drug that fights AMS and the first treatment doctors give to somebody suffering from mountain sickness. It works by acidifying the blood, which stimulates breathing, allowing a greater amount of oxygen to enter into the bloodstream.

A lot of climbers were initially a bit sceptical about Diamox, worrying whether it actually helped to fight AMS or merely masked the symptoms. Now, however, it seems widely accepted that it really is the most effective drug against altitude sickness. That's not to say that it works for everyone, however; for some reason, some people just don't seem to derive any benefit from the drug at all.

It's worth noting that while Diamox is widely regarded as a boon, there are still many questions to be answered about it. It's not unusual, for example, for climbers to be given different prescriptions by their doctors: some will have 125mg tablets, for example, and will be expected to take them twice a day; others (the majority) will have 250mg tablets and will be told to take them either once or, more often, twice per day; while still others will be issued with a single 500 or even 750mg tablet and told to take it only if they are feeling ill.

That last prescription leads us neatly onto the second major question about Diamox. Should the drug be used as a cure for when someone starts developing symptoms of mountain sickness? Or should it be used prophylactically, taking it at the start of the walk to prevent AMS occurring in the first place? The disadvantage with doing this, according to one doctor serving on the Annapurna Circuit in Nepal, is that by using Diamox prophylactically, you are using up one possible cure. That is to say, should you begin to suffer from AMS despite taking Diamox, doctors are going to have to look for another form of treatment to ensure your survival.

At the moment the jury is still out as to what is the best dose and prescription for Diamox, though for what it's worth I find that most people take them prophylactically, either at the very start of the trek or on day three when they are at an altitude of around 3500m or so; 250mg twice a day is the usual regime prescribed from here.

However you decide to take it, there are a couple of rules that you should always follow: always consult with your doctor before taking Diamox to discuss the risks and benefits; and secondly, if you do take it, remember to try it out first back at home to check for any allergic reaction, as Diamox is a sulfa derivative and some people do suffer from side effects, particularly a strange tingling sensation in their hands and feet.

Oxygen Giving the victim extra oxygen from a bottle or canister does not immediately reverse all the symptoms, though in conjunction with rapid descent it can be most effective.

OTHER POTENTIAL HEALTH PROBLEMS

Coughs and colds

These are common on Kilimanjaro. Aspirin can be taken for a cold; lozenges containing anaesthetic are useful for a sore throat, as is gargling with warm salty water. Drinking plenty helps too. A cough that produces mucus has one of a number of causes; most likely are the common cold or irritation of the bronchi by cold air which produces symptoms that are similar to flu. It could, however,

SAFE TREKKING & MINIMUM IMPACT

If you're farting well, you're faring well — other effects of altitude and acclimatization on the human body

In addition to AMS, there are other symptoms suffered by people at high altitude that are not in themselves usually cause for any concern. The first is the phenomenon of **periodic breathing** (aka sleep apnoea). What happens is that, during sleep, the breathing of a person becomes less and less deep, until it appears that he or she has stopped breathing altogether for a few seconds — to the obvious consternation of those sharing the person's tent. The person will then breathe or snore deeply a couple of times to recover, causing relief all round. Another phenomenon is that of **swollen hands and feet**, more common amongst women than men. Once again, this is no cause for concern unless the swelling is particularly severe. Another one that is far more common among women than men, is **irregular periods**. The need to **urinate** and **break wind** frequently are also typical of high-altitude living and, far from being something to be concerned about, are actually positive indications that your body is adapting well to the conditions. As is written on an ancient tombstone in Dorset:

Let your wind go free, where e'er you be,
For holding it in, was the death of me.

point to AMS. A cough that produces thick green and yellow mucus could indicate bronchitis. If there is also chest pain (most severe when the patient breathes out), a high fever and blood-stained mucus, any of these could indicate **pneumonia**, requiring a course of antibiotics. Consult a doctor.

Exposure

Also known as hypothermia, this is caused by a combination of exhaustion, high altitude, dehydration, lack of food and not wearing enough warm clothes against the cold. Note that it does not need to be very cold for exposure to occur. Make sure everyone is properly equipped, particularly your porters.

Symptoms of exposure include a low body temperature (below 34.5°C or 94°F), poor coordination, exhaustion and shivering. As their condition deteriorates the shivering ceases, coordination gets worse making walking difficult and the patient may start hallucinating. The pulse then slows and unconsciousness and death follow shortly. Treatment involves thoroughly warming the patient quickly. Find shelter as soon as possible. Put the patient, without their clothes, into a sleeping-bag with hot water bottles (use your water bottles); someone else should take their clothes off, too, and get into the sleeping bag with the patient. Nothing like bodily warmth to hasten recovery.

Frostbite

The severe form of frostbite that leads to the loss of fingers and toes rarely happens to trekkers on Kilimanjaro. You could, however, be affected if you get stuck or lost in particularly inclement weather. Ensure that all members of your party are properly kitted out with thick socks, boots, gloves and woolly hats.

The first stage of frostbite is known as 'frostnip'. The fingers or toes first become cold and painful, then numb and white. Heat them up on a warm part of the body (eg an armpit) until the colour comes back. In cases of severe frost-bite the affected part of the body becomes frozen. Don't try to warm it up until you reach a lodge/camp. Immersion in warm water (40°C or 100°F) is the treatment. Medical help should then be sought.

Gynaecological problems

If you have had a vaginal infection in the past it would be a good idea to bring a course of treatment in case it recurs.

Haemorrhoids

If you've suffered from these in the past bring the required medication with you since haemorrhoids can flare up on a trek, particularly if you get constipated.

Snowblindness

Though the snows of Kilimanjaro are fast disappearing, you are still strongly advised to wear sunglasses when walking on the summit – particularly if you plan on spending more than just a few minutes up there – to prevent this uncomfortable, though temporary, condition. Ensure everyone in your group, including porters, has eye protection. If you lose your sunglasses a piece of cardboard with two narrow slits (just wide enough to see through) will protect your eyes. The cure for snow-blindness is to keep the eyes closed and lie down in a dark room. Eye-drops and aspirin can be helpful.

Sunburn

Protect against sunburn by wearing a hat, sunglasses and a shirt with a collar that can be turned up. At altitude you'll also need sunscreen for your face.

Care of feet, ankles and knees

A twisted ankle, swollen knee or a septic blister on your foot could ruin your trek so it's important you take care to avoid these. Choose comfortable boots with good ankle support. Don't carry too heavy a load. Wash your feet and change your socks regularly. During lunch stops take off your boots and socks and let them dry in the sun. Attend to any blister as soon as you feel it developing.

Blisters There are a number of ways to treat blisters but prevention is far better than cure. Stop immediately you feel a 'hot spot' forming and cover it with a piece of moleskin or Second Skin/Compeed. One trekker suggests using the membrane inside an egg-shell as an alternative form of Second Skin. If a blister does form you can either burst it with a needle (sterilized in a flame) then apply a dressing or build a moleskin dressing around the unburst blister to protect it.

Sprains You can reduce the risk of a sprained ankle by wearing boots which offer good support. Watch where you walk, too. If you do sprain an ankle, cool it in a stream and keep it bandaged. If it's very painful you'll probably have to abandon your trek. Aspirin is helpful for reducing pain and swelling.

Knee problems These are most common after long stretches of walking down-hill. It's important not to take long strides as you descend; small steps will lessen the jarring on the knee. It may be helpful to wear knee supports and use walking poles for long descents, especially if you've had problems with your knees before.

SAFE TREKKING & MINIMUM IMPACT

Minimum impact trekking

Manya ulanyc upangenyi cha ipfuve – 'Do not foul the cave where you have slept' (A Chagga proverb that refers to the habits of the baboon who are said to 'foul their caves' until there comes a point where the stench compels them to find alternative accommodation.)

KINAPA does try to keep Kilimanjaro clean. At all huts and campsites, trekking groups have their rubbish weighed by the ranger and if there's any evidence that some rubbish has been dumped (ie if the rubbish carried weighs less at one campsite than at the previous camp) then the guide could have his licence temporarily revoked and/or have to pay a heavy fine. It's a system that would appear to have loopholes but until recently Kili *was* a very clean mountain, and though it can be frustrating to have to wait for your guide every morning while the rubbish is weighed, it's a small price to pay for a pristine peak. Sadly, standards appear to have slipped recently and there is now serious concern amongst trekking agents and environmentalists about the state of some of the trails. While it's easy to blame the authorities for the sorry state of Lemosho and other routes, trekkers are just as culpable. After all, much of it is our rubbish.

You can help Kilimanjaro become beautiful once more by following these simple rules that apply to almost every mountain anywhere in the world:

TOILET ETIQUETTE

The toilets at the various camps come in for a lot of stick from trekkers. And rightly so, too, because for the most part they're bloody awful. KINAPA recognizes as much and is currently attempting to improve the facilities; the smart new toilets at Mweka Huts (see p330) are the loos of the future. But for the moment in most campsites you'll have to make do with the standard rough wooden sheds with a hole in the floor, the more sophisticated examples of which come with a door.

There's no doubt about it, many of these 'long-drop' toilets are disgusting. But whatever their state and no matter how unpleasant they may be, you still have a duty to use them (unless you've paid to have a private toilet dragged up the mountain for your use, which costs around US$10 per day). There are few sights on Kilimanjaro more depressing than the clods and streamers of used toilet roll hidden behind rocks and hanging from bushes surrounding each campsite. It's hard to understand why some people think it's OK to sleep in a campsite surrounded by their own shit, rather than spending two minutes inside one of the public loos; but if you happen to be one of them, the following tips may help you overcome your fear of the latrine:

● If you're worried about being disturbed by a fellow trekker, then on hearing someone approach try coughing, whistling, screaming or otherwise alerting them to your presence *before* they have a chance to invade your space.

SOME GUIDELINES FOR KEEPING THE MOUNTAIN PRISTINE

● **Dispose of litter properly**. In theory, all you should have to do is give your litter to your crew: given the stiff punishments they receive for leaving rubbish behind (see opposite), this should ensure all waste is taken off the mountain. Unfortunately, despite all the cleaning crews and the weighing stations at each campsite, some think the litter situation is getting worse. Whatever you decide to do, don't give **used batteries** to porters; keep them with you and take them back to the West where they have the facilities to dispose of them properly (the batteries that is, not the porters).

● **Don't start fires**. The account on p122 gives you an idea of how damaging an out-of-control fire can be. There's absolutely no need for fires on Kilimanjaro: for cooking, your crew should use kerosene, while for heat, put another layer of clothes on or cuddle up to somebody who doesn't mind being cuddled up to.

● **Use the purpose-built latrines**. True, some of them could do with emptying (especially the central toilet at the Barranco campsite, which is now so full that the pile of human waste is in danger of developing a snowy summit all of its own), but this is still better than having piles of poo behind all the bushes on the trail and toilet paper hanging from every bough.

● **Leave the flora and fauna alone**. Kili is home to some beautiful flowers and fascinating wildlife, but the giant groundsels rarely thrive in the soils of Europe and the wild buffalo, though they may look docile when splashing about in the streams of Kili, have an awful temper that makes them quite unsuitable as pets.

● Conversely, when approaching the toilet, give any occupants inside fair warning of your presence by approaching noisily and knocking before entering. It's only polite.
● If it's the smell that worries you, a bandanna round the nose and mouth can help.
● Visiting the toilet in the early morning – when the stuff inside the toilets is frozen solid and the stench is reduced – is also a good plan.
● While you're inside the toilets you have a responsibility to keep things tidy. It can be difficult to maintain balance and aim but if you do miss, do the decent thing and tidy up.

Going outside

If you really, really, really can't wait to reach one of the toilets, the least you can do is deliberate before you defecate. Firstly, make sure you're at least 20m away from both the path and any streams – the mountain is still the main source of water for many villages and they would prefer it if you didn't crap in their H_2O. Secondly, take a trowel with you so you can dig a hole to squat over, and cover this hole with plenty of earth when you've finished. And finally, dispose of your toilet paper properly. One way is to try burning it. One reader has written in to say that it's very difficult to burn soggy toilet paper. My editor, however, has conducted a controlled experiment and gives this advice: 'If you light the dry corner of partially wet loo paper and twirl it round so the flame dries the wet bit it *does* all burn up'. Give it a go next time you need to, er, go. Even better, why not adopt the 'pack it in–pack it out' method, ie put the used paper in a bag for disposal in the next toilet – the best approach for keeping the mountain clean.

If we all follow these rules then maybe, just maybe, Kilimanjaro will remain Earth's most beautiful mountain – rather than resembling one massive, 5895m-high pile of poo.

It's illegal to take the flora and fauna out of the park, so leave it all alone. That way, other trekkers can enjoy them too.

● **Boil, filter or purify your drinking water**. This will help to reduce the number of non-returnable, non-reusable, non-biodegradable and very non-environmentally friendly plastic mineral water bottles that are used on Kili.

● **Stay on the main trail**. The continued use of shortcuts, particularly steep ones, erodes the slopes. This is particularly true on Kibo: having reached the summit, it's very tempting on your return to slide down on the shale like a skier and you'll see many people, especially guides, doing just that. There's no doubt that it's a fast, fun and furious way to get to the bottom, but with thousands of trekkers doing likewise every year, the slopes of Kibo are gradually being eroded as all the scree gets pushed further down the mountain. Laborious as it sounds, stick to the same snaking path that you used to ascend.

● **Wash away from streams and rivers**. You wouldn't like to bathe in somebody else's bathwater; nor, probably, would you like to cook with it, do your laundry in it, nor indeed drink it. And neither would the villagers on Kili's lower slopes, so don't pollute their water by washing your hair, body or clothes in the mountain streams, no matter how romantic an idea this sounds. If your guide is halfway decent he will bring some hot water in a bowl at the end of the day's walk with which you can wash. Dispose of it at least 20m away from any streams or rivers.

PART 7: MOUNT MERU

INTRODUCTION

Mount Meru, which overlooks Arusha from the north, is used by many trekkers as a warm-up trek – an *hors d'oeuvre* to the main course of Kili if you like. And a perfect starter it is too: though smaller, it's also quite similar in that to reach its volcanic summit you have first to climb through a number of different vegetation zones before embarking on the final night-time march to the highest point on the crater rim and thus the summit itself. What's more, at 4562.13m (according to the sign at the top) it provides the trekker with the perfect opportunity to acclimatize to Kilimanjaro's rarified atmosphere. In other words, the mountain offers a taste of the challenges that lie ahead on Kilimanjaro, whilst also whetting the appetite for the thrills and beauty of that mountain.

However, Meru is worth doing as much for the differences as for the similarities that it shares with its neighbour. In particular, there's the greater abundance of wildlife. Lying at the heart of Arusha National Park, a reserve that's teeming with animals, it's an odd trekker who doesn't finish the trek with his or her camera filled with pictures of buffalo, giraffe, elephant, bushbuck, dik dik, suni, colobus, blue monkey and warthog. Luckier ones may also see leopard and hyaena, while twitchers will be more than content with the number of birds on offer, from the noisy Hartlaub's turaco to the silver-cheeked hornbill and black-and-white bulbul.

If all this sounds like your idea of a perfect holiday – a safari-and-trek all rolled into one – then you're probably right, though there is one point that needs to be emphasized: do not underestimate Meru. Though it may be more than a thousand metres lower than Kili, it's still well above the altitude necessary to bring about altitude sickness and with almost everybody taking just over two days before reaching the summit, the risks are great. Indeed, though we've climbed Kilimanjaro on a number of occasions, without a shadow of a doubt our most nerve-racking ascent was on Meru. True, this had much to do with the fact that there had been heavy rain on the evening before the night-time walk to the summit, a downpour which quickly froze and caused the entire trail, from Saddle to summit, to become covered with a layer of ice. Inconvenient on the first part of that night-time walk, on the second half it became positively dangerous, causing us to scribble hurriedly a last will and testament in our notebooks. Indeed, it was thanks only to the hard work of the guides, who dug out footsteps in the ice with a piece of rock or the back of their heels – footsteps in which, taking our lead from King Wenceslas, we then trod – that we gained the summit at all. And it was only by inching our way back down, bottom pressed into the ice, limbs looking for any piece of rock or other non-slippery material to put our weight upon, that we made it back down to write this guide. So though Meru may not carry the cachet, prestige or the sheer scale of Kili, it's no pushover. Meru remains an awfully big mountain – the tenth highest peak in Africa, in fact, – and as such it should be treated with the utmost respect.

PRACTICALITIES

The route

There is only one main route up Meru. The route begins at **Momela Gate**, around 15km from the main Ngongongare entrance gate where you pay your park fees. Having paid up and driven those 15km, past the plain known as Little Serengeti (Serengeti Ndogo) because of its similarity to Tanzania's most famous park, you arrive at Momela where you pick up your ranger and hire your porters.

The route from Momela Gate (altitude 1597m) to the summit is punctuated by two sets of accommodation huts: the first are the Miriakamba Huts (2503m), a day's walk from Momela Gate; and the second are the Saddle Huts (3560m), lying a short day's walk from there. From the Saddle Huts it's a further day's walk – or rather, a night's walk – to the summit.

The cost

Trips up Meru are usually offered by the agencies in Arusha (the best place to organize such a trek) for either three or four days. Note that, unlike Kili, you don't actually need to book this trek through an agency and can do it independently; see opposite for the pros and cons of such an approach. Don't be misled, as we were, into thinking that if you book a four-day trek you are more likely to reach the summit because of the extra day's acclimatization; that extra day is actually spent on the *way down*, not up. So while we were glad to have the extra day to descend – it's a bit too much of a rush otherwise to go from the summit to Momela Gate in one day, and we were grateful to spend a second night at Miriakamba – if you're on a tight budget you'll save yourself a small fortune in park fees by taking a day less.

Regarding these park fees, they tend to be a little cheaper than the equivalent charges on Kili and are as follows:

Park entrance fee: US$35 per day (US$10 per day for under 16s).
Hut fee: US$20 per night
Rescue fee: US$20 per trip
Guide/ranger fee: US$15 per day

Thus for a four-day/three-night trip you're looking at a total figure of US$280. On top of this you'll probably need to pay the equivalent **porters/guide fees** to enable them to enter and stay in the park. Their entrance fees are charged at Ts1500 per day, while their hut fees are just Ts1000. So, for example, if your agency has supplied you with a guide and three porters, the total amount you'll be paying for them will be:

Entrance fee: Ts1500 x 4 people x 4 days = Ts24,000
Hut fee: Ts1000 x 4 people x 3 nights = Ts12,000
Making a grand total of: Ts36,000

All of these fees will be factored into the total amount the trekking agency charges for your trek and so needn't concern you too much here. However, you may have noticed in the above that there are in fact two guides in the party: one supplied by the agency and one by the park (whom we have called a ranger to avoid confusion). The ranger/guide supplied by the park is compulsory, for it is he who carries the gun that, should any of the local fauna take an unhealthy interest in your party, could come in very handy. However, these rangers in our experience are also better guides, with better English and a greater knowledge of the park, mainly because they spend most of their time in it. Indeed, on one of our treks we didn't even see the guide that had been supplied by the trekking agency until we got to the Miriakamba Huts at the end of the first day!

Doing it independently

It is this over-supply of guides that leads several tourists to consider doing the whole thing independently without signing up to any trekking agency. True, it is tempting but there are a few things to consider first. For one thing, you will need to arrange transport to and from the park, for there is no public transport. Secondly, you'll need to bring with you all the food and supplies you need, and some form of stove in order to cook. Thirdly, all this luggage means you'll probably need to hire porters, which can be done at Momela Gate at the start of the trail, though you'll need to work out how much to pay them (the Kilimanjaro Porters Assistance Project, see pp46-49, recommends Ts6000 per day) and to organize them yourself. What's more, you will still need to take with you one of the park rangers – they're compulsory. So while the idea of doing the whole trek independently may sound attractive, you do need to have a certain amount of confidence to bring it all off, especially when it comes to organizing your porters, a job that's outside of the ranger's remit but is perhaps the most useful purpose of the trekking agency guide.

So yes, it is possible to go up Meru independently but the saving, money-wise, will be negligible. Indeed, only if you've a real aversion to agencies or really fancy the challenge should you attempt it.

Trekking with an agency

Perhaps not surprisingly, therefore, most people choose to sign up with an agency in Arusha. Rates start at around US$400 for four days. You may want to factor into this fee a night or two at one of the lodges near the park. This will enable you to make an early start in the morning (though treks are officially not allowed to start until 10am anyway, so as not to disrupt the animals' dawn hunt). Some of these jungle lodges are paragons of charm. One such is *Colobus Mountain Lodge* (☎ 027-250 2813, 🖥 www.colobusmountainlodge.com), near the western Ngongongare Gate to the park. A good-value 18-banda lodge built around a large *makuti*-thatched reception-cum-bar, the rooms are all clean, airy and bright, while the gardens are flower-filled and attract a range of birds (as does, occasionally, the thatched roof of your banda). Rates start at around US$80 per room, half-board US$15 extra.

Another choice is the rather more eccentric **Hatari Lodge** (PO Box 3171, Arusha; ☎ 027-255 3456; 🖳 www.hatarilodge.com), which has real history and character. The lodge is named after the John Wayne film that was shot on the farm. Indeed, one of Wayne's co-stars, a German actor called Hardy Krüger, actually ended up giving up Hollywood for Arusha, and bought the farm on which the lodge is set soon after the film was completed. Lying just outside the park's northern boundary, the only realistic way of getting to it is via the park itself so you will have to pay the park fees. With a small library, long bar, breakfast terrace and great views of both Kili and Meru, this is a refreshingly different safari lodge with décor and location that are best described as quirky. Prices are US$280 per night full board. If you have the time, come here for a drink even if you're not staying.

STAGE 1: MOMELA GATE TO MIRIAKAMBA HUTS [MAP A, opposite]

Distance: 13.8km; altitude gained: 906m

Though we stated in the introduction to this trek that there's only one path to the summit of Meru, that's not entirely true for, in fact, on this first day there are two possible paths, the split between the two occurring just five minutes along the trail. Most trekkers, of course, will want to take both paths, one on the way up and the other on the way down. The question is, therefore, which path to take first?

Regarding these two trails, the first is a longer and more circuitous route that follows a 4WD dirt track as it swerves drunkenly and only very approximately along the course of the Ngare Nanyuki (the river you cross on a bridge right at the beginning of the trek) and Jekukumia rivers before turning north to cross the Crater Plain to the huts. As for the second option, this is a much more direct path and, on first sight at least, would appear to be the more tempting. It includes a crossing of the Meru Plain that's alive with Africa's tallest mammal (the giraffe) and its most bad-tempered (the buffalo), and should also take in a diversion to the beautiful Tululusia waterfall that lies just off the trail.

Trail map key					
/	Main trail	⋎	Cliff	☐	Building
⫽	Other trail	🜲	Bridge and river	◪	Toilet
⫽	4WD track	🌳	Trees	⬦	Hut
⫽	Road	🌿	Groundsel	⬧	Accommodation
↗	Slope	🌿	Tree fern	X	Campsite
⇗	Steep Slope	♥	Heather	008	GPS waypoint
		°°°	Boulders	21	Map continuation

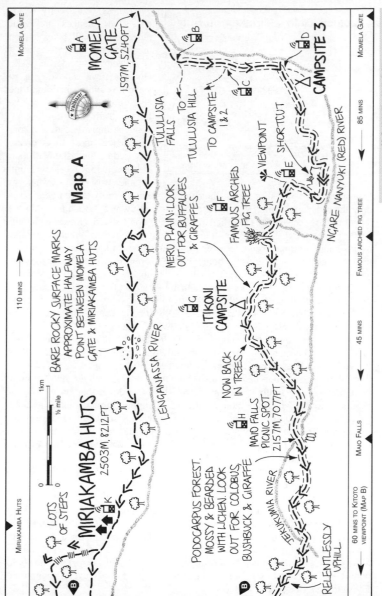

Map A

MOMELA GATE
1597M, 5240FT

TULULUSIA FALLS

TO TULULUSIA HILL

TO CAMPSITE 1 & 2

VIEWPOINT

SHORTCUT

CAMPSITE 3

FAMOUS ARCHED FIG TREE

NGARE NANYUKI (RED) RIVER

MERU PLAIN: LOOK OUT FOR BUFFALOES & GIRAFFES

ITIKONI CAMPSITE

BARE ROCKY SURFACE MARKS APPROXIMATE HALFWAY POINT BETWEEN MOMELA GATE & MIRIAKAMBA HUTS

LENGANASSA RIVER

NOW BACK IN TREES

MAIO FALLS PICNIC SPOT 2157M, 7077FT

PODOCARPUS FOREST. MOSSY & BEARDED WITH LICHEN. LOOK OUT FOR COLOBUS BUSHBUCK & GIRAFFE

RELENTLESSLY UPHILL

TEKUKUMIA RIVER

MIRIAKAMBA HUTS 2503M, 8212FT

LOTS OF STEPS

1km
½ mile

110 MINS
45 MINS

MIRIAKAMBA HUTS

60 MINS TO KITOTO VIEWPOINT (MAP B) | MAIO FALLS | 45 MINS | FAMOUS ARCHED FIG TREE | 85 MINS | MOMELA GATE

MOUNT MERU

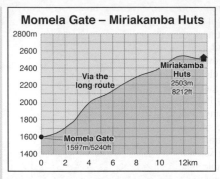

Momela Gate – Miriakamba Huts

Miriakamba
Huts
2503m
8212ft

Via the
long route

Momela Gate
1597m/5240ft

Unless you specify otherwise the chances are your ranger/guide will take you on this shorter, steeper path; and it is indeed a wonderful walk. However, we advise you to leave this shorter path until the end and instead opt for the longer trail for your ascent. Why? Simply because, in our experience, most trekkers are too tired on the last day of their trek to attempt the longer trail on the way down, whatever their intentions when they began their trek. (Indeed, if you've given yourselves only three days to complete the trek, you probably won't have time to do the longer trail on the last day.) In other words, if you don't take the longer path now, for the ascent, the chances are you'll miss out on it it altogether. Which is a shame, as this longer trail has plenty to offer including a pretty little waterfall-cum-picnic spot and a fantastic fig tree (about which, see opposite). There's also the matter of acclimatization to consider, for taking over four hours to climb the 906m to Miriakamba Huts is a lot more sensible than taking just two or so, as you would on the shorter trail. So don't be too eager to get amongst the animals on the plain at the foot of Meru but instead choose the longer trail for your ascent and save the shorter trail for the way down; and this is how we've described the trek below.

Though this longer trail avoids the **Meru Plain**, there's still an abundance of wildlife to be seen. In addition to the beasts of the plain that could still be espied behind the screen of acacias, within the first five minutes – no, make that three – of starting our trek we also encountered dik dik and suni standing motionless in the scrub lining the path, while a little further on a troop of baboons showed what they thought of our interrupting their elevenses by turning their backs and displaying their red-raw backsides. It's a hot and dusty start to the trek – but a distinctly memorable one. Indeed, even on this longer route we guarantee you'll see more animals within the first half-hour of your expedition than you would in a month on Kili.

The scenery changes slightly as you reach the junction with the path to Campsite 3 and the path bends right (west), with both the gradient and the size of the trees increasing. The first junipers, bearded with lichen, appear and the whole trail now takes on a lusher, greener aspect. Continuing up the hill, your guide, bored with the repetitive twists and turns of the official trail, may take you on a well-known short-cut, emerging back onto the trail just before a stream with a marshy patch of grassland to the left – often populated by bushbuck – and the Meru summit beyond. A good opportunity for a photo, methinks. A second photo opportunity occurs just a minute later with the first of several signposted **Kilimanjaro viewpoints**.

Regardless of whether you took photos of these places or not, one sight which we can almost guarantee will have you reaching for your Rolleiflex is the **arched fig tree**, a magnificent strangler fig (*Ficus thonningii*) which has now completely enveloped its host and arches across the track. It is reminiscent of those pictures you see of giant redwoods in California which have cars driving through them – though here it is elephants that have passed through the tunnel formed by the tree, widening the gap as they do so.

The path, now illuminated by Popcorn cassia (*Cassia didymobotrya*; incorrectly called candle bushes by many guides), heads north soon after to cross an open area with a good view of the summit and possible sightings of buffaloes in the depression to the left of the trail. The northerly direction is but temporary, however, the path soon reverting south to acquaint itself with the sweet-water **Jekukumia River** (the last available water source on this climb) at **Maio Falls**, at 2157m altitude a picturesque spot and a delightful place to break for lunch.

Rested and replete, you now return to the main track as it continues its weaving, wriggling way westwards up the slope. It's a pleasant stroll, the gradient seldom steep and the stands of juniper and podocarpus providing essential shade. The forest is still alive with animals, too, even though they may be more difficult to see. Your ranger/guide, however, should be able to point out the tracks of hyaena and snake, and your walk will, more than likely, be accompanied by the bark of the bushbuck, call of the colobus monkey (which sounds curiously like a frog) and the broken-klaxon honk of Hartlaub's turaco (which, just to confuse matters, sounds curiously like a monkey). If you're lucky, a crash in the undergrowth or in the branches will give away the precise location of these shy creatures, or indeed of giraffe or buffalo. The scenery is just as pleasant as before lunch too, but by now tiredness and a desire for change will probably have set in, along with a wish that the track, for a few metres at least, would follow a straight line. Thankfully, about an hour after leaving the falls the first red hot pokers appear (*Kniphofia thomsonii*), a flower that heralds the imminent arrival of **Kitoto Viewpoint** (Map B), with views east-north-east over the Momela Lakes and east-south-east over the fauna-filled Ngurdoto Crater, the original centre and raison d'être of Arusha National Park before it merged with Meru to create the current park you find today.

From now until the end of this first stage the path feels more alpine. It's still upwards, at least until you reach a clearing with unrestricted views of the petrified lava flow that runs down from the ash cone to the plateau on which you stand – the so-called **Crater Plain**. This plain, though more than 2600m above sea level, still attracts an abundance of game including giraffe, hyaena, leopard and, to judge from the number of skulls littering the area, would also seem to be the place where old buffaloes come to die. On the northern edge of this mini plain is the dry, rocky river-bed of the seasonal **Lenganassa River**, which you follow downhill to your first night's destination. The **Miriakamba Huts** (Map A) are a smart pair of accommodation huts and accompanying buildings sitting at an altitude of 2503m above sea level. The huts are divided into rooms for four people and are popular not only with tourists but also, if the amount of dung is anything to go by, with buffalo and elephant too; for this reason, we advise you to take care when nipping out to the loo at night. There are also good views across to Kilimanjaro from the toilets.

STAGE 2: MIRIAKAMBA HUTS TO SADDLE HUTS
[MAP A, p233; MAP B, opposite]

Distance: 6.1km; altitude gained: 1057m

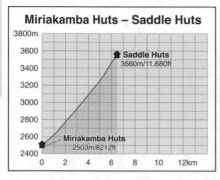

Miriakamba Huts – Saddle Huts

Saddle Huts
3560m/11,680ft

Miriakamba Huts
2503m/8212ft

Everybody has their favourite section of the Meru trek, and the walk from the Miriakamba Huts to the lunch stop at Mgongo Wa Tembo is ours. There's something gentle and gorgeously pastoral about the grassy slopes that put one in mind of the rolling hills of England for some reason – the exotic flora and piles of buffalo and elephant crap notwithstanding. Indeed, it's the unusual flora – the *Hagenia abyssinica* with its heavy pink/brown blossom, for example, or a species of lobelia (see below) which resembles in no way the lobelias you'll find in your garden at home – and the continuing presence of the park's larger fauna that add so much to the day. Even the path is impressive, a wooden staircase leading west up the slopes of the ridge towards the Saddle. Then of course there are the views over your shoulder of Kilimanjaro glowering at its little brother, its white summit glistening in the sun. It's a great morning's walk. Nor does the interest for trekkers wane much after lunch as the path enters the alpine zone. The trees diminish in size before disappearing altogether, to be replaced by the heathers and ericas that flourish at this altitude. The only problem with the latter half of this second day is that it can become slightly monotonous after a while and impatience and ennui can set in. But don't be in too much of a hurry: from the moment you set off it's vital that you take it *pole pole* because of the altitude.

So from Miriakamba adopt a funereal speed from the word go. After a few minutes traversing the ridge, the trail then heads off up the steps of the mountain's eastern flanks. The path zig-zags for much of the morning, with juniper and hagenia lining the way together with the occasional stand of *Lobelia gibberoa*, whose younger plants display an impressive phallic brush growing out of their tops. Elephants can occasionally be seen along this stretch, so do make sure you stick close to the man with the gun. The path soon bends in a more northerly direction, with great views of Kili to your right framed by the local vegetation. There are some great old fallen trees here with some vivid red mountain gladioli growing from the trunks. Following the zig-zags, **Mgongo**

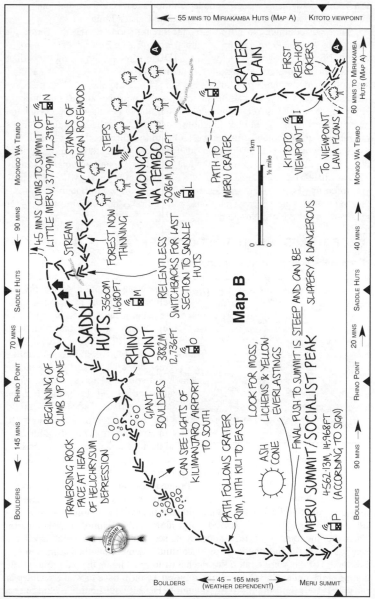

Wa Tembo ('Elephant's Back'; about 3086m) is reached, the usual lunch-stop on this second stage with views south over the **Crater Plain**.

The path continues to climb after the break, soon leaving the forest for something altogether more alpine with *Philippia excelsa* and *Erica arborea* now proliferating. If you're lucky, you may also come across chameleons that, despite being cold-blooded creatures, somehow thrive in this region. It's a bit of a relentless, monotonous trek but it's not long before the **Saddle Huts** (3560m) are reached. As with Miriakamba, these are smart huts that almost put those on Kilimanjaro to shame. Yet despite the altitude the huts still get the occasional visitor from Africa's animal kingdom, including elephants and buffaloes migrating to the grasslands further west. One of the huts has a fine collection of lobelias growing outside its door but other than examining those there's little to do up here, allowing you to spend the rest of the afternoon climbing the nearby 3779m **Little Meru**, a simple 45-minute trudge that the guides will often allow you to do by yourself – remember to climb *pole pole* even though there's no-one to regulate your speed! That done, you can relax and prepare yourself for the exertions of the night to come...

STAGE 3: SADDLE HUTS TO SOCIALIST PEAK   [MAP B, p237]

Distance: 5.5km; altitude gained: 1002.13m

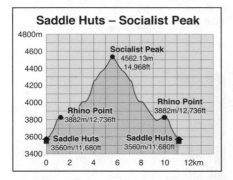

And so to the final ascent, and if the height of Meru is invaluable for acclimatizing, so this night-time march is wonderful preparation for that final push to Kili's Uhuru Peak. True, this walk is shorter and, unlike the relentless zig-zags taking you up Kibo's slopes, more varied and direct too. But the experience of waking up at some godforsaken hour to undertake a chilly high-altitude trek up a very big African volcano, before contouring around the crater rim to reach the highest point as the sun rises to the east, is useful training indeed.

The stage begins with a crossing of the Saddle before bending south to the start of the climb. It's a walk that sees you leave behind the larger vegetation – the ericas and philippias – on a winding path that eventually joins the crest of a ridge that brings you out at **Rhino Point** (3882m), the climb's first landmark. Thereafter the route bends west and, having descended to cross a rockface at the head of a lush (by the standards of this altitude) depression, then climbs to follow the lip of the Meru Crater. For the next couple of hours the path follows the course of the crater rim. Being night, of course, you'll have to wait for views of the crater itself until the morning, though beyond it you should be able to see, in the distance, the lights of various settlements as well as Kilimanjaro International Airport and even, in the far distance, the Mererani tanzanite mine, working away through the night. Eventually, about three and a half hours after setting off, the crater rim begins to bend noticeably south. As it does, hopefully at the same time the eastern horizon will be starting to turn pink and orange with the onset of the new day, and the silhouette of Kili can clearly be discerned, with both Kibo and Mawenzi summits visible.

The summit also seems tangibly closer, too, so it's disheartening to discover that it's still a minimum of an hour away – or nearer three if it's been snowing and your guides have to create a path in the ice using nothing but the heels of their boots as spades and bits of rocks as shovels! It can be a little terrifying, too, with one false step sending you plummeting down the icy slopes. Take care!

At the summit there's little save a flag, a sign and a box containing a book where you can sign your name. There are also, of course, great views over Arusha to the west and Kili to the east, with Meru's perfect ash cone below you. Photos taken and hands shaken, it's time for the descent – and isn't it wonderful to be able to walk at a speed of your choosing again! It's also interesting to see how different in daylight the path looks. Look back from Rhino Point, for example, to the climb up to the crater rim – was it really that steep? Notice, too, while renegotiating the descent from the summit, all the mini bumps and craters to the north and west of Meru which were hidden on the way up.

The descent, though wearying, shouldn't take more than a couple of hours. Those who've opted to spend four days on the mountain will take an hour or so

Mount Meru – Route to the Summit

back at the Saddle Huts, packing their bags, eating some well-earned food and maybe getting a little shut-eye, before the two-hour return stroll down to Miriakamba where they'll be spending the night. Those on the three-day trip will also have an hour to recover at the Saddle Huts, though for them the walk down is that much longer. If you're reading this at the Saddle Huts after your ascent to the summit, you'll probably appreciate now why we suggested taking the long route on the first stage, and saving the shorter route for now.

STAGE 4: MIRIAKAMBA HUTS TO MOMELA GATE   [MAP A, p233]

Distance: 7km, or 7.5km via Tululusia Falls; altitude lost: 906m

One of the advantages Meru has over Kilimanjaro is that this last stage, though

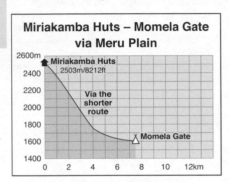

Miriakamba Huts – Momela Gate via Meru Plain

short, is in no way an anti-climax, whereas the last day on Kili often feels like something to endure rather than enjoy. The descent from Miriakamba is hard on the knees, of course, but by way of compensation there's some unusual flora (check out the pink *Impatiens* growing right on the path and the hardy Sodom's apple trees, *Solanum sodomaeum*, growing by the side of it), a charming little river to cross and, of course, a crossing of the buffalo- and warthog-filled plain at the very end, with Kili as an awe-inspiring backdrop. This walk should also include a brief diversion to the impressive **Tululusia Falls**, just a few minutes off the path to the south before the plain.

Even with the diversion you should find yourself back at Momela Gate two to three hours after setting off. There'll just be time to distribute tips, collect your certificates (one for Mount Meru, possibly one for little Mount Meru too) and say your farewells to your companions. It's been a wonderful walk, hasn't it? You've seen some beautiful birds, flowers and animals, taken in some breathtaking views and through sheer bloodymindedness climbed to the very summit of Tanzania's second highest mountain.

Now it's time for the highest...

Colour section (following pages)

● **C1 (Opposite)** The view east from the summit of Mount Meru with the Ash Cone in the foreground and Kilimanjaro in the background. ● **C2 Left**: Traditional Chagga house (top). At the market in Marangu (bottom). **Right**: Under the canopy of the cloud forest, Marangu Route. ● **C3 Top**: Kibo and the Saddle. **Bottom left**: Camping on the Shira Plateau. **Bottom right**: Crossing the Shira Plateau with Meru in the background. ● **C4 Left – Top**: Walking on the Lemosho Route across the Shira Plateau towards Kibo. **Middle**: Reflecting on Kibo. **Bottom**: Walking down the Marangu Route towards the Saddle, with Mawenzi in the distance. **Right – Top**: The groundsel forest above Barranco Campsite. **Bottom left**: Lava Tower Campsite from the tower itself. **Bottom right**: The Breakfast or Barranco Wall.

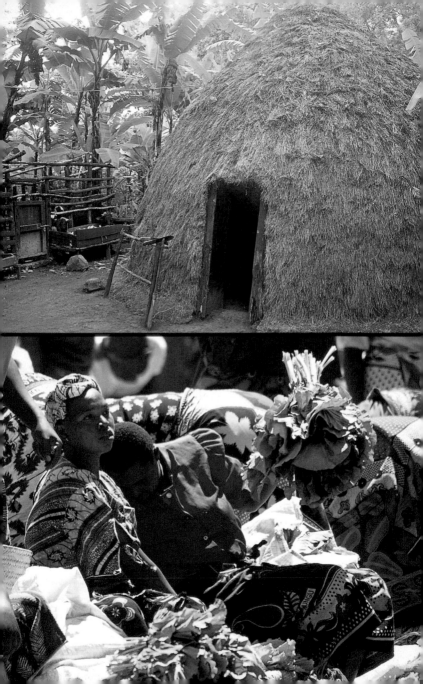

C2

C3

PART 8: TRAIL GUIDE AND MAPS

Using this guide

ABOUT THE MAPS IN THIS GUIDE

Scale

Most of the **trekking maps** in this guide are drawn to the same scale, namely 26mm to 1km (1²/₃ inches to the mile). The exceptions are those maps depicting the routes up to the Kibo summit – ie, those maps that depict the final ascent to the top, which is usually made at night (maps 6, 13 and 18). On these maps the scale has been doubled (ie 52mm to 1km or 3¹/₃ inches to the mile) to allow for more detail to be drawn upon them.

Walking times

The times indicated on the maps should be used only as an approximate guide. They refer to **walking times only** and do not include any time for breaks and food: don't forget to add on a few minutes for breaks when estimating the total time for a particular stage. Overall you may find you need to **add around 30-50%** to our times depending on your walking speed and the time taken for rest breaks to get an idea of the total time you'll spend on the trail.

Gradient arrows

You will also notice that we have drawn '**gradient arrows**' on the trekking maps in this book. The arrows point uphill: two arrows mean that the hill is steep, one that the gradient is reasonably gradual. If, for example, you are walking from A (at 80m) to B (at 200m) and the trail between the two is short and steep, it would be shown thus: A– – – – >>– – – –B.

The Marangu Route

Because this trail is popularly called the 'Tourist Route' or '**Coca Cola trail**', some trekkers are misled into thinking this five- or six-day climb to the summit is simply a walk in the (national) park. But remember that a greater proportion of people fail on this route than on any other. True, this may have something to do with the fact that Marangu's reputation for being 'easy' attracts the more inexperienced, out-of-condition trekkers who don't realize that they are embarking on a **36.55km uphill walk**, followed immediately by a 36.55km

---

(Opposite) **Top**: Leaving Karanga Valley Campsite with Kibo looming behind.
Bottom: The top of Kibo from the slopes of Mawenzi.

❑ In the following descriptions, the treks have been divided into stages, with each stage roughly corresponding to a day's trekking. For this reason, throughout the text the words 'stage' and 'day' have been used interchangeably.

knee-jarring descent. But it shouldn't take much to realize that Marangu is not much easier than any other trail: with the Machame Route, for example, you start at 1811m and aim for the summit at 5895m. On Marangu, you start just a little higher at 1905m and have the same goal, so simple logic should tell you that it can't be that much easier. Indeed, the fact that this route is often completed in 5-6 days as opposed to the 6-7 days that it takes to complete Machame would suggest that this route is actually more arduous – and gives some idea of why **more people fail on this route** than the so-called 'Whiskey Route'.

The main reason why people say that Marangu is easier is because it is the only route where you **sleep in huts** rather than under canvas. The accommodation in these huts should be booked in advance by your tour company, who have to pay a deposit per person per night to KINAPA in order to secure it. To cover this, the tour agencies will probably ask you to pay them some money in advance too. This deposit for the huts is refundable or can be moved to secure huts on other dates, providing you give KINAPA (and your agency) at least seven days' notice.

Unfortunately, those booking with a cheaper agency in Tanzania should exercise caution: some of the cheaper agencies prefer to trust to luck when it comes to accommodation on the Marangu Route, deciding that it is too much bother to travel all the way to Marangu Gate to pay a deposit. Instead, they prefer to assume/pray that there will be room in the huts for their clients when they get there. In days gone by this resulted in some trekkers sleeping on dining tables or hall floors in situations where the huts were overbooked. More and more frequently, however, KINAPA are refusing to

Kilimanjaro seen from Lake Jipé
(from *The Kilima-njaro Expedition – A Record of Scientific Exploration in Eastern Equatorial Africa* **HH Johnston**, 1886)

allow trekkers without a reservation even to start their walk if the huts are fully booked. For your own peace of mind, therefore, you should ask your agency to show you a receipt confirming that they have paid a deposit for your accommodation on the trek. Furthermore, be suspicious of any agency that doesn't ask for at least some of **your trekking fee upfront to cover these deposits**, or who agrees to accept a last-minute booking for the Marangu Route: they should have at least a day's notice in order to book the huts and pay the deposits. Of course, mostly these agencies get away with their lackadaisical approach to hut booking simply because the huts aren't always fully booked and there are usually enough spaces for you, especially if your party is a small one of only two or three trekkers. But don't be surprised if, having booked with one of the cheaper and less reputable agencies, it transpires that there is no room for you at the huts and you get turned away at Marangu Gate. Incidentally, there are 84 spaces at Mandara Huts, 160 at Horombo – the extra beds are necessary because this hut is also used by those *descending* from Kibo – and 60 at Kibo. If any one of those is already booked to capacity on the night you wish to stay there, you won't be allowed to start your trek and will have to change your dates.

The fact that you do sleep in huts makes little difference to what you need to pack for the trek, for sleeping bags are still required (the huts have pillows and mattresses but that's all) though you can dispense with a ground mat for this route. You may also need some small change should you give in to temptation and decide that the exorbitant price of sweets and drinks that are available at the huts is still a price worth paying. Regarding the sleeping situation, it does help if you can get to the huts early each day to grab the better beds. This doesn't mean you should deliberately hurry to the huts, which will reduce your enjoyment of the trek and increase the possibility of AMS. But do try to **start early each morning**: that way you can avoid the crowds, beat them to the better beds, and possibly improve your chances of seeing some of Kili's wildlife too.

In terms of **duration**, the Marangu Route is one of the shorter trails, taking just five days. Many people, however, opt to take an extra day to acclimatize at Horombo Huts, using that day to visit the Mawenzi Huts Campsite at 4535m. From a safety point of view this is entirely sensible and aesthetically such a plan cannot be argued with either, for the views from Mawenzi across the Saddle to Kibo truly take the breath away; assuming, that is, that you have some left to be taken away after all that climbing. *(Continued on p246)*

❏ **Mobile reception on the Marangu Route**
Those with mobile phones will find that the Marangu Route has poor mobile reception in general. It depends which network you're with, but I found that there is little to no reception at the **Mandara Huts** (though I did get reception at the nearby Maundi Crater), and the first real chance of getting reception was at Horombo Huts; reception there was patchy but walk around and you should be able to find some places where you can connect with the outside world. After that, mobile phone reception at Kibo Huts was pretty much non-existent and so you have to wait until Stella Point and Uhuru Peak before regaining contact with the outside world again.

WHAT'S IT LIKE ON THE TRAIL?

Fun. It really is. Sure, the last push to the summit is hard, as some of the quotes used later in this book clearly indicate, but don't let that put you off. Kilimanjaro is a delightful mountain to climb:

But we had much to compensate us for all we had to give up. The charm of the mountain scenery, the clear, crisp atmosphere, the tonic of 'a labour we delight in' and the consciousness now and again of success achieved, all went far to make our fortnight's arduous toil a happy sequence of red-letter days. **Hans Meyer** *Across East African Glaciers*

The days are spent walking through spectacular landscapes which change every day as you pass through different vegetation zones. The pace is never exhausting, as you have to walk slowly in order to give yourself a chance to acclimatize. What's more, at the end of the day, while the guides are cooking your dinner, you are free to wander around the campsite and, as you bump into the same people time and again over the course of the trek, a sense of community soon develops. Then as night falls, and you tuck into the huge plates of food cooked by your crew, the stars come out, stunning everyone into silence. This is the favourite time of day for most people: rested, replete with food and with a day of satisfactory walking behind and a good night's sleep ahead, it's natural to feel a sense of comfort and contentment, with the thought of wild animals possibly lying nearby serving to add a pleasing frisson of excitement.

Bed? It's too early. I feel too good. Aaah, I wonder if there'll ever be another time as good as this.   **Gregory Peck**, in the film version of *The Snows of Kilimanjaro*

Of course, walking up from less than 2000m or thereabouts to 5895m does, as you can probably imagine, take a lot of effort and the night walk to the summit is unarguably tough. But short of actually carrying you up, your crew will do everything in their power to make your entire experience as comfortable as possible. In fact, they'll spoil you: not only do they carry your bag, but at the end of the day's walk you'll turn up at camp to find your tent has already been erected, with a bowl of hot water lying nearby for you to wash away the grime of the day. A few minutes later and a large plate of popcorn and biscuits will be served with a mug of steaming hot tea or coffee.

Accommodation on the trail

I got back in time to see P.D. lying on sloping ground, slipping off the stretcher, and in great pain. Small fire had been made under the root of a great tree. Rain soon came on and wiped out the fire ... tent was not put up and we were all in great misery. Men with tent lost in the darkness. Thought if the rain stopped we could go on in the moonlight. Rain did not stop.   **Peter MacQueen** *In Wildest Africa* (1910)

Unless you are on the Marangu Route, accommodation on the mountain will be in tents brought up by your porters. (Do not be tempted to sleep in any of the caves, which is against park regulations.) On the Marangu Route, camping is forbidden and instead people have to sleep in huts along the route. (You will see people camping on this route but they are trekkers who took the Rongai Route to ascend and are now descending on Marangu.) The sleeping arrangements in these huts are usually dormitory-style, with anything from four to twenty beds per room.

Confusingly, away from the Marangu Route many of the campsites are actually called 'huts' but don't be fooled: they are called huts because of the green shacks that you'll find at these campsites which are usually inhabited by the park rangers. Trekkers used to be allowed to sleep in these huts too, but no longer.

Porters and guides, however, do still sometimes sleep in them depending on the ranger's mood and the space available. The only other buildings you will possibly see along the trail are the toilets. Most are of the same design, namely a little wooden hut with a hole in the floor. Some are in better condition than others; all we will say is that some people are terrible shots, while other latrines are in desperate need of emptying before the contents become Kilimanjaro's fourth peak. Smart new ones are being built at certain big camps.

Food on the trail

Remember to tell your agency if you have any special dietary requirements – because meat, nuts and gluten form a substantial part of the menu on Kilimanjaro.

A typical **breakfast** will involve eggs (boiled or fried), porridge, a saveloy (possibly with some tomatoes too), a piece of fruit such as a banana or orange, some bread with jam, honey or peanut butter and tea, hot chocolate or coffee.

Lunch is sometimes prepared at breakfast and carried by the trekker in his or her daypack, though the more expensive companies have tables set up and cook food on site. This packed lunch often consists of a boiled egg, some sandwiches, a banana or orange, and some tea kept warm in a flask and carried by your guide.

At the end of the day's walking, **afternoon tea** is served with biscuits, peanuts and, best of all, salted popcorn. The final and biggest meal of the day, **dinner** usually begins with soup, followed by a main course including chicken or meat, a vegetable sauce, some cabbage or other vegetable, and rice or pasta; if your porters have brought up some potatoes, these will usually be eaten on the first night as they are so heavy.

Drink on the trail

Porters will collect water from the rivers and streams along the trail. Some of this they will boil for you at the start of the day to carry in your water bottles. On the lower slopes you can collect water yourself from the many streams and purify it using a filter or tablets. Note, however, that as you climb ever higher the water becomes more scarce. On the Machame trail, for example, the last water point is at the Karanga Valley, the lunch-stop before Barafu; on Marangu, it's just before the Saddle. For this reason it is essential that you carry enough bottles or containers for *at least* three litres.

In camp, coffee and tea is served and maybe hot chocolate too – all usually made with powdered milk. Remember that caffeine, present in coffee and tea, is dehydrating, which can be bad for acclimatization. Caffeine is a diuretic too (ie you will want to urinate frequently – something you will already be doing a lot as you adapt to the higher conditions).

What to put in your daypack

Normally you will not see your backpack from the moment you hand it to the porter in the morning to at least lunchtime, and maybe not until the end of the day. It's therefore necessary to pack everything that you may need during the day in your bag that you carry with you. Some suggestions, in no particular order:

- sweets
- water and water purifiers
- camera and batteries plus spare film or memory card
- this book/maps
- sunhat/sunglasses and suncream
- toilet paper and trowel
- plastic bag for rubbish
- rainwear
- walking sticks/knee supports
- medical kit, including chapstick
- lunch (supplied by your crew)

One aspect of the Marangu Route that could be seen by some as a drawback is that it is the only one where you **ascend and descend via the same path**. However, there are a couple of arguments to counter this perception: firstly, between Horombo and Kibo Huts there are two paths and it shouldn't take too much to persuade your guide to use one trail on the ascent and a different one on the way down; and there's a Nature Trail alternative on the descent to the gate too. Secondly, we think that the walk back down the Marangu Route is one of the most pleasurable parts of the entire trek, with splendid views over the shoulder. Furthermore, it offers you the chance to greet the crowds of sweating, red-faced unfortunates heading the other way with the smug expression of one for whom physical pain is now a thing of the past, and whose immediate future is filled with warm showers and cold beers.

STAGE 1: MARANGU GATE TO MANDARA HUTS
[MAP 1, p249; MAP 2, p251]

Distance: 8.3km (8.75km if taking the Nature Trail); altitude gained: 818m

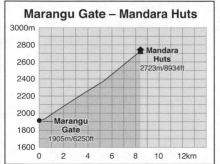

The woods are lovely, dark & deep,
But I have promises to keep,
And miles to go before I sleep.
Robert Frost as seen on a sign-writer's wall in Moshi

As the headquarters of KINAPA (Kilimanjaro National Park), you might expect Marangu Gate (altitude 1905m) to have the best facilities of all the gates and it doesn't disappoint. Not only does the gate have the usual **registration office**, but there's also a picnic area, a smart new toilet block and a **shop** that has a good collection of books and souvenirs. There's also a small booth run by the Kilimanjaro Guides Cooperative where you can **hire any equipment** you may have forgotten to bring along, from essentials such as hats and fleeces, sleeping bags and water bottles, to camping stuff that you almost certainly won't need on the trail such as stoves and so forth, which should be provided by your agency. (Incidentally, the authorities have even bigger plans for this gate, with blueprints for a whole new visitor centre already drawn up, including a conference hall, internet café and a museum dedicated to the mountain.)

Having gone through the laborious business of **registering** (a process that usually takes at least an hour, though it can be quicker if you manage to get here before the large tour groups arrive), you begin your trek by following the new trekkers' path which heads left off the road (which is now used solely by porters). Note the eucalyptus trees around the gate, one of the few non-native plants on the mountain. They were introduced, according to the version I've heard, by the first

Trekkers' experiences

Of course, everybody's experience of climbing Kili is different. The majority of letters we get are of the 'had the time of my life' variety, which are always lovely to receive, particularly as it's always nice to know that other people enjoy the experience as much as we do:

What a fab trip! And yes, We all made it to the top (one of us with a humungous, vice-like headache, but our good guide carried her pack on the last leg)!! And best of all, we all came back friends!   Anneliese Dibetta (Canada)

A few letters also contain some useful advice:

If I can make any strong recommendations it is the truth and value of 'pole pole'... I redefined the phrase pole pole and from the first step to the last I went the pace I needed to do to keep my heart rate even and not get out of breath. More often than not I was way behind the group, always had one of the guides or assistant guides with me and not once did I feel pressured to go faster. It was the key to my success.   Clare Wickens (US)

I found the trail up the Western Breach to be tough but not necessarily dangerous. I think the 'toughness' came from being at the altitude we were at causing the level of exertion needed to climb and the fatigue I was experiencing from the trip so far, more than the trail itself. As I watched the porters trot by with large loads (five dozen eggs on one guy or our dining table and chairs) I realized how easy the trail really was even though at the time I was feeling taxed by it.   Patti Wickham (US)

One general observation would be that although everyone said how much it was to do with altitude, I didn't realise the extent of it. I thought I'd tire easily and be breathless, but didn't understand how half the people would have headaches, and people would be running out of the dining hall to vomit. I was mentally prepared for something physically demanding, but not for feeling ill and having a headache for days on end...

As you come up to Kibo, a few people said they start to get excited and want to get it over with quickly. I'd say it's worth advising them to make sure they keep going slowly, and warn them that a lot of people suddenly feel really tired during the last 5-10 minutes of the walk.   Richard Evans (UK)

One or two of them were quite encouraging too:

Two of us were not really in good enough shape to complete Kili by any route, no scrambling experience, and no strong expectation of summiting, but by taking seven days and by doing the scramble in the daylight, all made it to the summit, and back down to Mweka Gate, happy, safe and sound.   John Wickham (US)

That's not to suggest, of course, that everyone has a pleasant time...

I've had a lovely few days but now I have a headache and feel like shit. Please leave me alone. Thank you. Unknown German, instructing his guide from inside his tent at Barafu Camp before undertaking the final push to the summit.

For a couple of days I thought you must have a great job: travel around the world and write about it. I now know better. I feel sorry for you. I thought climbing Kilimanjaro was hell. I would ask for a big raise in your salary if I were you...   Mark Burgmans (Holland)

TRAIL GUIDE AND MAPS

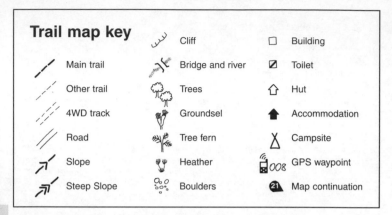

Trail map key

Symbol	Name	Symbol	Name
	Cliff	□	Building
Main trail	Main trail	☒	Toilet
Other trail	Other trail	⬦	Hut
4WD track	4WD track	⬆	Accommodation
Road	Road	⋏	Campsite
Slope	Slope		GPS waypoint
Steep Slope	Steep Slope	㉑	Map continuation
	Bridge and river		
	Trees		
	Groundsel		
	Tree fern		
	Heather		
	Boulders		

chief park warden of Kilimanjaro, a man who married a relative of Idi Amin – the former despot of Uganda later shooting him in an argument. As an 'alien' species and one that consumes a lot of water, the eucalyptus trees are slowly being eradicated by the authorities from the national park itself. (It has to be a gradual process, however: look through the trees to your right just after you start out and you'll see a big open area – the ugly result of eradicating the trees too quickly.)

This first day's walk is a very pleasant one of just over 8km and though the route is uphill for virtually the entire time, there are enough distractions in the forest to take your mind off the exertion, from the occasional troop of **blue monkeys** to the vivid red *Impatiens kilimanjari*, a small flower that has almost become the emblem of Kilimanjaro. The path soon veers towards and then follows the course of a mountain stream; sometimes through the increasingly impenetrable vegetation to your right you can glimpse the occasional small **waterfall**.

After about an hour and a quarter a wooden bridge leads off the trail over this stream to the picnic tables at **Kisamboni** and a reunion with the 4WD porters' trail. This is the halfway point of the first stage, and in all probability it is here that you will be served lunch.

At a height of 6,300 feet, however, all these were merged in the primaeval forest, in which old patriarchs with knotted stunted forms stood closely together, many of them worsted in the perpetual struggle with the encroachments of the parasitical growths of almost fabulous strength and size, which enfolded trunks and branches alike in their fatal embrace, crippling the giants themselves and squeezing to death the mosses, lichens, and ferns which had clothed their nakedness. Everything living seemed doomed to fall prey to them, but they in their turn bore their own heavy burden of parasites; creepers, from a yard to two yards long, hanging down in garlands and festoons, or forming one thick veil shrouding whole clumps of trees. Wherever a little space had been left amongst the many fallen and decaying trunks, the ground was covered with a luxurious vegetation, including many varieties of herbaceous plants with bright coloured flowers, orchids, and the modest violet peeping out amongst them, whilst more numerous than all were different lycopods and sword-shaped ferns.
Lieutenant Ludwig von Höhnel *Discovery by Count Teleki of Lakes Rudolf and Stefanie* (1894)

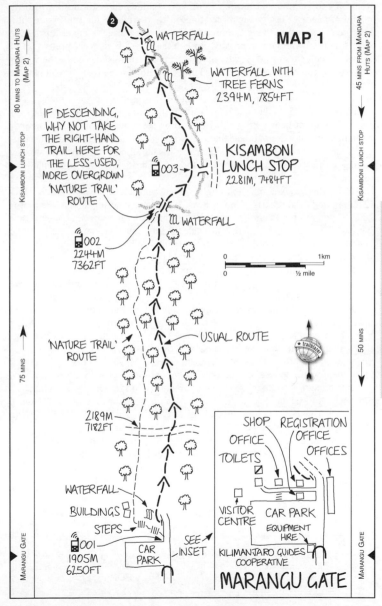

MAP 1

WATERFALL

WATERFALL WITH
TREE FERNS
2394M, 7854FT

IF DESCENDING,
WHY NOT TAKE
THE RIGHT-HAND
TRAIL HERE FOR
THE LESS-USED,
MORE OVERGROWN
'NATURE TRAIL'
ROUTE

003

KISAMBONI
LUNCH STOP
2281M, 7484FT

WATERFALL

002
2244M
7362FT

0   1km
0   ½ mile

'NATURE TRAIL'
ROUTE

USUAL ROUTE

trailblazer

2189M
7182FT

SHOP   REGISTRATION
OFFICE OFFICE
OFFICES
TOILETS

WATERFALL
BUILDINGS
STEPS

VISITOR
CENTRE

CAR PARK
EQUIPMENT
HIRE

SEE
INSET

001
1905M
6250FT

CAR
PARK

KILIMANJARO GUIDES
COOPERATIVE

MARANGU GATE

80 MINS TO MANDARA HUTS (MAP 2)

KISAMBONI LUNCH STOP

75 MINS

MARANGU GATE

45 MINS FROM MANDARA HUTS (MAP 2)

KISAMBONI LUNCH STOP

50 MINS

MARANGU GATE

TRAIL GUIDE AND MAPS

Returning to the trail and turning right, you continue climbing north for thirty minutes to another bridge, again leading off to the right of the trail; your path, however, heads off to the left, directly away from the bridge. The trail is a little steeper now as you wind your way through the forest. It is a very pretty part of the walk, with varieties of *Impatiens* and, draped amongst the trees, the white-flowered *Begonia meyeri-johannis* edging the path; though by now you may be feeling a little too tired to enjoy it to its fullest.

Press on, and fifteen minutes later yet another bridge appears which you *do* take. Like some sort of botanical border post, the bridge heralds the first appearance of the **giant heathers** (*Erica excelsa*) on the trail, with masses of **bearded lichen** liberally draped over them; and though the forest reappears intermittently up to and beyond the Maundi Crater, it's the spindly heathers and stumpy shrubs of the second vegetation zone, the alpine heath and moorland, that now dominate.

From this bridge, the first night's accommodation, the **Mandara Huts** (2723m), lie just thirty-five minutes away. There are some smaller private rooms here, though most trekkers sleep in the large dormitory in the roof above the dining hall. If you have the energy, a quick fifteen-minute saunter to the parasitic cone known as the **Maundi Crater** (see Map 2, opposite) is worthwhile both for its views east over Kenya and north-west to Mawenzi and for the wild flowers and grasses growing on its slopes. On the way to the crater, look in the trees for the bands of semi-tame monkeys, both blue and colobus, that live here and are particularly active at dusk.

Incidentally, the Mandara Huts are the only huts on the mountain to be named after a person rather than a place. Mandara was the fearsome chief of Moshi, a warrior whose skill and bravery on the battlefield was matched only by his stunning cupidity off it. Mandara once boasted that he had met every white man to visit Kilimanjaro, from Johannes Rebmann to Hans Meyer, and it's a fair bet that all of them would have been required to present the chief with a huge array of presents brought from their own country. Failure to do so was not an option, for those who, in Mandara's eye (he had only one, having lost the other in battle), were insufficiently generous in their gift-giving, put their lives in peril. The attack that led to the death of Charles New (see p113), for example, was said to have been orchestrated by Mandara after New had 'insulted' him by refusing to give the chief the watch from his waistcoat. Read any of the nineteenth-century accounts of Kilimanjaro and you'll usually find plenty of pages devoted to this fascinating character – with few casting him in a favourable light.

❏ In all the route descriptions, do remember that the times we quote are approximations and, more importantly, refer to walking times only and no time spent resting, taking photos etc. Add on 30-50% to get an estimate of the total time spent on the trail.

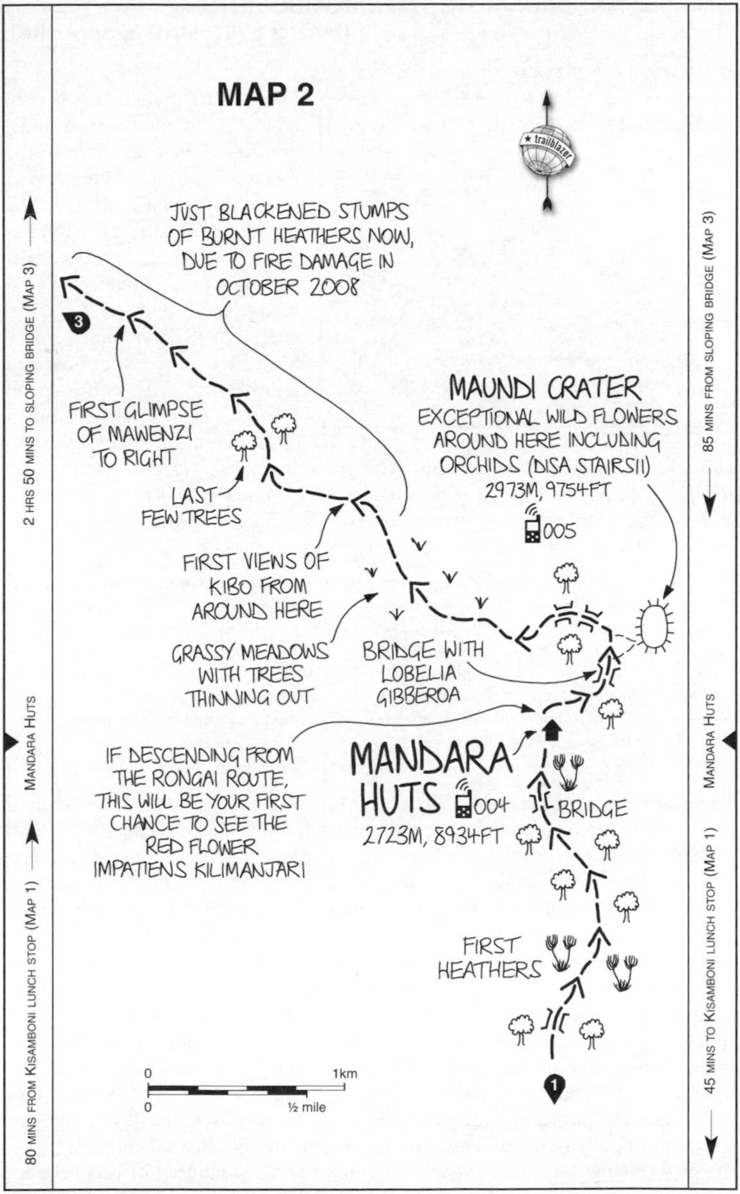
MAP 2
trailblazer
2 HRS 50 MINS TO SLOPING BRIDGE (MAP 3)
85 MINS FROM SLOPING BRIDGE (MAP 3)
MANDARA HUTS
MANDARA HUTS
80 MINS FROM KISAMBONI LUNCH STOP (MAP 1)
45 MINS TO KISAMBONI LUNCH STOP (MAP 1)
JUST BLACKENED STUMPS OF BURNT HEATHERS NOW, DUE TO FIRE DAMAGE IN OCTOBER 2008
3
FIRST GLIMPSE OF MAWENZI TO RIGHT
LAST FEW TREES
FIRST VIEWS OF KIBO FROM AROUND HERE
GRASSY MEADOWS WITH TREES THINNING OUT
MAUNDI CRATER
EXCEPTIONAL WILD FLOWERS AROUND HERE INCLUDING ORCHIDS (DISA STAIRSII)
2973M, 9754FT
005
BRIDGE WITH LOBELIA GIBBEROA
IF DESCENDING FROM THE RONGAI ROUTE, THIS WILL BE YOUR FIRST CHANCE TO SEE THE RED FLOWER IMPATIENS KILIMANJARI
MANDARA HUTS
004
2723M, 8934FT
BRIDGE
FIRST HEATHERS
0
1km
0
½ mile
1

STAGE 2: MANDARA HUTS TO HOROMBO HUTS
[MAP 2 p251; MAP 3, opposite]

Distance: 12.5km; altitude gained: 998m

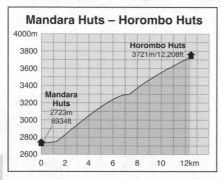

Mandara Huts – Horombo Huts

Horombo Huts
3721m/12,208ft

Mandara Huts
2723m
8934ft

On this stage, in which you gain almost a kilometre in altitude, you say a final goodbye to the forest and spend the greater part of the day walking through the bleaker landscape of Kilimanjaro's moorland. If the weather's clear you will get your first really good look at the twin peaks of Kili, namely spiky Mawenzi and snow-capped Kibo; they will continue to loom large, and will doubtless appear in just about every photo you take, from now to the summit. The giant groundsels (*Dendrosenecio kilimanjari*) and phallic lobelias (*Lobelia deckenii*) also make their first appearance in this stage, with the former growing in some abundance towards the latter part of the walk and especially around Horombo Huts.

The whole landscape as far as the eye could reach was a medley of dull grey lava slabs, dotted with the red-leafed protea shrub (Protea Kilimandscharica) and stunted heaths, which became smaller and smaller as we rose higher. Not a sound disturbed the silence of this uninhabited mountain mystery; not a sign of life broke the stillness save a little ashy-brown bird that hopped about the boulders, flipping its tail up and down. And to add to the impression created by the eerie scene, huge senecios lifted to a height of 20ft their black stems and greyish-yellow crowns and stood spreading out their arms in the deep moist gullies, like ghostly sentinels of the untrodden wilds.

Eva Stuart Watt *Africa's Dome of Mystery* (1930)

The day begins with a stroll through the monkey forest towards the Maundi Crater. After fifteen minutes you cross the small bridge and, leaving the last significant expanse of forest behind, enter a land of tall grasses and giant heathers. **Wild flowers** rarely seen elsewhere, such as the pinkish *Dierama pendulum*, abound in this little bumpy corner of the mountain. Crossing bridges over (often dry) water courses, you eventually come to a pretty depressing sight: acre after acre of burnt vegetation, blackened by a fire that raged in October 2008. Hopefully a new growth of green heathers will soon emerge between the blackened sticks of burnt bushes as they have on other fire-damaged parts of the mountain. If it's a clear day you may be able to make out, atop one of the many undulations, some picnic tables and toilets amongst the heather; this will be your lunch stop, reached after a fairly trying thirty-minute climb from the sloping bridge. The guides typically call this the halfway point in the day but they're being unnecessarily pessimistic: the Horombo Huts lie just 90 minutes away, the path tracing a generally westward course across a number of (dry) stream

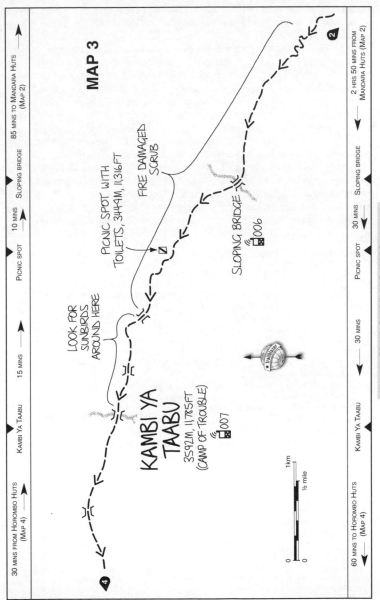

MAP 3

85 MINS TO MANDARA HUTS (MAP 2) →

SLOPING BRIDGE →

10 MINS →

PICNIC SPOT →

15 MINS →

KAMBI YA TAABU →

30 MINS FROM HOROMBO HUTS (MAP 4) →

PICNIC SPOT WITH TOILETS, 3444M, 11,316FT

FIRE DAMAGED SCRUB

LOOK FOR SUNBIRDS AROUND HERE

SLOPING BRIDGE
📷006

KAMBI YA TAABU
3592M, 11,785FT
(CAMP OF TROUBLE)
📷007

2 HRS 50 MINS FROM MANDARA HUTS (MAP 2) →

SLOPING BRIDGE →

30 MINS →

PICNIC SPOT →

30 MINS →

KAMBI YA TAABU →

60 MINS TO HOROMBO HUTS (MAP 4) →

1km

½ mile

0
0

beds including the head of the Whona River that runs through a valley known as **Kambi Ya Taabu**, which translates, rather melodramatically, as the 'Camp of Trouble'!

The **Horombo Huts** (3721m) are generally regarded as the most pleasant of those on the route: small A-frame shelters partitioned down the middle, with each side holding beds for four people. They cater for a transient population of around 160 trekkers plus porters and guides, as well as a more permanent population of four-striped grass mice whose numbers are now almost at plague proportions; indeed, some of them have now forsaken their grassy homeland to scavenge in the main dining hall. The huts are also the busiest on the mountain, catering not just for those ascending the mountain but those coming back down from Kibo too, as well as those who spend the day here acclimatizing. As such the whole place tends to get rather busy, which can be a problem when it comes to feeding-time, there being only one dining hut at Horombo and sometimes a rather officious warden who refuses to allow eating in the dorms. By the time you read this, however, the second dining hut should be finished; if not, try to arrange with your guide to have dinner slightly earlier than normal to avoid the main dinner-time rush, or you could be waiting for hours.

Mawenzi

Though less than 8km of nothingness (namely the Saddle) separates the foot of one from the foot of the other, the twin peaks of Kibo and Mawenzi could not be more different. Where Kibo is all gentle slopes and a perfectly circular crater, Mawenzi is spiky, steep, and rises to a series of peaks like the back of a stegosaurus; where the former is at least partially covered in glaciers, the other stands naked, or at least wears no permanent raiment of ice, its sides too steep to allow the glaciers a secure enough footing; and while Kibo is easily accessible to walkers, any assault on Mawenzi involves some serious preparation, specialist equipment and no small amount of technical skill.

Indeed, the only similarity between the two peaks is their enormity: Mawenzi's **Hans Meyer Peak**, at 5149m, is the third highest in Africa (after Kibo and Mount Kenya, 50m taller). Its smaller size when compared to Kibo can be ascribed to the fact that the Mawenzi volcano died out first, while the forces that formed Kibo continued to rage for a few thousand years after Mawenzi had become extinct, pushing Kibo above the height of its older brother. Erosion then caused the collapse of Mawenzi's entire north-east wall, releasing the waters of a lake that had formed in its crater down into the valley below.

The jagged appearance of its summit is due to the formation of **dykes**. This is where lava, pushed into gaps in the crater rim, solidified over time and, being harder than the original rock, remained while the softer rock eroded. Today, this hardened lava is also rather shattered, which, combined with its steep gradients, makes Mawenzi extremely dangerous to climb. John Reader, in his book *Kilimanjaro*, tells of two Austrian climbers who perished on their descent from the summit of Mawenzi, with the body of one of them found dangling by a rope snagged to the rocks. Such is the difficulty associated with any climb of Mawenzi that, rather than risk climbing up the peak to recover the corpse, the park authorities decided instead to hire a marksman to shoot at the rope with a rifle.

If you have opted for the **acclimatization day** tomorrow the chances are you'll be led by your guide on the northern route (aka Mawenzi Route, see box p325) past the **Zebra Rocks** and up to the **Mawenzi Huts** at 4535m (see Map 4, p256). Not only will this exercise help you to cope with the thin air of Kibo later on but it also affords magnificent views of your ultimate destination across the Saddle. It is also near enough to allow you to return to Horombo for a late lunch.

STAGE 3: HOROMBO HUTS TO KIBO HUTS
[MAP 4 p256; MAP 5, p257]

Distance: 9.5km (10.3km on the Mawenzi alternative); altitude gained: 993m

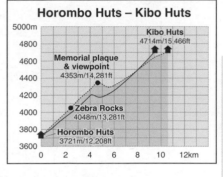

Horombo Huts – Kibo Huts

The path to Kibo from Horombo now divides into two; almost invariably you will be led along the southern (left-hand) route, which we describe now. If your guide is amenable, however, you may like to ask him on the return from Kibo to use the more northerly route, particularly if you did not take a day to acclimatize at Horombo (those who did will be familiar with much of this northerly path, which we have called the Mawenzi Route and describe, starting at Kibo Huts, on p325).

The 9.5km **southern path** seems rather steep at first as it bends left (north-west) and up through the thinning vegetation of the moorland. Looping north, just under 30 minutes after leaving Horombo you come to the tiny mountain stream known as the **Maua River** (3914m). You should fill up your water bottles here, for the water from this point on is rather brackish. The terrain climbs steadily after Maua, passing the junction with the **Southern Circuit** (a porters' path) as it does so, and some of Kili's many parasitic cones move into view for the first time. The **Last Water Point**, well signposted and rather incongruously furnished with picnic tables, marks the beginning of the uphill approach to **Mawenzi Ridge**, beyond which lies the approach to the **Saddle**, the dry, barren terrain separating Kilimanjaro's two major peaks. With the **Middle Red Hill**, a large parasitic cone, ahead of you to the right, you find yourself descending into a rather flat, extremely windswept and dramatic landscape, the only decoration provided by a few tufts of grass, some hardier floral species such as the aptly named everlastings, and a number of boulders and smaller stones, some of which have been arranged into messages by previous trekkers. It is for these kind of views that you brought your camera, for the light at this altitude is frequently superb, and while many of your photos may end up in the fire it's a fair bet that a few of them will be destined for the mantlepiece too. The path loops almost due north between the Kibo summit on your left and the Middle Red on

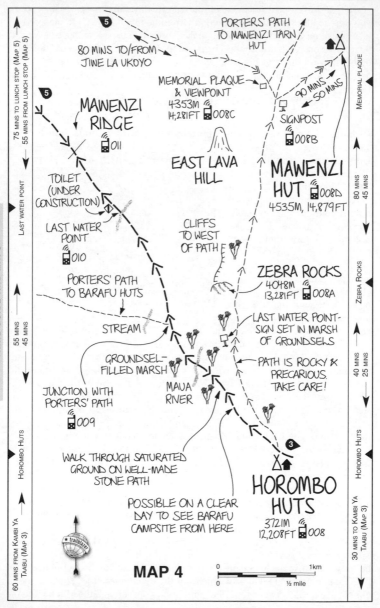

PORTERS' PATH
TO MAWENZI TARN
HUT

80 MINS TO/FROM
JINE LA UKOYO

MEMORIAL PLAQUE
& VIEWPOINT
4353M
14,281FT 008C

90 MINS
50 MINS

MEMORIAL PLAQUE

SIGNPOST
008B

MAWENZI
RIDGE
011

EAST LAVA
HILL

MAWENZI
HUT 008D
4535M, 14,879FT

80 MINS
45 MINS

TOILET
(UNDER
CONSTRUCTION)

LAST WATER
POINT
010

CLIFFS
TO WEST
OF PATH

ZEBRA ROCKS
4048M
13,281FT 008A

ZEBRA ROCKS

PORTERS' PATH
TO BARAFU HUTS

LAST WATER POINT
SIGN SET IN MARSH
OF GROUNDSELS

STREAM

PATH IS ROCKY &
PRECARIOUS.
TAKE CARE!

GROUNDSEL-
FILLED MARSH

MAUA
RIVER

JUNCTION WITH
PORTERS' PATH
009

40 MINS
25 MINS

55 MINS
45 MINS

HOROMBO HUTS

WALK THROUGH SATURATED
GROUND ON WELL-MADE
STONE PATH

POSSIBLE ON A CLEAR
DAY TO SEE BARAFU
CAMPSITE FROM HERE

HOROMBO
HUTS
3721M
12,208FT 008

HOROMBO HUTS

trailblazer

MAP 4

0   1km
0   ½ mile

your right, whose western slopes shelter trekkers from the often howling wind and more often than not provide the venue for **lunch**.

Your path for the afternoon continues northwards across the Saddle; it's a bit of a weary trudge on a steadily inclining path to **Jiwe La Ukoyo**, a former campsite with some toilet huts and a huge boulder (*jiwe* means 'rock' in Swahili.) It is also the meeting point between the two main paths from Horombo. Thereafter the path turns sharply westwards towards the **Kibo Huts**, which nestle snugly at the foot of the summit after which they were named. Though the huts look close, you still have around an hour and a quarter of walking from Jiwe La Ukoyo and it's a tough walk too, a gradual but relentless uphill slog to round off what has already been a fairly wearying day.

The huts themselves are basic, built of stone and rather chilly. A sign on the door of the main hut tells you that you are now at 4750m (though we think it's a little bit lower than this at 4714m); a second sign warns you that Gillman's Point is still five hours away...

TRAIL GUIDE AND MAPS

KIBO HUTS 45 MINS → JIWE LA UKOYO 50 MINS → LUNCH STOP 55 MINS TO LAST → WATER POINT (MAP 4)

TO OUTWARD BOUND SCHOOL HUT

015

24

6

JIWE LA UKOYO 014

SIGN FOR KIBO CIRCUIT 013

KIBO HUTS

4714M 15,466FT 016

TOILETS & PICNIC TABLE

BIG BOULDER

THE SADDLE
OFTEN EXTREMELY WINDY

80 MINS BETWEEN JIWE LA UKOYO & MEMORIAL PLAQUE

4

TRIPLETS

MAP 5

LUNCHSTOP & TOILETS 012

MIDDLE RED HILL

0   1km
0   ½ mile

FEELS LIKE A ROAD – A WIDE TREK CROSSING THE ALPINE DESERT

4

KIBO HUTS ← 75 MINS JIWE LA UKOYO ← 50 MINS LUNCH STOP ← 75 MINS FROM LAST WATER STOP (MAP 4)

STAGE 4: KIBO HUTS TO GILLMAN'S POINT AND UHURU PEAK
[MAP 6, p259; MAP 32, p335]

Distance: 6.25km; altitude gained: 1181m

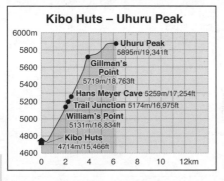

Kibo Huts – Uhuru Peak

- Uhuru Peak 5895m/19,341ft
- Gillman's Point 5719m/18,763ft
- Hans Meyer Cave 5259m/17,254ft
- Trail Junction 5174m/16,975ft
- William's Point 5131m/16,834ft
- Kibo Huts 4714m/15,466ft

And so you come to the testing part of the walk. No matter how tough you have found the trekking so far, it has been but a leisurely stroll compared to what lies ahead of you tonight. The path to Gillman's Point on the crater rim has been in your sights since the previous after-noon when you crossed the Saddle and saw it rearing up at an angle of 16° (John Reader's estimate) behind the Kibo Huts. We think that one of the rea-sons why this route has a higher failure rate than any of the others is down to the difficulty of this last stretch, which seems steeper and the ground less solid than on other routes. The stretch between Gillman's and Uhuru Peak also sees a high percentage of people giving up, even though the gradient is less steep and the hard stuff is, in theory at least, largely behind them.

All of which means that the chances of failure on this route are high – and of making it, but throwing up or passing out along the way, are even higher. Just remember the golden rule: when it comes to climbing Kibo, there is no such thing as too slow. The mountain was formed around 500,000 years ago and has remained much the same ever since, so I think it's reasonable to assume it will still be there in the morning, no matter what time you arrive at the top.

I find a rhythm and try to lose my thoughts to it but feel the first pain of a stomach cramp and then another, and I feel the nausea starting and the headache that I recognise all too well ... The pain is sharp in my head and my cramping is still with me; if I feel this way how is Danny doing with no sleep and nothing in his stomach from the vomiting after dinner?
Rick Ridgeway, *The Shadow of Kilimanjaro – On Foot Across East Africa*

What you can't see from Kibo Huts, and yet what is rather good about this path, is that there are a number of landmarks on the way – the main ones being William's Point at 5131m and Hans Meyer Cave at 5259m – that act as mile-stones, helping both to break up the journey and to provide you with some meas-ure of your progress. **William's Point** – or rather, the large east-facing rock immediately beneath it – lies 1hr 45min from Kibo Huts and is usually the first major resting point. **Hans Meyer Cave**, a small and undistinguished hollow adorned with a plaque commemorating the Hungarian hunter, Count and *bon viveur* Samuel Teleki, who rested here in 1887, is another 30min further on from William's Point.

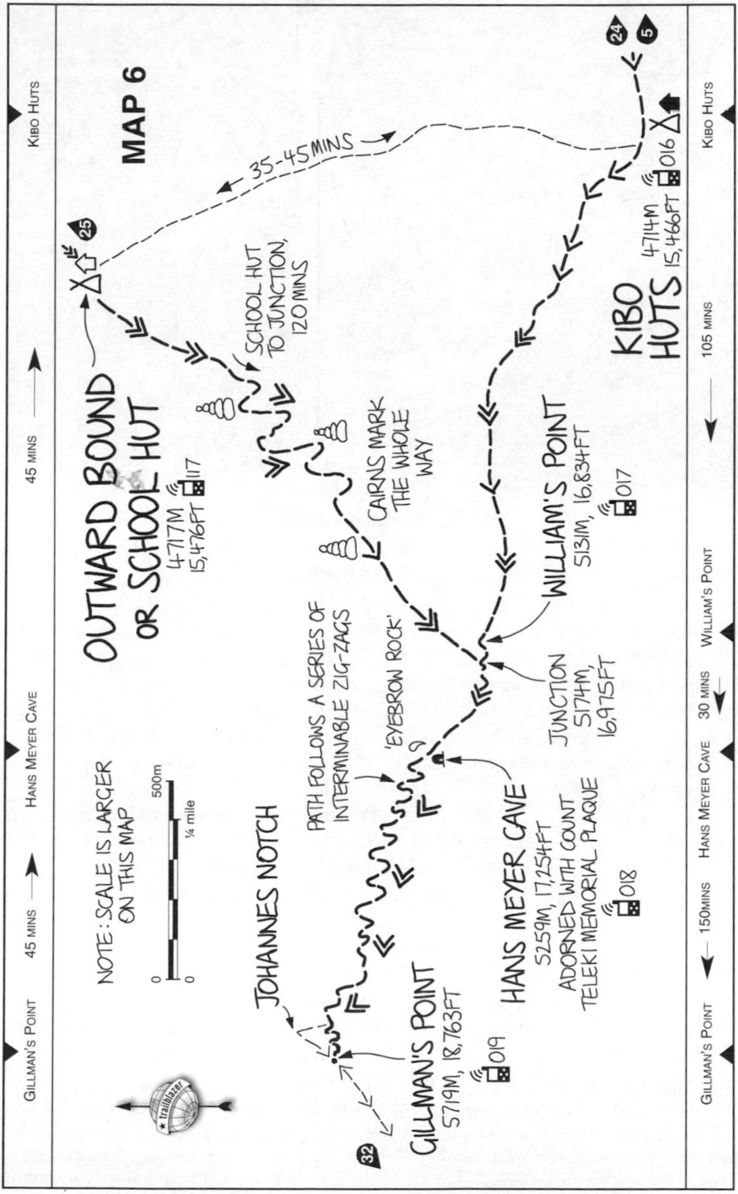

MAP 6

KIBO HUTS

45 MINS

KIBO HUTS

OUTWARD BOUND
OR SCHOOL HUT
4717M, 15,466FT 🏕117

35-45 MINS

SCHOOL HUT
TO JUNCTION,
120 MINS

CAIRNS MARK
THE WHOLE WAY

KIBO
HUTS 4714M
15,466FT 🏕016

WILLIAM'S POINT
5131M, 16,834FT 🏕017

NOTE: SCALE IS LARGER
ON THIS MAP

0   500m
0   ¼ mile

'EYEBROW ROCK'

PATH FOLLOWS A SERIES OF
INTERMINABLE ZIG-ZAGS

JUNCTION
5174M,
16,975FT

HANS MEYER CAVE
5259M, 17,254FT
ADORNED WITH COUNT
TELEKI MEMORIAL PLAQUE
🏕018

JOHANNES NOTCH

GILLMAN'S POINT
5719M, 18,763FT 🏕019

GILLMAN'S POINT ← 45 MINS → HANS MEYER CAVE ← 45 MINS → KIBO HUTS

GILLMAN'S POINT ← 150MINS → HANS MEYER CAVE ← 30 MINS → WILLIAM'S POINT ← 105 MINS → KIBO HUTS

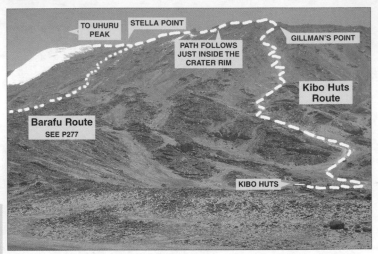

Kibo Huts Route

From Hans Meyer Cave, it's a case of following the scree **switchbacks**; if you've mastered the art of walking in a zombie-like trance, now is the time to put that particular technique into action. This part, as you pinball back and forth on a stretch of fine scree bounded by two boulder-strewn slopes, is extremely exposed and if there's any wind about, you will almost certainly feel it here. If you bought one in Moshi, now is the time to put on your balaclava: your friends will be too concerned with their own situation to laugh at you now anyway. By the way, look behind you and you'll see a line of torches snaking up the slope behind you in a scene that feels almost Biblical.

Gradually the switchbacks begin to reduce in size like the audiograph of an echo. You are now entering the final phase of the climb to Gillman's, though it takes an hour to complete and you'll probably be breathless the whole way. It's easy to get lost in the dark on this final stretch, so don't be too surprised if you see other trekkers to the left and right of you on a different path. If your guide is at least halfway competent, however, you should find yourself at the crater's edge at **Gillman's Point** (5719m; if, upon arrival at the crater rim, you find no signpost welcoming you to Gillman's, then the chances are the guide has got his bearings slightly wrong and has led you to the slightly lower point of **Johannes Notch**. No matter: Gillman's is just a three-minute scramble up to your left.)

Gillman's Point is 960m above Kibo Hut, that is almost the equivalent of three Empire State Buildings standing one on top of another. The horizontal distance between Kibo Hut and Gillman's Point is roughly 3000 metres, so the gradient averages about 1:3.3 and the distance covered on the way up is about 3300m – the equivalent of nine Empire State Buildings laid end to end up the incline. **John Reader** *Kilimanjaro*

If the wind is not too high, Gillman's is a good spot to sit for a few minutes, get your head together, contemplate the star-spangled night with the silhouette of Mawenzi to the east, and congratulate yourself on having earned a nice green certificate after completing the hardest part of the trek. At least, it's the hardest part physically; the hardest part from a psychological point of view now awaits you, as you try to muster up the energy and enthusiasm to tackle the walk to **Uhuru**. Though the time varies throughout the year, as a rough guide you need to be at Gillman's at around 4.45am in order to have a chance of seeing the sunrise at Uhuru at around 6am. If you've no chance of making it by then, consider seeing the sunrise from somewhere along the way: from Stella Point, for example, or overlooking the Rebmann Glacier, or from one of the lesser peaks before Uhuru.

See Map 32 on p335 for details of the summit. The first part of this walk is undulating as you ride the peaks and troughs of the crater rim, and you may well need your head torch as you walk in the moon-shadow. From **Stella Point**, around 30-45 minutes to the south of Gillman's, the path begins to climb more steadily. Though nothing like as steep as that which has gone before, at this stage any incline is a major challenge. Don't be too disheartened by the many false summits you will encounter along the last part; instead, distract your mind from the pain you are feeling by looking at the huge and beautiful icefields to your left and the sheer, desolate enormity of the crater on your right. A gorgeous dawn at the summit, and a certificate back at Marangu Gate, are the prizes that await...

> *Is it so small a thing*
> *To have enjoy'd the sun,*
> *To have lived light in the spring,*
> *To have loved, to have thought, to have done;*
> *To have advanc'd true friends, and beat down baffling foes?*
> **Matthew Arnold**, *Empedocles on Etna* (1852)

For details of what you can actually see at the summit, turn to p334, while for a description of the designated descent route, turn to the **Marangu Route descent** on p324.

TRAIL GUIDE AND MAPS

The Machame Route

Then they began to climb and they were going to the East it seemed, and then it darkened and they were in a storm, the rain so thick it seemed like flying through a waterfall, and they were out and Compie turned his head and grinned and pointed and there, ahead, all he could see, as wide as all the world, great, high, and unbelievably white in the sun, was the top of Kilimanjaro. And then he knew that there was where he was going.
Ernest Hemingway, *The Snows of Kilimanjaro*

Ask any guide or tour agent which is their favourite walk to do on Kilimanjaro and often they will choose this, the Machame-Mweka Route (usually just shortened to the Machame Route, a convention we have adopted here). Though some of them doubtless say this because it's easier to organize – requiring no hut-booking or long-haul driving – it is not difficult to see why the route is so popular with everyone: beginning on the south-western side of the mountain, the trail passes through some of the mountain's finest features, including the **cloud forest** of Kili's southern slopes, the dry and dusty **Shira Plateau** and the delightful groundsel-clad **Barranco Campsite**. Furthermore, you have a choice of ascent routes to the summit, with the thrill-seekers opting for the daunting **Western Breach Route** to the summit, while the majority head for the lengthy, long-winded climb up the **Barafu trail**, with the Rebmann Glacier edging into your field of vision on your left as dawn breaks behind Mawenzi on your right. Furthermore, unlike the Marangu Route, on Machame you don't use the same path to descend as you took to climb up the mountain but instead you come down via the Mweka Route, a steep but very pretty descent encompassing inhospitably dry mountain desert and lush lowland forest in a matter of a few hours.

For all these reasons, Machame is now the busiest on the mountain. Indeed, it must be said that it is now, on certain days at certain times of the year, simply *too* popular. Such are the crowds on the route that KINAPA are now looking to limit the number of users per day to 100 – down from the 150-plus users who march on it every day in the high season.

❏ **Mobile reception on the Machame Route**
It depends which network you're with, of course, but mobile reception on the Machame Route seems to be OK by the standards of Kilimanjaro. I couldn't get any reception up to **Machame Huts**, however, and it was only on the second morning as we left the forest that reception was resumed. At **Shira Caves** the porters climb up the rocks surrounding the camp to use their phones, at **Lava Tower** there is fair reception, and while you have to wander around the camp to get anything at both **Barranco** and **Karanga**, it is good at **Barafu**, intermittent at **Stella Point** and fine, so we are told, at **Uhuru Peak**. The **Millennium Camp**, on the descent, also has good mobile reception. If you are taking the Western Breach Route, please see the box on p283 for a summary of your mobile reception from Lava Tower.

Curiously, though the Machame Route is widely reckoned to be that much harder than the Marangu Route (and is thus nicknamed the Whiskey Route, in opposition to Marangu's softer soubriquet of the 'Coca Cola trail'), the proportion of trekkers who reach the top using this route is marginally but significantly higher. This could be down to a number of factors: the Machame Route allows people to acclimatize better because it's longer (40.16km to the summit via Barafu, or 36.7km via the Western Breach as opposed to 35.5km on Marangu); when it comes to climbing the slopes of Kibo, the Barafu Route is more straightforward than the route from Kibo Huts to Gillman's, as it is largely conducted on the firm terrain of a ridge rather than sliding, shifting shale; or maybe the Machame's higher success rate is merely an indication that more experienced, hardened trekkers – ie the very people who are most likely to reach the summit – are more inclined to choose this route.

The following description assumes that you will be taking the Barafu Route to the summit. This walk via Barafu traditionally lasts for six days and five nights, though it is now more common for trekkers to opt for an extra night during the ascent, usually at Karanga Camp, halfway between Barranco and Barafu camps. Not only does the extra day aid acclimatization, but this also reduces from almost six to three the number of hours walked on the day that precedes the exhausting midnight ascent to the summit, thereby allowing trekkers more time to recover their faculties, relax and prepare themselves for the final push to the top.

For those daredevils wishing to try their hand at the Arrow Glacier/Western Breach Route, you leave the regular Machame Route on the third day; the map on p270 and the box on p271 indicate where. You can then find a description of that path to the summit on p294.

STAGE 1: MACHAME GATE TO MACHAME HUTS
[MAP 7, p264; MAP 8, p266]

Distance: 10.75km; altitude gained: 1210m

Coming from Moshi, the drive to the Machame Gate, at an altitude of 1811m, takes just under an hour; the tarmac doesn't last that long, petering out after about 40 minutes. On the way to the gate ask the driver to point out the house of the local chief, a simple yet large bungalow on the left-hand side of the road.

Passing through Machame village you'll soon arrive at the gate itself, a small collection of buildings huddled around a 4WD car park. Register in the

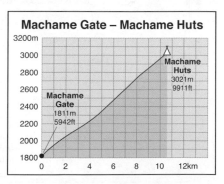

Machame Gate – Machame Huts

Machame Huts
3021m
9911ft

Machame Gate
1811m
5942ft

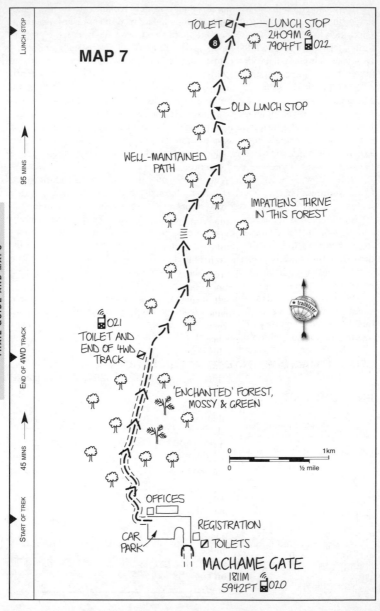

LUNCH STOP

95 MINS

END OF 4WD TRACK

45 MINS

START OF TREK

TOILET — LUNCH STOP
2409M
7904FT 022

MAP 7

8

OLD LUNCH STOP

WELL-MAINTAINED
PATH

IMPATIENS THRIVE
IN THIS FOREST

021
TOILET AND
END OF 4WD
TRACK

'ENCHANTED' FOREST,
MOSSY & GREEN

0   1km

0   ½ mile

OFFICES

REGISTRATION

CAR
PARK

TOILETS

MACHAME GATE
1811M
5942FT 020

office and make sure you use the toilet facilities on site – you may not think much of them now but, believe me, compared to some of the latrines on the trail these are heavenly.

Back at the car park, porters are busy haggling over who is going to take what, guides are reporting to the KINAPA reception to wrestle with the red tape, while the trekkers themselves are packing away their lunchboxes and quietly steeling themselves for the rigours ahead. To one side of this chaos is the beginning of the trail...

This 10km-plus first day is a long and sweaty one. It starts with a 3km amble up a 4WD track, a wide snaking trail that cuts through the kind of deep, dark enchanted forest that Hansel and Gretel would be familiar with. Green moss hangs thickly from the branches that creak and groan in the wind. It's a magical start to a wonderful adventure. After 45 minutes, the track arrives at a sign advising hikers that Machame is for those ascending the mountain only. The sign also marks the end of the 4WD road, the gentle curves and steady incline giving way to a narrower, steeper but now beautifully renovated pedestrians-only path that continues all the way to Machame Huts. Looking to the side of the path you'll notice that the vegetation is already changing as you progress deeper into the **cloud forest**, the scarlet and yellow *Impatiens kilimanjari* and pink *Impatiens pseudoviola* now flourishing between the roots of the huge 30-metre tall trees; tree ferns also proliferate here.

Ninety-five minutes or so from the end of the 4WD track, the path widens momentarily to form several small **clearings** (one of which has en-suite toilet facilities) that make for popular lunch stops. Those who've already drunk their water bottles dry can replenish their supplies from the stream down in the valley to the west. Listen out for the primate-like call of the black (actually dark green) and red turaco which nests around here, and watch your lunch too: it's not uncommon for the forest rodents to sneak into lunchboxes and drag off a samosa or two.

The post-prandial path varies little from that which has gone before, though the gradient increases slightly the higher you climb. As the forest gradually begins to thin out you'll notice that you are actually walking on a narrow forested spine between two shallow valleys. A stream – more audible than visible – runs briefly to the right of the trail.

Around two hours after lunch the second signpost of the day appears, this time warning against the careless discarding of cigarette butts; as well as dispensing some sound advice, this sign also marks the border between the cloud forest and the heath, where the long grasses dominate and the robust trees of the forest give way to the spindly, tree-like giant heathers. *Kniphofia thomsonii* (known to you and me as red hot pokers) make their first appearance at this altitude, as do several other wild flowers and shrubs such as the bushy *Phillippia excelsa*. With the forest thinning, the **Kibo peak** heaves into view for the first time to the east.

It is only twenty minutes from the signpost to **Machame Huts** (3021m), a series of level pitches cut into the grass, each with its own toilet. Make sure you sign your name in the **registration book** and aim to pitch your tent as high as possible for the best views: by the green hut is a good spot, affording views to

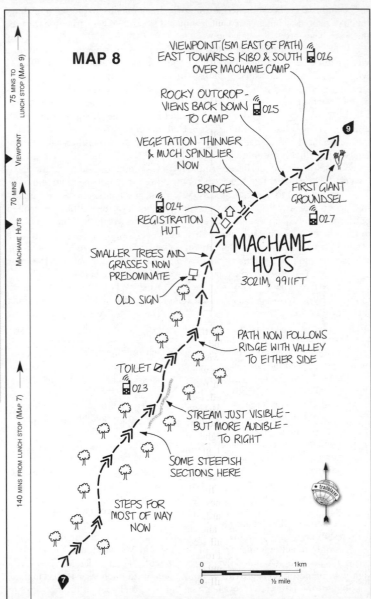

MAP 8

VIEWPOINT (5M EAST OF PATH)
EAST TOWARDS KIBO & SOUTH 📵026
OVER MACHAME CAMP

ROCKY OUTCROP -
VIEWS BACK DOWN 📵025
TO CAMP

VEGETATION THINNER
& MUCH SPINDLIER
NOW

BRIDGE

📵024
REGISTRATION
HUT

FIRST GIANT
GROUNDSEL

📵027

SMALLER TREES AND
GRASSES NOW
PREDOMINATE

OLD SIGN

**MACHAME
HUTS**
3021M, 9911FT

PATH NOW FOLLOWS
RIDGE WITH VALLEY
TO EITHER SIDE

TOILET
📵023

STREAM JUST VISIBLE -
BUT MORE AUDIBLE -
TO RIGHT

SOME STEEPISH
SECTIONS HERE

STEPS FOR
MOST OF WAY
NOW

9

7

75 MINS TO LUNCH STOP (MAP 9)

VIEWPOINT

70 MINS

MACHAME HUTS

140 MINS FROM LUNCH STOP (MAP 7)

TRAIL GUIDE AND MAPS

0   1km
0   ½ mile

the east up to Kibo and south-west towards Mount Meru. Look out for the birdlife too, which is abundant round here, with olive thrush, common stonechats and flocks of montane white-eye all resident, in addition to the usual seedeaters and alpine chats that are ubiquitous on the mountain.

By the way, having climbed to 3021m you are now higher than the top of Mawson Peak, at 2745m the highest point in Australia.

STAGE 2: MACHAME HUTS TO SHIRA CAVES
[MAP 8, p266; MAP 9, p268]

Distance: 5.3km; altitude gained: 818m

This leg of the trek is short but a little strenuous as you ascend from 3021m up to the Shira Plateau, finally coming to a halt at the Shira Caves at just over 3839m. Parts of this walk are a bit steep and the skinny, naked heathers at this altitude provide little shade from the heat; what's more, the path is extremely dusty, at least after lunch, so if you have gaiters you'll probably be thankful for the protection they provide (and

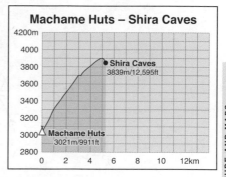

Machame Huts – Shira Caves

Shira Caves 3839m/12,595ft

Machame Huts 3021m/9911ft

remember to keep your camera bag tightly closed too). In spite of all this, by taking it slowly, resting frequently and enjoying the en-route views that encompass Kibo, Meru and all points in between, this day needn't be too taxing – indeed, it's probably the easiest day of the whole ascent.

The walk starts as it goes on for much of the day, with a steepish climb north up through forests of stunted, twisted heather bushes; while ahead of you in the distance is the lip of the **Shira Plateau**. The path winds its way up to the top of a ridge formed by a petrified lava flow, occasionally allowing trekkers some splendid views over last night's campsite, Machame village and the flat Tanzanian plains beyond. Giant groundsels (*Dendrosenecio kilimanjari ssp cottonii*), the squat, chunky trees with the green-leaf crown, begin to dot the path and Kilimanjaro's desiccated **helichrysums**, ubiquitous above 3000m, appear here for the first time too, like living pot pourri. Note, too, how most of the vegetation not only diminishes in size as you climb higher but the taller plants seem to bend as one towards the plateau, as if pointing the way. After passing a number of viewpoints and clambering from one side of the ridge to the other, the gradient of the trail increases exponentially towards the **lunch stop**, hidden from view behind a rocky outcrop. The effort expended in reaching there is worth it, for while munching your sandwiches you can savour yet more views of Kibo as well as all points south. Note, however, that the renovated path ends here.

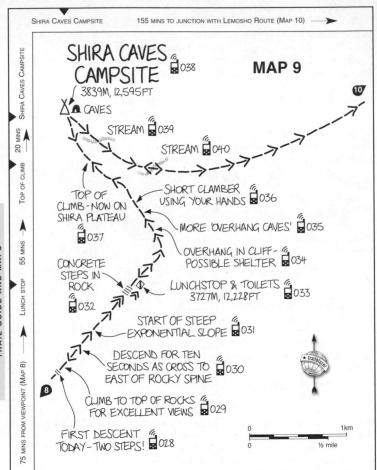

SHIRA CAVES CAMPSITE   155 MINS TO JUNCTION WITH LEMOSHO ROUTE (MAP 10) ⟶

SHIRA CAVES CAMPSITE

20 MINS — TOP OF CLIMB

55 MINS — LUNCH STOP

75 MINS FROM VIEWPOINT (MAP 8)

SHIRA CAVES CAMPSITE 038
3839M, 12,595FT
CAVES

MAP 9

10

STREAM 039
STREAM 040

SHORT CLAMBER USING YOUR HANDS 036

TOP OF CLIMB - NOW ON SHIRA PLATEAU 037

MORE 'OVERHANG CAVES' 035

OVERHANG IN CLIFF - POSSIBLE SHELTER 034

CONCRETE STEPS IN ROCK 032

LUNCHSTOP & TOILETS 033
3727M, 12,228FT

START OF STEEP EXPONENTIAL SLOPE 031

DESCEND FOR TEN SECONDS AS CROSS TO EAST OF ROCKY SPINE 030

8

CLIMB TO TOP OF ROCKS FOR EXCELLENT VIEWS 029

FIRST DESCENT TODAY - TWO STEPS! 028

trailblazer

0   1km
0   ½ mile

By observing the line of porters and trekkers on the path ahead you can pick out the afternoon's trail, which initially continues north and up, before bending fairly sharply to the north-west, cutting a near horizontal line beneath the rim of the plateau. But though the worst of the day's climbing is now behind you, don't be fooled into thinking this is an easy section, for the path on this north-westerly trail undulates considerably as it climbs over rocks and boulders and it can be tiring in the searing afternoon heat. As a distraction, the first of Kilimanjaro's celebrated moorland **lobelias** (*Lobelia deckenii*), both phallic and cabbage-shaped and growing to a height of around two metres, appear by the trail.

Just under an hour after lunch the plateau is gained and the path continues northwards. Look out for the Shira Plateau's distinctive, shiny black **obsidian** rock (see p93). Your camp for the night is the **Shira Caves Campsite**. (Note that this campsite is not on older maps, though the caves themselves are.) Looking west from the **Shira Caves Campsite**, ask your guide to point out the **Shira Cathedral** and the **East Shira Hill** which line the southern boundary of the Shira Plateau, and, behind them to the far west, **Johnsell Point** and **Klute Peak**, the highest points of the Shira Ridge, the western rim of the oldest of Kili's three craters. Mount Meru, too, is still visible to the west on the horizon.

Incidentally, by reaching this camp you are now at a higher altitude than Mafadi (3450m), the highest peak in South Africa.

STAGE 3: SHIRA CAVES CAMPSITE TO BARRANCO HUTS
[MAP 9, opposite; MAP 10, p270; MAP 11, p273]

Distance: 10.75km via Lava Tower; altitude gained: 147m (788m up to Lava Tower Camp, then 641m descent to Barranco)

Camp-life on Kilimanjaro is a capital school for the practice of self-denial.
Hans Meyer *Across East African Glaciers*

During this section of the trek you cover over 10km as you move from the western to the southern slopes of Kilimanjaro; by the end of it you may feel slightly disappointed to learn that, for all your efforts, you will have gained just 147m in height, from the Shira Caves at 3839m to Barranco, situated at an altitude of 3986m. Nevertheless, this leg of the trek is vital for acclimatization purposes, for during the day you will climb to a respectable

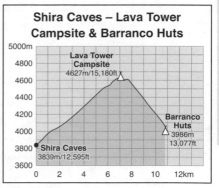

Shira Caves – Lava Tower Campsite & Barranco Huts

Lava Tower Campsite 4627m/15,180ft

Barranco Huts 3986m 13,077ft

Shira Caves 3839m/12,595ft

4627m if taking the path via Lava Tower. (There's another path available from the new and unofficial **Sheffield Campsite**, 4547m, which is great for those who can't quite manage the climb up to Lava Tower, and a third and older trail which is lower still.) Don't be surprised, therefore, if by the end of it you have a crashing headache: this is normal and is only cause for concern if it is accompanied by other symptoms of mountain sickness or if the pain hasn't disappeared by the morning.

The day begins with a steady, gentle ascent through the dry, boulder-strewn terrain of the Shira Plateau towards the western slopes of Kibo (the summit of which, from this angle, is said by some trekkers to resemble the profile of a Native American Indian chief at rest. No, I can't really see it either.) At first the path meanders somewhat, rising and falling regularly as it negotiates the gentle folds

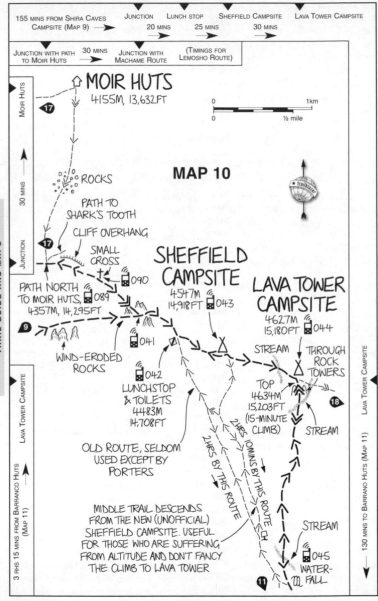

155 MINS FROM SHIRA CAVES CAMPSITE (MAP 9) →	JUNCTION 20 MINS	LUNCH STOP 25 MINS	SHEFFIELD CAMPSITE 30 MINS	LAVA TOWER CAMPSITE

JUNCTION WITH PATH TO MOIR HUTS →	30 MINS JUNCTION WITH MACHAME ROUTE	(TIMINGS FOR LEMOSHO ROUTE)

MOIR HUTS
4155M, 13,632FT

0 .... 1km
0 .... ½ mile

MAP 10

trailblazer

17

MOIR HUTS

30 MINS

JUNCTION

ROCKS

PATH TO SHARK'S TOOTH
CLIFF OVERHANG
SMALL CROSS
17
090

SHEFFIELD CAMPSITE
4547M
14,918FT
043

LAVA TOWER CAMPSITE
4627M
15,180FT
044

PATH NORTH TO MOIR HUTS,
4357M, 14,295FT
089

9

WIND-ERODED ROCKS

041

042
LUNCHSTOP & TOILETS
4483M
14,708FT

STREAM

THROUGH ROCK TOWERS

TOP
4634M
15,203FT
(15-MINUTE CLIMB)

18

STREAM

OLD ROUTE, SELDOM USED EXCEPT BY PORTERS

2HRS BY THIS ROUTE

2HRS 10MINS BY THIS ROUTE

LAVA TOWER CAMPSITE

LAVA TOWER CAMPSITE

3 RHS 15 MINS FROM BARRANCO HUTS (MAP 11)

130 MINS TO BARRANCO HUTS (MAP 11)

MIDDLE TRAIL DESCENDS FROM THE NEW (UNOFFICIAL) SHEFFIELD CAMPSITE. USEFUL FOR THOSE WHO ARE SUFFERING FROM ALTITUDE AND DON'T FANCY THE CLIMB TO LAVA TOWER

STREAM

045
WATER-FALL

11

> **❑ Ascent of Kibo via the Western Breach/Arrow Glacier Route**
> The Western Breach Route is a harder, shorter, more dangerous and less popular alter-
> native trail than the standard route via Barafu Huts. But it's also a great walk that
> allows you to explore the crater floor and all its features – the Furtwangler Glacier,
> Reusch Crater and Ash Pit, to name but three – as well as affording supreme views
> of the Shira Plateau, Barranco Valley and the summit of Mount Meru. The route starts
> at the Lava Tower Campsite. You can find a full description of the Arrow
> Glacier/Western Breach Route starting on p294.

of the plateau before finally settling on a roughly easterly direction, with a steady,
shallow incline for most of the next 6km. Notice how the vegetation has declined
until only a few everlastings and lichen manage to cling to life. Ahead, facing you
down, is the brilliant white smear of the Penck Glacier.

Soon after the **junction with the Lemosho Route** the path loops to the
south-east and divides into two. Not too long ago it was only those people who
opted to tackle the summit on the more difficult Western Breach Route who
headed east towards the **Lava Tower**; these days, however, most guides recognize the acclimatization benefits of taking this climb up to Lava Tower and so
also opt for this route, even if they will then divert off down to Barranco Huts.
As for the more southerly route, this is now largely the preserve of porters and
those trekkers who aren't doing so well and need to descend quickly to Barranco.

(This more gentle, southerly trail bends
round to the right past the **lunchstop** and
onto the highest point of this walk, 4530m,
before descending quickly via a series of
zigzags into a gully. It then bends south-
east once more, following the contours of
Kibo's lower reaches as it crosses two
more streams. Less than an hour later the
trail meets with the old **Umbwe Route** –
see p316 – a junction that is marked by a
proliferation of signposts, from where it's
downhill all the way to Barranco.)

From Lava Tower the path splits again.
The route up to Arrow Glacier soars above,
while the path to Barranco drops steeply
south to a stream, and rises and falls a couple of times before plummeting, finally and
fabulously, into the delightful **Barranco
Valley**, rich in groundsel and lobelia. A
huge gouge in the southern face of Kibo to
the south-west of Uhuru Peak, the valley is
in places 300m deep and was formed when
a huge landslide swept southwards down

'...an extraordinary arborescent
plant, since named *Senecio
Johnstonii*... Its trunk was so super-
ficially rooted and so rotten that, in
spite of its height and girth, I could
pull it down with one hand.
(from *The Kilima-njaro Expedition*,
HH Johnston, 1886; note that the
tree he is talking about and depicting is no longer called *Senecio johnstonii* but *Dendrosenecio kilimanjarii ssp cottonii*).

TRAIL GUIDE AND MAPS

from the summit about 100,000 years ago. From the **Barranco Huts campsite** (3986m) itself and its environs you'll have spectacular views of Kibo's southern face, the Western Breach and the mighty Heim Glacier, with glacial moraine tumbling southwards towards the camp. Few are the trekkers who do not rank this campsite as their favourite on this trail. Indeed, so beautiful is it that it's tempting to linger outside one's tent after dark and savour the sights and scenery of this most spectacular site – though in reality, the cold soon chases most people back into their sleeping bags.

By the way, though you have gained only 147m since this morning, by climbing to Lava Tower Campsite and 4627m you have reached an altitude that's just 7m shy of the highest mountain in Switzerland, the Dufourspitze; bother to climb up the Lava Tower itself, which takes about 15 minutes or so, and you'll be 57m higher.

STAGE 4: BARRANCO HUTS TO BARAFU HUTS
[MAP 11, opposite; MAP 12, p274]

Distance: 8.5km; altitude gained: 676m

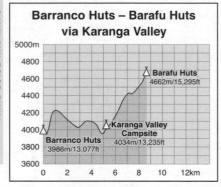

This is a long stage, so long that many trekkers now prefer to tackle it over two separate days, camping for the night above the Karanga Valley. Make sure you fill your containers in the valley below the campsite as this is the last place to get water on the Machame Route and, if the cold wind's rushing through, it's possibly the last place you'd want to be stopping at too, though its beauty cannot be denied. As you walk along the path today the great glaciers of Kili's **Southern Icefields** – the Heim, Kersten and Decken glaciers – will appear on your left one after the other. Curiously, although this stage sets you up nicely for the final push to the summit, by the end of the day you will actually be further away from Uhuru Peak (as the lammergeyer flies) than you were at the start of the day at Barranco.

The hardest part of the day occurs right at the beginning, with a near-vertical scramble up the **Great Barranco Wall** or **Breach Wall** (more commonly called the **Breakfast Wall** now, as it is usually tackled after breakfast) to the east of the campsite. In my experience most trekkers actually get a real kick out of this climb, probably because it provides such a welcome change from the relentless *pole pole* of the previous stage. You'll have to stash your walking poles away for this first section, because at times you'll need to use both hands to haul yourself up the groundsel-dressed slopes. False summits along the way shouldn't discourage you, for after about an hour and twenty minutes you'll reach the true summit of the wall; here you can sit on the bare rock and enjoy the views south and east, with the great **Heim Glacier** over your shoulder to the north, and relish the prospect of the relatively gentle descent into the next gully below.

At the bottom of this pretty little gully, and having crossed the small stream that flows through it, you come to a **flat gravel area**, possibly once a camping spot and, by the amount of loo roll hanging from the bushes, a popular pit stop too. To the north-east a path snakes towards a high pass, once open only to porters and now closed to everybody. Your guide will lead you away from this short-cut to Barafu and bring you instead along an easier trail cutting south-east into a series of mini-valleys. Climbing out of these valleys, the path then cuts across a barren, desert slope where the silence and stillness are positively deafening, before finally descending down the western, lusher slopes of the **Karanga Valley**. Ferns, heather and other greenery reappear for a while as you descend along the rock-and-mud path, a path that you share in places with a mountain

BARRANCO HUTS	TOP OF CLIMB	OLD PORTERS TRACK	KARANGA CAMPSITE
→ 80 MINS →	30 MINS →	70 MINS →	→

TRAIL GUIDE AND MAPS

10

GROUNDSEL GROVE

LARGE BOULDER AT START OF CLIMB

MAP 11

THE BARRANCO WALL
(AKA BREAKFAST WALL)

STREAMS

28

BARRANCO HUTS
3986M
13,077FT 047 046

UMBWE ROUTE

TOP OF CLIMB
4219M, 13,842FT
047

OLD PORTERS TRACK
(PROHIBITED)
4113M
13,494FT 049

048 STREAM

'DESERT SLOPE' 050

VALLEY FLOOR & STREAM
3946M
12,946FT 051

TORTOISE ROCK 052

KARANGA VALLEY

12

053

KARANGA CAMPSITE

IGNORE SIGNPOST THAT GIVES A DIFFERENT ALTITUDE – IT'S WRONG!

→ 4034M, 13,235FT

0   1km
0   ½ mile

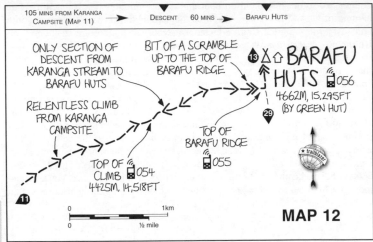

ONLY SECTION OF
DESCENT FROM
KARANGA STREAM TO
BARAFU HUTS

BIT OF A SCRAMBLE
UP TO THE TOP OF
BARAFU RIDGE

13 △ ⌂ **BARAFU HUTS** 056

4662M, 15,295FT
(BY GREEN HUT)

RELENTLESS CLIMB
FROM KARANGA
CAMPSITE

29

TOP OF
BARAFU RIDGE
055

TOP OF
CLIMB 054
4425M, 14,518FT

11

105 MINS FROM KARANGA CAMPSITE (MAP 11) → DESCENT 60 MINS → BARAFU HUTS

0 ——— 1km
0 ——— ½ mile

MAP 12

stream. The Karanga Valley is, in the words of John Reader, 'narrow, steep and exquisite'. It is also your last place to collect water before the summit, so it is vital you fill all your water bottles here. Try to collect your water from as high a point in the stream as possible and purify it: giardia could be present. The valley itself is like a small oasis of green, albeit a cold and windswept one; the beautiful shimmering green **malachite sunbirds** nest around here; you may spot them feeding on the lobelias.

Those who plan to cover this leg in two days rather than one will camp at the top of the next climb, a very steep twenty-minute ascent on a switchback path. This is the somewhat misnamed **Karanga Valley Campsite** (4034m; I say misnamed because, of course, it's above the valley and not in it), an unlovely place, windswept and ramshackled, with something of the atmosphere of a refugee camp about it. At this altitude it's often hemmed in by clouds which unfortunately obscure its best feature, namely the lovely views it affords of Kibo's southern face. By the way, for those who are staying here the night, the distance from Barranco to Karanga is **5.1km**, and despite all your efforts you will now be just **48m** higher than when you set off from Barranco.

At the campsite the trail takes a leftward turn, heading in a north-easterly direction on a steady incline, with the Kersten and Decken glaciers a permanent presence to your left. The scenery now becomes even more barren as you make your way between the boulders and over the shattered rocks and stones of this misty mountain slope. Even the trail is faint. Only the occasional cairn marking out the way gives an indication that man has passed this way before (unless, of course, some bastard has dropped some litter). If George Lucas is looking for somewhere wild, inhospitable and unearthly as a location for his next Star Wars instalment, he could do a lot worse...

TRAIL GUIDE AND MAPS

At the top the path bends more to the east and descends into a shallow valley that, if anything, is even drier and more blighted than the previous section. Once again, the Southern Icefields loom ominously to your left, with the **Rebmann Glacier** appearing for the first time.

Barafu Huts (4662m), your destination for this leg, lies at the end of this valley, reached after a short scramble up the cliff-face and a 15- to 25-minute walk almost due north. Barafu means 'Ice' in Swahili and the camp is probably called this because of its proximity to the Rebmann Glacier, away to the northwest. It's an appropriately chilly spot but it has its advantages: the views of the climb that you face are good, and they've started to install some new toilets too (and not before time; according to one popular rumour, a woman died at Barafu when the toilet she was sitting in collapsed and slid down the hillside – which is not the most dignified way of meeting your Maker).

Try to get some food and rest as soon as possible and sort out your equipment for the next stage before it gets dark: you've got a long night ahead.

STAGE 5: BARAFU HUTS TO STELLA POINT AND UHURU PEAK
[MAP 13, p276; MAP 32, p335]

Distance: 4.86km; altitude gained: 1233m

But now, apparently, the mountain was inhabited by fiery beings who baffled man's adventurous foot: the mountain receded as the traveller advanced, the summit rose as he ascended; blood burst from the nostrils, fingers bent backwards... even the most adventurous were forced back. **Richard Burton** in *Progress of Expedition to East Africa*, reporting the rumours he had heard about Kilimanjaro while residing in Tanga (circa 1857).

And so you come to the final ascent. For the past five days or so you've enjoyed some wonderful walking and miles of smiles; now it's time to do the hard yards.

The climb itself is a rigorous, vigorous push to Stella Point and the crater rim, followed by a 45-minute trudge up to Uhuru Peak, the highest point in Africa. It's tough, no doubt about it, but if you manage to avoid sickness or injury there's no reason why you, too, should not be clutching a certificate come tomorrow evening.

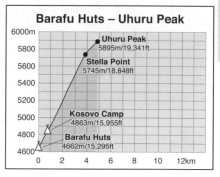

Barafu Huts – Uhuru Peak

- Uhuru Peak 5895m/19,341ft
- Stella Point 5745m/18,848ft
- Kosovo Camp 4863m/15,955ft
- Barafu Huts 4662m/15,295ft

This final stage usually begins at around midnight; this not only allows trekkers the chance to see sunrise from the summit but also leaves enough daylight to allow for the long descent to the next night's campsite, with an hour's recuperation back at Barafu on the way. As such, you can leave most of your **luggage** at Barafu while you tackle the ascent, though you should take any valuables with you (there have been a few robberies from tents left unguarded), as

TRAIL GUIDE AND MAPS

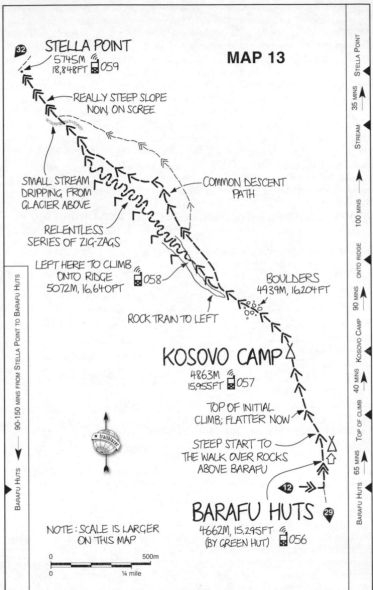

MAP 13

STELLA POINT
5745M
18,848FT 📱059

REALLY STEEP SLOPE
NOW, ON SCREE

SMALL STREAM
DRIPPING FROM
GLACIER ABOVE

COMMON DESCENT
PATH

RELENTLESS
SERIES OF ZIG-ZAGS

LEFT HERE TO CLIMB
ONTO RIDGE
5072M, 16,640FT 📱058

BOULDERS
4939M, 16,204FT

ROCK TRAIN TO LEFT

KOSOVO CAMP
4863M
15,955FT 📱057

TOP OF INITIAL
CLIMB; FLATTER NOW

STEEP START TO
THE WALK OVER ROCKS
ABOVE BARAFU

BARAFU HUTS
4662M, 15,295FT
(BY GREEN HUT) 📱056

NOTE: SCALE IS LARGER
ON THIS MAP

0   500m
0   ¼ mile

90-150 MINS FROM STELLA POINT TO BARAFU HUTS ← BARAFU HUTS

Stella Point ◄
35 MINS ▲
Stream ◄
100 MINS ▲
Onto Ridge ◄
90 MINS ▲
Kosovo Camp ◄
40 MINS ▲
Top of Climb ◄
65 MINS ▲
Barafu Huts

well as your **camera**, spare film and batteries and all your **water**, which should be kept in **insulated bottles** or it'll freeze up and be useless on the ascent. Cameras, particularly digitals and feature-heavy SLRs, have been known to freeze in these conditions as well so keep them (or at the very least their batteries) insulated, preferably by putting them in an inside pocket or wrapped in clothing in your daypack. Wear most of your **clothes** too – you can always take a layer or two off in the unlikely situation that you find yourself getting too hot – and have your **head-torch** readily to hand when you wake up so you don't have to spend time and energy looking around for it before you go.

Good luck!

At 4am by the light of a hurricane lamp, and wrapped in everything that could give warmth, I started with Mawala, the headman, and Jonathan, our guide, on the long uphill pull of 4000ft over loose scree and fissured rocks. The cold was intense, and Mawala got two of his toes frost-bitten ... our breathing had become so difficult that we could barely drag ourselves along and had to sit down every few yards to recover breath, now and again sucking icicles and nibbling Cadbury's Milk Chocolate. Yet the steep ascent was mostly over projecting ridges of lava slabs and presented no real obstacle beyond the extreme altitude. Here and there, however, we struck a bed of loose shingle, which mockingly carried us backwards at every footstep almost the whole distance of our tread.
Eva Stuart Watt *Africa's Dome of Mystery* (1930)

The way to the summit starts, as you've probably already observed from Barafu, by scrambling over the **small cliffs** at the northern end of the camp in what is the steepest part of the trek before the final push to Stella Point. Passing through the unofficial Kosovo Camp (4863m) about an hour and three-quarters

Barafu Route

into the trek, you may be pleased to find out that you are higher than Mont Blanc, the highest mountain in Western Europe (4807m).

Climbing still further, the path now ascends to a rocky ridge, in the shadow of which you initially walk before taking a sharp left to surmount it and walk along its spine. You are now heading directly for the summit and Stella Point, a direction you will maintain for nearly the entire night.

It seems like an age before Stella finally comes into view; when it does, it still seems an inordinate distance away. In my opinion, this is the hardest part of the climb, when the cold insinuates itself between the layers of your clothes, penetrating your skin, chilling your bones and numbing the marrow until finally, inevitably, it seems to freeze your very soul. The situation seems desperate at this hour and you can do nothing; nothing except keep going. It's one thing to fail to reach the summit because of altitude sickness; quite another to fail from *attitude* sickness.

The situation was appalling, there was a grandeur and a magnificence about the surroundings which were almost too much for me; instead of exhilarating, they were oppressive.
Charles New *Life, Wanderings, and Labours in Eastern Africa* (1873)

The **switchback path** begins in earnest now and continues for most of the next two hours or more. It is pointless describing the scenery on this section, for the chances are you won't be able to see much beyond the radius of your torch-beam and you probably won't be keen on surveying the landscape now anyway. If it's a clear night, however, you may be able to see the **Rebmann Glacier** ahead of you to your left, with the ice-free Stella Point a little to its right in the distance. Picking your way through the trail of knackered trekkers and exhausted assistant guides, ignore the sound of people retching and sobbing and remember to keep your pace constant and very slow, even if you feel fine: you've come this far, and now is not a good time to get altitude sickness.

Though you probably won't notice it, the path actually drifts slightly to the north over these three hours, before crossing a frozen stream. You are now just thirty-five minutes from Stella Point (5752m), but it's a painful, tear-inducing half-hour on sheer scree. The gradient up to now has been steep, but this last scree slope takes the biscuit; in fact, it takes the entire tin.

The ground underfoot is just one more obstacle at this stage, the distinctive **shale and gravel slopes** of Kibo causing you to slip back with every step. Everybody has their own way of tackling this, with some trekkers stabbing their poles hard into the ground to aid their balance, while others walk with a Chaplinesque gait, their feet splayed outwards to stem the slide back. Whatever way you choose, you'll find it hard work.

Lift one foot and then the other, just enough to place it higher; don't use any more energy than you need to and breathe deeply between each move. Rhythm is everything, rhythm and pacing, and when you are in it your thoughts go and it is dreamlike, but you are still here in the moment, the cone beam of light coming from your forehead tying you through the blackness to the lava slope of this mountain that in your mind you see rising to a rare glacial height above the acacia-studded plain of Africa.
Rick Ridgeway *The Shadow of Kilimanjaro – on Foot across East Africa* (1999)

Make it to Stella and you can afford to relax a little. To give you an idea of your achievement, you are now higher than the summit of Russia's Mount Elbrus, at 5642m the highest peak in Europe.

If you really, absolutely, positively, definitely can't do any more, take comfort from the fact that you have already matched the feat of respected climber HW Tilman, for whom Stella Point was the highest point reached on his first attempt on the summit; and you can always use his excuse – that he thought that this *was* the highest point – too. (Mind you, as if to prove that it was ignorance and not a lack of fortitude that prevented him from reaching Uhuru, he then went on to conquer the much harder Mawenzi Peak a few days later). Take comfort, too, from the fact that you have also earned yourself a certificate; a certificate, moreover, that's identical – save for a couple of words – to the one that they give you if you reach the summit. But for most trekkers, those two words – 'UHURU PEAK' – are everything. Words that are worth all the money, time and energy has spent in getting to this point; and which are certainly worth the extra 45 minutes that it takes to stagger around the crater rim (see Map 32, p335), passing minor pinnacles such as **Hans Meyer** and **Elveda** points before finally arriving, just as Hans Meyer himself did over a century ago, at Uhuru Peak: the true summit of the mountain and the highest point in the whole continent. You are now enjoying an unrivalled view of Africa – nobody on this great, charismatic continent is currently gazing down from as lofty a vantage-point as you.

From the summit, it's usual for trekkers who took the Machame Route up to take the **Mweka Route** back down; and this you'll find described on p328.

Machame village in the late nineteenth century. Engraving by **Alexandre Le Roy** from *Au Kilima-Ndjaro* published in 1893.

The Shira Plateau and Lemosho routes

Without doubt Kibo is most imposing as seen from the west. Here it rises in solemn majesty, and the eye is not distracted by the sister peak of Mawenzi, of which nothing is to be seen but a single jutting pinnacle. The effect is enhanced by the magnificent flowing sweep of the outline, the dazzling extent of the ice-cap, the vast stretch of the forest, the massive breadth of the base, and the jagged crest of the Shira spur as it branches away towards the west.
Hans Meyer *Across East African Glaciers* (1891)

These two treks have been put together simply because they have a lot of features in common, the main one being that both involve a crossing of the expansive Shira Plateau which stretches out for around 13km to the west of Kibo. This plateau is actually a **caldera**, a collapsed volcanic crater: when you are walking on the plateau, you are walking on the remains of the first of Kilimanjaro's three volcanoes to expire, over 500,000 years ago; it was then filled by the lava and debris from the later Kibo eruption.

The plateau also has a reputation for its **fauna**, largely thanks to its proximity to both Amboseli National Park in Kenya and the West Kilimanjaro Wildlife Corridor, from where herds of elephant, eland, buffalo, and big cats such as lion have been known to wander. Indeed, not so many years ago trekkers on these routes had to be accompanied by an armed ranger (for which they had to pay) to protect them against encounters with predators. That said, to be honest you will be very, *very* lucky to see any evidence of visiting wildlife on the plateau, save for the odd hoofprint or two and the occasional sun-dried lumps of scat and spoor. So while the proximity of Africa's finest wild beasts adds a certain frisson of excitement to the walk, don't choose either of these trails purely on the strength of their reputation for spotting game: it's an awful long way to come just to see some desiccated elephant shit.

The first thing to know about these two routes is that **it is common for the relatively new Lemosho Route to be referred to as the Shira Plateau Route** (or just the Shira Route), particularly by foreign agencies keen to promote the fact that you'll be walking across the Shira Plateau. This, of course, is confusing so you should ask your agency to indicate *exactly* which of the two routes you will be taking. Another way to check is to see where your first night's accommodation will be; if it's the Big Tree Campsite – or Mti Mkubwa in the local language – where you'll be staying, then it's actually the Lemosho Route that you'll be following, regardless of what your trekking agency calls it.

Furthermore, there are **many paths** on the plateau and a number of possible campsites too, and each year the guides slightly alter the routes taken by their trekkers. For these reasons, the following descriptions of the Lemosho and Shira Plateau trails may not tally exactly with your own experience on the plateau, though the difference should be negligible.

The journey to Londorossi

The starting point for both of these trails is the **Londorossi Gate**, reachable via a long drive from Moshi or an even longer one from Arusha. As a result of the extra effort and petrol required to get here, these two trails often cost a little more than the more popular, and nearer, Marangu, Umbwe and Machame trails.

Thus, for much of the first day you won't be walking anywhere but will be strapped into the back of a jeep as it glides along the Arusha–Moshi highway before turning off at **Boma Ya Ng'ombe** ('Cattle Corral'; 26km from Moshi). From there it bounces along for another hour past **Sanya Juu** (22km from the turn-off and virtually the last place to get supplies), **Ngarenairobi** and **Simba Farm** (a huge estate to the left of the road) before finally pulling up at the village and gate of Londorossi. It's a weird place, a Spaghetti Western outpost stuck in the middle of Africa, made entirely of wood, divided up and shut off from the outside world by high wooden fences designed to keep the local fauna at bay. At Londorossi you can register, pick up a **permit** (the only other place outside of Marangu and Machame gates where this is possible) and check out the troop of colobus monkeys that has been known to hang out in the trees near the park rangers' accommodation.

From here, the two trails divide and are described separately below.

The Lemosho Route

The Lemosho Route is a relatively new variation on the traditional Shira Plateau Route (described on p299), which is seldom used nowadays. Indeed, though many people book what they think is a trek on the Shira Route – as that is what the trekking agencies often call it – it is often the Lemosho Route on which they will actually be walking.

Although these things change quite often, currently the Lemosho route is one of the quietest on the mountain (only the Umbwe Route, which has a reputation for being the most difficult trail, and the Shira Route, which largely follows a road for its first couple of days, are less popular). At the risk of this situation changing (we can't help but feel somewhat responsible for the explosion in popularity of the Rongai Route due to our warm review of it in the last edition), it is currently our favourite of the official trails on the mountain, a seven- to eight-day yomp (though some companies take

Colobus monkey
(from *The Kilima-njaro Expedition,* **HH Johnston**, 1886)

as many as ten) through the remote and pristine rainforest of West Kilimanjaro and across the Shira Plateau to the highest point in Africa and back down again. The assault on the summit is conducted via either the tricky **Western Breach Route** (see p294) or via Barranco, Karanga Valley and Barafu to Stella Point on the **Barafu Route** (a description of which begins on p271). Either way, the usual **descent route is the Mweka trail**.

It is the first day or so, when you are walking through the forests on Kilimanjaro's western slopes, that is the main reason why this trail has overtaken the old Shira Plateau Route as the main path attacking Kilimanjaro from the west. With the latter you often take a car all the way up to the plateau, thereby missing out not only on some fine forest, which you experience only through a car window, but also on some useful acclimatization. And although the walk up to the plateau on the Lemosho Route is an exhausting one, the benefits of trekking rather than driving up will manifest themselves later on as you saunter up Kibo with little more than a headache, while littering the trail around you are the weeping, retching bodies of the AMS-sufferers who took the car instead. Indeed, take the Cathedral diversion and use the Barafu route to get to the summit and it's the **longest ascent route on Kilimanjaro at 46.26km** (though it can be just 32.8km if taking the direct route to Shira Huts and then the Western Breach).

Other advantages with this route? Well from personal experience I think that the birdlife on this route is the most diverse and interesting of any on the mountain (though I admit that I can't actually back this up with any statistical proof). What's more, the Lemosho Route allows for variations and diversions from the main route, with side trips to the minor peaks of Kilimanjaro's third summit, the Shira Ridge. In particular the **Shira Cathedral**, on the southern side of the plateau, has become a very popular excursion on the third day of the trek. Again, such a side trip is useful for acclimatization purposes and no extra days need to be taken to do this either. Other side trips that *do* require an extra day include a trek to the Moir Huts, on the north-western side of the mountain; and, if taking the Western Breach Route to the summit, a diversion to see the Reusch Crater and Ash Pit. Indeed, one of the joys of the Lemosho Route is the variety of different trails one can take and itineraries one can build – there is no one standard 'Lemosho Route'.

Though it's a great route, Lemosho is not without its drawbacks. For one thing, we reckon it to be the wettest route; though meteorology doesn't back us up, in our experience it always seems to rain on this side of the mountain more than anywhere else. Though it varies from month to month, the amount of **rubbish** on the trail and especially at the campsites can be distressing too. How anyone could be stupid enough to drop sweet wrappers in somewhere as lovely as the western forest is beyond me, while those who leave used batteries lying on the ground at campsites deserve shooting. Don't hesitate to leave messages in the suggestion boxes at Shira Huts or write to KINAPA if the trail and campsites are in a bad state when you arrive. I, too, would welcome your reports on the latest situation – for better or worse; send us an email to the usual address (🖳 postmaster@climbmountkilimanjaro.com) and I promise to reply – get enough of them and I'll let KINAPA know too.

STAGE 1: LONDOROSSI GATE TO MTI MKUBWA/BIG TREE CAMP
[MAP 14, p285]

Distance: 4.8km; altitude gained: 396m

Getting to the start of the Lemosho Route is a bit of a bind. First you have to suffer a two-hour African massage (the local euphemism for any sort of vehicular ride on a typically rutted African thoroughfare). Your first port of call is Londorossi, though before you even reach there your guide will have to alight briefly at a small hut to pay a fee to the Forest Authority. Park fees paid and luggage weighed at Londorossi, you

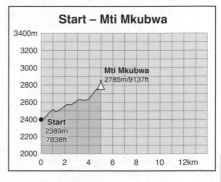

Start – Mti Mkubwa

Mti Mkubwa
2785m/9137ft

Start
2389m
7838ft

jump back on the coach/car as it takes you up the slopes past largely denuded hills and little wooden shacks incongruously furnished with satellite dishes. (As these dishes indicate, the inhabitants aren't particularly poor even though the conditions of their houses would indicate otherwise; in fact, the reason why they live in crudely erected wooden shacks is because they aren't actually allowed to build any permanent construction this high up on Kili.) Some of these settlements have actually been dignified with names, including **Gezaulale** and the last 'village' before the forest, **Chaulale**. Considering the cold climate, it won't surprise you to learn that as well as the tree plantations that abound, potatoes and carrots are the main crops in these parts.

Eventually, ten minutes after Chaulale and having entered the forest, your vehicle will give up trying to negotiate the muddy path – either at the official start of the track, marked by a couple of toilets, or some distance before it if the road or your vehicle is in a particularly poor state – and it will be time to alight, grab your rucksack and make your own way up the slopes. Even if you aren't having

---

❏ **Mobile reception on the Lemosho Route**

Trekkers with mobile phones will find little opportunity to use them on the first half of the Lemosho Route. The first place we have ever managed to get reception was after leaving the forest on the second morning, though this happened only once; the first place where it's just about certain you'll get reception is by the **Cathedral** on the third morning. **Shira Huts** has reception if you're prepared to search for it on the boulders around the campsite, and reception is OK at **Lava Tower**. Thereafter it depends on which route you're taking. For the Western Breach, reception is fair at **Arrow Glacier**, you can sometimes get it at **Crater Camp** too and, so it is said, at the **summit**. While if you're taking the Barafu Route to the summit, see the box on p262 for a summary of mobile reception on this route.

your lunch here and have no need for the toilets, do delay setting off just for a few moments to see if the colobus monkeys that hang around here will put in an appearance. (This place, by the way, is sometimes called **Lemosho Glades**.)

It may already be late in the day by the time you start walking, although the first night's camp lies only around two hours from the end of the road. There are enough steep gradients in these two hours to check all your equipment is comfortable and your limbs are in full working order. The conditions are often misty and quite cool on this first stage through the forest; ideal weather for walking, if not for taking photos.

As you can tell from the map opposite, landmarks in the forest are few; nevertheless, it's still a splendid start to your trek. At times there is an almost Jurassic quality to the trail, a feeling that you've stumbled into some Lost World – a feeling that I can ascribe only to the untamed nature of the forest on this side of the mountain and the complete lack of any evidence that humanity has passed this way. It's just wonderful.

It helps, of course, that throughout today you'll be sharing the forest with colobus and blue monkey and the rarely encountered buffalo, elephant, lion and leopard. Indeed, it wasn't uncommon a few years back for trekkers to be accompanied by armed rangers to ward off buffalo attacks. In addition to the fauna, you'll be sharing the path itself with many of the celebrities of Kilimanjaro's floral kingdom, including the two most prominent *Impatiens* species, *kilimanjaro* and *pseudoviola*, as well as millions of soldier ants; while watching over the

Dracaena afromontana – the Chagga's constant companion

Known as *masale* by the locals, the inedible and – at least compared to some of the beautiful plants on Kilimanjaro – rather unedifying *Dracaena afromontana* has nevertheless been cultivated and used by the Chagga since time immemorial, to the extent where it's now almost their tribal emblem. Nobody knows why this should be but it's clear that where the outside world sees an unspectacular green plant of little practical use, the Chagga see a shrub whose spiritual qualities and symbolism are far more important than the practical and nutritional value inherent in other plants.

You'll probably first come across the *dracaena* in one of the mountainside villages where it's still commonly used as a boundary marker, with a row of them planted to form a fence to demarcate the extent of a person's property. According to some Chagga guides, this is because the *dracaena* is able to ward off evil spirits, which are unable to pass through a line of them. The plant was also traditionally a symbol of contrition and an appeal for clemency. If you were in dispute with a neighbour, for example, or had somehow wronged somebody, the best way to ask for forgiveness would be by giving them a *dracaena* plant. Do so, and they'd have to have a very strong reason for not forgiving you.

Indeed, in some Chagga villages it is said that the *dracaena* is a Chagga's constant companion, accompanying a person throughout their life from their first breath to their last. There's some truth to this, too, because in some Chagga villages it was customary to give the sap of the plant to newborns before they took their mother's milk for the first time; while when it came to burying a village chief, the corpse would traditionally have been wrapped in dracaena leaves before being interred.

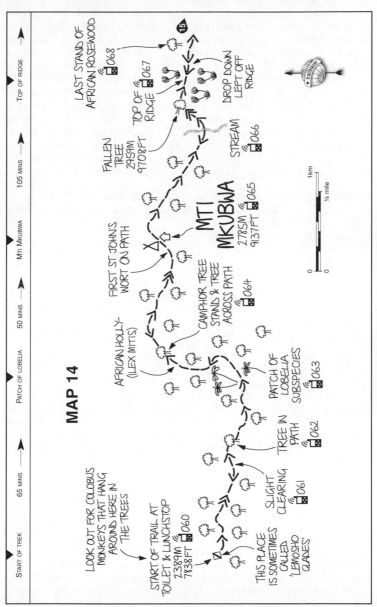

MAP 14

START OF TREK — 65 MINS — PATCH OF LOBELIA — 50 MINS — MTI MKUBWA — 105 MINS — TOP OF RIDGE

LOOK OUT FOR COLOBUS MONKEYS THAT HANG AROUND HERE IN THE TREES

START OF TRAIL AT TOILET & LUNCHSTOP 2389M 7838FT 📷060

THIS PLACE IS SOMETIMES CALLED 'LEMOSHO GLADES'

SLIGHT CLEARING 📷061

TREE IN PATH 📷062

PATCH OF LOBELIA SUBSPECIES 📷063

AFRICAN HOLLY- (ILEX MITIS)

CAMPHOR TREE STAND & TREE ACROSS PATH 📷064

FIRST ST JOHN'S WORT ON PATH

MTI MKUBWA 2785M 9137FT 📷065

FALLEN TREE 2959M 9708FT

STREAM 📷066

TOP OF RIDGE 📷067

DROP DOWN LEFT OFF RIDGE

LAST STAND OF AFRICAN ROSEWOOD 📷068

15

TRAIL GUIDE AND MAPS

1km
½ mile
0
0

whole shebang are those giants without which there would be no forest, in particular the camphor, podocarpus and hagenia trees. Look out, too, for the *Lobelia gibberoa*. Ask your guide, too, to point out the *Dracaena afromontana*, locally known as the yucca plant, which though seemingly unimpressive is held in high esteem by the Chagga (see box p284).

Your destination for this first stage is the campsite known officially (ie by nobody) as the **Forest Camp**, and unofficially (ie by everybody) as Mti Mkubwa, or the **Big Tree Camp** (2785m), for obvious reasons. Lying at the top of a ridge in the shade of a wonderful spreading podocarpus, as with all the campsites on Kili there's little to it other than a piece of flat ground, a couple of long-drop toilets and a ranger's hut. But it's still many people's favourite stopping point on the trail, with the noise of the turaco and colobus in the trees at both dusk and dawn making for a quintessential African night.

STAGE 2: MTI MKUBWA/BIG TREE CAMP TO SHIRA 1
[MAP 14, p285; MAP 15, opposite]

Distance: 7.9km; altitude gained: 719m

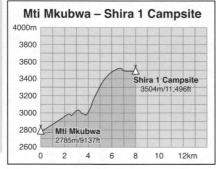

Mti Mkubwa – Shira 1 Campsite

Shira 1 Campsite
3504m/11,496ft

Mti Mkubwa
2785m/9137ft

You've spent a whole day travelling, registering and walking and you are still some way short of the plateau, which you will finally reach towards the end of this second stage, leaving the forest for the moorland as you do so. Many trekkers' favourite stage on the trail, this four hour-plus walk (though with all the breaks you'll need it will take a full day) is something of a red-letter day too. For not only do you forsake forest for moorland and get your first proper views of the Shira Plateau and its accompanying ridges and peaks but it is on this stage that, finally and famously, you get your first views of Kibo.

These rewards are not gained without effort, however, and during today you'll be climbing almost 750m, taking you above 3500m and into the realm of dastardly HACO and its evil twin, HAPO (see p219). So do make sure you go *pole pole* if you don't want to feel poorly poorly.

Today begins just as the last one left off, as you head in a general easterly direction and generally upwards too, though with plenty of minor variations as you negotiate the folds and creases of Kili's forested slopes. Eventually you find yourself heading north-east to climb to the top of a ridge, the point where you actually gain the top being marked by a large fallen tree. As with many of the larger trees in this neck of the woods, this giant used to show signs of having

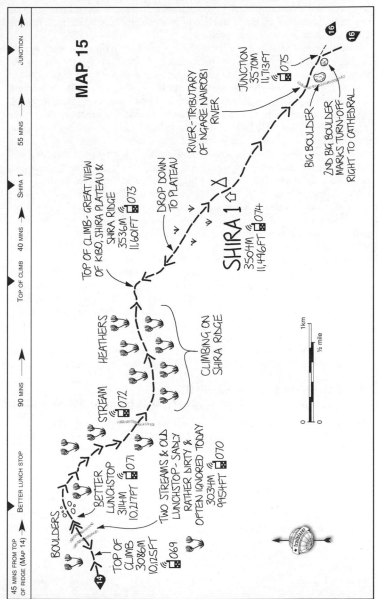

TRAIL GUIDE AND MAPS

been scorched around the trunk – the unmistakable handiwork of honey-seekers who burn the hollow inside of the tree in order to smoke out the bees, making it easier to gain access to their produce.

Heading east and up along the ridge, it's not long before the trees start to diminish in size and number, to be replaced by their hardier cousins of the heather and stoebe family. These soon begin to crowd you in on both sides but not enough to obscure your view north over the valley. It's a valley you eventually join, too, as you continue your eastward and upward progress, contouring gently to the valley floor to reacquaint yourselves with the decorative *Hagenia abyssinica*, here making one last stand.

The relentless uphill is finally interrupted by a short descent to what was once a popular **lunchstop** – popular, that is, until the litter left by these lunching parties drove guides and their trekkers to find another dining-room to frequent and, no doubt, despoil too. That alternative lunchspot lies at the top of the next ridge and while there's no water up here (whereas there is in the older picnic site down below) the views are better, particularly to the north over the Ngare Nairobi River and the 4x4 road of the Shira Plateau Route beyond. From this new lunchspot the path once again points east before bending south, following the ridge, before heading east once more to contour around the slope of what is – though you may not realize it just yet – the northern extremity of the **Shira Ridge**.

The path's gradient, steep since lunch, flattens out as you contour along this northern slope and drops at the first sight of Shira Plateau. This is the moment you've been waiting for all day: standing at 3536m above sea level, the Shira Ridge to your right, snow-capped Kibo ahead, the plateau unfurled at your feet with your next two day's trekking mapped out for you upon its face. More immediately, beneath you lies the green uniport of the **Shira 1 Campsite** (3504m), a spot that's popular with four-striped grass mice, streaky seed-eaters and white-necked ravens as well as the usual foreign itinerants in lurid Gore-tex.

STAGE 3: SHIRA 1 TO SHIRA HUTS
[MAP 15, p287; MAP 16, p290; MAP 17, p293]

Distance: 6.9km (10.1km via the Cathedral); altitude gained: 391m

As mentioned in the introduction, one of the advantages of the Lemosho Route is the number of different variations one can take. And this third stage is perhaps the one with the greatest number of options, for not only are there a number of different destinations, there are a number of different ways of reaching them too.

In order to introduce some sort of clarity and simplicity, we've chosen as our destination for this third stage the most common destination, Shira Huts (also known as Shira 2). But it is not unheard of for some companies, such as Tusker Safaris, to head on to Moir Huts, on the north-western side of Kibo. The gain in altitude of doing this is large – but then your company will have built in acclimatization days after this to compensate.

There are two main ways of getting to Shira Huts from Shira 1: the regular direct trail slicing north-west to south-east across the plateau, or the new and increasingly popular alternative detour via the Shira Cathedral on the plateau's southern rim. Though it's not too strenuous, this latter option does provide some useful acclimatization as you climb to 3862m before dropping again. Furthermore, as if the lack of a blinding AMS headache later on wasn't reward enough, there are also the views from the top of the Cathedral across the plateau and towards Kibo; and as it takes only a day, and thus no more time than the regular route, we recommend you to select this option if given the choice. (Though if you do choose this variation try to set off early as the clouds often roll in by mid morning, obscuring any decent views.) However, as it is the alternative route to the main trail, we have described it second (beginning on p291) after the regular, traditional trail which we look at now.

Shira 1 to Shira Huts: the regular route

This 'traditional' trail may lack the pzazz of the younger alternative but that's not to dismiss it altogether. After all, no stroll across the Shira Plateau could ever be described as dull! Shira Huts is the main campsite on the plateau, equipped with a rangers' office, some smart toilets and a particularly prominent suggestion box, as if to invite criticism from trekkers;

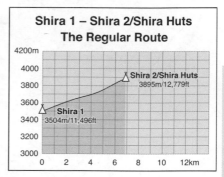

**Shira 1 – Shira 2/Shira Huts
The Regular Route**

Shira 2/Shira Huts
3895m/12,779ft

Shira 1
3504m/11,496ft

and given the filthy state of the campsite, it's probably going to get it too. The ranger here also oversees the campsite at Shira Caves on the Machame Route.

To get to Shira Huts involves just under three hours of steady uphill walking. From Shira 1 you head south-east through the heath and moorland of the plateau; watch out for buffalo tracks and those of other animals – klipspringer, dik dik – that cross the plateau in search of salt and fresh grazing. Come to think of it, watch out for the buffaloes themselves – encountering one can ruin your holiday. Crossing the unimpressive trickle of the waterway that will, further down the slopes, become the torrent of the Ngare Nairobi, about an hour and forty minutes from breaking camp you reach the plateau's major junction. It is here that the Lemosho Route meets the 4x4 track of the Shira Plateau Route; here too that you meet the deep-ish creek of the Simba River. Shame, then, that such an important landmark should be marked only by a couple of toilets belonging to the **Simba Cave Campsite** (3640m), used largely by those on the (old) Shira Route. The cave itself a rather forlorn effort lying north-east of the junction.

From here it's another 40 minutes or so up to the top of a ridge, from where you can see the green roof of your destination, **Shira Huts** (3895m). It's a fairly direct 35-minute path that takes you there, crossing a couple of shallow ridges and a stream along the way.

By the way, on arriving at Shira Huts you will be higher than the top of Großglockner, at 3798m the biggest mountain in Austria.

TRAIL GUIDE AND MAPS

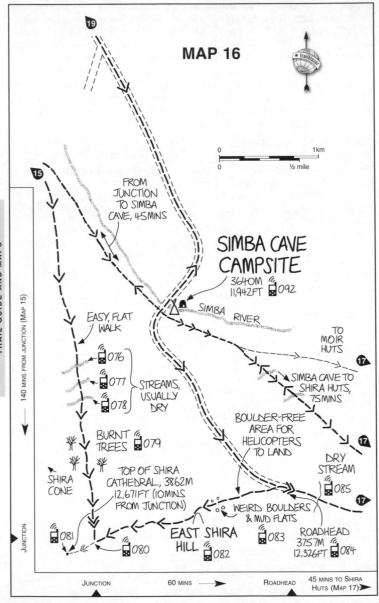

MAP 16

FROM JUNCTION TO SIMBA CAVE, 45 MINS

0   1km
0   ½ mile

SIMBA CAVE CAMPSITE

3640M
11,942FT 📱092

🏕 SIMBA RIVER

TO MOIR HUTS

19 ➜

15 ➜

EASY, FLAT WALK

📱076

📱077

📱078

STREAMS, USUALLY DRY

SIMBA CAVE TO SHIRA HUTS, 75 MINS

BURNT TREES 📱079

BOULDER-FREE AREA FOR HELICOPTERS TO LAND

17 ➜

17 ➜

SHIRA CONE

TOP OF SHIRA CATHEDRAL, 3862M 12,671FT (10MINS FROM JUNCTION)

DRY STREAM

📱085

📱081

📱080

WEIRD BOULDERS & MUD FLATS

EAST SHIRA HILL 📱082

📱083

ROADHEAD 3757M 12,326FT 📱084

JUNCTION

JUNCTION   60 MINS ➜   ROADHEAD   45 MINS TO SHIRA HUTS (MAP 17) ➜

140 MINS FROM JUNCTION (MAP 15)

TRAIL GUIDE AND MAPS

Shira 1 to Shira Huts via the Shira Cathedral

This route begins by following the regular trail as it heads south-east across the southern half of the plateau, turning off south by a big and distinctive boulder just after crossing the Ngare Nairobi. (Note that from this boulder you can already see your final destination on this stage, the Shira Huts, in the far distance.) It's a long trek across to the foot of the Cathedral, with the **Shira Cone** (aka Cone Place) the only major landmark nearby, but it's

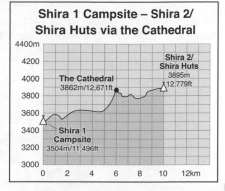

Shira 1 Campsite – Shira 2/ Shira Huts via the Cathedral

not a trek that's lacking in interest. In all probability you should see the first lobelias of your trek, standing sentinel-straight as they peer above the grass to check on your progress. You may also see many animal tracks on the trail, including klipspringer, eland and dik dik, hoofprints that betray this path's origins as a trail used by animals in search of salt and fresh grazing. Crossing many (probably dry) stream-beds, all of which, when filled with water, feed into the Ngare Nairobi, you start to climb through burnt heather trees – the legacy of another fire, though thankfully new heather bushes are flourishing amongst the roots of the blackened remains – to the foot of the rounded hump known as the **Cathedral** (3862m). The summit is gained soon after, the whole expedition from Shira 1 taking just under three and a half hours. Panorama-wise, not only are there the delights of the plateau ahead, including Moir Huts to the north-east and Kibo to your right, but behind and to the east of the Cathedral your guide should be able to point out the faint traces of the Machame Route etched into the slopes.

From the summit you make your way north-east across the **East Shira Hill** and the other undulations of the crater rim, eventually arriving at a strange muddy area sprinkled with boulders, the lack of vegetation being due to poor drainage according to one guide. The eastern end of this area has been converted into a **helipad** that may one day, God willing, be used by Flying Doctors, though until now it has been used largely by film crews to fly in supplies, including the IMAX crew during the 40 days they spent on the mountain to film their *Kilimanjaro: To the Roof of Africa* documentary. Just a couple of minutes later you come to the **roadhead** – the final termination of the 'rescue road' that emergency vehicles use when ferrying people from the mountain (and the continuation of the road that those on the old Shira Route take to gain access to the plateau, though they alight at the Morum Barrier – see p299). It may be the end of the road, but you still have a further 45 minutes up to the **Shira Huts** (3895m) and the day's end.

STAGE 4: SHIRA HUTS TO LAVA TOWER CAMP/BARRANCO HUTS
[MAP 17, opposite; MAP 10, p270]

Distance: 10.1km to Barranco Huts (6.7km to Lava Tower); altitude gained: 91m (732m to Lava Tower Campsite, then 641m descend to Barranco Huts)

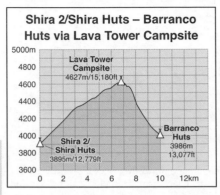

Shira 2/Shira Huts – Barranco Huts via Lava Tower Campsite

If you've spent the last three days marvelling at the silence and solitude of the Lemosho Route and wondering what all those reports about overcrowding on Kilimanjaro were about, today should answer that. For it is on this stage that the tranquil Lemosho Route (where, if you're lucky, it is still possible to feel like you're the only group on the mountain) merges with the over-popular Machame Route. Nor is it just solitude that you'll be bidding farewell to on this stage. The Shira Plateau also takes a final bow and as a result you'll be leaving the World of Heather for the Land of Lichen. True, those opting for the trek round the southern side of Kibo will reacquaint themselves with heathers, stoebes, lobelias and senecios at the magical Barranco Valley. But from now until the summit, the Barranco and other valleys excepted, it is the alpine desert that prevails.

What's more, as we are joining the Machame Route so there are two alternative routes to the summit – and it's on this stage that the two paths diverge. You can read about both of them on p271 onwards (regular route via Barranco Valley and the Barafu Route) and p294 onwards (Western Breach Route).

But you have to get to the Machame Route first and that involves about three hours of uphill walking. As you probably expect, it's an easterly climb up the fairly gentle slope of the Shira Plateau, gradually forsaking the heather and

---

❏ **The path to Moir Huts** [Map 10, p270]

From the junction with the main trail a thirty-minute path picks its way between boulders and around or over petrified lava flows before descending steeply down to the **Moir Huts** (4155m). Used mainly by those taking a 'rest' day to acclimatize – or by those few doing a complete circuit of Kibo – this campsite is set in a lovely sheer-sided valley. The valley sees few visitors and, as a result, the campsite is cleaner, tidier and certainly more peaceful than almost any other on the mountain. Indeed, even the white-necked ravens don't bother scavenging around here, the pickings presumably being too slim, and the silence as a result can be positively deafening. Apart from the three toilets, the only other building is a ruined pyramid-shaped hut, built as a sleeping shelter but now sadly vandalized. There are also some old elephant bones that somebody has carefully placed on one of the boulders, presumably to replace the buffalo bones that were once here but have now disappeared we know not where.

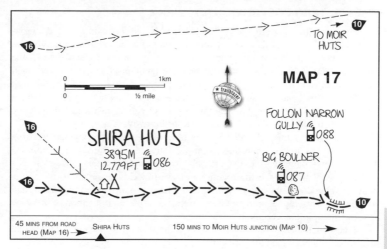

MAP 17

FOLLOW NARROW GULLY 088

BIG BOULDER 087

SHIRA HUTS
3895M
12,779FT 086

TO MOIR HUTS

0 — 1km
0 — ½ mile

45 MINS FROM ROAD HEAD (MAP 16) ▶   SHIRA HUTS   150 MINS TO MOIR HUTS JUNCTION (MAP 10) ▶

TRAIL GUIDE AND MAPS

moorland for something altogether more barren, where lichen-covered boulders predominate. Look out for the shiny black obsidian rock on the trail, not forgetting to look up occasionally to see Meru in the distance over your right shoulder. There are few steep passages to this stage, save for a brief clamber up a narrow gully on the route from Shira Huts. Ten minutes more of clambering on a fairly steep gradient and suddenly you find the path flattening out, just before the junction with the path to Moir Huts (Map 10, p270), which lie about 30 minutes away (see box opposite). This junction is a popular place to rest and, if the mist that swirls around Kibo is in a particularly benign mood, a great place for photos too. There's also a 25-minute path from here to the foot of **Shark's Tooth**, the pointy little peak sitting to Kibo's north-west. The regular trail, however, bends right (south) to chop through a gully, from where it bends again to follow, approximately, a line of overhanging rocks. Bending south again, you now climb up to the top of the neighbouring ridge... and there, marked by some weird mushroom-rock formations, you meet the main Machame Route that has been contouring that ridge from the Shira Caves.

Soon after, the path loops to the south-east and divides into two. It is here that those who have opted to tackle the summit on the more difficult Western Breach Route branch off east towards the Lava Tower. The majority of trekkers heading to Barranco will also follow this deceptively lengthy and fairly steep uphill trek, passing through the unofficial **Sheffield Campsite** (from where there is a further trail heading south to Barranco) and on to the **Lava Tower Campsite** (4627m), squeezed between Kibo and the tower itself. Though not the most direct path to Barranco, this route is useful in order to gain some much-needed altitude that could be vital in the battle against mountain sickness.

If you are taking the longer route via Barafu, turn to p271 for a description of your trek; while if you're continuing on the Western Breach, read on.

THE WESTERN BREACH ROUTE

Over the years the Western Breach Route has acquired a certain aura and a reputation as the hardest of the summit routes. Nor is this reputation entirely unde-
served. Though it's the shortest route, time-wise, it's also the steepest (with the
mean gradient of the route said to be 26 degrees) and there's a bit of non-technical
and very basic scrambling involved. What's more, and most worryingly, this trail
is subject to frequent rockfalls and there are a couple of places where your guide
will stop and listen out for any heading in your direction. In January 2006 three
American climbers perished in a rockslide near Arrow Glacier (see box p297).
Following on from this, KINAPA brought in some legislation to regulate trekking
on this route. All trekkers must now wear protective helmets during their climb on
this route, and many agencies ask their clients to sign disclaimers too.

It's interesting to see the reactions of the trekking agencies to the route.
Some, such as Zara, the biggest operator on the mountain, avoid it; others, such
as SEME, positively recommend it. Such reactions are an indication of just how
diverse the opinions are about this path.

That said, to hear some people talk about the Western Breach you'd think that
you'd have to have the climbing capabilities of your average bluebottle in order
to make it to the top. Suffice to say: you don't. Yes, this route is a little trickier in
parts. And yes, after snowfall the route up can be icy and an ice axe may be
required in really extreme conditions, though it is *only* in extreme conditions. But
as with all the trails in this book no technical climbing know-how is necessary –
just the ability to haul yourself up by your hands on occasion when required.

So what are the benefits of doing this route? Well, firstly, the Western Breach
is the only one that enters directly into the crater as opposed to peaking at the top
of the rim that rises above the crater floor. As such, this is the route to take if you
want to explore the Ash Pit, Reusch Crater, Furtwangler Glacier and other features of the summit. (Though it's possible to visit these features even though you
climbed to the summit on other routes, few actually do so; whatever their intentions before they reach the top of Kibo, by the time trekkers get there via
Gillman's or Stella Point they're usually too knackered or in too much pain to
spend the two hours-plus necessary to explore the crater.) And the other main
benefit of climbing via the Western Breach is, of course, the kudos that comes
with having conquered the hardest non-technical route Kilimanjaro has to offer.

Note that once upon a time the Western Breach was the one trail to the summit that was often tackled during the day rather than at night, traditionally by
those intending to camp on the summit. Despite this, the general consensus
amongst Kili connoisseurs is that it is still much easier to tackle 'The Breach'
at night, when the scree, shale and rocks are frozen and thus less likely to move
when you step on them. Furthermore, after dark the occasionally vertiginous
drops are invisible, which makes climbing for vertigo sufferers much easier.
Indeed for safety reasons KINAPA now insist that everybody is away from Arrow
Glacier Campsite by 5am, in order that they are clear of the area with the greatest
risk of rockfall by 7am (ie the first hour after sunrise). There are still a few groups
who tackle it by day but, like both of the other routes up Kibo, the Western Breach

is now mostly attempted at night. Do note, finally, that this route, though the shortest way to the top, is often the most expensive if you intend to camp at the summit because it is usual for porters to receive a premium to climb up Kibo. This is understandable; on all other routes they don't go above around 4700m (ie the altitude of the last campsite/huts), whereas here they have to go to the crater (above 5700m), and carry all their load up the trickiest route too.

Stage 5: Lava Tower to Arrow Glacier Campsite [Map 18, p296]
Distance: 2.5km
Altitude gained: 244m

By our reckoning this particular leg, even if taken *pole pole*, lasts little longer than an hour and a quarter, yet it's not unusual for trekking agencies to set aside an entire day for it. In one respect this seems a little over-cautious and does lead to a situation where, that hour aside, you'll be spending the rest of your day freezing your butt off inside your tent. On the other hand, it's a good idea to take your time at this altitude. After all, save for

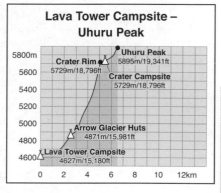

Lava Tower Campsite – Uhuru Peak

the crater camp this is the highest place where you can pitch your tent on the mountain (the altitude of Arrow Glacier Campsite being 4871m); and that kind of altitude should always be taken seriously.

Furthermore, the walk, though only sixty minutes or so in duration, is still quite exhausting, it being uphill all the way. You begin by crossing a stream or two (one of which, Bastions Stream, runs below Lava Tower) before climbing steeply in a south-easterly direction to the top of a ridge. Near the top of the climb you pass an old trail running directly from Lava Tower to the Western Breach Route that bypasses the Arrow Glacier Campsite altogether; it's a path that's seldom used these days and unless your guide points it out to you, it's easily missed. Descending for a few seconds to a stream and then climbing to a second ridge, by following the direction of that ridge eastwards you soon come to the **Arrow Glacier Campsite**. Engulfed by avalanches and often subject to the vagaries of the extreme conditions up here, this place has always been a bit of a mess and little has changed. Whilst the rubbish is depressing, it's the toilets that are the most revolting spectacle, with the ones that haven't been destroyed now home to an entirely new geological form: neither stalactite nor stalagmite, but stalacshite. Console yourself with the thought that if you're not spending a night on the summit, you probably won't be spending a full night here but should be away by 2am. Happy Camping!

Incidentally, you are now just 6m lower than the summit of the Vinson Massif – at 4877m, the highest point in Antarctica.

TRAIL GUIDE AND MAPS

TRAIL GUIDE AND MAPS

| LAVA TOWER CAMPSITE | 75 MINS → | ARROW GLACIER CAMPSITE | 50 MINS → | RED ROCK BAND | 150 MINS → | CRATER RIM |

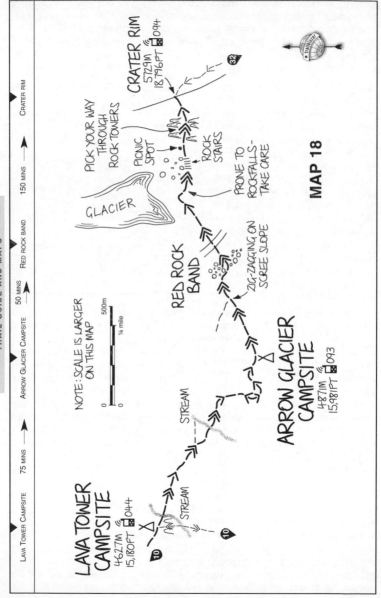

MAP 18

CRATER RIM
5729M
18,796FT 094+

PICK YOUR WAY THROUGH ROCK TOWERS

PICNIC SPOT

ROCK STAIRS

PRONE TO ROCKFALLS - TAKE CARE

GLACIER

RED ROCK BAND

ZIG-ZAGGING ON SCREE SLOPE

NOTE: SCALE IS LARGER ON THIS MAP

500m
¼ mile
0

STREAM

ARROW GLACIER CAMPSITE
4871M
15,981FT 093

LAVA TOWER CAMPSITE
4627M
15,180FT 044+

STREAM

STREAM

Stage 6: Arrow Glacier Campsite to Uhuru Peak
[Map 18, p296; Map 32, p335]
Distance 4km; altitude gained: 1024m
Though we've talked as if there is one set path from campsite to crater rim, this isn't actually the case; the path changes as snow and rockfalls dictate. Every guide has his own way of tackling the ascent, too. As such, the map opposite and the description that follows may differ from the exact route you end up taking. But whatever route you take, rest assured it will be steep, and it will be exhausting.

Having said that each path up the Western Breach is unique, your guide will doubtless aim for the rocky ridge that you can see from the Arrow Glacier Campsite which runs from the rock towers near the crater down towards the camp (and is often called the 'Stone Train'). It will take around an hour and three quarters before you properly join this ridge (soon after crossing a second stream), a walk that includes the most dangerous part of the ascent, where rockfalls are frequent. Furthermore, this area is often also covered in snow and many a guide has lost the path here. Successfully gain the ridge and about 15 minutes later you'll find yourself at the foot of the so-called **Rock Stairs** – natural steps that, after the shifting scree and rocks of the previous hour and three quarters, come as something of a relief. These stairs are also viewed as a 'Point of No Return' by the

The Western Breach disaster
On Wednesday 4 January, 2006, three climbers were killed in a rockfall on the Western Breach Route. Another member of their party, together with four porters, were injured in the incident.

The rockslide was caused by the collapse of a glacial deposit, estimated to weigh up to 39 tonnes. The rocks are believed to have tumbled some 150m and were travelling at 39m per second when they hit the climbers.

Following the tragedy, the route was closed for over a year while studies were made into the accident and its causes, finally reopening in late 2007. Yet there are many in the trekking community who are unhappy that it has been reopened at all. In particular, the decision to reopen without changing the course of the path has angered some: following the accident a 'death zone' – the part of the path where trekkers were considered to be most at risk from rockfalls – was identified. Lying between 5210m and 5310m (17,120ft and 17,417ft), it was this part of the trail that lay directly beneath the source of many rockfalls, and where trekkers were particularly vulnerable to being hit.

Some agencies were thus dismayed when KINAPA reopened the path without any modifications or reroutings away from this area. Instead, KINAPA's only concession to safety was to insist that trekkers wear safety helmets on the route – a stipulation that some agencies consider to be futile in the face of a full-scale rockfall. These days, in addition to helmets, many agencies also insist that their trekkers sign waiver forms that clear the agency from any liability for any accident that may occur.

While we don't want to dissuade people from choosing the Western Breach as their ascent route up Kibo, before opting for that trail you may want to consider why the agencies are taking these extra precautions and whether the authorities have really done enough to prevent another catastrophe on this route.

You can read a first-hand report of the accident by one of the guides at 🖳 www.jo-anderson.com/pages/20060104_kili_popup.html.

porters who, once they see that you've reached here, consider that there's no turning back and thus break camp and march off to Mweka (unless you're planning to sleep at Crater Camp, of course, in which case they'll be right behind you).

The stairs take about 40 minutes to tackle altogether, at the end of which you find yourself on a small, flat space that's often used as a **picnic spot** by those tackling the Western Breach during the day. Dirty and chilly, a more inhospitable picnic spot it would be hard to find, though you do get great views down to the Barranco Campsite. Beyond the picnic site the stairs are replaced by a path that's just as steep, though you have to tackle this section without the benefit of any steps. The trail picks its way between the rocky towers guarding the crater; but persevere for another 40 minutes and you'll find yourself finally gaining the crater rim, with the **Furtwangler Glacier** on your left the first of many spectacular sights up here. Walking on level ground for a change, it takes around ten minutes to reach the **Crater Campsite**, set amongst boulders at the foot of the climb up to Uhuru. The path up to the **Reusch Crater** and **Ash Pit Viewpoint**, 40 minutes away, bends north round and behind the Furtwangler Glacier. For more details on what's up here, see p334.

The stiff switchback climb up to Uhuru, 50 minutes away, lies to the south of the campsite, clearly etched into the crater wall. It's a hard climb and you'll be cursing every zigzag and switchback on the way. But keep going: the sense of achievement at the top is beyond compare. And it's a feeling that will stay with you all the way down, and all the way back to your home country. Because if you get to the summit, you'll believe you can do anything.

Oh, to be able to bottle that feeling...

Western Breach Route

The Shira Plateau Route

[MAP 19 p300; MAP 16, p290; MAP 17, p293]

Distance: From Londorossi Gate to Morum Barrier, 6.3km; Morum Barrier to Simba Cave, 6km; Simba Cave to Shira Huts, 3.6km. Altitude gained: 1187m from Londorossi Gate (2213m) to Morum Barrier (3400m), 495m from Morum Barrier to Shira Huts (3895m).

This is the older of the two trails and definitely inferior. The main problem is that for much of the first part you'll be walking on a 4WD road. Of course you could opt to drive to the end of the road, or at least the Morum Barrier which is as far as non-emergency vehicles are allowed; but then you'll be missing out on the entire forest zone and, more importantly, some precious acclimatization, for you'll be starting your trek at around 3400m. Still, if this route does have one thing in its favour it is that, apart from the odd rescue car zooming past, you'll be just about certain to have the first part of the walk all to yourself.

Assuming you choose to start your walk at the gate, the first day is about six hours long (depending on where, exactly, the car drops you). During those six hours you'll leave the forest – which is, to be fair, gorgeous around here – for the heather and moorland zone, with the Ngare Nairobi River an almost permanent presence to your right. The **first campsite** on the trail is sandwiched between the road and the river. It's used so seldom that there are several different names for it though **River Camp** (approximately 3100m) seems the most popular. Away to the south the northern slopes of the Shira Ridge loom up, while to your east lies the Morum Barrier. But that's for tomorrow...

For the first couple of hours of the **second stage** the path winds mercilessly up the slope towards, and then to the south of, **Morum Hill**. Beyond the hill is the **Morum Barrier**, where many Shira trekkers are dropped off – only emergency vehicles are allowed beyond here. If you *have* alighted here, depending on what time of day it is you can either walk for a couple of hours to one of the campsites on the plateau, or set up tent by the barrier and begin walking tomorrow.

This barrier marks the start of the Shira Plateau, where you'll be spending the next couple of days. The road continues south-south-east from the barrier, from where it's about another two hours to the junction with the Lemosho route and the **Simba Cave Campsite** (3640m). For details of the trail from here, please see p289.

TRAIL GUIDE AND MAPS

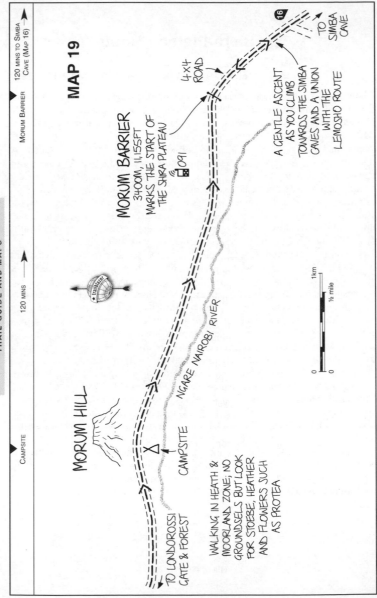

CAMPSITE

120 MINS

MORUM BARRIER

120 MINS TO SIMBA CAVE (MAP 16)

MAP 19

MORUM HILL

TO LONDOROSSI GATE & FOREST

CAMPSITE

NGARE NAIROBI RIVER

WALKING IN HEATH & MOORLAND ZONE; NO GROUNDSELS BUT LOOK FOR STOEBE, HEATHER AND FLOWERS SUCH AS PROTEA

MORUM BARRIER
3400M, 11,155FT
MARKS THE START OF
THE SHIRA PLATEAU

📷 091

4×4 ROAD

A GENTLE ASCENT AS YOU CLIMB TOWARDS THE SIMBA CAVES AND A UNION WITH THE LEMOSHO ROUTE

16

TO SIMBA CAVE

0   1km

0   ½ mile

The Rongai Route

Please convey to the seven blind climbers who reached the summit of Kilimanjaro my warm congratulations on their splendid achievement. **Queen Elizabeth II** in a telegram to Geoffrey Salisbury who, with his team of young, blind African trekkers, used the Rongai Route for their attempt on the mountain.

Whether it was the praises we heaped on this route in the last edition or the improvement in the road heading from Marangu to the Kenyan border that leads to the start of this trek, the Rongai Route has become inordinately popular over the past couple of years. Where once you had a 50:50 chance of having the trail to yourself, these days you'll be lucky indeed to avoid the hordes.

While many will see the Rongai's new found popularity as a drawback, it can't be denied that it is deserved – even though, at first glance, this trail seems decidedly unattractive. The lower slopes at the very start of the trail have been denuded by farmers and present a bleak landscape, the 'forest' for the first hour here being nothing more than a pine plantation. Nor is the 'proper' native forest that you do eventually walk through that spectacular either, being little more than a narrow band of (albeit pretty) woodland which soon gives way to some rather hot and shadeless heathland. Indeed, the parched character of Kili's northern slopes often means trekking parties have to carry water along the way (often all the way from the Third Cave Campsite to the Outward Bound Hut if taking the regular Rongai Route without the diversion to Mawenzi Tarn); your agency should have supplied you with enough porters for this. And then there's the expense: if you are booking your trek in Moshi, Arusha or Marangu, the cost of a Rongai trek can be higher than all other trails except Lemosho/Shira due to the expense of travelling to the start of the trek.

So why, if this route is more expensive, far-flung and barren than all the others, has it become so popular? Well for one thing, there's the **wildlife**. Because

---

❏ **Mobile reception on the Rongai Route**

Mobile reception on the the Rongai Route is not great, though it's better if you are taking the Mawenzi Tarn variation. As always, mobile reception depends a lot on which network you are with. Guides say that you can get reception by the **Hut at Simba Camp** – though I have to say I've never managed it. One place where I do always get reception, however, is at the popular resting place on the large flat rock during the second morning. Second Caves also has reasonable reception. Thereafter, however, on the regular Rongai Route the chances to use your phone are limited. Those taking the trail via Mawenzi Tarn will find reception at **Kikelelwa** comes and goes; while at **Mawenzi Tarn** it is also intermittent, though more reliable by the toilets. Crossing the Saddle there is usually no reception, so the next time you'll be able to use your mobile phone will be at **Gillman's** (possibly), **Stella** or **Uhuru Peak**.

❏ **What's this route called again?**

The name **Rongai Route** is actually something of a misnomer. It may be the name that everybody uses but, strictly speaking, it's not the correct one. The real, original Rongai Route used to start at the border village of the same name but was closed several years ago by the authorities who decided that two trails on a side of the mountain that few trekkers visit was unnecessary. You will still see this route marked on older maps, but today all trekkers who wish to climb Kilimanjaro from the north now follow a different trail, also known as the **Loitokitok Route** after the village that lies near the start. Just to confuse the issue still further, this isn't officially the correct name either, for along the trail you'll see various signs calling this trail the **Nalemuru Route** – or, occasionally, Nalemoru – though this name is rarely used by anyone.

of its proximity to Amboseli, your chances of seeing the local wildlife here are greater than on any other route bar those starting in the far west on the Shira Plateau. During the research for the first edition of this book we encountered a troop of colobus monkeys, while later that same day we came across an elephant skull, with elephant droppings and footprints nearby; and at night our little party was kept awake by something snuffling around the tents (a civet cat, according to our guide, though presumably one wearing heavy hobnail boots to judge by the amount of noise it was making). Buffaloes also frequent the few mountain streams on these northern slopes (though, as previously mentioned, these streams, never very deep, are almost always dry except in the rainy season, and consequently the buffaloes choose to bathe elsewhere for most of the year). The **flora** is different here too, with its juniper and olive trees. And if at the end of the **26.8km** (37.65km if taking the Mawenzi Tarn Diversion) ascent to Uhuru Peak you do feel you've somehow missed out on some of the classic features of Kili – lobelias, for example, or the giant groundsels, which don't appear regularly on the northern side except near the Kikelelwa Camp on the diversion up to Mawenzi Tarn – then fear not, as both can be found in abundance on the 35.5km-long Marangu Route, **the designated descent** for those coming from Rongai. Furthermore, opt for the extra day – which we strongly advise, for reasons not only of acclimatization – and you will spend that extra night at the **Mawenzi Tarn Hut**, which not only allows you to savour some gobsmacking views across to Kibo from the top of the ridge above the tarn but also gives you the chance the following day to walk across the Saddle, many people's favourite part of the mountain. And finally, when it comes to the ascent, we found the walk from the Outward Bound Huts to Gillman's Point to be *marginally* easier than that from Kibo Huts, (though admittedly the two do share, for the last three or four hours or so to the summit, the same path).

Other advantages include the drive to the start: from Moshi the road passes through a rural Chagga heartland, so giving you the chance to see village life Chagga-style (see p136), which we heartily recommend. Furthermore, if you manage to find other trekkers to join you and split the cost, the transport should not be too expensive.

PREPARATION

When booking your trek, it is important to get details right: are you staying at the cottages by Rongai Gate for the first night? (In which case you won't need to pay any park or camping fees to the authorities for that first day, though you will have to pay something to Snow Cap – see p209 – for using their campsite)? Check too that lunch on the first day is included, either taken at a café in Tarakea or, more usually now, at the gate itself. Finally, permits have to be collected at Marangu Gate; make sure your guide has that permit before embarking on the long drive to the gate.

The journey to Loitokitok

From Marangu Gate, the car returns down the hill to Marangu Mtoni before continuing round the dry, eastern side of the mountain, through the villages of Mwika and Mrere, host to a big market on Saturday, in the heart of the **Rombo District**. After them, in order, the villages of Shauritanga (site of a horrific tragedy in June 1994, when 42 schoolgirls were burnt to death in a dormitory fire started by a candle), Olele, Usseru, Mashima and Kibaoni emerge through the dust before, finally, around an hour and a quarter from the Marangu junction, you arrive at Tarakea, the largest settlement.

There is also a border post with Kenya in Tarakea; presumably your driver will know *not* to take the road leading to it but instead to keep on hugging the track which now heads north-west. The road is currently in a poor state up until about 18km from Rongai Gate, when tarmac makes a welcome return. Before then you'll need to keep your windows wound up and maybe even carry a face mask or a bandanna to prevent dust inhalation.

The wooden settlement of Loitokitok lies thirty minutes on from Tarakea, where a track on the left branches up to the park gate, situated at around 2000m. From the gate you can see the smart *Snow Cap Cottages*, which resemble (from this distance at least) Swiss-style chalets. It's a pleasant spot, with an open fire, TV room and a well-stocked bar. Book through Snow Cap in Moshi (see p209 for contact details).

STAGE 1: RONGAI GATE TO SIMBA CAMPSITE
[MAP 20, p305; MAP 21, p308]

Distance: 7km; altitude gained: 638m

It is an inauspicious start to the trek. Having registered with the park official in his wooden booth, and possibly having taken your lunch in the smart little tourist shelter behind it, your guide will then take you up the slopes through what, for many trekkers, is the ugliest part of Kilimanjaro, a hot and dusty blemish of **pine plantations** followed by fields of potato and maize, pockmarked here and there with the wooden shacks of those who eke out a living from the soil. (The pine in question, incidentally, is *Pinas caribas*, or Caribbean pine; native, according to one trekker, to a small valley in Belize where it struggles to grow but which thrives in the climatic conditions present on this side of the mountain.) True, there is more native forest just off the path to the right – but for some reason the

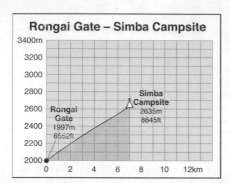

Rongai Gate – Simba Campsite

Rongai Gate 1997m 6552ft

Simba Campsite 2635m 8645ft

path for this first hour stead-fastly refuses to enter it, prefer-ring instead to stick to the perimeter of the plantations; and while there may be some interest to be had in studying the living conditions of rural Tanzanians, I'm guessing that the opportunity to walk past fields of vegetables was not one of the main reasons why you signed up to climb this mountain.

It is just about an hour before you turn right and escape into the lush green haven of the forest. When you do so, you'll be disappointed to find just how quickly the tall trees of the montane forest give way to the more stunted vegetation of the **heathland**, such as giant heathers and St John's Wort. It's tempting to blame the untrammelled agricul-ture for the paltry amount of decent rainforest here. No doubt the farmers have played their part but the truth of the matter is that this side of Kili has never had much in the way of rainforest – simply because it never gets much in the way of rain. Besides, this narrow band of forest is still teeming with wildlife, in particular **colobus monkeys**, with a troop often grazing by the entrance to the forest.

Leaving the forest on a trail that slowly steepens, about 50 minutes after-wards you cross a stream and a few minutes later reach the first campsite on this route, known as the **Simba** or **Sekimba Campsite**, at an altitude of 2635m. It's always good to get to a campsite, and this one in particular is pleasant: sur-rounded by heathers, with creatures snuffling about the tent at night and birdsong to wake you in the morning, this spot has a pleasingly wild, isolated ambience.

STAGE 2: SIMBA CAMPSITE TO THIRD CAVE CAMP
[MAP 21, p308; MAP 22, p309]

Distance: 5.8km to Second Cave; 3.3km to Third Cave Campsite (9.1km in total); altitude gained: 852m to Second Cave; Second Cave to Third Cave 449m; 1301m in total

This stage perhaps lacks the variety of other stages. For most of the day you will be walking up slopes flanked with heather and erica, with the twin peaks of Kilimanjaro keeping a watchful eye as you progress. If you're on a five-day trek, during this stage you will bid farewell to those lucky trekkers who opted to take the extra day and visit the Mawenzi Tarn Hut; they will go their own way after lunch. (That route is described on p308.) For the 'five-dayers', by the end of today you will have ascended more than 1300m. But there's no gain without pain and today is long, involving almost four and a half hours of steady walking on a steep, dusty path. Take comfort from the fact that tomorrow is much easier,

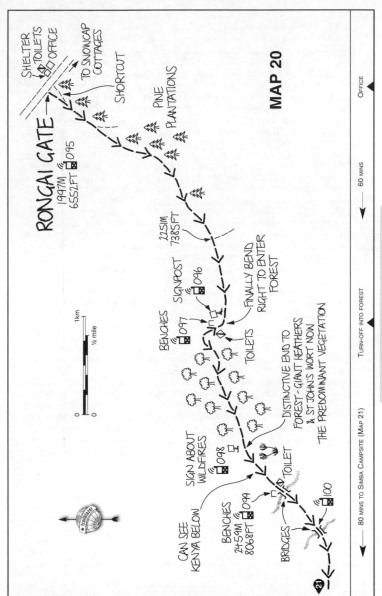

MAP 20

SHELTER
TOILETS
OFFICE

TO SNOWCAP COTTAGES

RONGAI GATE
1997M
6552FT 095

SHORTCUT

SHORTCUT

PINE PLANTATIONS

2251M
7385FT

SIGNPOST
096

FINALLY BEND RIGHT TO ENTER FOREST

BENCHES
097

TOILETS

DISTINCTIVE END TO FOREST-GIANT HEATHERS & ST JOHN'S WORT NOW THE PREDOMINANT VEGETATION

1km
½ mile
0
0

Trailblazer

SIGN ABOUT WILDFIRES
098

CAN SEE KENYA BELOW

BENCHES
2459M
8068FT 099

TOILET

BRIDGES

100

21

TRAIL GUIDE AND MAPS

OFFICE ◄ 60 MINS ◄ TURN-OFF INTO FOREST ◄ 80 MINS TO SIMBA CAMPSITE (MAP 21)

Wheelchair ascents

Getting to the top of Kilimanjaro is an achievement, no matter what your health, age or lifestyle. But there are some ascents that, in my opinion, really stand out. In particular, there are those who have attempted to reach the summit despite being confined to wheelchairs.

The first serious attempt to climb Kilimanjaro in a wheelchair was in 1998 by Brit **John Amos**, who was left paraplegic in 1976 in a traffic accident. In the end, John was prevented from reaching the summit by bad weather, although he did manage to attain the impressive altitude of 4812m (16,040ft). John's book about his climb, *The Roof of Africa on Wheels*, is a good read, giving one a good idea of the almost insurmountable obstacles wheelchair users face on the mountain.

John's record stood for five years until, on 1 October 2003, **Bernard Goosen** turned up at Africa's highest mountain with both his specially modified chair and incredible reserves of determination. Goosen has been disabled since birth as a result of cerebral palsy and is classified as quadriplegic. This wasn't enough to stop him, however, and twelve days later, on 13 October 2003, he became the first man to navigate his wheelchair to the summit of Africa's highest mountain. Unfortunately, the authorities were not so willing to recognize Bernard's climb, as there had been no way of checking that he had conformed to their strict rules. In particular, the guidelines for wheelchair record attempts stipulates that the person can be helped over obstacles for no more than 10% of the entire climb.

Rather than taking the perfectly justifiable option of telling the official bodies exactly what they can do with their rules, Bernard instead chose to return to Kilimanjaro to try again. A second attempt in 2005 ended in failure but he returned for a third time in 2007. Beginning at 12.40pm on 9 October, Mr Goosen chose the Rongai Route for his attempt this time. It was a good choice, being one of the shorter routes, though he diverted from it when better ground conditions for the wheelchair were available, until the actual path he took measured 27.1km (16.8 miles) from gate to summit. It took Bernard just 6 days, 3 hours and 20 minutes in total, reaching the summit at 4pm on the 15 October. What's more, despite requiring help over the rocks near the Second Cave (see opposite), and again at the crater rim at Gillman's Point, Goosen covered virtually all of the rest of the climb by himself, and well within the 10% maximum stipulated by the authorities who were pleased to verify his achievements this time. (Incidentally, there were 46 members that took part in the climb and amongst the other successful trekkers was Neil Stephenson, who lost his leg in a shark attack in his native South Africa a few years previously.)

Such an extraordinary effort on the part of Bernard was not without its cost, however, for having spent the night following the summit at Hans Meyer Cave, on the slopes of Kibo, he eventually arrived back at Marangu Gate, from where he was immediately evacuated to hospital and put on a drip after suffering from exhaustion.

Bernard Goosen's feat has since been emulated only once. On 30 September 2009 **Chris Waddell**, a paralympian skier from Park City, Utah, who had previously earned renown as the most decorated male skier in Paralympic history, winning twelve medals over four winter games (as well as participating in three summer games too), reached the summit via the Marangu Route with his One Revolution team. Waddell also became the first paraplegic to complete the climb all the way to the summit, beating fellow American and army veteran **Darol Kubacz** who in October 2008 make it to an altitude of 18,400ft (around 5608m) before having to turn back through exhaustion.

and that you have already ascended almost 2000m from the gate, and are now well over halfway to the summit.

If you haven't already been doing so, this is also the time to take things deliberately *pole pole* ('slowly slowly' in Swahili) – you're reaching some serious altitudes now, and mountain sickness stalks the unwary.

The path at the start of this 9.1km stage is, perhaps surprisingly, a westward one, its goal seeming to be the northern

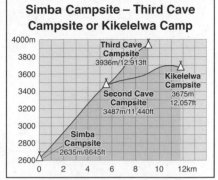

slopes of Kibo rather than the eastern slopes that you will eventually climb. The heathers are gradually shrinking in size now too, and while there are still some trees clinging on at this altitude, they are few in number and scattered. For these reasons, the first part of this stage is rather shadeless and very hot. After 45 minutes a **river bed** (dry for the best part of the year) joins you from the left and the path follows its course for most of the next hour. Look back occasionally and, weather permitting, you should be able to see a number of villages on the Kenyan side of the border, the sunlight glinting off the metal roofs. Continuing upwards, the path steepens slightly and begins to turn more to the south. The terrain up here is rather rocky and bumpy. The path continues south-south-west, rounding a few minor cliffs and hills and crossing a number of false summits, before eventually flattening out and arriving at a small, waterless cave. As inviting as the cave and the shade it offers now appear, this is not your lunch stop. That lies twenty minutes further on through lizard country of bare rocks and long grasses and is known as the **Second Cave** (3487m).

Before setting off in the afternoon, make sure you are on the right trail, for the path to the Mawenzi Tarn Hut branches off at this point (see p308): if your destination is the Third Cave Campsite but you find yourself heading south-east, reconsider.

The path to the Third Cave begins behind and above the caves, from where it now bears off in a more southerly direction than previously. Crossing a wide and usually dry riverbed, which in the rainy season is sometimes used as a playground by buffaloes, the path continues drifting southwards across increasingly arid terrain, the 'dry flower' helichrysum now interspersed amongst the heathers. As huge rocks begin to appear to left and right, temporarily obscuring Mawenzi and Kibo, the unmistakable outline of toilet huts appear ahead on the trail, a sure sign that the campsite is nearing, this time to your left across another broad riverbed. This is the **Third Cave Campsite** and the **last water point** before the summit.

For a continuation of this route, please go to p313.

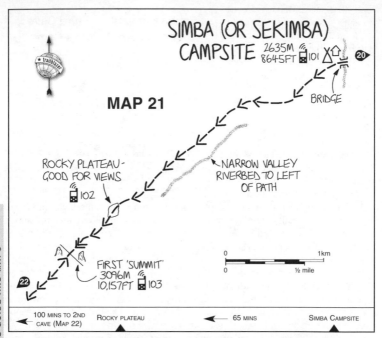

SIMBA (OR SEKIMBA) CAMPSITE 2635M 8645FT 📱101 △ ⬆️ ➡️ 20

BRIDGE

MAP 21

ROCKY PLATEAU-
GOOD FOR VIEWS
📱102

NARROW VALLEY
RIVERBED TO LEFT
OF PATH

0   1km
0   ½ mile

FIRST 'SUMMIT'
3096M
10,157FT 📱103

22

| ← 100 MINS TO 2ND CAVE (MAP 22) | ROCKY PLATEAU | ← 65 MINS | SIMBA CAMPSITE |

❏ THE MAWENZI TARN HUT ROUTE
[MAP 22, opposite; MAP 23, p311; MAP 24, p312]
This alternative path is wonderful. Great views, lovely scenery and a useful way to acclimatize. If you can afford the extra day on the mountain, don't hesitate.

Second Cave to Kikelelwa Campsite
Distance: 5.95km; altitude gained: 188m

From the Second Cave, the usual lunchstop on the second day, the path takes an abrupt south-easterly turn directly towards the jagged peak of Mawenzi. Traversing open moorland past vegetation blackened and damaged in a fire in 2007, the path meanders and undulates and, assuming you've already walked from Simba Camp this morning, you will feel rather drained by the time you stumble into **Kikelelwa Camp**, situated by a couple of caves by the Kikelelwa River, with giant groundsels and lobelias flourishing nearby. (Incidentally, I don't know why this should be so but whenever I have walked this stretch of the path – which must be a good half-dozen times now – it has always been either raining or very misty. That said, it has always brightened up in the evening to reveal Kibo's snowy summit peaking over the ridge that separates the campsite from the Saddle.) Compared to the morning where you gained over 850m, this afternoon's walk increases your altitude by less than 200m, though the distances of the two legs are about the same and, given the amount of climbs and falls, this latter walk is just as exhausting.

21

LOOK OUT FOR LIZARDS
IN THIS ARID ENVIRONMENT

SECOND 'SUMMIT'
3376M
11,076FT 104

1ST
CAVE

2ND CAVE
LUNCHSTOP
3487M
11,440FT 105

MAP 22

STREAM

UNDERGROUND
SPRING

MAIN
RONGAI
ROUTE

MAWENZI
TARN HUT
ROUTE

SERIES OF STREAMS-
OFTEN DRY EXCEPT
AFTER RAIN

MUCH OF THE
VEGETATION
ON THIS SECTION
WAS BURNT BY A
FIRE IN 2007

TRAIL GUIDE AND MAPS

THIRD CAVE
CAMPSITE
3936M
12,913FT 106

25

STREAM

23

0   1km
0   ½ mile

Kikelelwa Camp to Mawenzi Tarn Hut Campsite
Distance: 3.75km; altitude gained: 627m

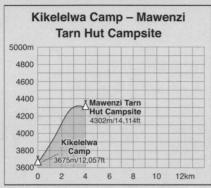

Kikelelwa Camp – Mawenzi Tarn Hut Campsite

Mawenzi Tarn Hut Campsite
4302m/14,114ft

Kikelelwa Camp
3675m/12,057ft

Though this stage to Mawenzi Tarn is relatively short at less than 4km and is usually completed in a morning (allowing time for a brief acclimatization trek in the afternoon for those who feel up to it), it's also steep as you gain over 600m, the path shedding the moorland vegetation as it climbs steadily. The **Mawenzi Tarn Hut** (4302m) is situated in one of the most spectacular settings, in a cirque beneath the jagged teeth of Mawenzi. There's a small ranger's hut here (though often nobody to staff it) and a smart new toilet block. Assuming the walk here was trouble-free you will have most of the afternoon to go on an acclimatization climb up the ridge to the west; if you're lucky, the sky will be clear, affording you fantastic views of Kibo, though in all probability you'll merely catch the odd glimpse through the clouds that usually roll in across the Saddle in the afternoon. But no matter, for you'll get the same views tomorrow morning when the skies should be clearer and the sun will be behind you too. The views back down to the Tarn – which, to be honest, is little more than a puddle with delusions of grandeur – are great too.

Mawenzi Tarn Hut Campsite to Kibo Huts
Distance: 8.9km; altitude gained: 412m

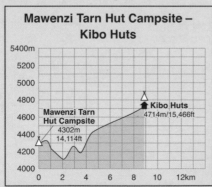

Mawenzi Tarn Hut Campsite – Kibo Huts

Kibo Huts
4714m/15,466ft

Mawenzi Tarn Hut Campsite
4302m
14,114ft

This lovely day begins with a slight retracing of your steps before you strike out westwards, crossing the ridge and dropping down the slope to tiptoe along the beautifully barren Saddle's northern edge. With views like screensavers to east and west, it's a rare trekker indeed who doesn't rate this day as their favourite on the mountain. The flora is sparse but do look out for eland which are said to stroll up here. You have two destinations at the end of this third day: the School Hut (Map 6) or, more usually these days, Kibo Huts. Both lie on the lower slopes of Kibo and both are just a few hours' walk away. Depending on which hut you end up at, please see either p314 or p258 for the continuation of your walk up to Gillman's and Uhuru.

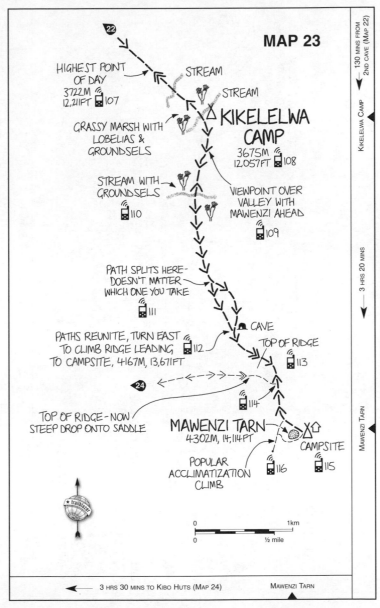

MAP 23

HIGHEST POINT
OF DAY
3722M
12,211FT 📱107

STREAM

STREAM

△ KIKELELWA
CAMP

3675M
12,057FT 📱108

GRASSY MARSH WITH
LOBELIAS &
GROUNDSELS

STREAM WITH
GROUNDSELS
📱110

VIEWPOINT OVER
VALLEY WITH
MAWENZI AHEAD
📱109

PATH SPLITS HERE–
DOESN'T MATTER
WHICH ONE YOU TAKE
📱111

PATHS REUNITE, TURN EAST
TO CLIMB RIDGE LEADING
TO CAMPSITE, 4167M, 13,671FT
📱112

CAVE

TOP OF RIDGE
📱113

24

📱114

TOP OF RIDGE – NOW
STEEP DROP ONTO SADDLE

MAWENZI TARN
4302M, 14,114FT

X⌂
CAMPSITE

POPULAR
ACCLIMATIZATION
CLIMB
📱116

📱115

0   1km

0   ½ mile

trailblazer

130 MINS FROM
2ND CAVE (MAP 22)

KIKELELWA CAMP

3 HRS 20 MINS

MAWENZI TARN

TRAIL GUIDE AND MAPS

◄— 3 HRS 30 MINS TO KIBO HUTS (MAP 24)   MAWENZI TARN

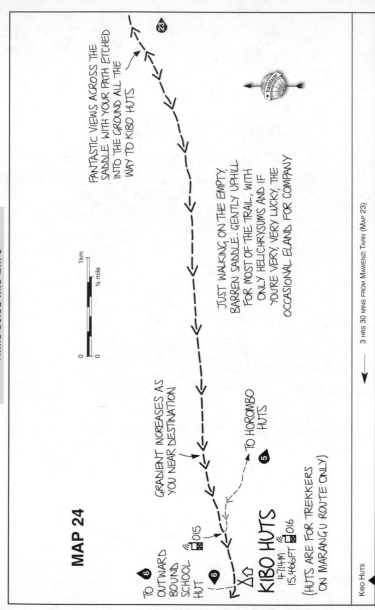

MAP 24

FANTASTIC VIEWS ACROSS THE SADDLE WITH YOUR PATH ETCHED INTO THE GROUND ALL THE WAY TO KIBO HUTS

23

JUST WALKING ON THE EMPTY, BARREN SADDLE. GENTLY UPHILL FOR MOST OF THE TRAIL, WITH ONLY HELICHRYSUMS AND IF YOU'RE VERY, VERY LUCKY, THE OCCASIONAL ELAND FOR COMPANY

GRADIENT INCREASES AS YOU NEAR DESTINATION

TO HOROMBO HUTS 5

TO OUTWARD BOUND SCHOOL HUT 6

015

016

KIBO HUTS
4714M
15,466FT

6

(HUTS ARE FOR TREKKERS ON MARANGU ROUTE ONLY)

1km
½ mile
0
0

3 HRS 30 MINS FROM MAWENZI TARN (MAP 23)

KIBO HUTS

STAGE 3: THIRD CAVE CAMPSITE TO SCHOOL HUT
[MAP 22, p309; MAP 25, p314]

Distance: 4.8km; altitude gained: 781m

This stage is little more than an *hors d'oeuvre* for the main course, which will be served at around midnight tonight. Yet it may surprise you to find out that over the course of this stage you climb 781m. By the end of it you'll be on the eastern slopes of Kibo, with splendid views across the Saddle to Mawenzi just a few minutes' walk away.

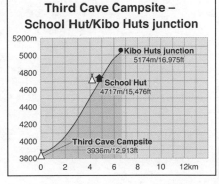

Third Cave Campsite – School Hut/Kibo Huts junction

- Kibo Huts junction 5174m/16,975ft
- School Hut 4717m/15,476ft
- Third Cave Campsite 3936m/12,913ft

Looking south-west from the Third Cave Campsite, you should be able to see today's path snaking over the undulations of Kibo. The path begins by retracing the last few steps of yesterday back to the river bed, which forks just a few minutes after the campsite into two distinct tributaries. The path, too, divides at this junction and is signposted, with your trail heading off to the right (west), crossing the western tributary and continuing on towards the foot of Kibo. It's a slow slog southwards up the hill. Even the heathers struggle to survive up here, disappearing for the last time less than an hour outside camp; only the *helichrysum* and the occasional yellow senecio continue to thrive, providing a welcome relief from the relentless greys and browns of the rocky soil.

After about 75 minutes a summit of sorts is reached, whereafter the path now heads more to the west, directly towards Kibo. The Northern Circuit bisects our trail around here, a path so seldom used that the junction is easily missed. No matter, for your path is clear as it bends more to the south, traversing Kibo's eastern slopes with the western face of Mawenzi now in full view to your left. This last bit of the walk is steep and, with the drop in air pressure at this altitude, quite exhausting. But after just over an hour from the western bend in the path, you finally reach the **School Hut** (marked as the Outward Bound Hut on some maps, its former name and one that KINAPA would prefer you didn't use), sitting in the shadow of some rather daunting cliffs. The huts sit at an altitude of about 4717m – virtually the same as Kibo Huts.

Officially you should still sleep in your tent rather than the hut; for a small consideration, however, (namely a beer or two) the caretaker may consider letting you use the hut if you prefer. Incidentally, if you need to fetch help for any reason, the Kibo Huts, larger and permanently manned by park staff, lie just 35-45 minutes to the south, the path beginning by the southernmost toilet hut.

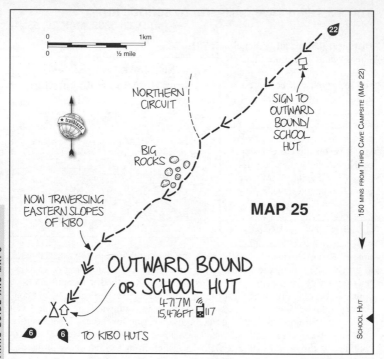

Within the map:

0 ——— 1km
0 ——— ½ mile

NORTHERN CIRCUIT

SIGN TO OUTWARD BOUND/ SCHOOL HUT

BIG ROCKS

NOW TRAVERSING EASTERN SLOPES OF KIBO

MAP 25

OUTWARD BOUND OR SCHOOL HUT
4717M
15,476FT
117

TO KIBO HUTS

150 MINS FROM THIRD CAVE CAMPSITE (MAP 22)

SCHOOL HUT

STAGE 4: SCHOOL HUT TO KIBO HUTS JUNCTION AND UHURU PEAK
[MAP 6, p259]

Distance: 1.9km to Kibo Huts junction, plus 4km to Uhuru Peak (5.9km in total); altitude gained: 457m to Kibo Huts junction, plus 721m to Uhuru Peak, 1178m total

The higher we climbed the rarer grew the atmosphere and the more brilliant the light of the stars. Never in my life have I seen anything to equal the steady lustre of this tropical starlight. The planets seemed to grow with a still splendour which was more than earthly, ... Assuredly, the nights of lower earth know nothing of this silver radiance.

Hans Meyer *Across East African Glaciers* (1891)

There is no direct trekking route from the School Hut to the crater rim. Instead, the path heads south from the huts to join up with the 'Tourist trail' running from Kibo Huts towards Gillman's Point – the trail that we have dubbed the Kibo Huts Route. Your trail joins it between William's Point (5131m) and Hans Meyer Cave (5259m). In our experience, it takes slightly – though only slightly – less time from School Hut to this junction than it does from Kibo Huts, so you may wish to start this stage a little later than you would if walking from Kibo Huts – say at 12.15-12.30am rather than midnight.

Finding the start of the path from the School Hut can be a little tricky in the dark so we recommend that you or your guide conduct a little reconnaissance while it's still light to ensure you know where you're supposed to go. Once you're on the path, which starts with a scramble up the rocks behind the School Hut, the trail becomes fairly clear, being marked with cairns the whole way. A repetitive pattern emerges during the walk: generally you are walking in a south-westerly direction over scree, but every so often the path turns more westerly and climbs more steeply over solid rock – these being petrified lava flows. At the end, a short descent brings you into the Kibo Huts 'valley' and a union with the path up to Gillman's. After the isolation of the previous two hours, the number of trekkers on this path comes as something of a shock. Hans Meyer Cave lies just twenty minutes above you along a series of switchbacks. For details of the path up to Gillman's Point from Hans Meyer Cave, turn to p260.

For the descent you'll be using the Marangu Route, details of which can be found on p324.

Common in the forests on the southern and western sides of the mountain, blue monkeys are nevertheless seen less often than their more flamboyant cousins the colobus mainly because their olive or dark grey coat makes them much harder to spot in the canopy.

The Umbwe Route

If Marangu is the 'Coca Cola Route' and Machame has the nickname 'The Whiskey Route', then what does that make Umbwe, (in)famous as the shortest (**24.35km** from gate to summit if taking the Western Breach Route, though it's **27.71km** if trekking via Barafu, making it longer than the standard Rongai Route), steepest and hardest of the trails on Kili? Sure, Machame is *fairly* steep here and there. But on Umbwe, the gradient is such that in a couple of places on the first day you can stand upright on the trail and kiss it at the same time. What's more, since the Machame path has been renovated, it's now only on the Umbwe trail that you'll be trekking on tree roots for much of the first day. So while Machame is still popularly called 'The Whiskey Route', since its recent renovation that whiskey has been rather watered down; and when compared to the unadulterated Umbwe Route, Machame starts to seem like pretty small beer.

That said, the Umbwe Route is still **a non-technical climb**. Taxing, but not technical. All you need are an iron will and calves of steel; this is truly a trek to test your mettle. The difficulty is that it's so damn relentlessly uphill. Indeed, looking back on the first couple of days we can think of very few places where you actually descend, the longest being the five minutes or so at the end of the second stage when you walk down to the Barranco Campsite.

As far as rewards go, while your calves and thighs will curse the day God paired them with somebody who would want to undertake such a climb, your heart and lungs will be thankful for the workout. Your eyes, too, will be grateful you chose Umbwe as they feast upon the scenery, particularly on the second morning as you leave the forest and find yourself walking on a narrow ridge between spindly heathers. The gobsmacking views on either side of the trail here are amongst the most dramatic the mountain has to offer, save for those on the summit itself. Your ears, too, will be glad that they're stuck to the side of your

---

❏ **Mobile reception on the Umbwe Route**

Mobile reception on the Umbwe Route is not great, though as always it depends a lot on which network you are with. I've never managed to get reception in the forest on this route, though on the second morning after struggling through the giant heathers I do often get reception – intermittently – then. At Barranco reception is not good, though on the ridge before entering camp it's OK. Then up to Lava Tower and Arrow Glacier it is fine, and even up to Crater Camp and, so I've been told, the summit. As for those heading to the summit via Barafu, while it's not great at Karanga I've always got pretty good reception at Barafu and at Stella, if you walk around enough, you can get it there too.

On the descent, it's usually OK at Millennium Camp but declines after that until you leave the forest.

head rather than anyone else's for they'll enjoy the break, this being the quietest trail of them all – at least until the second day when you find yourself joining the hordes at Barranco Camp, the busiest on the mountain. Once at Barranco, you can either follow the majority round to Barafu and access the summit via Stella Point; or, if you hanker after the quieter, more dramatic option once again, you can join the path up to Lava Tower and continue to the summit via the Western Breach (see p294). This latter option is the connoisseur's choice, no doubt, though be warned that it's an extremely risky strategy unless you take at least one – and preferably two – acclimatization days en route to the Arrow Glacier Campsite. Otherwise, the trip from Moshi up to Arrow Glacier Campsite, an increase in altitude of almost 4000m, will have taken you just three days which is far too rapid. Do this and you can kiss your summit certificate – and possibly a lot more – goodbye.

So that's Umbwe: dramatic views, blessed solitude and some terrific, invigorating walking – and all without the clutter and chatter of other trekkers. Those who know the mountain consider it Kili's best-kept secret. And it's hard to argue with that.

STAGE 1: UMBWE GATE TO UMBWE CAVE CAMPSITE
[MAP 26, p318; MAP 27, p321]

Distance: 9.6km; altitude gained: 1293m

The first stage of this trek transforms itself from a tiring tramp on a 4WD trail to a terrific trek on tree roots. It's normal to start this stage fairly late in the day for permits for this route are issued not at Umbwe Gate but at Marangu; if you specifically want to start early it might be worth asking your agency if they can fetch the permit the day before. (This may not be such a bad idea, for one guide told us of one occasion when, owing to

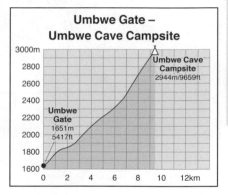

torrential rain that washed away the road leading to Umbwe, the group he was leading didn't actually arrive at Umbwe Campsite until 10pm!)

As the closest gate to Moshi, getting to the start of the trail should be uncomplicated. Turning off the Moshi-Arusha road just ten minutes after leaving the former, you bid farewell to the joys of tarmac by heading north on a mud track to Umbwe. Passing banana plantations (with much of the produce in this region going to make banana wine, bottled in Arusha) you soon reach the gate itself, where there's little save for some toilets and a couple of friendly and under-worked rangers. This is also the place where you should pay your forest fee – the only route other than Lemosho where you must fork out for the forest

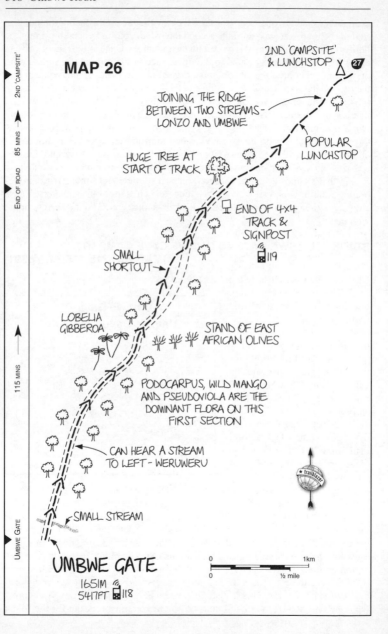

MAP 26

2ND 'CAMPSITE' & LUNCHSTOP △ 27

JOINING THE RIDGE BETWEEN TWO STREAMS – LONZO AND UMBWE

POPULAR LUNCHSTOP

HUGE TREE AT START OF TRACK

END OF 4X4 TRACK & SIGNPOST
📱119

SMALL SHORTCUT

LOBELIA GIBBEROA

STAND OF EAST AFRICAN OLIVES

PODOCARPUS, WILD MANGO AND PSEUDOVIOLA ARE THE DOMINANT FLORA ON THIS FIRST SECTION

CAN HEAR A STREAM TO LEFT – WERUWERU

SMALL STREAM

UMBWE GATE
1651M
5417FT 📱118

2ND 'CAMPSITE' | 85 MINS → | END OF ROAD | 115 MINS → | UMBWE GATE

TRAIL GUIDE AND MAPS

0 ___ 1km
0 ___ ½ mile

before you can begin (as usual, your trekking agency should have already sorted this out).

After the usual faffing around at the gate, you eventually begin your walk by setting off on a 4WD road. With monkeys (blue and colobus) crashing in the trees, turacos gliding above them, chameleons stalking amongst the shrubbery and some of Kilimanjaro's more celebrated flora putting in an appearance, including a profusion of *Impatiens pseudoviola* and, further on, its more glamorous, beautiful, and rarer cousin, *Impatiens kilimanjari*, it's a fine start. Look out, too, for *Lobelia gibberoa*, with its strange phallic brush growing out of the top of the plant. This route is one of the few places where you can find them on the mountain, though they appear in greater abundance on Mount Meru. If it's the weekend, you'll also be sharing the path with dozens of kids collecting fodder, probably illegally, from the forest.

No matter how interesting this initial walk is, after almost two hours it comes as something of a relief when the road finally ends and the Umbwe trail 'proper' begins. It's a path that continues the north/north-north-east trend of the road, though in our opinion it's considerably more charming. For much of it you'll be walking not on the soil but actually on tree roots. These can be your best friend, providing steps up a trail which would otherwise be too steep; or, if it's been raining, they can be your worst enemy, causing you to slip and swear.

Almost an hour after leaving the road you reach the first of two lunch-stops; halfway between here and a second possible campsite/lunchstop you realize that you've actually joined a ridge – and a spectacular one at that, with the great forested ravine of the Umbwe River on one side and the more modest dip of the Lonzo Stream on the other. No doubt you've also noticed that the trail is getting increasingly steeper. Indeed, this ridge is one of the steepest parts of the entire trek, and in places you'll be using the tree roots to haul yourself up with your hands. Luckily, there are plenty of tree roots around. The forest around here is rich and dark, the forest canopy minimizing the amount of light that filters through to the path. Distract yourself from the muffled screaming coming from your calf muscles by admiring the beauty of the forest here, the trees all knobbled, gnarled and heavy with moss. In between breaths, check out the beautiful red *Impatiens kilimanjari*, too, growing between those same tree roots that are helping you progress along the path.

An hour after joining the ridge you reach the first heathers on the trail. As those who've trekked on other routes will know, this often heralds the end of the first day and so it is here with the destination on this first stage, **Umbwe Cave Campsite** (2944m), lying just ten minutes away. More a glorified overhang than a proper cave, the adjacent campsite dribbles up the ridge and is a charming spot, a quiet place hidden in the upper reaches of the forest with *Impatiens kilimanjari* dotted here and there amongst the tents.

Let's just hope you started your trek in time to reach it.

STAGE 2: UMBWE CAVE CAMPSITE TO BARRANCO HUTS
[MAP 27, opposite; MAP 28, p322]

Distance: 4.75km; altitude gained: 1042m

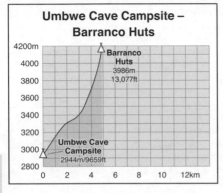

Umbwe Cave Campsite – Barranco Huts

Barranco Huts
3986m
13,077ft

Umbwe Cave Campsite
2944m/9659ft

This second stage of the Umbwe Route is a showcase for the weird and wonderful. It's the stage where you move from the forest, past a magical stretch of giant heathers and on to the moorland zone where giant groundsels – surely the strangest plants on Kilimanjaro – grow in abundance. The walking, as with yesterday's stage, is pretty much uphill all the way, though again is tiring rather than technical and thus nothing to fear. By the end you will have reached Barranco Huts, a wonderful spot at the junction of a number of routes and on the border of the alpine desert. Note that Machame Route trekkers will have taken three days to get to this camp, and those on the Lemosho Route four. It gives you some idea of just how steep the Umbwe Route is; it should also remind you, if you didn't know before, of the importance of building in rest days and of taking it *pole pole* from now on.

The stage starts with a tramp through one of the prettiest sections – no, make that *the* prettiest section – of heathland on the entire mountain, the sunlight penetrating through the giant heathers to dapple the carpet of soft mossy grass. We've never seen heather forest so thick, so uniform, so laden with bearded lichen nor so gorgeous. Though normally lumped together with the moorland above it, here, as with the Mweka Route that you'll be tackling on the way down, the heather zone is so very distinct from it. As the path veers to the left you notice you're overlooking the vertiginous valley of the Lonzo Stream (a tributary of the Weru Weru) while veer right and you find yourself staring down the giddying ravine of the Umbwe – and you suddenly realize you're balanced on a knife-edge ridge. Vertigo sufferers should perhaps concentrate instead on Kibo which, if the weather's on your side, glistens magnificently ahead.

Around 40 minutes after breaking camp you reach **Jiwe Kamba**, or 'Rope Rock', the name providing a clue as to how trekkers used to tackle this section. The rope's gone now and though the larger groups still bring their own, it's no problem if you didn't – it's just a few careful steps to the top, rope or no rope. The going is a little rockier from now on and you'll soon find yourself using the vegetation flanking the path to haul yourself up. As you progress further north the first helichrysums appear, their paper texture and white colour contrasting with the scarlet mountain gladioli, *Gladiolus watsonides*, which survives in

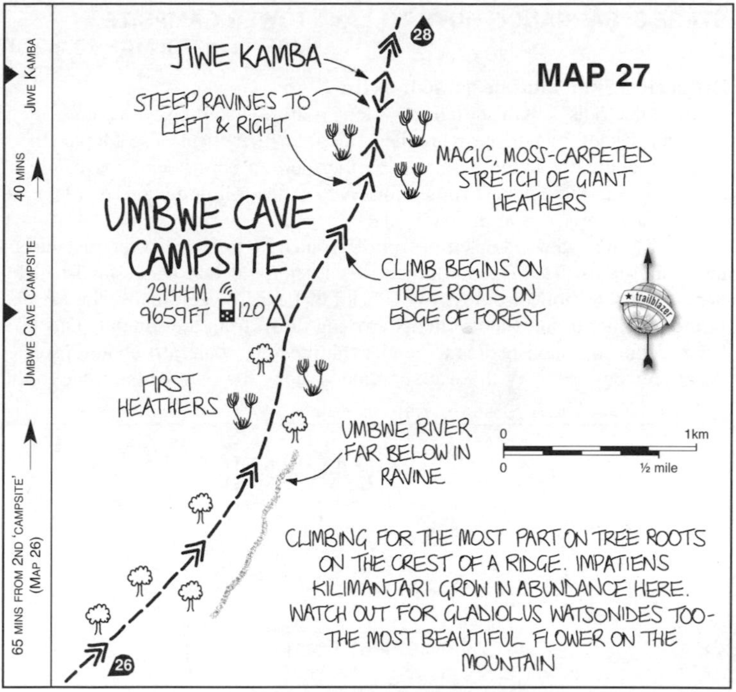
MAP 27
JIWE KAMBA
STEEP RAVINES TO LEFT & RIGHT
MAGIC, MOSS-CARPETED STRETCH OF GIANT HEATHERS
UMBWE CAVE CAMPSITE
2944M 9659FT
120
CLIMB BEGINS ON TREE ROOTS ON EDGE OF FOREST
FIRST HEATHERS
UMBWE RIVER FAR BELOW IN RAVINE
0 1km
0 ½ mile
CLIMBING FOR THE MOST PART ON TREE ROOTS ON THE CREST OF A RIDGE. IMPATIENS KILIMANJARI GROW IN ABUNDANCE HERE. WATCH OUT FOR GLADIOLUS WATSONIDES TOO- THE MOST BEAUTIFUL FLOWER ON THE MOUNTAIN
28
26
Jiwe Kamba
40 mins
Umbwe Cave Campsite
65 mins from 2nd 'campsite' (Map 26)
trailblazer

both the forest and heathland zones and is surely the most beautiful flower on the mountain. Continue still further and amongst the tussock grass and rocky outcrops the first groundsels also put in an appearance.

The ridge which you've been following eventually merges with a new one which you also climb and then follow, still heading north and with Mount Meru now a spectator in the distance to the west. Climbing to yet another rocky ridge, this one with clear signs of having suffered fire damage, you continue your progress north towards what we will call Barranco Ridge, which you start to climb before turning off right and down to the **Barranco Huts** campsite (3986m). For a description, please turn to p272.

It is at Barranco that you have a choice to make: left, north-west and up for the Lava Tower Campsite, Arrow Glacier Campsite and the path via the Western Breach to the summit. Or right, east and up to Karanga, Barafu and the path up to the summit via Stella Point. Presumably you will have already decided one way or the other. If you've opted for the more popular route via the Barafu Huts, turn to p272 for the continuation of this trail. Whereas if you're gunning for the Western Breach, read on...

STAGE 3: BARRANCO HUTS TO LAVA TOWER CAMPSITE
[MAP 11, p273; MAP 10, p270]

Distance: 3.5km; altitude gained: 641m

Many of the trails on Kili started as porters' routes. That is to say that the porters originally established them before the guides and their clients also adopted them and, eventually, the authorities too. Furthermore, it is of course the nature of porters to find the quickest route from A to B, with little thought given as to whether it's a pretty or attractive route.

And so it is with today's trail from Barranco up to Lava Tower, the start of the climb up to the Western Breach. It's a short-cut that was established by porters hurrying down from Arrow Glacier or Lava Tower round to the Mweka Route, in order to meet their clients arriving down from the summit. This trail has become so established as to render the previous route just about obsolete. (That previous route, by the way, continued along the crest of the ridge to the

TRAIL GUIDE AND MAPS

BARRANCO HUTS

↑ 65 MINS

ROCKY OUTCROP

55 MINS

ROCKY OUTCROPS

65 MINS FROM JIWE KAMBA (MAP 27)

DRIFT EAST OFF RIDGE TO...

BARRANCO HUTS
3986M
13,077FT 🔋046

CLIMB UP SOUTHERN SLOPE OF 'BARRANCO RIDGE' WHERE LOBELIAS AND HELICHRYSUMS DOMINATE

NOW ON NEW ROCKY RIDGE

ROCKY OUTCROP SURROUNDED BY EVIDENCE OF FIRE

🔋121
POPULAR LUNCH STOP ON RIDGE - VIEWS OF MOSHI

PATH DRIFTS NE TO JOIN RIDGE

PATH GOES THROUGH ROCKY OUTCROPS - FIRST GROUNDSELS APPEAR

ROCKY & STEEP - USE HEATHERS TO PULL YOURSELF UP

27

★ trailblazer

MAP 28

0   1km
0   ½ mile

west of the Barranco Campsite to the signposted junction at the head of the Barranco Valley and is still marked on most maps, though it's a rare guide – indeed, anyone – who'll follow it these days.)

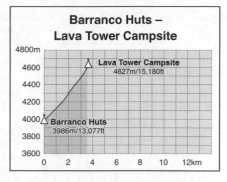

**Barranco Huts –
Lava Tower Campsite**

The only problem with this new route is that, as previously mentioned, it *is* a short-cut, and one moreover used by porters to *descend* from the mountain. As such, as an ascent route many people find it entirely too short and will have succumbed to the pain of altitude sickness by the stage's end. We therefore recommend you take this into consideration and maybe factor two nights at Barranco into your itinerary, with the rest day spent sauntering up to the head of the valley to help you get used to the rarified atmosphere.

The stage begins with a walk up the Barranco Valley. Come here later in the day and you'll find yourself hiking against a tide of trekkers on the Machame, Lemosho and Shira trails all coming the other way down the same path. But assuming that you've started walking in the morning it will probably be just you and your crew, allowing you to enjoy undisturbed views of Kibo through the stands of groundsels. About 25 minutes after setting off you leave the main path by a waterfall as you continue north, eventually crossing the stream you've been following since the day's beginning (and, indeed, as further down it turns into the Umbwe River, since the start of the whole trek). Recrossing it further upstream, you'll find yourself on a slightly gentler trail which continues straight ahead over two streams and on, steeply, up to Lava Tower. The entire walking, without breaks, would have taken you just three-and-a-quarter hours and you'll probably be at Lava Tower by lunch, allowing you plenty of time to savour this grim campsite's uniquely chilly, god-forsaken 'charm'.

For details of the rest of the walk from Lava Tower to the summit, please turn to p294.

Lammergeyer in flight

The descent routes

MARANGU ROUTE

Stage 1: Uhuru Peak to Gillman's Point to the Horombo Huts
[Map 32, p335; Map 6, p259; Map 5, p257; Map 4, p256]

Distance: 15.75km; (16.55km for Mawenzi alternative); altitude lost: 2174m

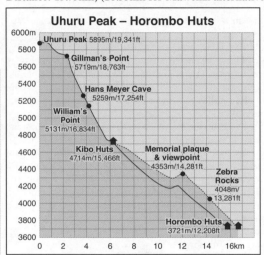

Uhuru Peak – Horombo Huts

Uhuru Peak 5895m/19,341ft
Gillman's Point 5719m/18,763ft
Hans Meyer Cave 5259m/17,254ft
William's Point 5131m/16,834ft
Kibo Huts 4714m/15,466ft
Memorial plaque & viewpoint 4353m/14,281ft
Zebra Rocks 4048m/13,281ft
Horombo Huts 3721m/12,208ft

TRAIL GUIDE AND MAPS

Few people remain at the summit for long: weariness, the risk of hypothermia and the thought of a steaming mug of Milo at the Kibo Huts are enough to send most people scurrying back down. There are two main ways of doing this: the first is to follow exactly the course from Gillman's to Kibo that you took getting up here, carefully retracing every zig and zag like somebody who has dropped a contact lens on the way up but can't quite remember when or where. It is precisely those people who are in greatest need of getting down fast who are the ones who usually use this slower method to descend.

The second way is to cut straight through the switchbacks and simply head vertically downwards in a sort of ski-style, using the now defrosted scree to act as a brake on your momentum. After the tedium of the previous night's heel-to-toe exercise, the sheer abandon of this method and the rapid progress made – it takes just over 90 minutes to travel from Gillman's to the huts this way – comes as something of a relief. Take care, however: far more people are injured going down than going up. Furthermore, do remember that every year at least ten thousand other pairs of feet tread on this part of the mountain and, at the risk of sounding like a killjoy, pushing down all that scree cannot be doing the mountain any good. Indeed, may we politely request that you use this faster method only if you need to descend rapidly? Otherwise, stick to the switchbacks which will be far less damaging to the mountain – and safer too!

❏ **Returning via the Mawenzi Route**   **[Map 5, p257; Map 4, p256]**
This is the more interesting path between Kibo and Horombo, encompassing entire groves of giant groundsels (*Senecio kilimanjari*), Zebra Rocks and the best panorama of them all on Kili. It is also seldom used.

From Kibo Huts the path descends once more to **Jiwe La Ukoyo**. Though there appears to be but one path from Jiwe, there is in fact another, much fainter path heading more directly towards Mawenzi across the Saddle. If you cannot make it out at first don't worry, just aim for Mawenzi and you will soon notice a faint but distinct path etched into the earth bisecting the Saddle. Ten minutes after Jiwe a junction with the even fainter **Northern Kibo Circuit** is reached (a signpost is the only evidence that there is a junction here at all), and thirty-five minutes after that the path begins to rise and fall as it follows the contours of Mawenzi's lower reaches. After another thirty-five minutes of following this undulating terrain you come to a summit of sorts, from where you can rest by a memorial plaque and gaze back over the finest **panorama** this mountain has to offer: the alpine desert of the Saddle, with a string of parasitic cones leading from the foreground to the foot of Kibo and with Mawenzi just over your shoulder. Spectacular. From here, the path runs due south through heather, past the path leading to Mawenzi Hut and on to the **Zebra Rocks** (a collection of rockfaces that resemble the flanks of a zebra), then down between the groundsel gullies until, 70 minutes from the unforgettable panorama and 2 hours 30 minutes since leaving Jiwe La Ukoyo, the roofs of the **Horombo Huts** appear beneath you.

Upon returning to camp, your guide should allow you to rest for an hour at least before moving on again to the **Horombo Huts**. If you ascended on the Marangu Route, heed the advice given at the beginning of Stage 3 (see p255) and ask your guide to take you back via a different route to the one on which you ascended. This usually means returning via the Saddle on the Mawenzi Route, a route we have described in the box above. If you return via the southerly, 'usual' route, expect it to take three hours fifteen minutes from Kibo Huts.

If you took the Marangu Route up the mountain, you'll be sleeping in the huts again; while those who took a different route (eg the Rongai Route which also uses this path to descend) will be camping outside them.

Stage 2: Horombo Huts to Marangu Gate
[Map 3, p253; Map 2, p251; Map 1, p249]

Distance: 20km (20.75km on Nature Trail – see p326); altitude lost: 1816m
Don't be in too much of a hurry to finish your trekking, for today holds lots of treats for those who take the time to enjoy them. If you have come from the Rongai Route this is the first time you will have seen forest so thick and vast on Kilimanjaro, and it's worth taking the time to appreciate the different flora on this side of the mountain. But even if you ascended by the Marangu Route, it still warrants a second look on the way down. Much of the scenery may be old hat to you by now but remember that you've still paid US$60 in park fees alone for the privilege of walking in the forest today, so you may as well make the most of it. And just as Lee Marvin in *Paint Your Wagon* sang that he'd never seen a town

❏ **The Marangu Nature Trail** [Map 1, p249]
A nice alternative for those who have already climbed via the Marangu Route and don't fancy taking exactly the same route back down is to divert off after one of the trail's many bridges onto the signposted nature trail. Only fractionally longer than the regular route, this trail's main attraction is that it is so rarely used; indeed, when we last walked along this path it was quite overgrown and it was clear that it hadn't been used in a while. This attraction could also be its main disadvantage – the path does have to divert around the occasional fallen tree and there are places where a number of alternative trails present themselves, so you do need a guide whom you trust to know where he is going if you are going to take this path. Assuming you have one of those then this really is a pleasant alternative to the main trail, and possibly for the first time on your entire trek you may get an inkling of just how Meyer, New, Teleki, von der Decken and all the other explorers of the nineteenth century must have felt as they carved their path through the forest. As a reward for taking the route less travelled the path culminates in a lovely waterfall – though it's only really 'active' during the rainy season. From there it's a simple climb up some steps back to the main trail, with the gate just yards away.

'that didn't look better looking back', so most people will agree that the forest seems so much more welcoming when you're walking *downhill* through it; and the views of Kibo are that much more appealing from over the shoulder, knowing that you'll never have to climb it again.

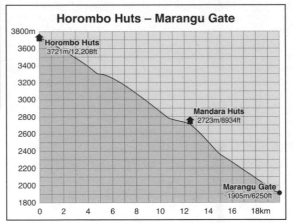

It takes about 2 hours 20 minutes to return from Horombo to the **Mandara Huts** which are, typically, the final lunch-stop of the trail. This is also your last chance to buy beer while it's still cheaper than water. From there, it's back into the forest and down to the **gate**, a journey of some 95 minutes. Name registered, tips dispersed and with certificate clutched close to your bosom, it's time to return to the land of hot showers and flush toilets. Your adventure is at an end – and civilization will rarely have felt so good.

Waterfall at the foot of Kilimanjaro. Engraving by Alexandre Le Roy from *Au Kilima-Ndjaro (Afrique Orientale)* published in 1893.

THE MWEKA ROUTE

The Mweka Route (20.6km from summit to civilization) is the designated descent route for the Machame, Lemosho/Shira and Umbwe Routes. As such, it is a very busy route though renovations a few years ago have ensured that it is once more in good condition.

Stage 1: Uhuru Peak to Barafu Huts and Mweka Huts
[Map 32, p335; Map 13, p276; Map 29, opposite; Map 30, p330]

Distance: 11.5km; altitude lost: 2789m

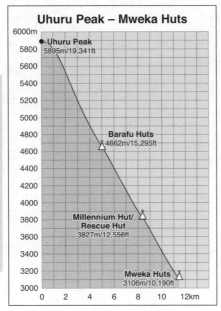

Uhuru Peak – Mweka Huts

- Uhuru Peak 5895m/19,341ft
- Barafu Huts 4662m/15,295ft
- Millennium Hut/ Rescue Hut 3827m/12,556ft
- Mweka Huts 3106m/10,190ft

What goes up must come down, and that includes you. The path back to Barafu is little more than a retracing of your steps of the previous night (assuming you climbed this way and not the Western Breach Route), though there is a slightly quicker, if more hair-raising approach: descending from Stella Point, after ten minutes or so you reach a boulder which earlier that morning you would have walked around: it's the same boulder that marks the very steep last thirty minutes or so to the crater rim. This boulder also marks the start of a straight ski-run down through the gravel that bypasses the zigzags of the regular route. Some people prefer to make it down as quickly as possible and so choose this trail; others find it too taxing on both nerves and knees, and opt for the gentler descent. Before deciding which is for you, read the advice about erosion in the last paragraph on p324 and if possible take the gentler descent. Note, too, that with this 'faster' descent it's not so easy to find your way back to Barafu: at one point you must turn right to rejoin the main path to camp or you risk ending up lost in the valley below. A Korean trekker was believed to have done this in 2008 – and has never been seen again. The entire descent takes about two hours from Stella Point, less if you take the 'fast' route.

You probably feel, on returning to camp, that you have earned the luxury of a brief rest at Barafu, and indeed you have. But make sure it *is* brief, for you still have another two hours and twenty minutes of knee-knackering downhill before you reach Mweka Huts, your probable home for the night. A pretty monotonous two hours and twenty minutes it is, too, as you head off due south and down for the entire 6.64km. In its defence, the descent is both large (dropping from 4662m to 3106m) and fairly gradual, which can only be good news for AMS sufferers. There is also some interest to be had in seeing how the vegetation changes along the way: at first, only the incredibly hardy yellow senecios are able to survive at the high altitude, but they are soon joined by their dry-looking cousins in the *helichrysum* family, and soon after that the first heathers appear, to be joined a little later by the proteas.

After forty minutes or so you come to a huddle of **signposts** warning you about the danger of starting fires around here. The signs also mark the junction with the little-used Southern Circuit: to your left on the slopes you can see paths from the Horombo Huts on the Marangu Route, while to your right are those coming from the Karanga Valley. Another path, an emergency trail from Karanga Campsite for those suffering from altitude, joins the Mweka Trail just above the green-roofed rescue hut. This hut was originally established to help out the suffering during the millennium when the mountain was swamped by thousands hoping to see the new era in from the summit. It's remained ever since and, now called the **Millennium Huts** or **Rescue Hut** (or even **High Camp**; 3827m), is a

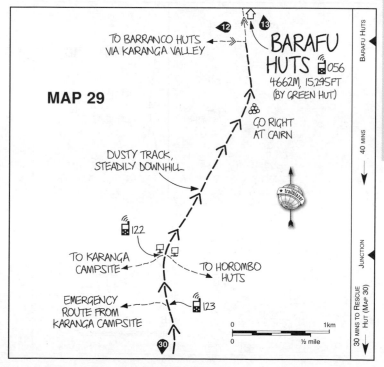

TO BARRANCO HUTS ←
VIA KARANGA VALLEY

MAP 29

BARAFU
HUTS 📱056
4662M, 15,295FT
(BY GREEN HUT)

GO RIGHT
AT CAIRN

DUSTY TRACK,
STEADILY DOWNHILL

📱122

TO KARANGA
CAMPSITE ←

TO HOROMBO
HUTS

EMERGENCY
ROUTE FROM
KARANGA CAMPSITE ←

📱123

0   1km
0   ½ mile

TRAIL GUIDE AND MAPS

BARAFU HUTS

40 MINS

JUNCTION

30 MINS TO RESCUE HUT (MAP 30)

campsite for those who prefer something a little quieter than the Mweka Huts; it's also a useful site to use when the Mweka has been flooded by heavy rain. It also has a water source nearby – another advantage over the Mweka Huts and one of the reasons, perhaps, why more and more groups are choosing to stay here. Coke and beer are available here too.

Immediately afterwards, giant heathers grow for the first time by the dusty path and, further down, the vanilla-coloured **protea** makes its first appearance, and thereafter dominates the pathside vegetation. The protea's presence ensures a healthy population of **malachite sunbirds** live around here too, as well as the little green **montane white-eyes** – so-called because of the distinctive white ring around their eyes. **Chameleons**, surprisingly, also make the heather their home.

You first glimpse **Mweka Huts** (3106m) about 40 minutes before you actually get there as you descend on a ridge between two valleys towards a small heather-clad hill. Rounding this, the path widens and flattens before turning south-west and climbing for one minute to the camp – the only ascent of the entire walk from Barafu. Mweka Huts is unremarkable save for the new toilets they've installed, by some distance the smartest on the mountain with a choice of

TRAIL GUIDE AND MAPS

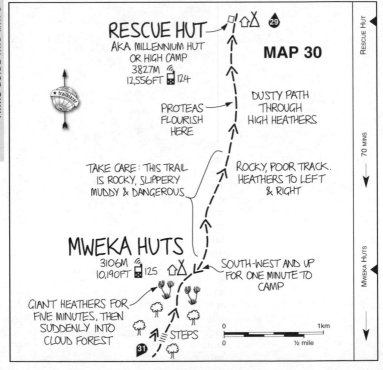

RESCUE HUT
AKA MILLENNIUM HUT
OR HIGH CAMP
3827M
12,556FT 📵 124

MAP 30

DUSTY PATH
THROUGH
HIGH HEATHERS

PROTEAS
FLOURISH
HERE

TAKE CARE: THIS TRAIL
IS ROCKY, SLIPPERY
MUDDY & DANGEROUS

ROCKY, POOR TRACK.
HEATHERS TO LEFT
& RIGHT

MWEKA HUTS
3106M
10,190FT 📵 125

SOUTH-WEST AND UP
FOR ONE MINUTE TO
CAMP

GIANT HEATHERS FOR
FIVE MINUTES, THEN
SUDDENLY INTO
CLOUD FOREST

STEPS

31

0   1km
0   ½ mile

RESCUE HUT

70 MINS

MWEKA HUTS

Western-style sit-down toilets or the traditional squat-over-the-hole long-drop, as well as lockable doors, tiled floors, and even, on occasions, toilet roll(!). Nor are all the advantages of this toilet visible, for beneath there is a newer, greener and more efficient decomposition system. Depending on whether this new decomposition system is a success, the toilets will then be rolled out to other campsites; Shira Huts already has some, and the ones at Barafu are under construction.

By the way, you may wish to share out your tips at Mweka Camp before you depart on this last leg: as porters all walk at different speeds, this may be the last time the whole group is together.

Stage 2: Mweka Huts to Mweka Gate   [Map 31, p332]

Distance: 9.1km; altitude lost: 1473m

By now you'll probably just want to get off the mountain as quickly as possible – which would actually be rather a shame, for this last section follows a very pretty forest trail alive with birdsong and flowers. Indeed, the variety, quantity and sheer beauty of the flora is incredible. This path has now thankfully been fully restored following years of over-use. Towards the end of 2001 it was so eroded that in parts trekkers found themselves walking in a two-foot deep trench. The worst bits of that path have now been abandoned altogether (in one place a bridge has actually been built to convey

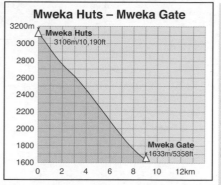

the new path across the old), and the new trail is in much better shape. The only complaint we have is that the authorities have decided to build steps on the steep parts, which we are sure is good for combatting erosion – but after five days or so of climbing, your knees will be screaming for mercy by the end. It's a lovely section of forest, but whether your mind can concentrate on anything other than the pain in your joints is another matter.

This stage begins in similar fashion to much of the previous one, by heading south and down. Less than five minutes after you start walking, you find yourself in cloud forest, the border between this and the giant heather forest so definite and distinct that you could almost draw a line in the ground between the two. Once again walking on a narrow ridge between two valleys, look around and notice how the trees now grow in height and girth, how the moss that grows upon them is thick, green and hearty where before it was stringy and limp, and how flowers such as the *Impatiens kilimanjari* once again make an appearance on the trail, and in abundance too. Its cousin *Impatiens pseudoviola* also lines the path, while the occasional beautiful vivid red mountain gladiolus flourishes

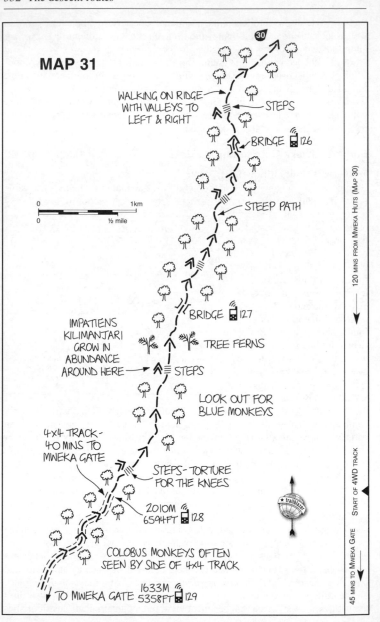

MAP 31

30

WALKING ON RIDGE
WITH VALLEYS TO
LEFT & RIGHT

STEPS

BRIDGE 126

STEEP PATH

BRIDGE 127

IMPATIENS
KILIMANJARI
GROW IN
ABUNDANCE
AROUND HERE

TREE FERNS

STEPS

LOOK OUT FOR
BLUE MONKEYS

4×4 TRACK-
40 MINS TO
MWEKA GATE

STEPS - TORTURE
FOR THE KNEES

2010M
6594FT 128

COLOBUS MONKEYS OFTEN
SEEN BY SIDE OF 4×4 TRACK

TO MWEKA GATE
1633M
5358FT 129

0 ____ 1km
0 ____ ½ mile

TRAIL GUIDE AND MAPS

120 MINS FROM MWEKA HUTS (MAP 30)

START OF 4WD TRACK

45 MINS TO MWEKA GATE

★ trailblazer

here and there, the delicate white flowers of the wild blackberry grow in clusters and the alabaster-white petals of the *Begonia meyeri johannis* litter the trail towards the end.

Around two hours after breaking camp, you'll find yourself walking on the start of the 4WD track down to **Mweka Gate** (1633m), a further 45 minutes away. At the gate you can buy a souvenir T-shirt to advertise the fact you reached the summit (curiously, there are no suitable T-shirts for those that did not). You must also sign the last **registration book** at the nearby park office, from where those who were successful can collect the appropriate certificate. If you're with a company that has four-wheel drive vehicles you might be met at the gate; the rest have to walk ten minutes further down the hill to the lower station, where there are a couple of shops and a bar. Those who succeeded in reaching Uhuru Peak can usually be seen standing around, their certificates dangling casually yet deliberately from their hands so that they are clearly visible to passers-by, in much the same way that Ferrari owners are wont to display their car keys. Your mountain odyssey is almost at an end: from here, it's a 30-minute drive back to the land of power showers, flush toilets and cold, cold beer. You've earned it – though if you do plan to celebrate in Moshi, please take more care than Meyer did upon his return to town:

In the evening, to show there was no ill-feeling, I treated the natives to a display of fireworks, in the course of which a spark from a rocket set fire to one of the men's huts.

TRAIL GUIDE AND MAPS

PART 9: THE SUMMIT

What's at the top?

The crater of Kilimanjaro is a primeval place and decidedly uncomfortable, yet I was drawn to it. The idea of spending some days and nights awoke a compelling mixture of reverential fear and wonder; similar, I suspect, to the compulsion which draws some people unquestioningly to church. And like churches, the crater also invites contemplation of the eternal mysteries. **John Reader** *Kilimanjaro* (1982)

It's only when you reach the top of Kibo that you realise that the mountain really is a volcano, and all you have done is climb to the crater rim.

The rim itself is largely featureless, though as the highest point on the mountain it has assumed a pre-eminent role and is the focus of all trekkers. The few bumps and tumescences on it have been dignified with the word 'Spitze' or 'Point' as if they were major summits in their own right. Heading clockwise around the rim from **Gillman's**, these bumps in order are: **Stella** (the aim of those climbing from Barafu), **Elveda**, **Hans Meyer**, **Uhuru** and **Furtwangler**; while just to the north of Gillman's is **Leopard Point**. The distance between Gillman's and Uhuru is a little over 2km, with the crater rim rising 176m between the two. The floor of the crater, covered in brown shale and rocks and boulders of all shapes and sizes, lies between 25m (at Gillman's) and 200m (at Uhuru Peak) beneath this rim.

Trudging around the rim to Uhuru is achievement enough. There are, however, plenty of other diversions to keep you on the summit for longer ...

WALKING ON THE SUMMIT [Map 32, opposite]

For most people, the conquest of Uhuru Peak, and a nice certificate that says as much is reason enough to climb Kilimanjaro. Some trekkers, however, always want to do just that little bit more, and if you still have some energy to burn once you've reached the summit you may care to take a quick tour around the crater itself. **Warn your guide in advance** of your intentions – preferably before you've even started your trek – for some react badly to the idea of spending any longer on the summit than is absolutely necessary; a little gentle cajoling along with a few hints about the size of the tip that awaits them at the end of the trip should do the trick. Make sure, too, that your guide knows his way around up there: you'll probably be a little short of humour as well as breath on the crater rim and following an ignorant guide while he tries in vain to locate the correct path to the Reusch Crater will do little to lighten your mood.

The standard way to reach the **Reusch Crater**, the Kibo summit's very own parasitic cone, is to ascend via the Western Breach, where a trail of sorts heads off to the north round the Furtwangler Glacier away from Uhuru Peak to the

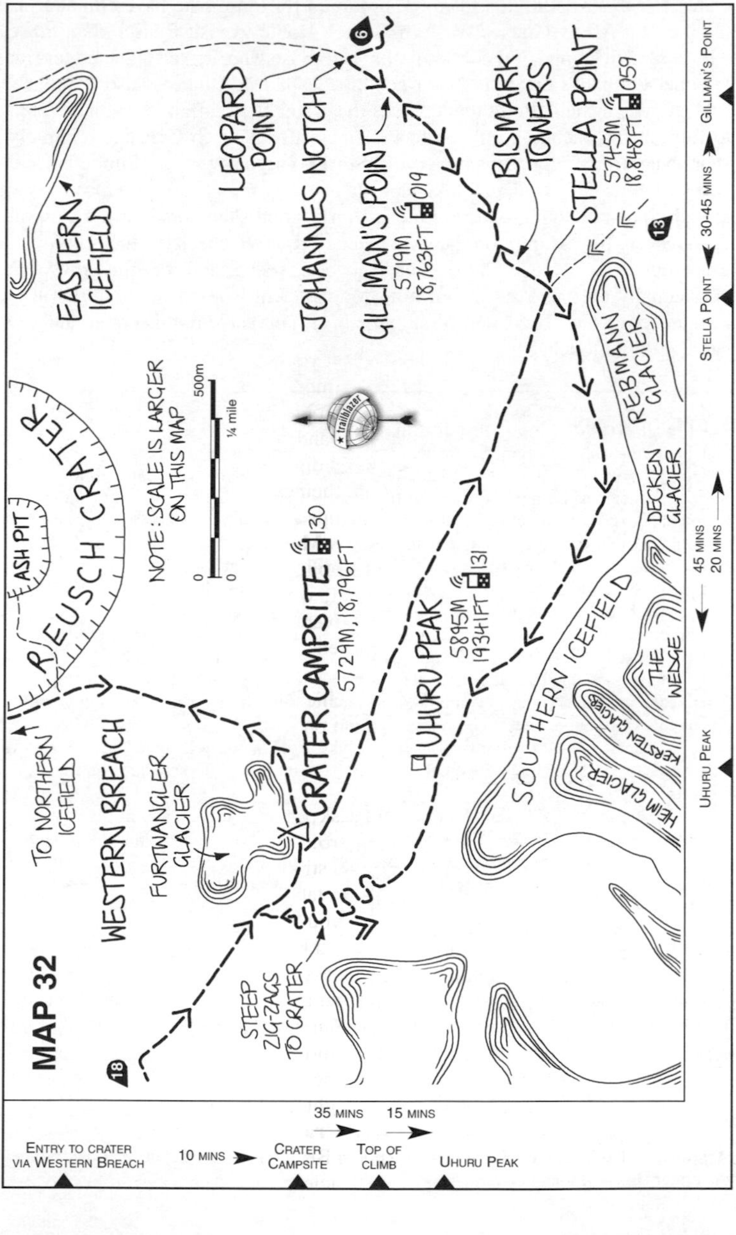

MAP 32

ASH PIT

REUSCH CRATER

EASTERN ICEFIELD

LEOPARD POINT

JOHANNES NOTCH

GILLMAN'S POINT
5719M
18,763FT 📷 019

BISMARK TOWERS

STELLA POINT
5745M
18,848FT 📷 059

To NORTHERN ICEFIELD

WESTERN BREACH

FURTWÄNGLER GLACIER

CRATER CAMPSITE 📷 130
5729M, 18,796FT

NOTE: SCALE IS LARGER ON THIS MAP

500m

¼ mile

trailblazer

REBMANN GLACIER

DECKEN GLACIER

UHURU PEAK
5895M
19341FT 📷 131

SOUTHERN ICEFIELD

THE WEDGE

HEIM GLACIER

KERSTEN GLACIER

STEEP ZIG-ZAGS TO CRATER

6

13

18

GILLMAN'S POINT ◄ 30-45 MINS ► STELLA POINT

STELLA POINT ◄ 45 MINS ► 20 MINS

UHURU PEAK

THE SUMMIT

ENTRY TO CRATER VIA WESTERN BREACH — 10 MINS ► CRATER CAMPSITE — 35 MINS ► TOP OF CLIMB — 15 MINS ► UHURU PEAK crater. For this reason, it is far more common for those who have climbed via the difficult Arrow Glacier/Western Breach Route to visit Reusch than those who ascended by one of the other paths. But those who arrived at the crater rim at either Gillman's or Stella Point needn't despair, for there is also a porters' trail from near Stella Point that crosses the crater floor to join up with the path to Reusch. The actual climb up to the rim of the Reusch Crater is relatively short but surprisingly tiring; if you didn't know you were at altitude before, you will now! This walk can take as little as thirty minutes from the campsite, though that's assuming that you are in fairly good shape; and on the summit this is a very big assumption. Having reached Reusch, check out the bright yellow sulphurous deposits, largely on its western side, and the fumaroles that occasionally puff smoke – proof not only that Kili is a volcano, but that it is also an active one. The smell of sulphur is all-pervasive in this crater, and the earth is hot to touch.

❑ **Is Uhuru Peak the true summit?**

Uhuru Peak and its unremarkable wooden sign (unremarkable, that is, except for the fact that some poor porter must have had to carry it up here once upon a time) has been accepted as the highest point in Africa for so long that it seems almost a heresy to challenge its claim. But recently a couple of people with GPS systems have cast doubt on this record by saying that they think that there's a spot that's actually, according to their GPS receiver, a little higher than Uhuru. Normally I would dismiss such claims as the work of a mind clearly befuddled by altitude. But there's just one problem with this: I myself, using a GPS receiver, happen to agree with them. The difference is not great – we are probably talking centimetres – but each time I have walked west past Uhuru Peak for a couple of hundred metres I have found my GPS telling me that I am at a higher altitude. (The exact spot where the slightly higher reading is taken is usually marked by a small pile of stones; not enough to be called a cairn but enough to be noticeable.)

This, of course, poses a whole series of questions. Should we move Uhuru Peak? Or at least the sign? Should we call this new summit by a different name, and if so, what?

Given the veritable can of worms that this opens up, I think it's probably best to leave Uhuru as it is, and where it is, if only to save the back of that poor porter who lugged the sign up the mountain in the first place and who is presumably in no hurry to run back up and move the sign a couple of hundred metres to the west. And besides, presumably many thousands of people have in the past measured the height of Uhuru Peak, and none have mentioned that it's not the highest spot.

So we'll leave it as it is at the moment. And if it should by some chance turn out that there is a higher point than Uhuru on the rim of Kilimanjaro, its name should change continually, and it should be named after whoever happens to be standing on it at the time, looking down (literally) on those celebrating at Uhuru.

(**Opposite**) Trudging past the Southern Icefield just after dawn on that final push round the crater rim. Not long now...

Within the Reusch Crater is the 120m-deep **Ash Pit** which, though it does not conspicuously contain ash, is said to be one of the most perfect examples of this sort of formation in the world. At 360m across, it's also one of the largest. If you reach the Ash Pit, you can truly say that you have conquered this mountain.

The faces behind the features

Most Kilimanjaro climbers are aware that Uhuru is Swahili for 'Freedom' and the highest point in Africa was christened this after Tanzania achieved independence in 1961. But do you know after what or whom other features of Kibo are named? Some of them are relatively easy: the Rebmann Glacier is obviously named after the first European to see Kilimanjaro (see p105), while neighbouring Decken Glacier is named after another eminent Victorian, Baron von der Decken, the first man to seriously attempt to climb the mountain. His travel partner, Otto Kersten, has his own glacier named after him next to the Baron's. Next is the Heim Glacier, named after Albrecht Heim, world renowned glacier expert. There's also the Furtwangler Glacier, sadly much reduced recently, which sits on the crater floor and is named after the first man to ski down the side of Kilimanjaro.

Herr Furtwangler also has a point on the crater rim named after him, as does Hans Meyer – the first man to the summit, of course – and the leopard which was found frozen in the ice back in the early years of the twentieth century. Curiously, however, two of the most well-known points on the crater rim, Gillman's and Stella Point, are named after quite obscure figures. The former, for example, was *probably* named after the first man to reach the crater rim after the mountain had come under British protection, one Clement Gillman, who reached this point (but no higher) in 1921. While Stella Point is named after the wife of Dr Kingsley Latham, a member of the Mountain Club of South Africa, and marks the point that they both reached in 1925. Latham then went on to discover the frozen leopard mentioned above, from which Pastor Richard Reusch took an ear as a souvenir (see p121) – and after whom the inner crater is named.

THE SUMMIT

APPENDIX A: SWAHILI

Of the two main languages you will encounter, Swahili, the national tongue, is undoubtedly the more useful and the one you will see written on signs and notices. There are plenty of Swahili dictionaries around: street vendors sell little green versions in Arusha or you can pick one up in souvenir stores for about a sixth of the price they charge. The other language, Chagga and its various dialects, is common around Kili but it is unlikely you will hear it outside the region. You will, however, curry favour with porters and guides on Kilimanjaro by learning a few words; see the box on p135 for a brief introduction to the language. Chagga dictionaries are rare, though you'll find one mentioned in *Appendix E*.

Basics

Yes	Ndiyo
No	Hapana
Good Morning	Jambo
My name is...	Jina langu ni...
How are you?	Habari gani?
Please...	Tafadhali...
Thanks (very much)	Ahsante (sana)
Do you speak English?	Unasema Kiingereza?
Help!	Saidia!
How much is it?	Kiasi gani?
Slowly, slower	Pole, pole-pole
Let's go!	Twendai!

Numbers

1	moja
2	mbili
3	tatu
4	nne
5	tano
6	sita
7	saba
8	nane
9	tisa
10	kumi
11	kumi na moja
12	kumi na mbili
20	ishirini
21	ishirini na moja
30	thelathini
40	arobaini
50	hamsini
60	sitini
70	sabini
80	themanini
90	tisini
100	mia
200	mia mbili
1000	elfu
2000	elfu mbili

Places

Bank	Banki
Laundry	Kufulia
Post office	Posta

Days of the week

Monday	Jumatatu
Tuesday	Jumanne
Wednesday	Jumatano
Thursday	Alhamisi
Friday	Ijumaa
Saturday	Jumamosi
Sunday	Jumapili

Travel

Bus station	kituo cha mabasi
Airport	kiwanja cha ndege
Port	bandari
Train station	stesheni
Ticket office	wanapouza tikiti
When will we arrive at...?	tutafika...jini?
Is this the direct way to...?	hii ni njia fupi kwenda...?

Food and drink

Beans	Maharagwe
Bread	Mkate
Chicken	Kuku
Coffee	Kahawa
Cold	Baridi
Eggs	Mayai
Fish	Samaki
Meat	Nyama
Orange	Chungwa
Pork	Nyama ya nguruwe
Vegetables	Mboga
Venison	Nyama ya porini
Water	Maji

APPENDIX B: SCHEDULES FOR KILIMANJARO INTERNATIONAL AND ARUSHA AIRPORTS

FLIGHTS TO KILIMANJARO

With the suspension of Air Tanzania international flights, there are currently just three main **international carriers** flying into Kilimanjaro: Kenyan Airways (who actually use their partners Precision Air to fly to Kilimanjaro), Ethiopian Airlines, and the Dutch airline KLM.

KLM (⌨ www.klm.com) used to fly every day in the high season to Tanzania, touching down in Kilimanjaro on their way to Dar. Unfortunately, it looks to us suspiciously like they are winding down their service to East Africa: their office in Arusha is now closed, and they are currently offering only three flights per week on Mondays, Wednesdays and Fridays. The flights leave Schipol (Amsterdam) at around 10.10am, arriving the same day at Kili at 8.35pm (total travel time 8hr 25min). This is certainly the most convenient way to get to Kili from Europe, particularly if you're coming from the UK where KLM have a great network linking various airports around the country to Schipol. Those flying from the US will also find KLM the most convenient option: flights from New York to Amsterdam fly around twice daily except Mondays, the flights arriving in time (no later than 7.35am) to catch the flight to Kilimanjaro; they also fly from Los Angeles daily except Monday but don't arrive until 1pm, so any onward connection to Kilimanjaro would involve an overnight stop in Amsterdam.

Ethiopian Airlines (⌨ www.ethiopianairlines.com) operate a pretty comprehensive pan-African network and are renowned for being cheap, and one of the most reliable of African airlines. They fly daily from Addis Ababa to Kilimanjaro via Nairobi, departing at 10am and arriving at 1.50pm. To connect with that flight, from London they have flights to Addis Ababa six times weekly, leaving 9pm twice weekly and 9.35pm twice weekly, both arriving after 7am but in time to catch the connecting flight to Kilimanjaro. They also have a flight that leaves at 1.50pm, arriving at 2am – less convenient if you then want the connecting flight to Kilimanjaro. From the States, they have a flight from Washington Dulles Airport five times a week, with their 10.05am flight arriving at 8.20am three times a week – perfect for the connecting flight to Kilimanjaro as long as everything runs smoothly.

Kenya Airways (⌨ www.kenya-airways.com), partners of Virgin Atlantic, also advertise flights to Kilimanjaro, though they will actually carry you only as far as Nairobi and another of their partners, Precision Air, will fly you from there. Nevertheless, it's a good service, flying daily at 8pm from London to Nairobi, arriving at around 6am, with a second one at weekends at 10.20am. This last one arrives at 8.50pm in Nairobi, which all being well should allow you to catch the last flight with Precision Air to Kilimanjaro at 9.30pm.

Regional and Domestic airlines to Kilimanjaro Airport

For the best overview of regional airlines – and the chance to book tickets – visit the website ⌨ **www.alternativeairlines.com**.

Air Tanzania (currently no website) have one flight a day to Kilimanjaro from Dar es Salaam via Zanzibar, the flight leaving at 2pm. **Precision Air** (⌨ www.precisionairtz.com), partners of Kenya Airways, fly on average around three times per day between Nairobi and Kilimanjaro. They also have around 3-4 flights from Dar every day. **Fly540** (⌨ www. fly540.com) fly daily from Nairobi at 11.30am, arriving at 12.15pm.

FLIGHTS FROM KILIMANJARO

KLM's flight leaves Kilimanjaro Airport for Dar at about 8.50pm before returning to Europe. **Ethiopian Airlines'** planes tend to hang around for an hour at Kilimanjaro Airport from the moment they arrive (see p340) before returning to Addis.

    Air Tanzania have one flight a day from Kilimanjaro to Dar es Salaam via Zanzibar, the flight leaving at 3.20pm. **Precision Air** have three flights a day from Kili to Dar, at 7.30am, 10.30am and 7.30pm, the middle one flying via Zanzibar first. They also fly to Nairobi four times a day (currently 6am, 9.05am, 3.30pm and 7.40pm), and also to Mwanza (9.15am), from where they continue on to Entebbe four times a week. **Fly540** also fly to Nairobi, and from there onto Entebbe, their flight leaving at 3pm.

FLIGHTS TO ARUSHA AIRPORT

Air Excel (☎ 027-254 8429; 💻 www.airexcelonline.com) have daily flights from various destinations in the Serengeti (Grumeti, Kleins, Seronera) as well as Lake Manyara, before finally arriving at Arusha at 12.10pm. They also have a daily flight from Dar at 4.20pm, and one from Zanzibar at 4.55pm.

Coastal Aviation (💻 www.coastal.cc) have daily flights from Grumeti, Kleins, Lobo, Mwanza, as well as the south and Ruaha and Selous.

Regional Air (💻 www.regional.co.tz) operate flights from Serengeti and Manyara.

Zanair (💻 www.zanair.com) operate a daily flight (except Thursday) from Zanzibar to Arusha, arriving at 12.50pm.

FLIGHTS FROM ARUSHA AIRPORT

Air Excel (💻 www.airexcelonline.com) have daily flights to the Serengeti (Grumeti, Kleins, Seronera) as well as Lake Manyara and a daily flight to Dar and Zanzibar.

Coastal Aviation's (💻 www.coastal.cc) 12.15pm flight arrives at Dar at 2.20pm (US$230), then continues on to Selous, Mafia and Kilwa. They also serve the Serengeti, Ngorongoro, Tanga and other Tanzanian destinations.

Regional Air (💻 www.regional.co.tz) also run daily flights to Manyara and on to the Serengeti, with another route taking in Zanzibar and Dar.

Zanair (💻 www.zanair.com) have a daily flight to Zanzibar at 2.15pm.

ZantasAir (💻 www.zantasair.com) run private charters all over Tanzania and are useful if none of the above offers a flight that fits your schedule.

APPENDIX C: TANZANIAN AND KENYAN DIPLOMATIC MISSIONS

TANZANIAN EMBASSIES AND CONSULATES ABROAD

Australia 3rd Fl, MPH Building 23 Barrack Street, Perth WA 6000; ☎ +61 (0)8 9221 0033; 🖳 www.tanzaniaconsul.org; also Level 2, 222 La Trobe Street, Melbourne 3000; ☎ +61 (0)3 9667 0243

Belgium 363 Avenue Louise, 1050 Brussels; ☎ +32 2 640-6500; 🖳 tanzania@skynet.be

Canada 50 Range Road, Ottawa, Ontario KIN 8J4; ☎ (613) 232 1500; 🖳 tzottawa@synapse.net

China 53 Dong Liu Jie, Beijing; ☎ (86-1) 532-1491, 532-1719; 🖳 tzbejing@info.iuol.cn.net

Congo (DRC) 142 Boulevard 30 Jin BP 1612, Kinshasa; ☎ (0982) 34364

Denmark Klintebjerg vej 105, Otterup; ☎ +45-64822702; 🖳 anni@post7.tele.dk

Egypt 9 Abdel Hamid Loutfy, Street, Dokki-Cairo; ☎ 20-2 3374286; 🖳 tanrepcairo@infinity.com.eg

Ethiopia P.O. Box 1077, Addis Ababa; ☎ +251-1 51106

France 13 ave Raymond, Pointcare, 75116 Paris; ☎ (+33) 1 53 70 63 66; 🖳 ambtanzanie@wanadoo.fr

Germany 11 14050 Berlin, Charlottenburg, Westend, PO Box 191226; ☎ (+49) 0228-358051; 🖳 www.tanzania-gov.de

India 10/1 Sarv Priya Vihar, New Delhi 110016; ☎ +91 (11) 24122864; 🖳 tanzrep@del2.vsnl.net.in

Italy Viale Cortina d' Ampezzo 18, Rome; ☎ +39-6-33485801; 🖳 info@embassyoftanzania.it

Japan 21-9, Kamiyoga 4, Chome Setagaya-Ku, Tokyo 158; ☎ (03) 425 4531/3

Kenya Taifa Road Re-insurance Plaza, 9th Floor, Nairobi; ☎ +254 331 056/7; 🖳 tanzania@users.africaonline.co.ke

Mozambique Ujamaa House, PO Box 4515, Maputo; ☎ (263-4) 721870; 🖳 safina@zebra.uem.mz

Netherlands Parallelweg Zuid 215, 2914 LE Nieuwerkerk aan den IJssel, Amsterdam; ☎ 0180-320939; 🖳 http://www.tanzania.nl/

Nigeria 15 Yedseram Street, Maintama, PMB 5125, Wuse, Abuja; ☎ 234 9 413 2313; 🖳 tanabuja@lytos.com

Russia Pyatnitskaya, Ulitsa 33, Moscow; ☎ 231 8126; 🖳 tanmos@wm.west-call.com

Rwanda 15 avenue Paul VI, BP 3973, Kigali; 🖳 tanzrep@rwandatell.rwandal.com

South Africa 845 Goont Avenue, Pretoria; ☎ (+27-12)-3424371; 🖳 tanzania@cis.co.za

South Korea Hyundai Corporation, Hyundai Bldg 2F 140-2, Kye-dong Chrongro-ku, Seoul; ☎ +82-2-7446-1172

Sweden Wallingatan 11, Box 7255, 111 60, Stockholm; ☎ 46 8 503 206 00/1; 🖳 mailbox@tanemb.se

Switzerland 47 Avenue Blanc, CH 1202 Geneva; ☎ (004122) 731 8920; 🖳 mission.tanzania@itu.ch

Uganda 6 Kagera Road, PO Box 5750, Kampala; ☎ (41) 257357; 🖳 tzrepkla@imul.com

UK 3 Stratford Place, London W1C 1AS; ☎ +44 020-7569 1470; 🖳 www.tanzania-online.gov.uk

USA 2139 R Street, Washington DC 20008; ☎ +1 (202) 939 6125/7; 🖳 www.tanzaniaembassy-us.org

Zambia Ujamaa House, No 5200, United Nations Ave, PO Box 31219, 10101 Lusaka; ☎ 227698/227702; 🖳 tzreplsk@zamnet.zm

Zimbabwe Ujamaa House, 23 Baines Ave, Harare; ☎ (263-4) 721870, 722627

KENYAN EMBASSIES AND CONSULATES ABROAD

Australia Qe Insurance Building, 33-35 Ainslie Ave, Civic Square, Canberra, ACT 2601; ☎ +61 2 6247 4788; 🖳 www.kenya.asn.au/

Belgium Ave Winston Churchill 208, 1180 Brussels; ☎ +32 2 3401040; 🖳 www.kenyabrussels.com

Botswana Plot 786 Independence Ave, Private Bag Box 297, Gaborone; ☎ + 267 3951408; 🖳 Kenya@info.bw

Burundi PTA Bank Building, West Wing, Chaussée du Prince Louise Rwagasore, BP 5138, Mutanga, Bujumbura; ☎ +257-22-258160/62/63/67; 🖳 information@kenyaembassy.bi

Canada 415 Laurier Avenue East, Ottawa, Ontario, K1N 6R4; ☎ 000-1-613-5631773/4/6; 🖳 www.kenyahighcommission.ca

Congo (DRC) 4002 Avenue de Louganda, Commune de Gombe, PO Box 9667, Kinshasa; ☎ + 243 817008203/00/07; 🖳 kenem-drc@jobantech.cd

Egypt 29 El Kods EL Sharif St, Mohandesseen, Giza, PO Box 362, Cairo; ☎ 00-20-2-3453628; 🖳 info@kenemb-cairo.com

Ethiopia Fikre Mariam Road, High 16 Kebelle 01, PO Box 3301l, Addis Ababa; ☎ +251 11 6610033; 🖳 kengad@telecom.net.et

France 3 Rue, Freycinet, 75116 Paris; ☎ + 33 1 56622525; 🖳 paris@amb-kenya.fr

Germany Markgrafenstr. 63, 10969 Berlin; ☎ + 49 030 25926650; 🖳 www.kenyaembassyberlin.de

India 34, Paschimi Marg, Vasant Vihar, New Delhi, 110057; ☎ +91 11 26146537/38/40; 🖳 www.kenyamission-delhi.com

Ireland 11 Elgin Rd, Ballsbridge, Dublin; ☎ +353-1-6136380; 🖳 www.kenyaembassyireland.net

Israel 15 Abba Hillel Silver, 3rd Floor, Ramatgan 52136, PO Box 3621, Tel Aviv; ☎ + 972-3 5754633; 🖳 www.kenyaembassyisrael.org

Italy Via Archimede 164, 00197, Rome; ☎ + 39 06 8082717; 🖳 www.embassyofkenya.it

Japan 3-24-3 Yakumo, Meguro-ku, Tokyo 152-0023; ☎ + 81 3 37234006/7; 🖳 www.kenyarep-jp.com/embassy/access_e.html

Netherlands 21 Nieuwe Parklaan, 2597 LA The Hague; ☎ (+31)70-3504215

Rwanda Chancery Plot No 1716, Kacyiru Avenue Del Lumuganda; PO Box 6159, Kacyiru, Kigali; ☎ + 250 583332-6

South Africa 302 Brooks Street, PO Box 35954, Menlo Park, 0081 Pretoria; ☎ + 27 12 3622249; 🖳 kenrep@mweb.co.za

Spain Paseo De La Castellana 143 2 APL, 28046 Madrid; ☎ +34 91 571 09 25; 🖳 www.kenyaembassyspain.es/contact.htm

Sudan Premises No 516, Block 1 West Giraf, Khartoum; ☎ + 249 155772808; 🖳 kenemb@yahoo.com; also PO 208, Juba; ☎ + 249 811 823664; 🖳 keconju@yahoo.co.uk;

Sweden Birger Jarlsgatan 37, 2nd Floor, PO Box 7694, 103 95 Stockholm; ☎ + 46 8 218300/4/9; 🖳 Kenya.embassy@telia.com

Tanzania PO Box 5231, Dar-es-Salaam; ☎ + 255 22 2668285/6

Uganda Plot No 41, Nakasero Rd, PO Box 5220, Kampala; ☎ 006-41-258232/5/6; 🖳 kenyaahicom@africaonline.co.ug

UK 45 Portland Place, London W1B IAS; ☎ + 44 020 76362371; 🖳 www.kenyahighcommission.net

USA 2249, R Street NW, Washington DC 20008; 000-1-202-3876101; 🖳 www.kenyaembassy.com; also Park Mile Plaza, 4801 Willshire Blvd, Mezzanine Floor, Los Angeles CA 90010; ☎ 000-1-323-9392408

Zambia 5207 United Nations Ave, PO Box 50298, Lusaka; ☎ + 260 1 250722; 🖳 kenhigh@zmnet.zm

Zimbabwe 95 Park Lane, PO Box 4069, Harare; ☎ + 263 4 704820

APPENDIX D: RECOMMENDED READING, LISTENING AND WATCHING

MAPS

Maps of Kilimanjaro are available in Arusha, Moshi and your own country. The best one we've found, however, is only reliably available online: *Kilimanjaro Kibo* (1:80,000) is written in both English and German and is by some distance the most accurate map available on the mountain. With profiles of a couple of the routes, GPS points, town plans on Arusha and Moshi, descriptions of the vegetation zones and a review of the retreat of permanent ice, this is also the most informative and useful map. You can order a copy by visiting the publisher's website at 💻 www.climbing-map.com.

The most common map is the cartoonish *New Map of the Kilimanjaro National Park*, published by the safari-cum-trekking agency Hoopoe Adventure & Tropical Trekking (now Summits Africa). It's not a bad map, bright and colourful, though in all honesty it's a little inaccurate and the cartoon style means it's of little practical use. Still, it's packed full of information and the flora guide on the reverse is useful. The scale, by the way, is about 1.1cm to 1km (or 1:90,909), with a close-up of the summit on the reverse drawn at a scale of 5.4cm to 1km (about 1:18,518.5). They also publish a similar-style map to Meru. NB Make sure you get the *New Map* as the old one really is out of date these days.

The *Tourist Map of Kilimanjaro* (1:100,000) by the Ordnance Survey is the biggest and most beautiful, though once again of little practical use: the routes themselves have been drawn, seemingly without thought of precision, over the top of what looks an accurate topographical map. Well over a decade old, it's a little out of date too. Better in a frame on your wall at home than in your backpack.

A third map, *Kilimanjaro* (1:50,000), by Mark Savage, is harder to track down – though the shop at Marangu Gate stocks some. The descriptions of the trails are not brilliant and the map itself is a little ugly, though it is more up to date than the above and the black-and-white drawings of wild flowers are good – though would be far more useful in colour.

Finally, the Canada-based ITM (International Travel Maps) series has recently produced *Kilimanjaro*, a colourful 1:62,500 map of the mountain, as well as a separate 1:6,250,000 road map of the area.

Online maps

A couple of companies have produced GPS maps of the Kilimanjaro region that you can upload to your computer – and then plot the waypoints on it. I'm afraid that I am not entirely enamoured of either version. The best is by GPS travelmaps (💻 www.gpstravelmaps. com). There are some teething problems with it – the trails they've drawn are simply straight-line dashes and their altitude readings seem a tad awry (Uhuru Peak is at 5860m, for example, a whole 35m below the actual height). Still, the basic map itself seems very detailed and it's a useful base for putting on your own GPS readings. The other map is **Tracks 4 Africa**'s (💻 www.tracks4africa.co.za) map which to me is currently the inferior model.

RECOMMENDED READING

Please note that many of the following are rare and a number are extremely difficult to find. Among those that are readily available are Hemingway's *The Snows of Kilimanjaro* (and the recently published *Under Kilimanjaro*, the rather long-winded novel-cum-memoir-cum-tribute-to-Africa that recounts Papa Hemingway's time in Kenya); the comprehensive and wonderful book-of-the-IMAX-film *Kilimanjaro, Mountain at the Crossroads*, by Audrey Salkeld – possibly the most beautiful and absorbing souvenir of your climb that money can buy (the book that is, not Audrey); and John Reader's excellent (though rather bulky) *Kilimanjaro*, which you may have more luck tracking down in Tanzania than in your home country. If you're visiting Zanzibar after Kilimanjaro, you may want to wait and buy your reading material for the mountain there: some of the bookshops in Stonetown have fine selections.

Biography and personal accounts

Many of the following books, particularly those written during the great days of exploration in the 1800s, are now out of print and, short of a miraculous find in a secondhand bookstore, the only place you're going to find them is at the British Library or a similar institution abroad.

The internet is, of course, another source. For example, I've successfully tracked down online the English translation of Hans Meyer's account of his conquest of Kili (see first entry below); now all I've got to do is find the £5750 that the dealers are asking for it. The online auction house eBay is a good place to begin your search, with companies such as Bibliografi, who trade through eBay, occasionally offering some rare tomes. The Canadian-based Voyager Press also have some good stuff on Kili, particularly old reports from the Royal Geographic Society.

For those books that *are* still in print, your best bet is in Tanzania itself, either in the small souvenir shop by Marangu Gate or, somewhat surprisingly, in the large bookshops in Stonetown, Zanzibar. Failing that, you could always try online bookshops like Amazon, on which you will usually be able to track down a copy.

The explorers...

Across East African Glaciers – An Account of the First Ascent of Kilimanjaro Dr Hans Meyer, translated from the German by EHS Calder (George Philip and Son, 1891). Perhaps the most fascinating book ever written about the mountain, Meyer's beautiful work describes his unprecedented ascent of Kilimanjaro, all illustrated with some lovely sketches by ET Compton. Splendid stuff. Now available in a much less-charming – but much more affordable – reprint by Kessinger Press.

An Essay on the Sources of the Nile in the Mountains of the Moon Charles T Beke (Neill and Company, 1848). This short work is of interest not only because it was published at the same time as Rebmann's ground-breaking visit of Kilimanjaro but also, though written around 160 years ago, the author still takes as his starting point the work of Ptolemy written 1800 years before, thus giving an indication of just how little was known about Africa at that time.

Discovery by Count Teleki of Lakes Rudolf and Stefanie Lieutenant Ludwig von Höhnel, translated by Nancy Bell (Longmans, Green and Co, 1894). Lengthy, two-volume account of the Hungarian count as he shoots and slaughters his way through East Africa's fauna, written by his companion von Höhnel. Only about a sixth of the book deals specifically with Kili, though that sixth is interesting both for the account of their attempt to climb Kili, and their dealings with Chagga chiefs Mandara (whom they try to avoid) and Mareale.

Life, Wanderings, and Labours in Eastern Africa Charles New (Cass Library of African Studies, 1971, originally 1873). Charles New set off in 1871 to spread the gospel to Africa's heathen population but it was as an explorer that he is remembered, becoming the first white man to cross the African snow-line during a visit to the Chagga region. This book was written in the months spent in England between his first and second trips, on the latter of which he fell ill and died. Once again, though the account of his time on the slopes of Kili occupies only about a third of the book, it is for the most part fascinating, as much for his description of Mandara and the Chaggas as it is for his climb up the mountain.

The Church Missionary Intelligencer (Seeleys, 1850). Definitely one you'll have to look for in the British Library, this august organ was the first to publish Rebmann's accounts of his three trips to Kilimanjaro, as well as Krapf's subsequent visit to the Usambara region. Volume 1, May 1849, contains most of the relevant texts.

The Kilima-njaro Expedition – A Record of Scientific Exploration in Eastern Equatorial Africa HH Johnston (Kegan Paul, Trench and Co, 1886; republished by Gregg International Publishers Ltd, 1968). Widely dismissed as exaggeration going on fabrication, this is nevertheless a very entertaining read thanks to Johnston's sense of humour and the scrapes he gets into. Just possible to find secondhand or pick up the reprint by Kessinger Publishing.

Tracts Relating to Missions (Printed by A Lankester, 1878) Yet another work whose habitat is restricted almost entirely to the British Library these days, this collection of missionary accounts includes one by the Rev A Downes Shaw entitled *To Chagga and Back — An Account of a Journey to Moshi, the Capital of Chagga, Eastern Equatorial Africa*.

...and those who followed in their wake

Africa's Dome of Mystery Eva Stuart Watt FRGS (Marshall, Morgan and Scott Ltd, 1930). Brought up in East Africa, Ms Stuart-Watt describes her life among the Chagga people, including an account of her climb to Kibo's crater rim. Interesting, if only for the fact that there are few accounts of Kibo from this period under British rule.

Bicycles up Kilimanjaro Richard and Nicholas Crane (Oxford Illustrated Press 1985). These two cycled up Kili with Mars Bars taped to their handlebars to finance the construction of windmills for pumping water in East Africa. The only other person I met who had read this book said he enjoyed it, but I didn't.

Duel for Kilimanjaro Leonard Mosley (Weidenfeld and Nicolson, 1963). Account of the East African campaign during World War I. The fact that I stuck with it to the end, even though my interest in military history is slight, is testament to how well this book is written and what an absorbing story it is. The English, by the way, come across as comically incompetent.

Snow on the Equator HW Tilman (Bell and Son Books, 1937, republished as part of *The Eight Sailing/Mountain Exploration Books* by Baton Wicks, 1989). Inaccurate account (Kilimanjaro is not an extinct volcano, for example, but a dormant one) by coffee planter, explorer, mountaineer and all-round show-off Harold William Tilman. Nevertheless a very entertaining read and, for all his bluster, Tilman comes across as an entirely likeable fellow.

The Road to Kilimanjaro Geoffrey Salisbury (Minerva Press, 1997). Though mainly autobiographical, recounting Salisbury's busy life, this book includes a heart-warming, humbling account of an expedition in 1969 by the author to the summit of Kilimanjaro on the Loitokitok (Rongai) Route with a group of eight totally blind African youths, all but one of whom made it to the top.

Making the Climb: What a Novice Climber Learned About Life on Mount Kilimanjaro John C. Bowling (Beacon Hill Press, 2007). Tedious account of climb by the president of Olivet Nazarene University that's reminiscent of the dullest of sermons you used to have to sit through as a child – including a liberal sprinkling of prayers throughout the chapters. Read it if you must, but only as a way to build up stamina; for if you manage to finish it before your own trek then climbing the mountain will feel like a breeze. Very, very dreary indeed.

Kilimanjaro: Hakuna Matata Chris Baker (www.lulu.com, 2007). There's nothing unusual about this person's climb, nor is there anything special about Mr Baker or his writing style. Nevertheless, as a straightforward account of what it's like to climb Kilimanjaro I really think this book is very good, and the fact that profits go to KPAP can only be a good thing. Also has an accompanying website: 🖥 www.kilimanjaro-hakuna-matata.com/

The Shadow of Kilimanjaro – On Foot Across East Africa Rick Ridgeway (Bloomsbury 1999). Well-written account of a walk that begins on the summit of Kilimanjaro and ends at Malindi on the Kenyan coast. Though Kilimanjaro is dealt with in a matter of pages at the front of the book, the narrative style is absorbing and this book is well worth reading.

On Top of Africa – the Climbing of Kilimanjaro and Mount Kenya Neville Shulman (Element Books, 1995). Tale of the conquering of these two African giants by the author, along with the help of Zen philosophies and his own personal *shin* spirit.

In Wildest Africa Peter MacQueen, FRGS (George Bell and Sons, 1910). Account of one of the first tourists to visit Kilimanjaro, coming here during the German occupation. Includes a description of their ascent up Kili, during which some of their porters died, more were frightened by snow and fled (taking the food with them) and MacQueen himself only managed to find his way down by following the trail of porters' corpses left behind from an expedition five months previously. MacQueen went on to reach a highly credible 19,200 feet, the highest, at that time, by an English speaker.

Kilimanjaro via the Marangu Route – "Tourist Route" my ass Phil Gray (iUniverse Inc, 2006). This book has had some pretty negative reviews on the internet and it is indeed pretty negative, but it's not as bad as some people will have you believe. Mr Gray seems an amiable fellow, never one to tell it straight when there's the possibility of a gag, and I found the book a readable account of his climb.

Fiction

Home on Kilimanjaro Margaret Chrislock Gilseth (Askeladd Press, 1998). Novel written by a lady who spent four years teaching in Marangu for the Lutheran Church, written largely from the point of view of her 11-year-old son.

The Snows of Kilimanjaro Ernest Hemingway (Arrow Books, 1994). Short story about a writer plagued by both a gangrenous leg and a rich wife, written by an honorary game warden based in Loitokitok in the early 1950s. Was always regarded as his most autobiographical work until the publication of...

Under Kilimanjaro Ernest Hemingway (Kent State University Press, 2005). Hemingway called it fiction but with himself and his wife as the lead characters and the events that are described presumably pretty close to the truth, this book could just as easily have been pigeonholed in the Biography category above. Long and funereally paced, it has its moments but is probably for fans and aficionados only.

Kilimanjaro Burning John H Robinson (Birch Book Press, 1998). Entertaining enough, but other than in being set in Tanzania it's not really relevant to the mountain. Nevertheless, good at evoking the country, its sights and smells, for those who know the area.

Bingo Bear was here – A Toy Bear's Climb to the Top of Africa's Highest Mountain Gwill York Newman (Sunstone Press 2003). It goes against one's nature to criticize a children's book but when the author implies that Kilimanjaro is in Kenya in the preface, thereby insulting an entire nation, I think the gloves are off. Anyway, this is about the adventures of a stuffed koala from Cleveland, Ohio, as he accompanies the author and her husband to the top of Africa's highest mountain. Which is in Tanzania. The author lives in New Mexico, by the way, and has since climbed with Bingo in other mountainous places including Kashmir and the American Rockies. Which she probably thinks are in France.

Chagga language, history and lifestyle

Chagga – A Course in the Vunjo Dialect of the Kichagga Language of Kilimanjaro, Tanzania Bernard Leeman and Trilas Lauwo (published in Europe by Languages Information Centre). The best Chagga language book we could find, this tome, written by an Australian who worked as a teacher in the region, deals with the basic structure and grammar and is an ideal introduction to the tongue.

History of the Chagga People of Kilimanjaro Kathleen M Stahl (Mouton & Co, 1964). Highly detailed account of the Chaggas, probably more for those with an academic interest in the subject, but proof that contrary to popular opinion the Chagga do have an absorbing – and surprisingly lengthy – history.

Hunger and Shame – Child Malnutrition and Poverty on Mount Kilimanjaro Mary Howard and Ann Millard (Routledge). Comparatively rich by African standards it may be but, as this book proves, the Kilimanjaro region still suffers from more than its fair share of grinding poverty. With views from family members, health workers and government officials, this book discusses the moral and practical dilemmas of malnourishment.

Kilimanjaro and its People The Honourable Charles Dundas OBE (H, F and G Witherby, 1924; reprinted by Frank Cass & Co, 1968). Probably still the most authoritative account of the Chagga people, this tome is a little dry in places (particularly the rather involved history section), and outdated too (very few of the more extreme Chagga practices, described on pp138-41 of this book, are still conducted today); nevertheless the sections on religion, witchcraft and ritual ceremonies are completely fascinating and offer the most comprehensive insight into how the Chaggas *used to be*, at least, if not how they are today.

Field guides to the fauna
Pocket Guide to Mammals of East Africa Chris Stuart and Mathilde Stuart (Struik, 2009). Around 160 pages of nice photos of animals both fierce and fascinating.

Kilimanjaro – Animals in a Landscape Jonathan Kingdon (BBC Publications 1983). Born in Tanganyika, Kingdon is an artist specializing in the flora and fauna of his homeland. This book, based on a BBC series, contains examples of his work as well as an extended commentary on the creatures that live on the mountain.

Birds of East Africa: Kenya, Tanzania, Uganda, Rwanda, Burundi Terry Stevenson and John Fanshawe (Helm Field Guides, 2004). Bird guides tend to be amongst the most beautiful books around and this one is no different, with gorgeous drawings by Brian Small, John Gale and Norman Arlott. Reckoned to be *the* authoritative guide.

Birds of Kenya and Northern Tanzania Dale A Zimmerman (Helm Field Guides, 2005). Another in the series, just as beautiful – and only slightly less weighty than the one above.

Field guides to the flora
Strangely, there is no comprehensive book on the flora of the region or country. There is *Field Guide to Common Trees and Shrubs of East Africa* Najma Dharani (Struik, 2002) but this, alas, has little relevance to the mountain itself.

Coffee-table books
Kilimanjaro John Reader (Elm Tree Books, 1982). Excellent, beautifully written coffee-table book with detailed accounts both of the history and geology of Kili, and the author's own experience of photographing it.

Kilimanjaro: The Great White Mountain David Pluth (Camerapix, 2001). Another tome that will have your coffee-table groaning.

Kilimanjaro: To the Roof of Africa Audrey Salkeld, (National Geographic Books, 2002). The best-looking book on Kilimanjaro, this mighty tome includes detailed sections on history and geology as well as some excellent photographs of the mountain. If you only buy one book on the mountain – other than the one you're holding now, of course! – make it this one.

FOR YOUR LISTENING PLEASURE

The following is some appropriate music to take up the mountain with you; appropriate, but not necessarily any good. And we have to wonder: have any of the following artists actually been anywhere near the mountain?

Babyshambles *Kilamangiro* Celebrity junkie and Kate Moss's ex is also, apparently, a rock star. This 2005 offering was Pete Doherty's first single with new band Babyshambles following his acrimonious departure from The Libertines.

Miles Davis *Filles de Kilimanjaro* Before he went all funky and weird on us with his *Bitches Brew* album – great album cover, unlistenable tunes – Miles Davis recorded this album in 1968 with his 'second great quintet', featuring Wayne Shorter on trumpet and keyboard god Herbie Hancock.

Medwyn Goodall *Snows of Kilimanjaro* 'As uplifting as catching the first sight of the mountain rising up out of the African plains – as inspirational as gazing down from the summit – *Snows of Kilimanjaro* is a perfect musical tribute to the inner strength of those who rise above adversity.' At least, that's what the blurb says; and as it was made in support of a charity climb, I'm not going to disagree. Whatever I may really think.

Iration Steppas Meet Dennis Rootical *Kilimanjaro* A 1995 ten-inch single from British dubmasters. Rare; check out the Summit Mix on side two.

Lange presents Firewall *Kilimanjaro* Trance-dance CD from 2004, including 8-minute-long original mix, 9-minute 23-second Lange remix and 7-minute 51-second 'B-side', *Touched*. Not special.

Letta Mbulu *Kilimanjaro* Soulful disco with Afrobeats. Quite groovy but difficult to find except on compilation.

The Rippingtons *Kilimanjaro* Guitarist Russ Freeman's instrumental follow-up to *Moonlighting*, their successful debut. Jazzy, smoothish and with world-music influences.

Teardrop Explodes *Kilimanjaro* One of Britain's loveable oddballs, Julian Cope – last seen in public travelling around Britain to write about stone circles – first came to public attention with the release of this 1980 debut album. Includes their greatest hit, 'Reward', which is bound to stir up memories amongst those who grew up in the eighties. Like me. Described as post-punk by aficionados – shorthand for passionate, angry yet melodious.

Toto *Africa* Bearded eighties crooner's worldwide smash includes the line 'Sure as Kilimanjaro rises like Olympus above the Serengeti'. Which, of course, it doesn't.

The Twinkle Brothers *Kilimanjaro* A 2000 Roots-reggae release. I must confess, I've never actually heard it but I like the look of the cover.

...AND SIX FILMS WITH KILIMANJARO IN THE TITLE

Kilimanjaro – to the Roof of Africa The 2002 film of the book – or was it the book of the film? Whatever, this IMAX film recounting the experiences of a group of trekkers on the mountain is beautifully shot by film-maker David Breashears. It's the best documentary if you want to know what it's like to climb the mountain, as well as a gorgeous and evocative souvenir for those who have already done so.

Killers of Kilimanjaro With scarcely a swash left unbuckled, this 1959 tale follows the adventures of trouble-shooter Robert Adamson (Robert Taylor) who, arriving in deepest Africa with Jane Carlton (played by the luscious Anne Aubrey) to oversee the completion of a cross-continental railroad, finds he has all manner of continental clichés to contend with, from slave traders (ruthless) to tribes (savage) and, of course, the local fauna (Grrrr!). Will he make it out alive? And complete the railroad too? And get together with Jane? Probably, yes. It's not great but I quite enjoyed it, and it has a certain charm. Usually available on eBay, if you're interested.

The Mines of Kilimanjaro Italian offering from 1986 that's been dubbed into English. Tobias Hoesl stars as Dr Ed Barkely who travels to East Africa in search of his professor's killers. But as Robert Taylor (see *Killers of Kilimanjaro*, above) could have told him, this part of the world is chock-a-block with danger, from savage tribes (in this case, the Gundors), Chinese gangsters (?) and even Nazis (???). And after that, things get *really* weird! But as Robert Taylor could also have told him, there are compensations in the form of some lovely scenery and equally comely female company, with Elena Pompei as Eva Kilbrook.

All in all, an appalling film but unfortunately not bad enough to be funny – making it possibly the worst couple of hours of cinematic 'entertainment' you will ever experience.

In the Shadow of Kilimanjaro It's 1500 men versus 90,000 flesh-eating baboons that have been driven mad by a drought: the odds look bad but if anybody can find a way out of this 1986 dilemma, John Rhys Davis and Timothy Bottoms can.... Grab a beer and some chocolate, settle into your favourite armchair, disengage your brain and enjoy this truly rubbish but succulent slice of eighties' ham and corn. Available on eBay if you're interested.

Snows of Kilimanjaro Henry King's 1952 film version of Ernest Hemingway's semiautobiographical work, with Gregory Peck in the leading role, Susan Hayward as his devoted belle and Ava Gardner as the lost love he pines for – and when you see Ava in this film, you can't blame him. Of course it's the most highbrow film of the three here and I should like it – but, personally speaking, give me killer baboons anyday.

Volcano above the Clouds From the Nova PBS stable comes this hour-long documentary from 2003 about a team climbing the Lemosho/Western Breach Route. Ostensibly it's about the team's attempts to discover how much the glaciers' disappearance will affect the water supply and to see whether the volcano is still active, but really it's just a documentary of a climb – and for that it's OK. Contact Nova direct, or I found it via Amazon marketplace.

APPENDIX E: GPS WAYPOINTS

Each GPS waypoint was taken on the route at the reference number marked on the map as below. Note the position format we are using is known as UTM UPS; the map datum is WGS 84 (37 M); you can change both of these on a Garmin GPS by going to Units Setup on the Settings menu, then changing the Position Format and Map datum where necessary.

Note that by some of the waypoints there is a small 'c', which denotes that the waypoint was not found by us and thus we cannot vouch for its accuracy. Where waypoints are on more than one map, each relevant map number is given, separated by a forward slash (eg Map 5/24). Any comments on any of the waypoints and their accuracy will be gratefully received. Thanks.

MERU

Map	Ref	GPS waypoint	Description
Map A	A	37M 261065 9642331	Momela Gate
Map A	B	37M 260557 9642021	Turn-off to Tululusia Hill
Map A	C	37M 260452 9641613	Turn-off to Campsite 1 & 2
Map A	D	37M 260430 9640906	Campsite 3
Map A	E	37M 259270 9640892	Turn-off to viewpoint
Map A	F	37M 258686 9641090	Fig Tree
Map A	G	37M 258127 9641264	Itikoni Campsite
Map A	H	37M 256701 9640742	Maio Falls
Map B	I	37M 254592 9641371	Kitoto Viewpoint
Map B	J	37M 254338 9642470	Turn-off to Meru Crater
Map A	K	37M 255495 9642787	Miriakamba Huts
Map B	L	37M 253925 9643310	Mgongo wa Tembo
Map B	M	37M 252564 9644015	Saddle Huts
Map B	N	37M 252628 9644638	Little Meru
Map B	O	37M 251603 9643468	Rhino Point
Map B	P	37M 249943 9641219	Socialist Peak

KILIMANJARO

Map	Ref	GPS waypoint	Description
Map 1	001	37 M 335295 9641479	Marangu Gate
Map 1	002	37 M 335341 9644784	Bridge
Map 1	003	37 M 335676 9645120	Kisamboni
Map 2	004	37 M 334809 9648242	Mandara Huts
Map 2	005	37 M 335400 9648732	Maundi Crater
Map 3	006	37 M 330631 9651540	Sloping bridge
Map 3	007	37 M 328280 9652715	Kambi ya Taabu
Map 4	008	37 M 326490 9652894	Horombo Huts
Map 4	008A	37 M 325945 9654684	Zebra Rocks
Map 4	008B	37 M 326374 9656687	Signpost and junction
Map 4	008C	37 M 326240 9656836	Memorial plaque and viewpoint
Map 4	008D	37 M 327617 9657468	Mawenzi Hut
Map 4	009	37 M 325328 9654221	Junction with porters' path
Map 4	010	37 M 324892 9655246	Last water point
Map 4	011	37 M 324379 9655970	Mawenzi Ridge
Map 5	012	37 M 323192 9657409	Lunchstop with toilets
Map 5	013	37 M 322614 9658810	Sign for Kibo Circuit

Map	Ref	GPS waypoint	Description
Map 5	014	37 M 322447 9658958	Jiwe la Ukoyo
Map 5/24	015	37 M 321300 9659306	Junction with path to Mawenzi Tarn
Map 6/24	016	37 M 320991 9659232	Kibo Huts
Map 6	017	37 M 319713 9659625	William's Point
Map 6	018	37 M 319400 9659750	Hans Meyer Cave
Map 6/32	019	37 M 318632 9660028	Gillman's Point
Map 7	020	37 M 304266 9649064	Machame Gate
Map 7	021	37 M 304409 9650814	End of 4x4 track
Map 7	022	37 M 305373 9654229	Lunchstop
Map 8	023	37 M 306531 9656282	Toilet
Map 8	024	37 M 307321 9657714	Machame Huts
Map 8	025	37 M 307748 9658051	Rocky outcrop
Map 8	026	37 M 308080 9658257	Viewpoint
Map 8	027	37 M 308137 9658337	First giant groundsel
Map 9	028	37 M 308233 9658449	First descent of day
Map 9	029	37 M 308315 9658560	Climb to top of rocks for views
Map 9	030	37 M 308515 9658753	Ten-second descent
Map 9	031	37 M 308807 9659087	Start of steep slope
Map 9	032	37 M 309122 9659438	Concrete steps in rock
Map 9	033	37 M 309123 9659466	Lunchstop
Map 9	034	37 M 309299 9659975	Overhang
Map 9	035	37 M 309192 9660158	Further overhang caves
Map 9	036	37 M 309175 9660179	Clamber
Map 9	037	37 M 308977 9660464	Now on Shira Plateau
Map 9	038	37 M 308443 9661064	Shira Caves Campsite
Map 9	039	37 M 308730 9660835	Stream
Map 9	040	37 M 309299 9660600	Stream
Map 10	041	37 M 312517 9661462	Junction Machame/Lemosho Route
Map 10	042	37 M 312859 9661292	Lunchstop
Map 10	043	37 M 313415 9661041	Sheffield Campsite
Map 10/18	044	37 M 314131 9660747	Lava Tower Campsite
Map 10	045	37 M 313959 9658662	Junction of paths/waterfall
Map 11/28	046	37 M 314325 9657792	Barranco Huts
Map 11	047	37 M 315177 9657333	Top of Breakfast Wall
Map 11	048	37 M 315779 9657062	Stream
Map 11	049	37 M 316167 9656961	Old porters track
Map 11	050	37 M 316315 9656386	Desert slope
Map 11	051	37 M 316983 9656046	Valley floor and stream
Map 11	052	37 M 316851 9656077	Tortoise Rock
Map 11	053	37 M 317089 9655848	Karanga Campsite
Map 12	054	37 M 318707 9656657	Top of climb
Map 12	055	37 M 319724 9656918	Top of Barafu Ridge
Map 12/13/29	056	37 M 319762 9657263	Barafu Huts
Map 13	057	37 M 319592 9658015	Kosovo Campsite
Map 13	058	37 M 319249 9658326	Joining the Ridge
Map 13/32	059	37 M 318040 9659630	Stella Point
Map 14	060	37 M 294046 9667904	Start of Lemosho Route
Map 14	061	37 M 295058 9667784	Slight clearing
Map 14	062	37 M 295082 9667762	Tree in path
Map 14	063	37 M 295789 9667751	Patch of lobelia
Map 14	064	37 M 296078 9668489	Tree across path

Map	Ref	GPS waypoint	Description
Map 14	065	37 M 297174 9668591	Mti Mkubwa
Map 14	066	37 M 298279 9668000	Stream
Map 14	067	37 M 299074 9668169	Top of ridge
Map 14	068	37 M 299193 9668178	Last stand of rosewoods (left of path)
Map 15	069	37 M 299516 9668155	Top of climb
Map 15	070	37 M 299765 9668304	Old lunchstop
Map 15	071	37 M 300087 9668487	Better lunchstop
Map 15	072	37 M 300897 9667634	Stream
Map 15	073	37 M 302211 9667729	First view of Kibo
Map 15	074	37 M 303210 9666760	Shira 1
Map 15	075	37 M 304514 9665765	Junction
Map 16	076	37 M 304809 9663689	First stream
Map 16	077	37 M 304843 9663552	Second stream
Map 16	078	37 M 304873 9663387	Third stream
Map 16	079	37 M 304884 9662988	Burnt trees
Map 16	080	37 M 305059 9661945	Junction by cathedral
Map 16	081	37 M 304823 9661850	Top of cathedral
Map 16	082	37 M 306091 9662268	East Shira Hill
Map 16	083	37 M 306328 9662360	Boulders and mud flats
Map 16	084	37 M 306876 9662437	Roadhead
Map 16	085	37 M 307312 9662331	Dry stream
Map 17	086	37 M 308314 9662240	Shira Huts
Map 17	087	37 M 310497 9662179	Big boulder
Map 17	088	37 M 311028 9662077	Narrow gully
Map 10	089	37 M 311568 9661987	Path to Moir Huts
Map 10	090	37 M 312105 9661769	Cross
Map 19	091	c 37 M 304112 9669645	Morum Barrier
Map 16	092	c 37 M 305598 9664702	Simba Cave Campsite
Map 18	093	c 37 M 315109 9660256	Arrow Glacier Campsite
Map 18	094	c 37 M 316482 9660666	Crater Rim
Map 20	095	37 M 332794 9672735	Rongai Gate
Map 20	096	37 M 330548 9671175	Signpost
Map 20	097	37 M 330486 9671195	Benches
Map 20	098	37 M 329351 9670985	Sign about wildfires
Map 20	099	37 M 328834 9670717	Benches
Map 20	100	37 M 328371 9670227	Bridge
Map 21	101	37 M 327535 9670053	Simba Campsite
Map 21	102	37 M 325494 9668733	Rocky plateau
Map 21	103	37 M 324934 9668209	First summit
Map 22	104	37 M 324279 9667203	Second summit
Map 22	105	37 M 324041 9666423	Second Cave
Map 22	106	37 M 323390 9663383	Third Cave
Map 23	107	37 M 326938 9662833	Highest point of day
Map 23	108	37 M 327477 9662418	Kikelelwa Camp
Map 23	109	37 M 327418 9661909	Viewpoint and photo stop
Map 23	110	37 M 327332 9661625	Stream with groundsel
Map 23	111	37 M 327506 9660758	Fork in path
Map 23	112	37 M 327787 9660261	Paths reunite
Map 23	113	37 M 328098 9659970	Top of ridge
Map 23	114	37 M 328116 9659841	Junction of paths

Map	Ref	GPS waypoint	Description
Map 23	115	37 M 328485 9659458	Mawenzi Tarn Campsite
Map 23	116	37 M 328083 9659117	Top of acclimatization climb
Map 25/6	117	37 M 320681 9660721	School Huts
Map 26	118	c 37 M 308823 9647262	Umbwe Gate
Map 26	119	c 37 M 308500 9649200	End of 4x4 road
Map 27	120	c 37 M 312323 9654092	Umbwe Cave
Map 28	121	c 37 M 312900 9556000	Lunchstop on ridge
Map 29	122	37 M 319091 9654859	Junction with Southern Circuit
Map 29	123	37 M 319086 9654264	Emergency route from Karanga Valley
Map 30	124	37 M 319144 9653675	Millennium/Rescue Hut
Map 30	125	37 M 318558 9650985	Mweka Huts
Map 31	126	37 M 317765 9649028	Bridge
Map 31	127	37 M 317256 9647528	Second bridge
Map 31	128	37 M 316526 9645691	Start of 4x4 road
Map 31	129	37 M 315674 9643991	Mweka Gate
Map 32	130	37 M 316829 9660194	Crater Campsite
Map 32	131	37 M 317075 9659821	Uhuru Peak

APPENDIX F: ACUTE MOUNTAIN SICKNESS

The following was sent in by Gerald (Joe) Power, Director of Cardiac Anaesthesia at Princess Alexandra Hospital, Brisbane in Australia. It is a more scientific – and accurate – summary of altitude sickness, its causes and treatments, and we are very grateful to him for taking the time to write and send this in to us; nice one Joe!

Altitude sickness occurs as a result of there being less oxygen in the air you breathe as you ascend through the atmosphere. Although the percentage of oxygen stays the same, the amount of oxygen, best represented by the pressure it exerts, decreases. At sea level, the atmosphere exerts a pressure of 760 millimetres of Mercury (mmHg) or 101 kilopascals (kPa). Oxygen represents 21% of this total and correspondingly exerts a "partial pressure" of 152mmHg or 21kPa.

The importance of this pressure can be illustrated by the example of a river – water flowing from a high to a low point under the influence of gravity. The greater the difference in height between these two points will influence how rapidly the water flows. Likewise oxygen has to diffuse (flow) from the lungs, into the blood and then into the tissues. This process is influenced by many factors, the most important being the pressure of the oxygen in the air you breathe into your lungs. Human life has evolved to survive comfortably when that pressure is close to 21kPa.

As one ascends higher in the atmosphere, this pressure decreases and consequently the rate at which the oxygen is able to diffuse from the lungs into the tissues decreases. This, however, is not met with a decreased requirement of oxygen in the tissues.

At the summit of Kilimanjaro, the atmospheric pressure is approximately 349mmHg or 48kPa. This is roughly half the pressure at sea level. The partial pressure of oxygen is 9.2kPa, which represents a significant reduction from that at sea level. If a person were to be exposed to this pressure with no acclimatization (for example if you flew to the summit of Kilimanjaro in a helicopter), loss of consciousness would most likely be the result.

Altitude sickness comes as a result of the abnormal response of the human body to the oxygen starvation that occurs with altitude. The response of the brain to low oxygen supply is to dilate the arteries supplying blood to it. This results in an increase in the pressure in the brain and if the normal regulation breaks down, swelling (oedema) of the brain occurs and if severe, this can cause death.

The lungs have a normal physiological response to decreased levels of oxygen in the air, whereby the small arteries constrict and decrease the blood supply to an area of the lung. Under normal circumstances, this reflex is essential to allow the correct matching of blood supply and ventilation in the lungs. At altitude, this response can become unregulated and will result in fluid filling the air sacs (alveoli) in the lungs.

Not everyone responds in the same manner to altitude. Research done in the 1980s on Mt Everest, and in low pressure simulators, revealed that certain individuals do not respond appropriately to falling levels of oxygen. Under normal circumstances, the rate at which someone breathes is predominantly controlled by the level of carbon dioxide in the blood. A reserve reflex is to be able to respond to decreasing oxygen pressure by increasing your breathing. Individuals who lack this response appear to be susceptible to developing mountain sickness.

The key element to minimizing altitude sickness is through acclimatization. A gradual ascent of the mountain allows the heart, lungs, brain and blood to adjust to the decreased oxygen pressure. The physiological response includes an increased respiratory rate (made easier by the air being thinner) and increased heart rate to supply more blood to the tissues. Over time, the amount of haemoglobin in the blood will increase as this allows more oxygen to be carried to the tissues.

Factors that will increase the likelihood of developing altitude sickness are those that worsen the supply of oxygen to the tissues – dehydration, hypothermia, fatigue and drugs that depress or interfere with respiration.

Diamox (acetolzolamide) was first proposed as an aid to acclimatization in the 1960s. In brief, as a person breathes harder with altitude, the levels of carbon dioxide in the blood fall. This has the effect of removing some of the stimulus that a person requires to breathe. This effect is particularly important when one falls asleep. Diamox reduces the impact of the falling carbon dioxide levels and helps to maintain normal breathing.

The treatment of altitude sickness is to restore the oxygen pressures to normal. This is most effectively achieved by descending from altitude. Temporary measures include using bottled oxygen or a Gamow bag (portable pressure chamber). In the event of the development of cerebral oedema, intravenous steroids help to limit the swelling of the brain.

References

JF Nunn *Applied Respiratory Physiology*

JB Wes *Tolerance to severe hypoxia: lessons from Mt. Everest; Acta Anaesthesiol Scand 1990:34; S94 18-23*

INDEX

TRAILBLAZER'S BRITISH WALKING GUIDE SERIES

We've applied to destinations which are closer to home Trailblazer's proven formula for publishing definitive route guides for adventurous travellers. Britain's network of long-distance trails enables the walker to explore some of the finest landscapes in the country's best walking areas and they are an obvious starting point for this series. These are guides that are user-friendly, practical, informative and environmentally sensitive.

● **Unique mapping features**
In many walking guidebooks the reader has to read a route description then try to relate it to the map. Our guides are much easier to use because walking directions, tricky junctions, places to stay and eat, points of interest and walking times are all written onto the maps themselves in the places to which they apply. With their uncluttered clarity, these are not general-purpose maps but fully edited maps **drawn by walkers for walkers**.

● **Largest-scale walking maps**
At a scale of just under 1:20,000 (8cm or 3¹/₈ inches to one mile) the maps in these guides are bigger than even the most detailed walking maps currently available in the shops.

● **Not just a trail guide**
Includes where to stay, where to eat and public transport Our guidebooks are a complete guide, not just a trail guide. They include: what to see, where to stay (pubs, hotels, B&Bs, campsites, bunkhouses, hostels), where to eat. There is detailed public transport information for all access points to each trail so there are itineraries for all walkers, both for hiking the route in its entirety and for day walks.

Coast to Coast *Henry Stedman* ISBN 978-1-905864-09-6, £9.99
3rd edition, 240pp, 109 maps & town plans, 40 colour photos

Cornwall Coast Path *Edith Schofield* ISBN 978-1-905864-19-5, £9.99
3rd edition, 224pp, 112 maps & town plans, 40 colour photos

Cotswold Way *Tricia & Bob Hayne* ISBN 978-1-905864-16-4, £9.99
1st edition, 192pp, 55 maps & town plans, 40 colour photos

Hadrian's Wall Path *Henry Stedman* ISBN 978-1-905864-14-0, £9.99
2nd edition, 192pp, 60 maps & town plans, 40 colour photos

North Downs Way *John Curtin* ISBN 978-1-873756-96-6, £9.99
1st edition, 192pp, 60 maps & town plans, 40 colour photos

Offa's Dyke Path *Keith Carter* ISBN 978-1-905864-06-5, £9.99
2nd edition, 208pp, 88 maps & town plans, 40 colour photos

Peddar's Way & Norfolk Coast Path *Alex Stewart* ISBN 978-1-905864-28-7
1st edition, 224pp, 80 maps & town plans, 40 colour photos

Pembrokeshire Coast Path *Jim Manthorpe* ISBN 978-1-905864-03-4, £9.99
2nd edition, 208pp, 96 maps & town plans, 40 colour photos

Pennine Way *Keith Carter & Chris Scott* ISBN 978-1-905864-02-7, £11.99
2nd edition, 272pp, 135 maps & town plans, 40 colour photos

The Ridgeway *Nick Hill* ISBN 978-1-905864-17-1, £9.99
2nd edition, 192pp, 53 maps & town plans, 40 colour photos

South Downs Way *Jim Manthorpe* ISBN 978-1-905864-18-8, £9.99
3rd edition, 176pp, 60 maps & town plans, 40 colour photos

West Highland Way *Charlie Loram* ISBN 978-1-905864-13-3, £9.99
3rd edition, 192pp, 53 maps, 10 town plans, 40 colour photos

*'The same attention to detail that distinguishes its other guides
has been brought to bear here'*. **The Sunday Times**

TREKKING GUIDES
Europe
Corsica Trekking – GR20
Dolomites Trekking – AV1 & AV2
Scottish Highlands – The Hillwalking Guide
Tour du Mont Blanc
Trekking in the Pyrenees
Walker's Haute Route: Mt Blanc to Matterhorn

South America
Inca Trail, Cusco & Machu Picchu

Africa
Kilimanjaro
Moroccan Atlas – The Trekking Guide
Australasia
New Zealand – The Great Walks
Asia
Nepal Trekking & The Great Himalaya Trail
Trekking in the Annapurna Region
Trekking in the Everest Region
Trekking in Ladakh

Tour du Mont Blanc *Jim Manthorpe*
1st edition, 208pp, 60 maps, 30 colour photos
ISBN 978-1-905864-12-6, £11.99
At 4810m (15,781ft), Mont Blanc is the highest mountain in western Europe, and one of the most famous mountains in the world. The snow-dome summit is the top of a spectacular massif stretching 60 miles by 20 miles, arguably the most magnificent mountain scenery in Europe. The trail (105 miles, 168km) that circumnavigates the massif, passing through France, Italy and Switzerland, is the most popular long distance walk in Europe. Includes Chamonix and Courmayeur guides.

The Walker's Haute Route – Mt Blanc to the Matterhorn
Alexander Stewart,1st edn, 256pp, 60 maps, 30 colour photos
ISBN 978-1-905864-08-9, £12.99
From Mont Blanc to the Matterhorn, Chamonix to Zermatt, the 180km (113-mile) Walkers' Haute Route traverses one of the finest stretches of the Pennine Alps – the range between Valais in Switzerland and Piedmont and Aosta Valley in Italy. Includes Chamonix and Zermatt guides.

Corsica Trekking – GR20 *David Abram*
1st edition, 208pp, 32 maps, 30 colour photos
ISBN 978-1-873756-98-0, £11.99
Slicing diagonally across Corsica's jagged spine, the legendary red-and-white waymarks of the GR20 guide trekkers across a succession of snow-streaked passes, Alpine meadows, massive boulder fields and pristine forests of pine and oak – often within sight of the sea. Physically demanding from start to finish, it's a superlative 170km, two-week trek. Includes guides to gateway towns: Ajaccio, Bastia, Calvi, Corte and Porto-Vecchio. '*Indispensable*'. *The Independent* '*Excellent guide*'. *The Sunday Times*

New Zealand – The Great Walks *Alexander Stewart*
2nd edition, 272pp, 60 maps, 40 colour photos
ISBN 978-1-905864-11-9, £12.99
New Zealand is a wilderness paradise of incredibly beautiful land-scapes. There is no better way to experience it than on one of the nine designated Great Walks, the country's premier walking tracks which provide outstanding hiking opportunities for people at all levels of fitness. Also includes detailed guides to Auckland, Wellington, National Park Village, Taumarunui, Nelson, Queenstown, Te Anau and Oban.

Inca Trail, Cusco & Machu Picchu
Alexander Stewart, 4th edition, 352pp, 74 maps, 40 photos
ISBN 978-1-905864-15-7, £12.99

The **Inca Trail** from Cusco to Machu Picchu, is South America's most popular trek. Practical guide including detailed trail maps, plans of Inca sites, plus guides to Cusco and Machu Picchu. Route guides to other trails in the area: the **Santa Teresa Trek** and the **Choquequirao Trek** as well as the **Vilcabamba Trail** plus the routes linking them. This entirely rewalked and rewritten fourth edition includes a new history of the Incas by Hugh Thomson.

Nepal Trekking & The Great Himalaya Trail *Robin Boustead*
1st edition, 320pp, 8pp colour maps, 40 colour photos
ISBN 978-1-905864-31-7, £14.99   **Due mid 2010**

This guide includes the most popular routes in Nepal – the Everest, Annapurna and Langtang regions – as well as the newest trekking areas for true trailblazers. This is the first guide to chart **The Great Himalaya Trail**, the route which crosses Nepal from east to west. Extensive planning sections to help visitors choose a trek.

Trekking in the Everest Region   *Jamie McGuinness*
5th edition, 320pp, 30 maps, 30 colour photos
ISBN 978-1-873756-99-7, £12.99

Fifth edition of this popular guide to the Everest region, the world's most famous trekking region. Includes planning, preparation and getting to Nepal; detailed route guides – with 30 route maps and 50 village plans; Kathmandu city guide – where to stay, where to eat, what to see. Written by a professional trekking and mountaineering leader.

Trekking in the Annapurna Region   *Bryn Thomas*
4th edition, 288pp, 55 maps, 28 colour photos
ISBN 978-1-873756-68-3, £11.99

Guide to the most popular walking region in the Himalaya. Includes route guides, Kathmandu and Pokhara city guides and getting to Nepal. *'Good guides read like a novel and have you packing in no time. Two from Trailblazer Publications which fall into this category are* Trekking in the Annapurna Region *and* Silk Route by Rail'. **Today**

Trekking in Ladakh   *Charlie Loram*
3rd edition, 288pp, 72 maps, 24 colour photos
ISBN 978-1-873756-75-1, £12.99

Fully revised and extended 3rd edition of Charlie Loram's practical guide. Includes 72 detailed walking maps, guides to Leh, Manali and Delhi plus information on getting to Ladakh.   *'Extensive...and well researched'.* **Climber Magazine** *'Were it not for this book we might still be blundering about...'* **The Independent on Sunday**

Dolomites Trekking Alta Via 1 & Alta Via 2   *Henry Stedman*
2nd edn, 192pp, 52 trail maps, 7 town plans, 38 colour photos
ISBN 978-1-873756-83-6, £11.99

AV1 (9-13 days) & AV2 (10-16 days) are the most popular long-distance hikes in the Dolomites. Numerous shorter walks also included. Places to stay, walking times and points of interest, plus detailed guides to Cortina and six other towns.

TRAILBLAZER GUIDES – TITLE LIST

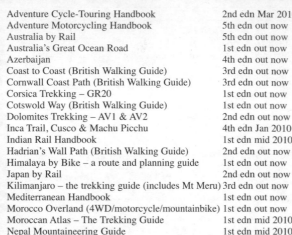

Adventure Cycle-Touring Handbook	2nd edn Mar 2010
Adventure Motorcycling Handbook	5th edn out now
Australia by Rail	5th edn out now
Australia's Great Ocean Road	1st edn out now
Azerbaijan	4th edn out now
Coast to Coast (British Walking Guide)	3rd edn out now
Cornwall Coast Path (British Walking Guide)	3rd edn out now
Corsica Trekking – GR20	1st edn out now
Cotswold Way (British Walking Guide)	1st edn out now
Dolomites Trekking – AV1 & AV2	2nd edn out now
Inca Trail, Cusco & Machu Picchu	4th edn Jan 2010
Indian Rail Handbook	1st edn mid 2010
Hadrian's Wall Path (British Walking Guide)	2nd edn out now
Himalaya by Bike – a route and planning guide	1st edn out now
Japan by Rail	2nd edn out now
Kilimanjaro – the trekking guide (includes Mt Meru)	3rd edn out now
Mediterranean Handbook	1st edn out now
Morocco Overland (4WD/motorcycle/mountainbike)	1st edn out now
Moroccan Atlas – The Trekking Guide	1st edn mid 2010
Nepal Mountaineering Guide	1st edn mid 2010
Nepal Trekking & The Great Himalaya Trail	1st edn mid 2010
New Zealand – The Great Walks	2nd edn out now
North Downs Way (British Walking Guide)	1st edn out now
Norway's Arctic Highway	1st edn out now
Offa's Dyke Path (British Walking Guide)	2nd edn out now
Overlanders' Handbook – worldwide driving guide	1st edn late 2010
Peddar's Way & Norfolk Coast Path (British Walking)	1st edn mid 2010
Pembrokeshire Coast Path (British Walking Guide)	3rd edn out now
Pennine Way (British Walking Guide)	2nd edn out now
The Ridgeway (British Walking Guide)	2nd edn out now
The Silk Roads – a route and planning guide	2nd edn out now
Sahara Overland – a route and planning guide	2nd edn out now
Scottish Highlands – The Hillwalking Guide	2nd edn out now
South Downs Way (British Walking Guide)	3rd edn out now
Tibet Overland – mountain biking & jeep touring	1st edn out now
Tour du Mont Blanc	1st edn out now
Trans-Canada Rail Guide	4th edn out now
Trans-Siberian Handbook	7th edn out now
Trekking in the Annapurna Region	4th edn out now
Trekking in the Everest Region	5th edn out now
Trekking in Ladakh	3rd edn out now
Trekking in the Pyrenees	3rd edn out now
The Walker's Haute Route – Mont Blanc to Matterhorn	1st edn out now
West Highland Way (British Walking Guide)	3rd edn out now

www.trailblazer-guides.com